The Promise Fulfilled

The University of Minnesota Press gratefully acknowledges the generous assistance provided for the publication of this book by The Research Council of Norway.

The Promise Fulfilled

A Portrait of Norwegian Americans Today

ODD S. LOVOLL

University of Minnesota Press
Minneapolis • London

Published in cooperation with the Norwegian-American Historical Association

Published by the University of Minnesota Press
111 Third Avenue South, Suite 290
Minneapolis, MN 55401-2520
http://www.upress.umn.edu

Library of Congress Cataloging-in-Publication Data

Lovoll, Odd Sverre.
    The promise fulfilled : a portrait of Norwegian Americans today / Odd S. Lovoll.
      p.   cm.
    "Published in cooperation with the Norwegian-American Historical Association."
    Includes index.
    ISBN 0-8166-2832-7 (hc : alk. paper). — ISBN 0-8166-2833-5 (pb : alk. paper)
    1. Norwegian Americans—Ethnic identity.   2. Norwegian Americans—History.   3. Norwegian Americans—Interviews.   I. Norwegian-American Historical Association.   II. Title.
E184.S2L686   1998   98-4000

Printed in the United States of America on acid-free paper

The University of Minnesota is an equal-opportunity educator and employer.

10 09 08 07 06 05 04 03 02 01 00 99 98   10 9 8 7 6 5 4 3 2 1

Dedicated to the Memory of My Brother
Magnar Bertel Lowell, February 10, 1931–October 9, 1950

Contents

Preface

The Promise Fulfilled is a story told by Norwegian Americans themselves through interviews and completed questionnaires, and also through the historical record as preserved in libraries and archives. It is an experiment in social history that marks a departure in the study of American ethnic groups. As a reviewer said, a major finding of the study is "the creation of an ethnicity through the interactions of ethnic institutions and American society and the impact on those who identify with that ethnicity." It is a case study that presents a comprehensive portrait of an "old" immigrant group toward the end of the twentieth century.

Initial preparations to conduct such a study would have come to naught save for the enthusiastic encouragement and support of Johan Fr. Heyerdahl, secretary general of Nordmanns Forbundet in Oslo, Norway, who secured the first large grant-in-aid of the project. My good friend Lawrence O. Hauge, president of the Norwegian-American Historical Association, contributed generously and was helpful at every turn. Terje Mikael Hasle Joranger of Oslo, Norway, traveled with me throughout the United States for a period of twelve months as my capable and optimistic research associate; the fieldwork benefited greatly from his innate talent for social history

and for relating to subjects of in-depth interviews. Our varied experiences in pursuit of the Norwegian American might even merit a book all their own. Terje deserves a special word of gratitude for his invaluable contributions to the project at the personal as well as professional level. Professor David C. Mauk of the Norwegian University of Science and Technology in Trondheim, and an authority on the Norwegians in the eastern United States, joined us for the two weeks devoted to research in New York. At St. Olaf College Michael H. Foote served as my reliable and knowledgeable administrative assistant, tending to correspondence and entering and analyzing information on the database he created.

I incurred a large debt of gratitude to many individuals and institutions in the course of the research. I owe most of all to my academic institution, St. Olaf College, for granting me a two-year special leave of absence, 1995–97, on generous terms. Without this institutional largesse the work could not have been done. President Melvin D. George and later his successor, President Mark U. Edwards, and the academic deans Jon Moline and Kathleen Fishbeck encouraged and supported the project.

It will not be possible within the confines of this preface to acknowledge adequately all those who in one way or another became a part of the project. Nearly three hundred individuals volunteered to work as local contact persons, a number that was multiplied many times over during our visits to local sites throughout the United States and in our correspondence with individuals in places we missed. In most cases, these people were the local experts of the history of their communities. Numerous newspapers, including the *Minneapolis Star Tribune,* which twice carried articles by staff writer Chuck Haga; the *Post-Bulletin* in Rochester, Minnesota; the *Wisconsin State Journal* in Madison; the two remaining Norwegian-language weeklies, *Western Viking* in Seattle and *Norway Times* in Brooklyn; and numerous local journals as well as major newspapers in Norway communicated our research to a large audience. Much of the latter resulted from an arrangement made by Odd Mølster, cultural attaché at the Royal Norwegian Embassy, for me to address the embassy staff and the Norwegian press corps in Washington, D.C.

We made visits to societies, organizations, and festivals. Disrespectful or disinterested encounters, though they did occur, were the rare exceptions. More typical were the enthusiastic receptions and interest we enjoyed at such Sons of Norway lodges as the Washington Lodge in the District of Columbia, which was the first lodge to extend an invitation to address its members and to give financial support. Kringen in Fargo and Gyda Varden in Grand Forks,

North Dakota; Sagatun in Brainerd, Nordmarka in Northfield, Lauris Norstad in Red Wing, and Storting in Austin, Minnesota; Vennelag in Mount Horeb, Wisconsin; Fjordland in Brookings, South Dakota; Trollheim in Denver, Colorado; Leif Erikson in Salt Lake City, Utah; Grieg in Portland, Oregon; and many others all made an evening's program of our visit. The Sons of Norway International early on spread the news about the project in an article in *The Sons of Norway Viking,* April 1995, for which I extend my sincere thanks, especially to the chief fraternal officer, Orlyn A. Kringstad, and the fraternity's president, Dennis Sorheim. In Texas the Norwegian Society took a special interest in our work; men's cod luncheon clubs, Norwegian-American chamber of commerce meetings, local historical societies, congregations, *bygdelag* conventions, family reunions, and clubs of many kinds welcomed us and encouraged our efforts.

Early in the study I visited Florida, where Sonja and Professor James T. Hillestad arranged for me to attend the Sons of Norway Viking Ship Regatta in Clearwater in May 1995. When our systematic fieldwork began in August, our first visits were to western and southern Minnesota, where Clara Swingseth in Benson, Leland Pederson in Glenwood, Elvera Bisbee and Laurie Ziemke in Tracy, Alma Jean Satran in Minneapolis, Carol Nelson in Milan, Dwight Boyum in Rochester, Jean R. Legried in Oakland, Georgia Rosendahl in Spring Grove, and Yvonne and Richard Blomquist in

Hanska were among those who made local arrangements.

In northern and northwestern Minnesota our main contacts and enthusiastic assistants were George Myers, Walter Spidahl, Joyce Bruns, Enid Ringdahl, and Christine Hefte in Fergus Falls; George Sands in Alvarado; Henry Gjersvig in Detroit Lakes; E. T. Lowell Smith in Elbow Lake; and Sue and Ted Leagjeld at their lovely resort on Upper White Fish Lake. In Little Falls, Minnesota, Susan Brekke Benson served as our local contact; in Duluth, Gerald R. Sime; and in Red Wing, William L. Christianson. As always Ambassador Sidney A. and Lois Rand in Minneapolis showed their friendship and deep interest in their Norwegian heritage by their generosity of means and spirit. In Minneapolis and environs a large number of people stepped forward to assist, both longtime friends and new ones, people like Consul General Bjarne Grindem; E. T. Fjelde; Arley R. Bjella; Marie Louise Markley; Deborah L. Miller; Gordon W. Strom; Don Omodt; Kenneth E. Broin; Nancy C. Nelson; Sharon Sayles Babcock; Robert Lee Ellingsen; Terry Johnson; Professor L. Sunny Hansen; Marilyn Somdahl, president of the Council of Bygdelag; and Andreas Jordahl Rhude, president of the Norwegian-American Genealogical Association. Warden Louis A. Stender at the Minnesota Correctional Facility in Faribault made it possible to interview Norwegian-American prison inmates.

In western Wisconsin we enjoyed the assistance of Arvalene and Jacob Vedvik, Judy and Wayne Gates, Else Bigton and Phillip Odden, and Borghild Olson. In the central and southern districts of the state Lois and Professor Joel Mickelson, Malcolm Rosholt, Bonnie and Harold Vastag, and Ingrid and Lars Graff were among many others who came to our aid. Senator Brian Rude arranged for interviews in Madison with Wisconsin state legislators of Norwegian origin. Ann and David Nelson, Doris and Chuck Hayes, Tom Rygh, Jeffrey J. Doerfer, Ron Larson, and the director of the Vesterheim genealogical center, Blaine Hedberg, were other friendly supporters. Professor Ann M. Legreid of Warrenburg, Missouri, assisted as well in our research in Wisconsin. Our main contact and guide to pioneer Norwegian settlements in Milwaukee and environs was Mylan E. Ottum.

Carrol T. Juven of Juven Travel became one of the most enthusiastic promoters of our research in North Dakota. But we were also well served by among others Debbie Shortino, Professor Virginia Anderson, Carol Ann and Kermit Bye, Iona M. Hystad and Rolland Loken, Orville Nelson, and Dan A. Aird. In South Dakota Sherry S. Stilley in Mitchell, Gertrude and Roswall Nearman in Sioux Falls, Maynard Molstad and Jerome Holter in Canton, Anna Haga in Hudson, and Doris Hanson in Elk Point were among those who made our visit both enjoyable and profitable. O. Jay Tomson, chair of the First Citizens National Bank in Mason City, served as our main contact in Iowa. He contributed generously to the project financially and assisted in our research. We are also greatly indebted to Professor J. R. Christianson; Darrell Henning, then director of Vesterheim Norwegian-American Museum; and Fran and Stanley Jeffers of the local genealogical society in Decorah; Katherine Munson in Story City; Helen and Clarence Stangeland of the Stavanger Friends Church in Marshall County; Ann Urness Gesme in Cedar Rapids; Virginia and Floyd Thomas in Lake Mills; and President William E. Hamm of Waldorf College in Forest City. Consul James P. Sites and Richard Fretheim were among those who provided information on the Norwegians in Montana.

In the pioneer settlement in Fox River, Illinois, Ralph Egeland became our knowledgeable guide together with Pat Ainsley Hayes, president of the Slooper Society; in Champaign Professor Earl Richard Ensrud served as our interested contact person. Nils I. Johansen provided information on Norwegians in Indiana. In Chicago our gracious hosts were Josefa and J. Harry Andersen, and research assistance was given by Alice and Ronn Toebaas, Grete Roland, Dorothy M. Stein, and Honorary Consul General Per and Liv Ohrstrom, among others. Our main contact in Michigan was Richard L. Lee of Lapeer, who arranged for meetings and provided transportation for an entire week of research; assistance came also from Consul Norval Eide Engelsen in Detroit and Owen Bahle in Suttons Bay.

In Washington, D.C., Marjory and Fred Olson vacated their apartment for our use; Lori Jo Olson and Paul Engelstad were our main contacts in the area; and in Norge, Virginia, Berit Mesarick. On the east coast of Florida Sandra and Finn Lorentzen and Ingeborg Nesheim Brinkman were helpful hosts. C. David Seng was an early and interested assistant in that state. In investigating the Norwegian colony in Brooklyn and Norwegians in Greater New York in general, Sandy Ginsberg, then president of the third district of Sons of Norway; Ruth Haanes Santoro, chair of the May 17 committee; Victoria Hofmo; Gary Alan Boardman; and Thomas Sandseth were especially involved. Grace Allen generously paid for our hotel in full. Ellen Skaar in Fairhaven and Charles S. Fineman in Cambridge assisted in Massachusetts. In Connecticut Laura Clementsen of Cheshire served as our principal contact, and in Pennsylvania Sally and Ivar Christensen and Odd B. Sundquist of Philadelphia guided us to Norwegian-American activities.

Our research on the West Coast was greatly aided in Seattle by Professor Terje I. Leiren; the publisher of *Western Viking,* Alf Lunder Knudsen; James F. Vatn; and Beth Kollé. Consul Anton Zahl Meyer in Anchorage, Alaska, provided information on the Norwegians in that state. Beverly Hansen was our faithful contact in Hawaii; in Portland, Oregon, Fern and Lewis J. Carlson and Johanna and Bernhard Fedde deserve special mention. Other significant contacts in the state were Beverly and Russell Hackleman and Stan Hultgren in Eugene, Ted Ahre in Woodburn, Ferne Hellie in Salem, and Jeanette Overen Habedanck in Klamath Falls. Our main contacts in San Francisco were Marie and Nils Lang-Ree, Trygve Morkemo, Jean Labadie, and Gary Olsen Schaefer. Mona and Olaf T. Engvig and Odd "Bud" Oimoen offered their kind services. Norwegian diplomats welcomed our work, among others, Consul General Hans Ola Urstad in San Francisco and Honorary Consul General Richard J. Fine in Los Angeles, who gave us free office space and the use of two telephones for the purpose of conducting interviews. Professor Jon Gjerde at Berkeley showed a warm interest and gave insightful perspectives on immigration history. Wanda Reiersgaard Collins in Sacramento was a major contact in California and arranged a day of interviews; David Ostby became an invaluable co-worker in Anaheim; as did Lorraine and Neil A. Hofland, Berit Austin, and Ruth Sylte in the Los Angeles area; Consul Knut Ivar Halvorsen in San Pedro; and Anne and Professor Oddvar Hoidal, Adolf M. B. Jacobsen, Bjarne Anthonsen, and Consul Oswald Gilbertsen in San Diego. In Phoenix, Arizona, Howard Barikmo was our main contact and did much to further our research; Bente Tingulstad and Per Aanestad were other helpful contacts; we were graciously received by Honorary Consul Allan Dale Solheim. Jason Sederquist in Albuquerque and Professor Michael L. Olson in Las Vegas, New Mexico, assisted in the work there.

In tracing the Norwegian-American experience in Colorado we had the assistance of Pam Aakhus in Lakewood, who drove us into the state's skiing paradise; Beverly and Robert King in Wheat Ridge; Jane and Irving "Bud" Lowell in Lakewood; and Bjørn Erik Borgen in Denver, who in addition to providing us with office space became one of our major sponsors. In Utah Dean Erlend D. Peterson and Professor Gerald M. Haslam, both at Brigham Young University in Provo, acquainted me with the state's spectacular scenery and introduced me to the Norwegian-American community of Latter-day Saints.

Research in Texas became our last distant excursion from our headquarters. Our main contacts were Sarah and Professor V. L. Mike Mahoney of Dallas; others who gave assistance were Gwen and Jim Workman in Plano. In the pioneer Norwegian Bosque County careful planning was made for our visit by especially Geneva Finstad, and also Elaine Bakke Bell and Judge Derwood Johnson. In Houston Joanne Ashland and Anne Brith Berge made similar arrangements, the Norwegian Lutheran Seamen's Church being our main base with the pastors Helge Boe and Audun Haga as our gracious hosts.

We thank all those who volunteered to be

interviewed or completed our questionnaire and for their forthrightness in answering difficult questions in regard to their personal life experiences. Our questions regularly elicited emotional responses. Unfortunately, only a few of the hundreds of interview responses can be included, and the identities of the more than seven thousand questionnaire respondents are for the most part lost in the tables based on their answers. These responses, both from the interviews and the questionnaire, are nevertheless the most essential contributions to the research effort. Our insights into the contemporary Norwegian-American experience came precisely through our respondents' sincere accounts of their lives and convictions. Many others sent family histories, pedigree charts, and books about pioneer life. All the assembled material will be permanently housed in the archives of the Norwegian-American Historical Association at St. Olaf College and will eventually be made available to researchers of the Norwegian-American experience. Lloyd Hustvedt, executive secretary; Ruth Hanold Crane, assistant secretary; and Forrest Brown, archivist, kindly tolerated our increased presence in our common association quarters.

Major donations came from Lutheran Brotherhood by Robert P. Gandrud, O. W. Caspersen Foundation by Finn M. W. Caspersen, the Nygaard Foundation at St. Olaf College, the Borgen Family Foundation by Bjørn Erik Borgen, and First Citizens National Bank by O. Jay Tomson. All the above gave from $10,000 to $30,000. The following contributed from $5,250 to $1,000: Ingrid and Lars Graff, the American-Scandinavian Foundation, Ellen McKey, Sundet Foundation by Louise and Lee Sundet, the Arthur B. Schultz Foundation by Arthur B. Schultz, Lois and Lawrence O. Hauge, Minnesota Humanities Commission, John K. and Luise V. Hanson Foundation, Beverly and Roe H. Hatlen, Leif W. Anderson, Nettie O. Mooney, Arley R. Bjella, Norsk Høstfest Association by Chester M. Reiten, Washington Lodge of Sons of Norway, and Geraldine M. and Herbert M. Stellner Jr., who in addition to fiscal generosity showed much enthusiasm and encouraged the work. The following contributed from $500 to $200: Sons of Norway Foundation, Consul Norval Eide Engelsen, E. T. Fjelde, Marie and Nils Lang-Ree, LaDelle and Alfred Olson, Judith Stenehjem, Ardis Munter, Aase Grethe Holby, Lois and Sidney Rand, Enid and John Ringdahl, Margaret Hanson, Barbara and Carrol T. Juven, Eleanor A. "Kek" Robien, Walter S. Rugland, C. David Seng, Kringen Lodge of Sons of Norway, and Lauris Norstad Lodge of Sons of Norway. A large number of individuals donated amounts below $200. I thank all donors most cordially.

My patient wife, Else Lovoll, who tolerated my extended absences and helped prepare the long research excursions, deserves a special thanks, and also my son, Ronald Lovoll, for his expertise and assistance in preparing appropriate illustrations. Mary R. Hove is responsible for the index.

I dedicate the book to the memory of my brother, Magnar Bertel Lowell, whose untimely death at the age of nineteen—washed overboard from our father's halibut schooner, the *Attu,* off the coast of California in 1950—deprived me of the counsel and comfort of an older brother. The harsh reality of the German occupation in Norway and the absence of our father, who spent the years of war in the United States, prematurely pushed him to assume adult responsibilities. Our family reunited in

Seattle, Washington, in 1946; there Magnar pursued his strong educational interests. At the time of his death, just out of high school, he had assembled an impressive private library and was making plans for his college career. I have cherished the memory of my promising, intelligent, and determined big brother and sorely missed him throughout my life.

Odd S. Lovoll
King Olav V Professor of
    Scandinavian-American Studies
St. Olaf College

CHAPTER 1

The Shifting Face of Norwegian America

The Contemporary Norwegian American

A Norwegian presence in America, excluding the failed Norse colonization efforts toward the end of the first millennium, dates from 1825 with the arrival of the sloop *Restauration* carrying the first boatload of Norwegian immigrants. Some Norwegians had joined in the Dutch New Amsterdam venture in the seventeenth century, and there were other individuals who made the crossing before 1825.[1] But that year is the beginning of a continuous Norwegian-American history of more than 170 years and eight generations of descendants of those pioneer immigrants.

Their story was pursued by ambitious field research in about thirty states; by extensive correspondence, telephone conversations, and electronic communication with Norwegian-American organizations, individuals, and institutions; by nearly eight hundred personal in-depth interviews with Norwegian Americans; and by specifically designed research instruments, questionnaires, and surveys. We visited Norwegian-American events of many kinds: conventions, reunions, festivals, athletic meets, and rallies. About three hundred local contact people assisted in making arrangements for research in their communities.

According to the 1990 federal decennial census, 3,869,395 Americans subjectively reported Norwegian as their first or second ethnicity, or ancestry, if you will. Of these, 65.1 percent claimed Norwegian as their first ethnicity.[2] Only 47,396 had been born in Norway, nearly 40,000 of these having arrived before 1980. The majority of Norwegian Americans, thus, are members of the third or fourth generation or later generations. In fact, a study based on census data for 1979 found that 84 percent of Norwegian Americans were third generation or later, and only 16 percent were immigrants and their children, the first and second generations. Norwegian Americans exhibit in this regard a typical pattern for ethnic groups generally described as "old."[3]

Geographical mobility has dispersed Norwegians throughout the United States. Nevertheless, the 1990 census indicates a persistent ethnic strength in their traditional regions of settlement. Of those who gave Norwegian as their first or second ethnicity, 51.7 percent resided in the Midwest that year. Minnesota continued to lead in numbers of people of Norwegian ancestry, Wisconsin ranked second, and North Dakota fifth. The West had 32.5 percent of all Norwegians, with California ranking third after Wisconsin, and the state of Washington fourth. The South had 9.5 percent of the Norwegian-American population, and the Northeast 6.2 percent.[4]

It is this population that I made the subject of an ambitious two-year research endeavor, from 1995 to 1997, in order to paint a portrait of an "old" immigrant group. The result constitutes a case study of one specific ethnicity. The extensive investigation was conducted under the premise, to quote Olivier Zunz, that migration and adjustment are "an individual as well as collective process."[5] The study is intended to answer questions concerning duration of ethnic loyalties, the role of an ethnic "hard core" in generating ethnic self-awareness,[6] and the shifting content and symbols of a Norwegian-American identity. I have adopted an intercultural and interactive frame of interpretation in order to demonstrate ways in which Norwegian Americans collectively and individually have interacted with the multiethnic American environment and to show the consequences of that interaction. The mingling of ethnic populations and the forces of assimilation continually create new ethnic configurations and new ways in which to define a personal and a collective ancestral identity. It is from this broad social and historical perspective that contemporary Norwegian Americans are viewed in this study.

A central thesis of the study is that Norwegian Americans throughout their history have evinced an exceptional degree of ethnocentricity, clearly more so than Danes or Swedes in America, and indeed, one might claim with possible—though not obvious—exceptions for the Icelanders and Finns, even more so than all other northern European nationalities. A striking example of ethnic cohesiveness in comparison to other Scandinavians is the Norwegian Memorial Church on Logan Square in Chicago, which as of 1997 still conducted services in the Norwegian language. On either side of the altar are, in addition to the United States and Norwegian flags, the Danish and the Swedish ones, these flags having been given to the church when the last Danish- and Swedish-language churches closed their doors. These closings occurred in spite of the fact that the Swedes in Chicago are much more numerous than the Norwegians.

Explanations for the high level of ethnic zeal must be sought on both sides of the Atlantic: at the aggregate level in Norway's position as an underdog among the three Scandinavian kingdoms, and in the country's understandable defensive feeling of national inferiority. A centuries-long union with Denmark ended in 1814. The constitution signed at Eidsvoll on May 17 of that year signified the rebirth of the Kingdom of Norway. But in November 1814 the newly established national assembly, the Storting, or Grand Assembly, surrendered Norway's claimed independence to the demands of big-power politics and accepted a union with Sweden under the Swedish king. The double monarchy, which lasted until 1905, gave Norway full independence in domestic affairs, but Sweden remained the preeminent partner in this uneven union. A fierce quest for a separate identity preoccupied Norwegians in the nineteenth century and throughout the era of mass emigration. Writers sought to transform the cultural and political sense of inferiority by producing proudly nationalistic and romantic literature. The goal was, as expressed by the nineteenth-century Norwegian historian P. A. Munch, "to stand in full equality together with the other Nordic nations"; Munch wished to show "the influence of the Norwegian nationality in Old Norse times and its Nordic genuineness at pre-

sent."[7] In this striving, the era of Norwegian national grandeur and independence during the Nordic Middle Ages and the dynamic expansion of the Age of the Vikings assumed an extraordinary and lasting importance. Mythologies surrounding the historical greatness of those distant times continue to supply Norwegians and Norwegian Americans with their most evocative ethnic symbols.[8]

Norwegians harbor a deep consciousness of local origins. Immigrants reared in one of the many isolated fjord communities or highland valleys, even as a part of a historical folk district, developed a sense of kinship with others from the area. The spectacular landscape left indelible mental imprints of every glen, mountain peak, and rushing waterfall. These communicated a sense of the primordial and permanent condition of their identity. Norway for most became the small rural community, the homestead, and the ancestral traditions in speech, food, and beliefs.

Parochial concerns affected Norwegians in America greatly in their patterns of settlement and in their social and religious associations. A unique ethnic intensity of religious observance, mainly expressed through the Lutheran faith, set ethnic and religious boundaries, and the extreme rural character of Norwegian settlement gave added force to congregational life and pastoral influence. The strong Lutheran pietism that prevailed in many Norwegian-American communities strengthened ethnocentric prejudices in the American environment and encouraged a segregated ethnic life. In *Elmtown's Youth,* written in the 1940s, August B. Hollingshead demonstrated how a pious Lutheran condemnation of "worldly pleasures," including adolescent dancing, cosmetics, motion pictures, cards, bowling, and high school parties, isolated Norwegian-American youth. Circumstances naturally change over time, however. Revisiting the same Illinois community thirty years later, in the 1970s, Hollingshead found that Norwegians were not "as ingrown as they were 30 years ago."[9] Both men and women were now marrying outside the Norwegian group. Still, Lutheranism is central to the identity of many people of a Norwegian background. "Norwegians took their religious tradition seriously enough to argue about it," Bishop H. George Anderson of the Evangelical Lutheran Church in America insists, and "it has lasted until today."[10] Thus, as this study shows, for many Norwegian Americans a nearly symbiotic relationship between Lutheranism and Norwegian ethnicity continues in force.

National peculiarities and circumstances, localism, patterns of settlement, religious loyalties, social interaction, and ethnic biases must all be considered in a study of Norwegian Americans. In this population these factors facilitated cultural maintenance and the transfer of ethnic traditions, values, and biases to American-born generations. Even so, no fully satisfactory explanation for the extraordinary ethnic fervor among Norwegian Americans may

ever be found. One may in a final analysis be left with only an enduring notion of cultural and even genetic qualities shrouded in mystical concepts of heritage and ancestry being subtly passed down through the generations. Opposing the precepts of assimilation, Horace Kallen in his 1915 essay "Democracy versus the Melting Pot" argued in similar cultural biological terms about the newer American, commenting that "behind him in time and tremendously in him in quality, are his ancestors; around him in space are his relatives and kin, carrying in common with him the inherited organic set from a remoter common ancestry."[11]

For this study, contemporary Norwegian Americans were invited to relate their own ethnic and family experiences. A manifest and vivid picture of the group as it appeared toward the end of the twentieth century emerged from their accounts. It is a story told by them. Due to the voluntary nature of most responses, no claim of scientific ethnographic evidence is made for conclusions based on the distributed questionnaires. In some respects the survey speaks to a "core" constituency. It moves beyond this central ethnic population, however, to give revealing information about the American experience of Norwegian Americans and their attitudes, values, and biases. Results are consistently compared to other evidence. Representativeness was furthermore sought by identifying individuals for in-depth interviews and by broadly distributing the questionnaire on which the survey is based. The detailed

recorded or written interviews that were conducted represented all age groups and generations, people in all walks of life and in all parts
of the United States. They responded to a fixed
set of questions regarding family, religious and
political views, beliefs and values, and their relationship to their ancestral heritage. What was
most striking was a pronounced consistency in
how ethnic identity and merits were perceived;
it was coupled with a visible defensive posture
when their perceptions of their cultural ethnic
identity were challenged.[12]

Few issues have generated more heated
debate within segments of the Norwegian-
American community than the question of the
authenticity of the so-called Kensington Stone
(figure 1). It is a stone with runic inscriptions
"discovered" by Swedish-American farmer
Olof Ohman in 1898 on a farm in Douglas
County, Minnesota, near Kensington, in a
strongly Norwegian and Swedish region of
settlement. The stone is today on exhibit in the
Runestone Museum in Alexandria, the county
seat, which in a chamber-of-commerce-
inspired statement declares itself as "the birthplace of America." The runes namely relate a
spectacular tale of "8 Swedes and 22 Norwegians on an exploration journey from Vinland
westward." The stone gives the year 1362 for
this incongruous Norse expedition to central
North America; if historical veracity could be
determined, the event would make Swedes and
Norwegians the first Europeans to reach
Minnesota, and claims of a special birthright

*Figure 1. The Kensington rune stone in the Runestone
Museum in Alexandria, Minnesota. Courtesy of the
Runestone Museum Foundation.*

would then be in order. It is no less than a
Norwegian-American national epic.

For many believers, supporting evidence
exists in the "Viking mooring holes," bored
indentations in rocks along the rivers of the
upper Midwest, which if really anchoring
places for ancient Norse mariners, as their supporters insist, would indicate because of their
great numbers that flotillas of Viking ships

once traversed these midwestern waterways. No authentic artifacts or skeletal remains lend credibility to these notions. Consistent expert opinions of the fraudulent character of the Kensington rune stone as a hoax and "clumsy forgery" have never convinced the faithful. A deathbed confession by Ohman or the yet to be clearly identified "rune smith" himself, it has been said, would not have changed their minds. As recently as 1994, an amateur researcher, trained in music and meteorology, published a book in the defense of authenticity, in order to, as he states in the foreword, "restore the record of a proud event in Norse and American history," that a named scholar "tried to destroy forever."[13] Fourth-generation Norwegian American and resident of Alexandria Doris Engen Burkey, born in 1926, insisted that "there is no doubt in my mind at all that the stone is authentic." "It is important to prove it," she continued, "to show that the Vikings were here before Columbus." Her most telling argument, however, related to her perception of her own ethnic group. "It sticks in my craw," Burkey stated forcefully, "that someone would think Norwegians would *do* something like that."[14] They were, in other words, too honest as a nationality to commit fraud.

The extent to which perceived ethnic qualities and ideals, all of course meritorious, really are ethnic, or are simply idealized and cherished mainstream American attributes, will, one expects, emerge from the subsequent deductive inquiry of the sources. Adopted ideals may reflect early assimilative strategies, or there may even be a self-consciously selected combination of ethnic and American identifying cultural and social patterns, which also reveals a spirit of accommodation. When all is said and done, pride in ancestry may be related to how freely an ethnic group can move about in society without facing extreme prejudice or barriers. In contemporary America few social restrictions would apply to persons of Norwegian ancestry.

Thousands of questionnaires were distributed, at organizational meetings, at public events, at family reunions, in places of employment, in restaurants and saloons, and through mailings to selected individuals and groups. The questionnaire was inserted into ethnic journals and newsletters, and it appeared in numerous local newspapers in regions of Norwegian settlement. Nearly seven thousand questionnaires were completed and returned. The geographical distribution of the respondents nearly matches the percentages in the 1990 federal census. Of the 6,701 who provided this information, 8.06 percent resided in what the census defines as the Northeast, including New England and the mid-Atlantic states; 9.94 percent in the South, with Texas and Florida having the most returns; 55.76 percent in the Midwest; and 26.22 percent in the West. The census distribution of Norwegians is strikingly similar to these percentages.[15] Geographically, then, the sampling accurately reflects the current situation.

Table 1. Ranges of ages and gender of respondents to questionnaires distributed in 1995–96

Age	Number	Percentage	Percentage female	Percentage male
< 20	74	1.16	59.46	40.54
20 to 29	216	3.37	62.50	37.50
30 to 39	434	6.77	62.44	37.56
40 to 49	597	9.32	59.13	40.87
50 to 59	985	15.38	60.30	39.70
60 to 69	1,632	25.48	57.41	42.59
70 to 79	1,743	27.21	56.17	43.83
80 to 89	657	10.26	61.49	38.51
> 89	68	1.06	64.71	35.29
Total	6,406	100.00	58.71	41.29

On the other hand, in terms of age the respondents do not well represent the Norwegian-American population as a whole, as table 1 indicates. Older people were more apt than younger to complete the questionnaire, and more likely to join ethnic organizations. These factors caused the older age groups to be over-represented. The survey does, however, show a broad age distribution among the respondents.

The census figures indicate a much higher percentage of Norwegian Americans who are third generation and later than the percentage of the survey respondents (table 2). An estimated actual figure for all Norwegian Americans approaches 90 percent, whereas close to 70 percent of the respondents were third generation or later. This situation is due to the age composition of the survey respondents. Nevertheless, the family and personal experiences of the respondents give an abundance of insightful and valid information about Americans of

Norwegian descent in general. Their stories are enlarged by personal interviews with individuals with as many as seven generations of Norwegian-American ancestors.

The Migration

On October 9, 1825, the "Sloopers" landed in the port of New York, taking their name from their crossing on the sloop *Restauration,* a frail vessel of only thirty-nine tons (figure 2). These pathfinders of Norwegian emigration numbered fifty-three, crew and passengers, counting a baby girl born during the fourteen-week voyage, which began on July 4 at the town of Stavanger on the southwest coast of Norway. They were Quakers, Quaker sympathizers, and Haugeans, followers of the lay preacher Hans Nielsen Hauge, and thus subject to persecution by the clergy of the religiously monopolistic Norwegian Lutheran state church. It was

Table 2. Distribution of ethnic generations of respondents to questionnaires distributed in 1995-96

Generation	Number	Percentage
First	539	8.40
Second	1404	21.87
Third	2807	43.73
Fourth	1285	20.02
Fifth	313	4.88
Sixth	56	0.87
Seventh	15	.023

Note: The immigrants constitute the first generation.

the religious liberties of America, perhaps communicated to them by English Quakers with whom they had contact, that encouraged their courageous move. America, of course, also held out hopes for economic betterment. Their agent, Cleng Peerson, after having investigated opportunities in the New World and reported back on favorable conditions, met them as they debarked and together with American Quakers guided them to Kendall Township on the shores of Lake Ontario in western New York. There they struggled through the hardships of pioneer life.[16]

But they had come to a nation on the move. In the mid-1830s most of the Sloopers, again guided by the wanderer Peerson, joined the westward movement by selling their small plots in Kendall and settling in the fertile Fox River valley southwest of Chicago. It was the first Norwegian settlement in the Midwest and became an important mother colony for later settlement. The Fox River settlement became the first destination when Norwegian group exodus commenced again in 1836; from then on group emigration was an annual occurrence. Communities of compatriots in the New World stood ready to receive and assist newcomers.

"America letters," communications back home from emigrated kin, former neighbors, and acquaintances, were the most common source of information about America. Famed letter writers like Gjert Gregoriussen Hovland, who emigrated in 1831 and settled in Kendall, told of equality and opportunity in America and gave advice and guidance. There were also guidebooks[17] and personal visits by emigrated countrymen, such as Knud Andersen Slogvig, who, like Hovland, had emigrated in 1831, returned to Norway in 1835, and served as leader on one of the two brigs that sailed from Stavanger in 1836 with emigrants, heralding the advent of annual group departures.

The "America fever," as people called the urge to go to America as early as 1837, was spread by such infectious literature and by the pressures brought to bear by emigrated kin and friends to join them in America. Social circumstances at home made footloose peasants receptive to the news of a better life across the ocean. Norway had a population of 883,487 in 1801, and more than 91 percent of the population lived in rural areas. It was a backward agricultural society in which about 83 percent of the population was directly dependent on live-

Figure 2. This full-size replica of the sloop Restauration *was built for the centennial of Norwegian immigration in 1925.
Photograph courtesy of the Minnesota Historical Society.*

lihoods from primary economic pursuits in farming, logging, and fishing. An explosive population growth mainly in rural areas outside small urban centers increased Norway's population to 1,701,757 by 1865. The growth caused the agrarian communities to burst all economic bounds and encouraged Norway's move toward modernization. It was a powerful dispersing force.

A constant pressure to move, overseas or to opportunities closer at hand, persisted and was most strongly felt in the regions that experienced the highest rates of emigration. In spite of economic growth, impoverishment occurred in all parts of the country, both rural and urban, and caused the bottom stratum of Norwegian society to grow faster than other social groups. Large segments of the population were looking for better opportunities wherever they might exist.

Norwegian emigration rose in the 1840s. By 1850, 18,200 had left their homeland, and nearly 70,000 had done so by the outbreak of the Civil War. The migration moved north from Stavanger along the coast and inland to the upland communities. The majority of Norwegian emigrants came from the inner fjord districts of western Norway and the central mountain districts. It was emigrants from these communities that first shaped a Norwegian immigrant community. Farmers who had sold their small land holdings to finance their trip, younger sons of independent farmers unable to continue in familiar pursuits, and, gradually, especially in the 1850s and later, cotters and members of the lower classes in rural society joined the movement overseas. They came from fjord districts, like Sogn, and mountain valleys, like Hallingdal, Numedal, Valdres, and Setesdal, and also to some extent from towns, like Bergen and Oslo (then Christiania). The emigrants were mainly family groups intending to find a permanent home in America.

In the decade before the Civil War, all of Norway's administrative units (*amt*) were touched by migration. During what may be regarded as a founding phase of Norwegian emigration, contacts from all parts of the kingdom were made with immigrant communities in America. These contacts prepared emigrants for the mass migration that occurred following the end of hostilities. The transition from sail to steam transportation in the 1860s made mass overseas migration possible. Norwegians crossed the Atlantic in three massive waves: the first began in 1866 and lasted through 1873, the second occurred from 1880 through 1893, and the final great wave took place in the first decade of the twentieth century. During the fifty years after 1865, nearly 677,000 Norwegians took part in the overseas migration.

The ebb and flow of migration can be explained by an interplay of domestic and international economic circumstances, by depression or economic expansion on either side of the Atlantic. The needs of the American marketplace may, however, have weighed heaviest in determining the magnitude of the movement, especially as the migration became more urban and industrial and less agrarian in nature. The move toward modernization was never adequate to satisfy the need for employment. Surplus labor was siphoned off through migration. It was a voluntary act—conditions and possibilities on both sides of the ocean were considered, and an effective communication network kept people informed. The earlier family emigration from the 1870s gave way markedly to individual departures. Toward the end of mass migration the overseas movement had to a great degree become a youth migration, and the proportion of men had consistently increased. Almost two-thirds of the emigrants in the final mass exodus were in their most mobile years, between the ages of fifteen and twenty-five.

They were mainly ordinary workers with only their labor to offer. But as Norway modernized and became more urban, engineers, artists, and other professionally trained people responded to the lure of America.

In the 1920s there was again a wave of emigration, but it was much smaller than the earlier ones. It was curtailed both by the quota laws, which in their final form in 1929 gave Norway an annual quota of 2,377, and by the Great Depression of the 1930s. The latter, together with the years of war, produced a long break in migration. Still, the post–World War II movement must be viewed as a continuation and a natural extension of an earlier tradition.

The postwar emigration never assumed dramatic proportions and dropped greatly after the Immigration and Nationality Act of 1965, effective on July 1, 1968, substantially altered the existing national quota system. But the downward trend of Norwegian migration overseas developed independently of immigration legislation in the United States. Somewhat more than 49,500 Norwegians immigrated to the United States between 1946 and 1978, showing a steady decline throughout this period. Those who arrived before 1960 have had a greater tendency to settle permanently in the United States than later immigrants, who have displayed a much higher rate of return migration. To be sure, Norway participated in the movement of skilled workers, the so-called brain drain, as America's dynamic and expansive economic growth provided the greatest opportunity for immigrants in this category. Reports of the U.S. Immigration and Naturalization Service show, however, that most postwar Norwegian immigrants entered various occupational pursuits, both skilled and unskilled. A near balance between the sexes suggests that the small immigration after World War II has to a great extent had a family character. The earlier youth migration thus definitely came to an end.[18]

Settlement in the Midwest

The nineteenth-century Norwegian pioneers who settled in the Fox River valley of Illinois turned northwestward within four years of the founding of this mother colony in the mid-1830s. By the 1840s Wisconsin had become the center of Norwegian-American life and activity and retained this position up to the Civil War. New farming communities arose in the southeastern region of the state, Jefferson Prairie in Rock County in 1838, and Luther Valley in the following year. The two most famous settlements in pioneer history, Muskego in Racine and Waukesha Counties and Koshkonong in Dane County, both dated from 1840. The latter was one of several Norwegian settlements that surrounded the city of Madison. The main concentration in eastern and northern Wisconsin is the so-called Indielandet around Iola in Waupaca County. In western Wisconsin an almost solid strip of Norwegian settlement runs along the Mississippi River in the coulee country from Crawford to Barron Counties. These three main regions of Norwegian settlement exhibit a surprising stability and remain as the major Norwegian districts in the state.[19]

Land was not very important to the Norwegians who settled in Michigan, since most good land had been taken by the time of their arrival. But there was immediate income from lumbering, mining, and employment as seamen and captains on the Great Lakes. Because of these opportunities, Norwegian settlement, and Scandinavian in general, has been to a greater extent than in any other state a direct immigration from abroad rather than from older immigrant colonies. Transplanted skills could immediately be employed in familiar occupations. The earliest Norwegians settled in the city of Muskegon in 1848; in western Michigan the heaviest concentration of Norwegian settlement centered on Muskegon County. In the Lower Peninsula Norwegians settled most heavily in the triple tier of counties northward from Allegan County to the peak of the peninsula that forms Leelanau County. In the latter county, settlement began in 1867, mostly by people from the Nordmøre district in Norway, who were offered employ-

ment in lumbering. Their settlement shows the role played by chance. They arrived aboard the lake vessel *City of Fremont,* which stopped for fuel at Northport in Leelanau County on its way to Chicago. A lumberman offered the newcomers work, but they declined and continued on to their destination. Failing to find work in Chicago, some of them went west, but the majority returned to Northport to accept the lumberman's offer. Economic interests of many kinds promoted settlement; railroad companies, business ventures, state agencies, land speculators, newspapers, and even settlers themselves, through their letters, attracted people from home and from older settlements.

Copper and iron mines coupled with the labor crisis caused by the Civil War moved Norwegians to the Upper Peninsula. The mines engaged in the importation of contract labor from Scandinavia and sent agents abroad to recruit workers. Well known is the ship that left Tromsø in 1865 with 589 persons on board headed for the Lake Superior mines. Many Norwegians were drawn to the Ishpeming region, to the iron mines of Marquette County.

While the majority of Norwegians wandered westward, a smaller pioneer party set out from the Fox River valley in 1853 to join compatriots in Texas who had come there directly from Norway. The aging Cleng Peerson had scouted Texas to find possibilities for Norwegian settlement. He strongly encouraged the move and accompanied the pioneer party, but not as a leader. Earlier, in 1845, Johan R.

Reiersen had led a small group of peasants from Agder to land he had selected in Texas. His two colonization ventures, Brownsboro in Henderson County in northeastern Texas and Prairieville, founded in 1848, in Kaufman and Van Zandt Counties southeast of Dallas, both failed. The company from the Fox River settlement led by the young Ole Canuteson, however, established a prosperous colony in Bosque County south of Dallas with the little town of Clifton as its center. This settlement attracted people from the two earlier failed ventures and from Norway. It was yet another offshoot of the mother colony by the Fox River. Peerson died there in 1865, and a large marker on his grave in the Lutheran cemetery near Norse in Bosque County commends him as "the first Norwegian immigrant in America."

There was a strong regional composition to settlement, especially in the early Norwegian farming communities. It is possible to speak of the *bygd* phase of Norwegian settlement, a *bygd* being defined as a Norwegian country community, neighborhood, or district. Norwegian rural communities had developed striking local differences in customs, traditions, and most vividly in speech patterns. The early settlements in the Midwest re-created the rural *bygd* to an astounding degree.

As settlement moved westward, there was an increased intermingling of people from different districts, although a tendency to associate with *bygd* folk persisted. Bonds of kinship to the pioneer colonies strengthened this re-

gional tendency as the older immigrant farming communities gave up their youth to new settlements. The pattern of settlement made the original *bygd* settlement function as a mother colony for numerous communities farther west. Familial relations also guided Norwegian newcomers to specific destinations. But not all were immigrants. Many of those who set out to new regions were American-born and had never experienced the dramatic scenery of their immigrant parents' homeland.

Norwegian settlement followed the general westward movement of the American population. In the 1850s Norwegian settlements emerged in northeastern and central Iowa, and soon the attention of Norwegian settlers shifted from Wisconsin to Minnesota. With the beginning of mass Norwegian emigration in the mid-1860s, immigrants and settlers from older farming communities in southeastern Minnesota pressed on to the western districts of the state, and subsequently to the Dakota frontier, reaching even to the northern part of Dakota Territory in the late 1870s. The majority of Norwegian agrarian settlements developed in the northern region of the so-called Homestead Act triangle between the Mississippi and Missouri Rivers. The opening of the frontier and the availability of land under the Homestead Act of 1862 coincided with the rise of Norwegian mass emigration as well as a general surge westward from farming communities farther east. Norwegians responded to the promotional efforts of the agents of land companies, town agents, state bureaus of immigration, railroad companies, and land speculators of many kinds.

Norwegians became the most rural of any immigrant group in the nineteenth century. And wherever they entered farming, they confronted the challenge of adjusting to the demands of American commercial agriculture. The 1900 federal census reveals that 49.8 percent of all Norwegian-born heads of households were engaged in agriculture, as owners or renters of farms, or as agricultural laborers. A major increase in the last-mentioned category in the second generation placed 63 percent of those with one or both parents Norwegian in agriculture; 54.3 percent of the second generation were in fact farm operators. No other ethnic group even came close to being this rural.[20]

Some commentators have identified a special rural orientation and bond among Norwegian Americans. Their economic adjustment in the upper Midwest states was, however, not fundamentally different from that of other nationalities from northern Europe. Perhaps the greatest impact of Norwegian-American farmers, as well as of other farmers from northern Europe, was their dedication to farming as a way of life. While retaining many traditional sociocultural traits, immigrant farmers were successful when measured by their farm size, livestock, and machinery. In other words, economic success did not mark immigrant farmers as different from Americans.[21]

Wisconsin, Iowa, and Minnesota all began as wheat-growing states, and wheat was the primary product of early farmers. Small grain had the advantage of being harvested only months after planting and could be consumed at home or become a commodity for sale. Norwegian farmers later diversified to corn and other grains, and as a consequence began dairy farming and raising hogs. In southwestern Wisconsin, and earliest in the Koshkonong settlements, Norwegians took up tobacco cultivation. This crop became closely associated with Norwegian identity in the state.

Norwegian farmers in Iowa, settling mainly in the gently rolling prairies in the central, north-central, and northeastern counties, helped make the state a major producer of corn, beef cattle, and hogs. In Minnesota, Norwegian farmers settled in large numbers in the three major agricultural regions of the state; these were the hay and dairying counties in the southeast, corn and hog raising counties in the southwest, and spring wheat and small-grain counties in western and northwestern Minnesota.

The hard-spring wheat region extended to the prairies to the west and north, to the region that in 1889 became the states of South and North Dakota. In 1914 Norwegians owned about one-fifth of all farm land in North Dakota; in South Dakota Norwegians occupied and farmed primarily in the eastern counties. These two states were among the most rural regions in the United States. They consequently reinforced and communicated a rural character to their residents.[22]

The Urban Experience

As recently as 1940 over half of all midwestern Norwegians lived on farms or in small villages and towns. Norwegian Americans did indeed appear to be moored by a rural bond. In later generations a lifestyle associated with the family farm and traditional rural values persisted, and a certain conservatism of spirit and mind prevailed with a distinct distrust of the city and its artificial and materialistic ways.

Such antiurban sentiments were sometimes even harbored by Norwegian city dwellers. In spite of their fear of the city, Norwegians settled early in urban environments and made a living in urban economic pursuits. Chicago is considered to be the third Norwegian settlement, after Kendall and the Fox River valley, though it for some time resembled a rural village more than a town. In 1832 half a dozen families resided in five log houses at the mouth of the Chicago River. In the summer of 1833 Chicago became a city, a separate administrative unit within Cook County. It could boast a population of only 350 citizens. Even though it remained for some time "a walking city," it experienced a rapid growth; by 1836 nearly 4,000 lived in the city, in 1850 some 29,000, and by the end of the 1860s Chicago had become a substantial city of close to 110,000 inhabitants. Census figures from both 1850 and 1860 reveal that more than half of all of Chicago's residents were foreign-born, a dramatic indication of the role of immigration in the urbanization of America.

A Norwegian colony came into existence in 1836 when a group of newcomers decided to remain in the city rather than continue on to the Fox River. It is significant that one of the families was Niels Knutsen Røthe, his wife, Torbjørg, and their three children from Voss. They were very likely the first emigrants from Voss and attracted others from that community to Chicago. A large Voss contingent, a rural group referred to as the "Voss Circle," came to play an important role in the history of this first Norwegian urban colony.[23]

The pioneer Norwegians settled in the unhealthy area north of the Chicago River, known as "the Sands," where it emptied out into Lake Michigan. By 1850 they numbered 562, though the exact number is difficult to determine because of the transient nature of the population. Many were stranded in this port city without funds to continue their journey; others stayed only long enough to earn the money they needed to purchase or claim the farm of which they had dreamed. Transients and sojourners characterized the early Norwegian enclave.

The building of warehouses, railroads, and factories pushed the Norwegians from their original settlement. They moved to the sparsely settled district west of the north branch of the Chicago River and established a viable colony centering on Milwaukee Avenue. In the 1860s more than 60 percent of all Norwegians in Chicago lived in this area. The Milwaukee Avenue colony flourished. By the late nineteenth century no fewer than one Baptist, two Methodist, and eight Norwegian Lutheran churches marked a strong Norwegian presence. Immigrant-owned factories and other places of employment, business establishments of many kinds, restaurants and saloons, club houses, professional services, banks, bookstores, mutual aid societies, and benevolent organizations responded to the social needs of the city. They all gave evidence of a self-sufficient immigrant colony.

Movement of Norwegians out of this district accelerated in the 1880s as other ethnic groups, mainly newly arrived Poles, Polish and Russian Jews, and Italians replaced the Norwegian residents. Crowding in these dirty, smoky industrial river wards made it an undesirable district. They were joined in their move to a new district by the children of Norwegian farmers who responded to the lure of the city and by others who came directly from Norway. The third and final Norwegian colony developed farther west in the Humboldt Park and Logan Square districts. New communications made these districts desirable. Here Norwegians could set up their cheap wooden frame houses. In the 1880s there were a little more than 18,000 Norwegians, immigrants and their progeny, in Chicago. By 1900 the colony was 41,551 strong, and by 1910 there were 47,235 Norwegians, again counting only the first two generations. The numbers did not change much during the following decade, but by 1930 the population had reached 55,948.

These were "the golden years" of what many called "Little Norway." It constituted the third largest "Norwegian city" in the world, after Oslo and Bergen. The Chicago colony was a major cultural and organizational center within the national Norwegian ethnic community.

In the urban economy Norwegians found a niche in the building trades and construction. And they became carpenters and tailors. Women who worked outside the home sought domestic service. In Chicago Norwegians played a significant part in shipping on the Great Lakes as seamen, captains, and shipbuilders as long as sailing ships dominated, into the 1870s. A greater diversity of occupations for both men and women slowly evolved, as they entered white-collar work and received professional training. The upward social mobility is most evident in the second generation. Those arriving from Norway with special skills may have entered an immigrant elite. Social distinctions within the group showed themselves in the more exclusive residential choices made by prosperous Norwegian Americans. They were, however, still a part of the community as ethnic leaders and as organizers of public events.

Minneapolis eventually assumed a position as the new "Norwegian-American capital" because of its location at the center of the Norwegian population in the upper Midwest, though it had a much smaller Norwegian population than Chicago. In 1870, 1,000 of the city's inhabitants were Norwegian. The whole town communicated a Norwegian, or Scandinavian, flavor and lacked the cultural and ethnic diversity of Chicago. Adjustment in the public sphere was thereby less interactional with other ethnic populations and was devoid of much of the tensions of ethnic competitiveness. The Norwegian-American newspaperman Carl G. O. Hansen, who as a newcomer came to an uncle and aunt in Minneapolis in 1882, felt that he had arrived in a Norwegian city. By 1900 the Norwegian colony in Minneapolis consisted of 11,532 first- and second-generation Norwegians.[24]

On the East Coast Norwegians were mainly found in an urban setting, although there they also made their homes in small towns and away from large urban centers. The main concentration of Norwegians was, however, in Greater New York City, initially in Lower Manhattan. But soon, in the 1870s, Brooklyn became the main urban concentration in the East. By 1930 the Bay Ridge district, considered the fourth area of Norwegian settlement in the city, together with other areas of Norwegians in the metropolis had surpassed Chicago to become the largest urban center of Norwegians outside Norway. There were nearly 63,000 Norwegians, 60 percent of whom had been born in Norway.

A historian has described the Norwegian settlement as "the colony that rose from the sea" to suggest its connection to maritime activities.[25] Its beginnings were associated with sailors deserting Norwegian ships, but immigrants also transferred skills to find employment in the shipyards, dock construction, and other forms of work associated with shipping. And Norwegian sailors traveled on American ships both on distant waters and along the coast. A pronounced "birds of passage" phenomenon—people moving back and forth across the Atlantic—the many calls by Norwegian ships, and regular visits by prominent Norwegians preserved a closer connection with the homeland than was possible in the Midwest. The Brooklyn colony has been dubbed a Norwegian suburb, which, even if a bit exaggerated, describes a circumstance that is a clarifying significant variable in interpreting adjustment to the demands of the American environment.[26]

The Pacific Coast

Norwegian settlement in the Far West and in intermediate regions may in part be viewed as an extension westward from the core Norwegian areas in the upper Midwest. Around 1900 some Norwegians moved from North Dakota into the Great Plains in eastern Montana. Later settlement in that state was part of the response to the opportunities in mining in the Far West, western Montana, Idaho, and Colorado. In this large area of settlement can be included the Norwegian Mormon agricultural settlements in Utah. The center of Mormonism in the 1830s was Nauvoo, Illinois, not far from the main Norwegian settlements. The teachings of the Church of Jesus Christ of the Latter-day

Figure 3. The Norwegian-American artist Torlief S. Knaphus beside his statue of the type of cart used in the Mormon trek westward. The model is in clay; in bronze it stands on the temple square in Salt Lake City. Photograph courtesy of Martin Knaphus.

Saints found converts in the Fox River community. One of the Sloopers, Gudmund Haugaas, a Haugean preacher, became a Mormon bishop, and other Norwegians rose in rank and influence within that religious body. Some Norwegians followed in the trek westward to Utah in 1846 and 1847 (figure 3), and after proselytizing began in Scandinavia in the 1850s,

others went directly from Norway to the Mormon state.

Pioneer settlement on the Pacific Coast was associated with the discovery of gold in the lower Sacramento valley of California. Norwegians in the Midwest as well as in Norway responded to the lure of riches, although gold fever played no significant part in the history of Norwegian immigration. In the 1850s a small urban colony of Norwegians, largely sailors and craftsmen, emerged in the San Francisco Bay area. In the early history of the colony, members were businessmen and men of finance attracted to the speculative spirit and the opportunity for easy riches. The Norwegian colony had an elite character.[27]

The Puget Sound area became the main destination for Norwegians. Employment was found in fishing, shipping, and logging operations, and some took land. The completion of the transcontinental railroads in the 1880s encouraged Norwegian settlement in larger proportions. A large movement from the Midwest commenced in the latter part of the decade. In the protected sea lanes and bays in the Puget Sound Norwegians formed separate communities.

Forestry was an important livelihood for all Scandinavians in Washington State. Tacoma and Seattle were important mill towns. Seattle, on Elliott Bay, became the commercial center of the area and had the largest number of Norwegians, most heavily concentrated in the Ballard district in the northwestern part of the city. As in other urban settings, Norwegians entered construction and the building trades. They worked in shipping along the coast, transporting lumber to California. In 1900 as many as 16 percent of all Norwegian men in Seattle were employed in transportation. After 1900 Norwegians working as deep-sea fishermen and trap fishermen became the major players in the fishing industry in the Pacific Northwest. They were most prominent in the development of the halibut fishery as fishermen, boat owners, and boatbuilders. They owned land stations and participated in processing the catch, totally dominating this industry.

They took advantage of the fishing possibilities in Alaska as well. Numerically Norwegians in Alaska were few, but they still constituted the largest immigrant group in the first decades of the twentieth century. The only real Norwegian colony was Petersburg in southeastern Alaska, named after Peter Thams Buschman for his contributions to the development of the fishing industry in Alaska. Buschman emigrated from Trøndelag in 1891.[28]

The Lutheran Identity

The recounting of Norwegian-American religious life is the history of Lutheranism in America, although not exclusively; in the nineteenth century the majority never formally joined any denomination. The difficult transition from a state-church system with automatic membership to a free-church arrangement with voluntary membership presented religious leaders with a formidable challenge. Though Norwegian immigrants were attached by tradition to Lutheran rituals associated with baptism, confirmation, marriage, and burial, they regularly sought such church services without joining any congregation. The Lutheran Church had an influence in the immigrant community through the force of tradition that far exceeded the number of member communicants.

None, of course, desired to duplicate precisely the authoritarian episcopally organized Lutheran state church that had existed in Norway since the Reformation. The Lutheran Church among Norwegian Americans was to a marked degree an immigrant church, plagued with disharmony and divisiveness but also with impressive growth. It became in its various manifestations the main institution erected by Norwegians on American soil. The common confessionalism of the many Norwegian Lutheran synods that came into being in America, from the liturgical high church to the pietistic low church, placed a distance between it and non-Lutheran denominations and distinguished it from American Lutheranism with its roots in the German Colonial immigration. Under the influence of American Protestantism, the latter Lutheran Church attached less importance to Lutheran dogma.[29]

No fewer than fourteen Lutheran synods came into being among Norwegian Americans between 1846 and 1900. The free environment of America and a sense of nearly unbridled personal liberties encouraged separate synodical or institutional expressions of the homeland's faith. The early immigrants were served by lay preachers, who held devotional meetings in the simple immigrant huts in the Norwegian settlements. They were Haugean pietists but remained within the Lutheran fold; in Norway lay religious evangelizing was illegal until the conventicle acts regulating religious life were abolished in 1842 and complete religious freedom was granted in 1845. It was therefore natural that the first immigrant church body was a denomination of the laity, organized within the Lutheran free-church movement by the Norwegian lay preacher Elling Eielsen and his followers in the Fox River settlement in 1846. It became known as Eielsen's Synod. This church organization led to the founding of Hauge's Synod in 1876. It was a church of believers and the main representative for a low-church ideal. It stood for a transfer to America of a deep puritanism rooted in the pietistic Haugean movement in Norway. But regardless of theological direction, the American environment reinforced a puritanical conviction. Puritanism became pervasive among Norwegian immigrants and demanded strict adherence to rigidly moral conduct.[30]

The high-church arrangement was transplanted by university-trained and ordained Norwegian ministers. Both in education and in social status these men differed greatly from the lay founders, usually of the peasant classes, in the low-church congregations. Prominent names from Norway's upper classes were well represented among the immigrant high-church leaders. The Norwegian clerics had traveled to the Midwest out of a personal sense of mission; they were not sponsored by the Church of Norway, which did not consider the spiritual life of the immigrants its responsibility. The first congregation that came out of the state-church tradition was organized in the Muskego settlement in 1843 on the initiative of the Danish theologian Claus L. Clausen. J. W. C. Dietrichson, who came to the Norwegian colonies in 1844, was the first Norwegian university-trained pastor. He was a conservative and authoritarian man and did much to establish church discipline among his compatriots. His work and that of Herman Amberg Preus, who emigrated in 1851, led to the establishment in 1853 of the church organization generally referred to as the Norwegian Synod. It considered itself a daughter church of the Church of Norway and adopted its rituals and traditions; it opposed lay preaching, was dogmatic in its teachings, and asserted church authority in all questions of doctrine. Preus, and the other powerful "church fathers" Jacob Aall Ottesen and Ulrik Vilhelm Koren, upheld the doctrine of literal inerrancy and verbal inspiration of scripture and rejected a historical-critical approach to the study of biblical truths. Its conservatism in doctrine in time led it to distance itself from the homeland's church as this state religion responded to new theological currents and positions and to a modernization of Norwegian society in general. The immigrant clerics objected to these developments, and in bitter debates and conflicts with other Norwegian Lutheran bodies, the synod preoccupied itself with retaining "pure doctrine" based on biblical authority. The Norwegian Synod was the largest gathering of Norwegian Lutherans. From its founding and for many

years thereafter, it can with some justification be called the Norwegian church in America.

The third trend within Norwegian-American Lutheranism expressed itself as an intermediate direction between the liturgical church of the clerics and the pietistic church of the laity. Perceptions of clericalism and dogmatism in the Norwegian Synod led to the formation in 1860 of the Scandinavian Augustana Synod by Swedish and Norwegian congregations; the group also rejected the extremes of piety of the low-church movement. This Lutheran persuasion was influenced by the new theological and spiritual orientations in Norway. In 1870 the Norwegians left and formed their own synod. In 1890 several factions and synods within the intermediate persuasion, including the congregations known as the Anti-Missourian Brotherhood, which had departed from the Norwegian Synod in the strife over the teachings in regard to predestination in the late 1880s, formed the United Norwegian Lutheran Church. The name of the brotherhood was a reference to the Norwegian Synod's long-standing relationship with the stagnant theology of the German Missouri Synod. The United Church was then by far the largest Lutheran synod among Norwegians.

Not until 1917 were these three directions in Norwegian-American Lutheranism able to reconcile their differences and dissensions. There was a strong desire for union among Norwegian Lutherans. In the work toward a merger, appeals were made to nationality, to have one Norwegian Lutheran Church in America. It was easier to find similarities than differences, and the new waves of immigrants, who were more urban and better educated, showed little appreciation for the conflicts rooted in an older immigrant tradition. In general, the spread of urban values and practices into the isolated Norwegian settlements and the blossoming of secular organizations and political participation lessened congregational influence. That many of the old and authoritarian religious leaders had passed from the scene also helped the work for union. On Saturday, June 9, 1917, the United Church, Hauge's Synod, and the Norwegian Synod merged to form the Norwegian Lutheran Church in America, consummating the union at a grand celebration in St. Paul, Minnesota.

Religious Diversity

The religious pluralism in America made the Lutheran faith only one of several religious options. Membership in non-Lutheran denominations tended, however, to isolate Norwegians, not only in religious matters but also socially. Much of social life was associated with the congregation. But in places where no Norwegian Lutheran Church existed, immigrants tended to be pragmatic in their choice of place of worship and frequently attended American Protestant churches. Norwegians became members of Congregational and Presbyterian churches, which in their missionary activity showed a disinterested benevolence

in their aid to immigrants. Furthermore, their congregational independence and low-church services appealed to many Norwegians. Norwegians who sought status and had attained a degree of success were more likely to join the Protestant Episcopal Church. The Episcopal St. Ansgarius Church founded in 1849 in Chicago by the Swedish Episcopal minister Gustav Unonius had both Norwegian and Swedish members. But the Episcopal Church made little headway among Scandinavians. Many turned away from it perhaps because in organization and practice it reminded them too much of conditions they had left behind in Scandinavia. In other instances, immigrants responded favorably to zealous activity by friendly American missionaries who invited them to join their faith.

Norwegian Quakers generally became members of American congregations of Friends. The sloop *Restauration* carried the first Norwegian converts to the church of the Friends. Their history, therefore, extends through the entire period of Norwegian settlement. Many of the members of the Quaker Society in Stavanger, Norway, followed in the path of the pioneers and moved to the United States. In the Midwest independent Norwegian societies of Friends developed in the mid-nineteenth century in Marshall County, Iowa. Some of their small congregations still retain a Norwegian-American identity.[31]

Methodist missionary activity, characterized by evangelism and revival meetings, had greater success among Norwegian Americans, but considering the enthusiastic reception in American society of the pietism in conduct and beliefs and of the emotional religious content of Methodism, it is somewhat surprising that there were not more Norwegian converts. Lutheranism obviously had a strong hold, but the American character of Methodism and its noticeable nativistic overtones may have alienated many Norwegians. An idiosyncratic Norwegian nationalism, as compared to the other two Scandinavian nationalities, may have heightened such sensitivity.

Still the Methodists' message of repentance and conversion found a response. The Methodist mission among Scandinavians began in New York in 1845 with the Bethel Ship mission of the Swede Olof G. Hedström, who preached to Scandinavian seamen.[32] Ole P. Petersen, a Norwegian sailor who had converted to Methodism in an American port and was an associate of Hedström, began missionary work west of the Mississippi River in 1851. He founded a Methodist church the following year in Washington Prairie, a conservative Lutheran district in northeastern Iowa.

Toward the end of the 1860s, revivalism was carried forward by zealous missionaries in Chicago, which became the center of Norwegian-American Methodism. In June 1868, thirty-five Danish and Norwegian members joined by other converts formed the First Norwegian-Danish Methodist Church. Most of these had earlier belonged to a Scandinavian Methodist

Church erected in 1854. A Norwegian-Danish cooperation was thus established, and in 1880 the Norwegian-Danish Conference became a national body within the Methodist church, with a separate theological seminary in Evanston, Illinois. Fewer than five thousand members in "full union" had joined by the end of the century.[33]

Advances for the evangelistic Baptists among Scandinavians were modest and uneven. Like the Methodists, they had most success among Swedes. Norwegians baptized by immersion joined groups of Swedish Baptists or Danish and American churches. The first converts were made as early as 1837 in the volatile religious climate in the Fox River settlement. There were Norwegians in the small First Danish Baptist Church formed in Chicago in 1864. The First Norwegian Baptist Church in Chicago came into being in 1877 with few members. Economic reality dictated Danish-Norwegian cooperation. The large Scandinavian Pilgrim Baptist Church in Chicago was a result of this cooperation. In 1910 Norwegians formed a separate Norwegian conference within the Baptist Church, which was eventually assimilated into the main church body.[34]

The Norwegian-American Press

As an institution, the immigrant press was second only to the religious ones in importance. In fact, it made a separate ethnic life possible. The immigrant newspapers served as local news sheets and urban community mediums, and in some cases strove to become national Norwegian-American organs. They thereby created a sense of a national community of Norwegian Americans. Only through the written word could ethnic solidarity be achieved, and the written language consequently assumed increased importance in immigrant circumstances.

The immigrant journals were all in the tradition of the penny press, written for and frequently about the common man. Their democratic tone encouraged a lively interaction with their readers. The ethnic newspaper frequently became like a personal friend. People related personal experiences, requested information, expressed opinions, and if the need was there, appealed for aid from compatriots. The significance of the immigrant press is suggested by the fact that per capita its circulation exceeded by far the distribution of newspapers in Norway. Immigrants became avid subscribers and readers of newspapers, attesting to the great need for information in the new and unfamiliar environment, as well as to the desire to associate with compatriots. The ethnic press kept immigrants informed about events and people in the homeland, but also reflected immigrants' desire to take part in the public life of America. Most immigrant newspapers showed a clear political affiliation; from the start they were players in American politics and a part of the process of immigrant adjustment.[35]

The Norwegian-American press estab-lished itself firmly in pioneer times. The first Norwegian-language newspaper, *Nordlyset,* came out in 1847 in the pioneer Muskego settlement but lasted only briefly. The major pioneer newspaper was *Emigranten,* published as a secular organ beginning in 1852 by the church-controlled Scandinavian Press Association, showing the strong influence of the Lutheran clergy in most aspects of early immigrant life. It began as a Democratic organ, but with new ownership and independence shifted to Republican colors in 1857, reflecting a general trend among Norwegian voters. *Emigranten* lasted well beyond the Civil War.

Newspapers sprang up in shifting centers of Norwegian settlement. As many as four hundred newspapers saw the light of day from 1847 to the present, even though the majority did so only briefly. A few journals became leading organs, growing with the Norwegian-American community and providing leadership in changed conditions. In the Midwest, *Skandinaven* in Chicago was published from 1866 to 1941, *Decorah-Posten* in Iowa existed for nearly one hundred years, from 1874 to 1972, and *Minneapolis Tidende* in Minnesota lasted from 1887 until 1935; all three were major newspapers with wide circulation. *Skandinaven* was for some time the largest Norwegian-language newspaper in the world, surpassing by a wide margin any newspaper published in Norway at that time.[36]

Outside the Midwest, *Washington-Posten,* started in Seattle in 1889, became a major organ on the Pacific Coast. It is currently published as *Western Viking*. And in the East, *Nordisk Tidende/Norway Times* has been published in Brooklyn since 1891. These two centers of more recent immigration still support ethnic publications, though the support is rapidly diminishing, and much of the material is presented in English. Both publications have sought a national circulation as the number of potential subscribers has fallen. Obviously their role is no longer what it once was. They still carry news of the homeland and articles about Norwegian-American activities but, of course, no longer inform a separate subculture.[37]

In Public Life

The immigrant press frequently served individual political ambitions among the immigrants, and political hopefuls sought the endorsement of influential journals. The press not only educated Norwegian Americans about public affairs, but it solicited their support for individual political positions and for political candidates. Norwegian Americans could, therefore, appear at times as major voting blocs for candidates of their own nationality and for specific issues that found favor within the Norwegian-American community. American politicians and political parties courted their support as a potential voting bloc. Since all male immigrants who had reached the age of maturity were granted the franchise by declaring their intent to become American

citizens—that is, by filing the all-important first papers—Norwegian immigrants appeared early to be a possible political force. At times their vote was split according to political convictions or because a favored candidate was running for office. Norwegians took part in shaping several political cultures in America and cannot be considered a hegemonic bloc, even though regional circumstances in America, such as those that generated an agrarian revolution in wheat-producing regions, their time of emigration, and even social class encouraged common political mobilization. Economic considerations may have been more important in political affiliation than ethnic solidarity.

Since the newspaper enjoying the widest circulation often became a county's official organ regardless of whether it was printed in English or a foreign language, in the nineteenth century a Norwegian-language journal was declared the official newspaper in some counties with large Norwegian populations. Because of this status, these newspapers enjoyed the advertising business generated by public announcements.

And it was in the local community that Norwegian immigrants initially entered political life. They first became politically active and learned about American democracy and its practices in township administration. In townships where they dominated, they had no choice but to assume responsibility. Where they were fewer, language barriers and a sense

Figure 4. Knute Nelson (1843–1923) was the first Norwegian-American politician to gain prominence in American politics. Photograph courtesy of the Minnesota Historical Society.

In the years after the Civil War the Norwegian-American press both reflected and encouraged a greater patriotism for the American homeland and greater political participation. The war was a watershed experience for Norwegians in America. The extreme hostilities had created Norwegian-American heroes, and at the same time members of an American-born generation appeared with the self-confidence to become ethnic political leaders. The war had also moved Norwegian Americans, guided by immigrant journals, completely into the fold of the Republican Party. It was, after all, nearly the only political organization in the upper Midwest, but in addition for Norwegian Americans it represented Protestantism, high moral ideals, and prohibition, as well as free land under the Homestead Act. A historian has claimed that to understand Norwegian political behavior, one has to realize the group's fierce anti-Catholicism. The Democratic Party was, they thought, infested with Catholicism, vice, and corruption.

Knute Nelson, U.S. senator from Minnesota from 1895 to 1923, was the most prominent politician among early Norwegian Americans (figure 4). He owed much of his success to his ability to rise above narrow parochialism and to even court the support of Catholic voters and other potential supporters. Initially, however, he had been carried forward on the shoulders of his compatriots as he entered state and national politics, being elected from

of ethnic inferiority may have kept them from actively taking part in local political affairs. The distance was short from township administration to political positions in the county. From these positions they might be elected to the state legislature or other state office, and even to the national arena. These ethnic politicians usually had grassroots support. But there were exceptions. James D. Reymert, publisher of *Nordlyset* in 1847, used his involvement in the immigrant press as a springboard for election to the Wisconsin legislature.

Minnesota to Congress in 1882. It was this victory that launched him on his career of national leadership.[38]

New issues and interests weakened the loyalty of Norwegian Americans to the Republican Party. In urban situations with strong Democratic Party ties, like Chicago, for instance, there was a continuous, though small, coterie of Norwegian voters who placed themselves in that political camp. Norwegians, in fact, joined the urban machine politics of both parties. During the politically turbulent 1890s, the Democratic Party moved toward a reform stance. In this historic change Democrats embraced economic radicalism, departed from their earlier laissez-faire conservatism, and mobilized small farmers and laborers to political action. Norwegian voters, along with other urban ethnic groups, followed the national trend in the first decades of the twentieth century toward support of the Democratic Party, bringing it to national prominence. Still, Norwegian-American loyalty to the Republican Party remained a political factor. The Republicanism of middle- and upper-class Norwegian Americans and other Scandinavians reflected the concerns of Americans in these classes—protection of their economic position and emulation of the leaders of society, who generally were strongly Republican.[39]

In the Midwest Norwegians involved themselves in reform movements. Some of the issues, such as temperance and prohibition, were restrictive rather than liberal reform measures.

Work for temperance and prohibition, an effort to eradicate the evils they thought manifested in alcohol and the saloon, drew many Norwegians into reform efforts. This work also became an avenue for Norwegian-American politicians to gain political office through the support of reform-minded compatriots. Many of the immigrant journals, such as *Reform* in Eau Claire, Wisconsin, and *Afholds-Basunen* (The Temperance Trumpet) in Hillsboro, North Dakota, made prohibition their main cause. In North Dakota the temperance forces, supported by Norwegian voters, put a prohibition plank into the state constitution in 1889. The efforts of Norwegian Lutheran pastors and lay people in agitating for reform and in organizing temperance societies were decisive in securing wide support from the Norwegian electorate.[40]

Defections from the Republican Party coupled with insurgency within the party gave evidence of strong reform convictions among Norwegian-American voters. But such protest actions were to a large extent generated by economic self-interest. In the wheat-producing regions in North Dakota and northwestern Minnesota, farmers endeavored to gain control over the marketing of their own products and to diminish the power of railroads and credit agencies. An agrarian revolt, intensified by a continual agricultural crisis, produced the Populist Party in 1890. Many Norwegians joined. The Norwegian-language *Normanden* (The Norseman) in Grand Forks, North Dakota, became its official organ. Prosperity around the turn of the century dissipated the Populist movement, but it left a legacy of political independence, even though most Populist defectors returned to the Republican Party.

There remained a Progressive wing within the Republican Party where many Norwegian voters seemed to place themselves. In Wisconsin Norwegian voters followed the Progressivism shaped by Robert M. La Follette. With *Skandinaven* as its Norwegian-language organ, La Follette and such prominent Norwegian-American politicians as Nils P. Haugen sought to enact laws to protect the poor, ignorant, and defenseless, and to pass legislation to hinder the accumulation and abuse of wealth and power by a few. The Progressive candidates gradually consolidated their hold over the Republican Party in Wisconsin.[41]

In North Dakota the Republican Nonpartisan League was organized in 1915 as a radical offspring of the Progressive movement. The league agitated for socialistic reforms such as state control and operation of grain silos and the sale of wheat. It was a new form of agrarian unrest and a renewed effort to lead the Republican Party. Some historians have attributed political radicalism in the state to Norwegian immigrants. Whether or not it might be accepted as an ethnic or even religious quality, as some commentators have suggested, can be debated; economic self-interest and local conditions where they settled may have encouraged radicalism among them more than ethnic or religious idiosyncrasy.

In Minnesota many of the protest groups found each other in the Farmer-Labor Party founded in 1922; in 1944 it merged with the Democratic Party. The more affluent Norwegian districts in the southeastern part of Minnesota rejected the reform message of Farmer-Laborism and remained in the conservative and traditional Republican camps. In many ways, of course, Norwegian and Scandinavian political behavior was not unique but followed a general political pattern in the Midwest.

A class-based philosophy produced a socialistic movement among Norwegian and other Scandinavian workers. Chicago became the center of Scandinavian radicals. They were united in the Scandinavian Socialist Union organized in 1910, a time when ethnic socialist leaders displaced old-stock American centrist and conservative socialists. They advocated not a revolutionary socialism, however, but one achieved through the ballot box in a democratic manner. The Scandinavian Socialist Union combined the efforts of Scandinavian socialist clubs from all over the United States. Urban centers such as Minneapolis and St. Paul had many labor activists, some of these being former Populists, and socialism entered smaller towns and rural communities in the western part of Minnesota, again in the so-called Populist wheat belt. Many Norwegians joined the socialist cause after the failed Populist movement. The oppression of the years of World War I, with its hysterical "100-percent Americanism," left little room for politically radical groups and led many Norwegian voters to seek social democratic reform within other responsive political constellations, such as the Farmer-Labor Party in Minnesota.[42]

Cultural Affairs

According to the 1910 census every third Norwegian, counting only the immigrants and their children, one million people in all, resided in the United States. The first generation reached its peak that year with 403,858 persons registered by the census takers; the second generation had surpassed the immigrants, numbering 607,267. About 80 percent of the Norwegian-American population lived in the states of the upper Midwest.[43] No Norwegian historian at the time took cognizance of these truly impressive statistics, although these are the years in which official Norway discovered and sought contact with a mature Norwegian-American community. A large Norwegian-speaking population gave impetus and support to cultural, social, and creative activities of many kinds. This is the time, if any, that may be described as Norwegian America.

In urban and rural settings a voluntary organizational life flourished, and there were events and celebrations that strengthened an ethnic impulse. The end of the Swedish-Norwegian Union in 1905 created national pride in the homeland's complete independence. As sociologist Herbert Gans has pointed out, the old country is particularly useful as an identity symbol; because of distance, it does not make arduous demands on American ethnics.[44] Still, greater prosperity made visits to the home sod commonplace for the immigrants and their descendants. In 1914 Norwegian Americans commemorated the centennial of the Eidsvoll Constitution, signed on May 17, 1814; a large number of them attended commemorative observances in Norway. The Eidsvoll Jubilee honored the rebirth of Norwegian nationality in 1814 after a nearly four-hundred-year-long union with Denmark. Public celebrations on May 17 in centers of Norwegian settlement were regular occurrences from the early 1870s on (figure 5). Public festivals became grand events from around the turn of the century. In large urban areas the many Norwegian societies cooperated in arranging colorful folk festivals, with children's parades, athletic competitions, choirs, musical contributions, and always speeches extolling the virtues and merits of Norwegian ethnicity. May 17 became the main identifying ethnic symbol.

Winter sports on snow and ice served as another romantic national image. They were a special ethnic forte, and skiing especially created celebrated ethnic heroes. Ski sports, in particular cross-country skiing and ski jumping, were introduced and developed by Norwegian immigrants in the 1880s. "Ski jumper" became a nickname for Norwegians. These initiatives blossomed at the end of the century. Numerous clubs built scaffolds and arranged meets and national tournaments. In 1905 the

Figure 5. May 17 celebration in the mid-1870s in Winequaw, in the vicinity of Madison, Wisconsin. Such folk festivals have been the most prominent Norwegian-American ethnic symbol. Note the device marking the union with Sweden in the upper left-hand corner of the flag. Photograph courtesy of the State Historical Society of Wisconsin [WHi (D31) 681].

National Ski Association of America was founded in Ishpeming, Michigan. Six of the seven founders were Norwegian.[45]

The large number of young male immigrants encouraged athletic activity of various types. Gymnastics or turn societies, following the German model, became popular, and they expanded to include soccer teams and skating competitions, and gradually admitted women athletes. Male choral singing was another common German and Scandinavian activity that found many practitioners, and women's choral groups were also formed. Grand singing festivals attracted large audiences. There were theater troupes in urban centers like Chicago from the late 1860s. The Norwegian Dramatic Society was founded in 1868 and in its repertoire displayed a distinct Norwegian national spirit. Dramatic art was cultivated in clubs and lodges and became one of the most conspicuous cultural activities among Norwegian immigrants. There were literary societies, which mainly chose literature from the homeland and classical fiction in Norwegian translation, but also read some of the modest works of Norwegian immigrant authors. Immigrant literary expression lasted for some seventy years, but it reached its height only toward the end with the masterful novels about immigrant life by Ole E. Rølvaag.[46]

Special interests, social cliques, and personal ambitions sought expression in a multitude of clubs, societies, and organizations. Within the fluid and occasionally chaotic bounds of the

ethnic community a veritable organizational mania existed. The proliferation of societies appeared as an inescapable aspect of immigrant social life. Men's clubs were common, and many of these had a clear social status above the ordinary immigrant as they arranged exclusive banquets and fashionable balls. A similar "high life" attracted prosperous and successful Norwegian Americans to elite clubs, a number calling themselves Norwegian Society, emulating—in name at least—the nationalistic and elitist society of Norwegian students at the university in Copenhagen in the 1770s. Such societies, and the numerous clubs with a more democratic character, may be said to have been united in their common concern for the preservation of a national heritage.

A unique organizational development found expression in the *bygdelag*, or old-home societies, that appeared on the immigrant scene around 1900. These groups gave the rural Norwegian American an organizational base. They were regional in character and assembled Norwegians from specific districts, valleys, and fjord regions, who came together for an annual reunion to cultivate their peasant cultural heritage in speech and in other cultural indicators. The reunion, or *stevne*, as it was called, recreated an eclectic and partly constructed version of their local peasant cultural heritage. It was a celebratory way of defining who they were. Though the content of the reunions varied from society to society in the approximately fifty national groups that came into being, a

general pious spirit prevailed, introduced by
the Lutheran clergy that gained control of
many of these societies. The first *stevne* was held
by immigrants from Valdres, in Norway's central highland, in Minnehaha Park in Minneapolis in 1899. Obviously, these groups clashed
with the refined ethnic culture embraced in
urban colonies of Norwegians, and their parochial attachment prompted attacks by those
who promoted a common Norwegian ethnic
identity. Yet, it was these groups that joined
forces to arrange a festival commemorating the
centennial of the Eidsvoll Constitution in 1914
in Minneapolis and St. Paul, and again in 1925
to organize the grand Norse-American Centennial, also in the Twin Cities, celebrating the arrival of the sloop *Restauration* a hundred years
earlier. It was the first large festival to observe a
historic immigrant event and was a rejection of
the oppressive advocacy of 100-percent Americanism generated by the xenophobia of World
War I.[47]

The *bygdelag* were social organizations. But
a few of the societies formed in the larger cities
based on a Norwegian regional origin, like
most ethnic urban organizations, functioned
when need dictated as mutual aid societies.
Such self-help societies, and also burial societies, were the most common form of immigrant organization. Dictated by social needs,
they became numerous in the Norwegian-
American community. Most were found in
urban centers, but a few also emerged in rural
and small town environments. These societies
gave a voice to urban workers outside the

control of the Lutheran Church. The most
successful of these societies was the Sons of
Norway, organized among Norwegian workers in Minneapolis in January 1895. As a fraternal group it grew to become a national, and
even international, organization with lodges
throughout the United States and Canada, and
lately even in Norway. It represented a general
effort from the 1890s to unite Norwegians in
America on a regional or nationwide basis.
Women were permitted as members after 1916.
In the manner of other fraternities it transformed itself, while giving outlet for social impulses, from mutual assistance into an insurance company.[48]

Immigrant Social Institutions

The social work of the church was a prominent
aspect of its mission. The congregation itself,
especially in rural settlements, became a focal
point and a conservative force. The congregation created a tight social network and touched
all aspects of life—religious, social, and economic. Familial relations were strengthened through
extensive in-marriage; it was expected that one
married within the congregation. The discord so
characteristic of Norwegian-American Lutheranism may even be seen as creating increased
interest in the church. Historians have interpreted Lutheran schism simply as a transformation
or reinterpretation rather than as a breakdown
of the rural community. The new community
structures in the divisions that resulted from
the controversy were more homogeneous and

intense in terms of personal interaction. Thus, as a central institution, the church, even as it engaged in internal religious warfare, nurtured a sense of community by adherence to a common set of values and traditions.[49]

The denominationalism of Norwegian-American Lutheranism produced a church responsive to the needs of its parishioners, corresponding to American Protestantism in general. Like the latter, it was formed in a rural environment, and its entry into the city was a missionary venture. It transferred its prejudices and fears to the new setting and viewed the city as a direct threat both to Lutheranism and to the Norwegian heritage. In the city the church assumed new responsibilities and competed more directly with temporal interests than in the Norwegian-American farming communities.

The Norwegian Lutheran Church adapted to the city, mainly in its expanded social services, again following the pattern of American Protestant denominations. The influence of the urban church was felt far beyond the congregational or denominational fold. The social needs became especially pressing in large urban centers, and the circumstances among the immigrants themselves called forth large charitable efforts by the church. Many immigrants arrived with few or no resources, and the hard reality of an urban existence required charitable action. Early on there were assistance societies that addressed the problem; there were especially many formed in response to the dire needs of immigrants during the 1860s. The church also collected money to respond to appeals for help and to the needs it identified within Norwegian neighborhoods.

The large systematic charitable enterprises, however, commenced only in the 1880s in urban colonies of Norwegians. Many orphanages, hospitals, and old-people's homes had their modest beginning in this decade and the following. Some of them are currently major institutions, though they in the main have lost much of their Norwegian identity.[50] Women played an important part in the voluntary charitable work. They were most frequently from what might be called a Norwegian-American urban middle class. Like their American contemporaries, married women of this class spent much of their time outside the home. Women's organizations grew in step with urbanization.

The American Matrix

The growth and transformation that occurred in those immigrant institutions—social, cultural, and educational—that adjusted and survived and in commercial and industrial enterprises become a measure of the overall changes, transitions, adjustments, and conformities within the Norwegian-American population as a whole. There were forces of assimilation located both inside and outside the group as it interacted with a multicultural American environment.

Industries founded by Norwegian immigrants functioned within an American economic system from the start, even those that catered to the immigrant community specifically and those that entered the American marketplace. Their identities as Norwegian-American commercial enterprises have now largely been lost as they have become, if not always in name, in reality part of major national and international corporations. Those that did not make this transition have largely disappeared.

The educational institutions founded by Norwegian immigrants have, while becoming totally integrated into the American educational system, retained more of a Norwegian ethnic identity, at least in superficial ways. It assumes at times an ornamental quality. Six four-year colleges and one two-year college are the survivors of the great number of institutions of higher learning founded by various factions of Norwegian Lutherans in America. They still receive royal visits from Norway, and their presidents are regularly decorated by royal orders. Their student bodies and faculties are, however, rapidly becoming less Lutheran and even less Norwegian.

What is occurring in these institutions is simply a reflection of societal developments in general. The 1990 census shows no particular concentration of Norwegian Americans in specific occupations and professions, save for a somewhat higher than average representation in the category of farming, forestry, and fishing, an economic niche that earlier had characterized the group.[51] An economic assimilation is thus much in evidence; Norwegian Americans are occupied in all levels in the workplace. In many respects, the Norwegian-American population is well adjusted, and most members view their situation in America in favorable terms.

Norwegian Americans conscious of a specific identity see themselves as descendants of the Vikings, insist on a Viking discovery of America by Leif Ericson and his fellow Norse mariners, celebrate the pioneer frontier history of Norwegian immigrants, commemorate Norwegian heroes of the Civil War, and take pride in their achievements as a nationality in American society. These are the images and mythologies that have shaped their self-perception, and it is how they continue to present themselves in public celebrations and festivals. Many of those who participate in Norwegian commemorative events and identify with Norwegian-American culture have through the ethnic mixing of the nationalities only a diluted bloodline to a Norwegian ancestry or *none* at all; ethnic identity has become a matter of subjective choice, not infrequently through choosing to identify with the ethnicity of a spouse. Some will call this a postethnic phenomenon, a cosmopolitan rejection of the narrowness of the involuntary dogma of cultural pluralism that *assigns* group identities. It is a voluntary affiliation, perhaps, as has been claimed, a step beyond multiculturalism. In any case, in their creation, or invention, if you will, of a Norwegian-American identity, based on self-consciously selected and refurbished elements of an ethnic heritage, Norwegian Americans have as a group unquestionably secured a respectable place in American history and society.[52]

CHAPTER 2

In the American Mosaic

Ethnic America

During the past few decades, ethnicity has become a basic concept in historical studies of immigrant adaptation to American society. It is a central theme in American life and suggests the origins of the American nation in the immigrant heritage. Immigrants move, it is said, in a process of ethnicization from their immigrant status to becoming some kind of ethnic Americans. A productive conceptualization of ethnicity by Werner Sollors, described as "the invention of ethnicity," will inform the analysis of the Norwegian-American experience.[1] This conceptualization echoes the notion introduced by Eric Hobsbawm in 1983 as "the invention of tradition": when traditions have recent origin in national cultures but because of repetition, give the impression of being sanctioned by long usage over the centuries, and thus imply continuity with the past.[2] Once stated as a general principle, however, the theory of invention may be amplified and redefined as an analytical tool and given a prescribed objective. For instance, in the context of this study of Norwegian Americans, invention must not be equated with fiction, or even a cultural construction accomplished over historical time, as Sollors seems to suggest. Admittedly, ethnic groups in modern societies respond to internal and external forces by constantly re-creating and reinventing their ethnicity. In the socialization of an ethnic group across the generations, aspects of its values, norms, and identifying patterns of behavior are increasingly altered. It is, thus, an ethnicity that is constructed in a historical process that incorporates and transmutes shared cultural heritages and historical memories. In other words, it rests upon social and cultural realities.

35

Ethnicity represents a negotiation and re-negotiation in which not only is the dominant American culture involved in a social dialogue with each ethnic group, but in which the different ethnic groups relate to each other in both positive and negative ways in a diverse environment of competing ethnic identities. The nature of the relationships among differing immigrant cultures has an impact on the formation of communal bonds, as ethnic boundaries are established, and on ethnic identities, as each group defines itself. In a certain sense ethnic identities may even be said to have been ascribed by the majority culture, although here also the perception and the stereotyping of minority cultures have varied temporally. This shifting attitude of the dominant society toward ethnic minorities has influenced evolving ethnic group identities.

A major point in regard to the theory of invention of ethnicity is that it allows for human agency in defining group identities and solidarities, rather than postulating the conventional idea of a passive assimilation into a dominant Anglo-American culture. Ethnic groups instead are regarded as engaging in a dynamic strategy of adaptation and accommodation. The process of invention briefly stated may be viewed as a selective and self-conscious refashioning of a particular ethnicity through historic time. The issue for contemporary Norwegian Americans is, consequently, not how much of a traditional culture has been preserved, or how their ethnic culture relates to modern Norway, but rather how the ethnic symbols and rituals of the group have found changing utilization in a multicultural American setting. As ethnicity applies to contemporary Norwegian Americans, the findings of this study agree with Thomas J. Archdeacon that ethnic background "can affect actions and attitudes whether the person involved is unconscious of his or her heritage, publicly rejects it, or chauvinistically flaunts it."[3]

In order to proceed, then, it is manifestly imperative to recognize ethnic cultures as legitimate and meaningful expressions of a historical process. Norwegians, like other nationalities, are a people divided by migration. As a consequence two separate cultures emerged; one developed among Norwegians in Norway, and one took shape among Norwegians in America. From the time of separation in the mid-1820s, these two cultures over time, from generation to generation, evolved in different directions. This is a major point of this study, which rejects both the idea that the Norwegian-American community and its culture are merely an extension of the homeland and the sense that its cultural manifestations are inferior. They are, of course, simply ethnic, having evolved in historic time in a multicultural American environment. By making modernization of the homeland the norm against which the ethnic community is judged, Norwegians on both sides of the Atlantic seem, however, to agree on the hybrid and diminished quality of ethnic cultural developments. Norwegian

Americans throughout their history have frequently felt embarrassed and have regularly been made fun of by their kin at home whenever comparisons are made between their ethnic traditions and linguistic habits and those in Norway (figure 6). Making value judgments on historical processes is in all cases unproductive. To approach ethnic adjustment over time from a biased point of view is to enter a blind alley intellectually. Avenues to a cogent knowledge of the group's history will as a consequence be barred. Accordingly, the Norwegianness of Americans of Norwegian ancestry deserves to be viewed with respect, as this study does, to be taken seriously, and to be understood on its own premises as a valid and logical outcome of the group's American experience.[4]

According to the federal census, in 1990 Norwegians constituted only 1.6 percent of the total American population, making it one of the smallest of America's definable ethnic groups.[5] Of European ethnic groups, 23.3 percent reported German ancestry; 15.6 percent, Irish; 13.1 percent, English; 5.9 percent, Italian; 3.8 percent, Polish; 1.9 percent, Swedish; and 0.7 percent, Danish.[6] Geographic dispersion and regional concentrations determined to a great extent the relative influence of the different nationalities. Norwegian-American experience would, therefore, be affected by the group's relative strength in specific regions and by the ethnic and racial composition in these areas. Accommodation, personal and group identities, and the symbols of these identities would as a consequence exhibit regional variations. Norwegian Americans residing in solidly Norwegian communities in western Wisconsin, for instance, would not face the multicultural tensions of their compatriots in a bustling urban center such as Brooklyn in the East, or of those living dispersed in the huge Los Angeles metropolitan area on the Pacific Coast, and hence the diverse settings would affect how Norwegian-American ethnicity manifested itself.

Newcomers and Old-Timers

Timing represents a second important variable alongside geography in immigrant adjustment. Those arriving in America following World War II may have understandably experienced a certain distance from the expressions of Norwegian ethnicity they encountered. The postwar immigrants harbored a greater piety toward the traditions and practices of the homeland. Furthermore, American immigration legislation affected the social makeup of Norwegians arriving in the United States. Whereas early postwar immigrants, especially those who immigrated before the Immigration and Nationality Act of 1965 became effective in 1968, represented a broad social spectrum of Norwegian society, those who immigrated after the act were progressively more elite in their composition. This tendency could be discerned even prior to the restrictions the new law imposed.

Figure 6. The "typical" Norwegian American who returned to the homeland was popularly perceived as a person with expensive habits but without culture. This caricature appeared in the satirical newspaper Trangviksposten, published between 1900 and 1907.

Highly educated people were still welcome after the act, and the financial rewards in America for this class of Norwegians were attractive. For Norwegians arriving with the benefit of skilled training, such as architects, engineers, bankers, and scientists, economic adjustment posed few problems. Many made their homes in affluent suburban neighborhoods. Those working in the United States for only a few years for Norwegian companies in banking, shipping, and in the oil industry—often referred to as "the new industries"—during the past decade, even more so than educationally privileged postwar immigrants, provide much evidence of exclusiveness in regard to the older immigrant tradition. They not infrequently simply dismiss Norwegian Americans as "Americans." This attitude shows the historical split between "colonist" and "newcomer," though in this case the newcomer from a prosperous and modern Norway is assuming the superior attitude.

From the late 1960s many Norwegian newcomers in the category of university-trained immigrants made their homes in the affluent Charbonneau suburb of Portland, Oregon. Lila Oftenæs Larsen, born in Oslo in 1944, belongs to this group of immigrants and relates her disappointing early encounter with the local lodge of the Sons of Norway. To her dismay she discovered that it consisted mainly of elderly people who "came together to play cards" and thus had little time to cultivate interest in Norway. They commemorated May 17 on the nearest Sunday, whereas the newcomers in Charbonneau piously wanted to observe Norway's constitution day on the day itself, as in Norway, and to speak Norwegian, which few of the lodge people could. Tensions were intensified by differences in age and economic status between the newcomers and the Sons of Norway members. The Norwegian identity of the recent arrivals was reinforced by the fact that the majority retained their Norwegian citizenship. They may even to some extent have viewed themselves as Norwegians in exile.

In the mid-1980s the Charbonneau gang, as Larsen described it, combined their efforts in a society called Syklubben, the sewing club, which had nothing to do with handiwork. Instead, its main purpose was to arrange traditional May 17 observances. In the following years this national Norwegian holiday was properly commemorated. But alas, even in this newcomer setting the inevitable intrusion of English and a surrender to the demands of the work place moved Syklubben toward the Norwegian-American pattern. May 17 was on its way to being reduced to an ethnic identifying symbol among the Norwegian-born. It could not be maintained as an unaltered traditional Norwegian national event. In January 1996, a committee of the Grieg Lodge of the Sons of Norway in Portland, of which Larsen had by then become social director, and representatives of the Syklubben constituency met to plan a joint observance—on the Sunday closest to May 17.[7]

Figure 7. One of the youngest participants of the thousands who lined the parade route during the May 17 celebration in Bay Ridge, Brooklyn, in 1996. The event continues to be advertised as the largest celebration of the day outside Norway. Photograph reprinted courtesy of the Norway Times.

An even greater cultural and social distance is evident between affluent representatives for Norwegian companies and more recently arrived Norwegians with their own businesses and residences in fashionable Stamford or Greenwich, Connecticut, and the older Norwegian-American community in the East. But even so, a common ethnic link exists, at least intermittently. On May 17 many become "Norwegian for a day"; it is that year's ethnic experience for some. May 17 in Bay Ridge in Brooklyn is still advertised as the largest celebration of the day outside Norway; the 1996 event was the forty-seventh May 17 parade there (figure 7). Thou-

sands of people marched while other thousands lined the parade route on Fifth Avenue. It was indeed ethnicity on parade. For several years social distinctions have surfaced dramatically when the May 17 committee, consisting of delegates from the Norwegian-American organizations, have invited people to a ferry ride following the parade for $15, not including refreshments. In the meantime, the elite have enjoyed a luxury cruise with full beverage and food service for $150, arranged by a successful Norwegian-born ship chandler in New York, Victor Samuelsen. Ethnic solidarity breaks down along social class lines.[8]

In Houston, Texas, the numerous younger arrivals from Norway—mainly in shipping and oil but also in engineering and banking—have apparently taken over the Snorre chapter of the Norwegian Society of Texas in Houston, a Norwegian-American organization formed in 1975. The membership is split between, on one side, short-term Norwegians, who are those who return to Norway after a few years, and, on the other, the permanent Norwegian immigrants and those of Norwegian descent. The short-term Norwegian residents in this port city center their activities around the Norwegian Seamen's Church and may regard it as an institution mainly for Norwegian-born individuals. They clannishly stay away from the Christmas ball arranged jointly by the Sons of Norway and the Scandinavian Club but may join the ball at the more elite Norwegian-American Chamber of Commerce.

Norwegian-American traditions, and their advocates, may appear foreign and quaint to many contemporary Norwegians, not just to the newcomers in Houston. Perhaps, one may speculate, descendants of Norwegian immigrants and their ways remind them of a previous Norway—a backward and poor agricultural nation that gave up a substantial portion of its population to overseas migration. It is a Norway many younger Norwegians do not know and may even wish never existed. Their perception of who they are favors instead an image of a prosperous and progressive Norway.[9]

Individuals born in Norway are naturally a minute minority of the Norwegian-American population of nearly 3.9 million, only about 1.2 percent; approximately 84 percent of them arrived before 1980. As stated previously, the earlier postwar immigrants were less elite and more representative of the social composition of the Norwegian population as a whole. In the 1980s, 7,555 Norwegians entered the United States. Those arriving before 1980 number 39,841, of which 30,536, about 77 percent, have become naturalized citizens of the United States, indicating identification with the new society and, to be sure, in some cases reflecting merely a pragmatic attitude or even a requirement of a particular occupational pursuit, for instance, fishing, where boat ownership is limited to American citizens.[10] A social variable in the rate of naturalization cannot be empirically observed, but anecdotal information suggests that it was those at the upper level of the Nor-

wegian-American community who most often resisted giving up Norwegian citizenship.

Separate social organizations and societies, however, emerged at all class levels among postwar immigrants, suggesting the greater comfort of associating with other newcomers, and also a certain distance from the older immigrant culture. Still, some postwar newcomers entered older immigrant organizations, took part in May 17 celebrations, and were leaders in many ethnic activities. Richard Berhow, a fourth-generation Norwegian American born in 1928 from the Midwest now residing on the West Coast, explained the split as it pertains to the Columbia Lodge of the Sons of Norway in Vancouver, Washington: "Certain groups of first-generation Norwegians clique to themselves and their own traditions. The lodges are too American for them, and they don't like American customs. Most of them are professional people who arrived in their late twenties and are now middle age. But there are others in our lodge who keep in contact with Norwegian Americans."[11] Karin Lier Brevig and her husband, Ola Brevig, now of Del Mar, California, may typify the early postwar immigrants. They were born in East Norway, in 1931 and 1928, respectively, married in the mid-1950s, and moved to California, where Ola was employed with General Dynamics. After additional studies in the United States he became a rocket scientist.

The Brevigs were clearly successful immigrants. Soon after their arrival, both became very active in the Valhall Lodge of Sons of Norway, and in time they enrolled their three children, Sigurd, Sidsel, and Kenneth, in the lodge. They feel at home in Norwegian-American circles. By their presence, newcomers like the Brevigs obviously strengthen a national Norwegian impulse in America and encourage the use of the Norwegian language. Both became United States citizens in 1962 (for Ola a requirement for security reasons). They vote conservatively as registered Republicans, consider Lutheran and Norwegian to be nearly synonymous terms, and tend to be critical of the liberal social-democratic welfare state Norway became in the postwar era.[12] The latter attitude frequently justified in the minds of many of the early postwar immigrants their decision to settle permanently in America. "All individual initiative is taken away from the people in Norway. I would never move back," insisted Jan H. Henricksen, who immigrated in 1950 at the age of twenty from Sandefjord, Norway.[13] Another immigrant of the 1950s stated that he had left Norway because "of total disgust with the Norwegian socialistic government and control of the economy."[14] Faith in the American free enterprise system made these immigrants, like earlier immigrants, see America as the land of opportunity, where perceived ethnic merits of hard work and reliability would be rewarded. Later immigrants, having reached maturity in an affluent and modern social-democratic welfare state, tend to be less receptive to traditional American ideals.

"The Roots Phenomenon"

Superficially observed, many Americans of Norwegian ancestry may appear less than serious when considering their heritage. There is an impression of a persistent levity when Norwegian-American subjects are introduced, more so in the midwestern heartland than on either coast or in the southern states. It is in the Midwest, if any place, because of numerical strength, that Norwegian Americans know who and what they are. References to ethnic symbols relating to such food items as *lefse* and lutefisk invariably produce humorous responses, and ethnic jokes about slow-witted Norwegian immigrants, generally dubbed "Ole and Lena," are regular fare at many events. One may ask if this attitude only reflects distance from the immigrant generation, and thus simple ignorance, or if in reality there exists a great indifference to a Norwegian-American past. On the other hand, a sense of humor about heritage may just as well be evidence of a secure ethnic identity. More to the point, later-generation Norwegian Americans are in fact invited into an ethnic fellowship through humor and disparaging remarks about ethnic stereotypes; it is a simple and acceptable means of signaling a sense of belonging.

That Norwegian Americans on occasion relate to their ethnicity by what admittedly constitutes "comic relief" may also appear to affirm sociologist Herbert Gans's contention that *identity* has become the primary way of being ethnic for the third generation and later. Gans says that because "people's concern is with identity, rather than with cultural practices or group relationships, they are free to look for ways of expressing that identity which suits them best, thus opening up the possibility of voluntary, diverse, or individualistic ethnicity." To Gans, "any mode of expressing ethnic identity is valid as long as it enhances the feeling of being ethnic." Subjecting one's ethnic identity to humorous ridicule can, as Gans might see it, obviously be one such mode. This pursuit of identity in later generations, freed from the constraints of commitment to an ethnic culture and behavior, Gans labels as "symbolic ethnicity." Most people will look for easy and intermittent ways of expressing an ethnic identity, Gans states, but because it no longer can be taken for granted, they must make this identity explicit and find ways to communicate it.[15]

Gans mainly dismisses the ethnic revival—referred to as the "new ethnicity"—of the 1970s as being only "symbolic." The ethnic renaissance associated with that decade, expressed in humorous as well as more substantive fashion, can in any event hardly—given the overwhelming evidence of ethnic mobilization and of ethnic cultural blossoming—be understood merely in terms of shallow symbolism. Michael Kammen in his *Mystic Chords of Memory* (1991) instead speaks—with reference to the publication in 1976 of Alex Haley's *Roots*—of "the Roots phenomenon," which in that decade and later, as he affirms, gave collective memories of ethnic groups, multigenerational families, and even individuals a new and greater visibility.[16] A sense of loss of human continuity, caused in part by the virtual disappearance in American society of the three-generation family—grandparents are no longer there to interact with youngsters—and the conviction that family continuities are precious may in part explain the high tide of interest in family history since the mid-1970s. Inspired by *Roots*, it was possible for every ordinary man and woman to become their own historians. Genealogical guides on how to trace "roots" became available.

Another distinctive American social phenomenon is the large reunions at regular intervals or occasionally organized by the family association that have proliferated among everyday people since that same decade. Some family associations are of greater vintage. The Aaker Family, descendants of Knud Saavenson Aaker and his wife, Mari Larsdatter Hegtvedt, who emigrated from Upper Telemark in 1845, have convened annually since 1923. The two pioneer ancestors are buried in the Holden Church cemetery in Goodhue County, Minnesota. "We are fortunate," the association president wrote in the Aaker Family newsletter, "in this time of constant moves and a widespread feeling of rootlessness, to *belong* to a visible and audible group, the Aaker Family."[17]

In all, 62 percent, or 4,156 individuals, of those who responded to the survey questions stated that their family had a written history of their time in America. Many Norwegian-American families presented their family histories or pedigree charts to become a part of the contemporary history investigation.[18] Most of these include accounts of family reunions. Nearly as many—61 percent—of all respondents answered affirmatively to the question of family reunions. These were by and large the same persons who said they had family histories. Norwegian-American reunions are generally based, as the Aaker Family conventions are, on the descendants in America of a specific immigrant or of an immigrant family and not on descent of a Norwegian progenitor. Though, there are, of course, exceptions. A unique family association is the Charcoal Burner Family, or in Norwegian, the "Kølabrenner Slekt," which traces its name to John Levorson Goplerud, who settled in 1760 at Goplerud in Hedalen in Valdres, where he made charcoal in the forest around the homestead and became known as "the burner." Today he is celebrated as the family's progenitor among descendants both in Norway and America. The family history indicates that Charcoal Burner descendants emigrated to America as early as the 1840s, and that others arrived in the 1860s and later; the author identifies thousands of names of generations of American descendants. The mountaintop memorial park Vatneberget in Valdres is, to quote, dedicated to "the glory of God and the honor of the Goplerud family." It serves as a family place of pilgrimage.[19]

A booklet published in 1978 for the 125th anniversary and celebration of "the Omsrud-Thordson-Torgrimson Emigration" is dedicated "In Gratitude to Our Pioneer Forebears Who Struggled Here Against Great Odds." It is a rather typical family history, containing accounts of the pioneer struggles and hardships and showing great pride in the immigrant heritage. Of Torgrim Torgrimson, who emigrated from Hedalen in Valdres in 1852 and settled on a farmstead by Omsrud Lake in Brown County in southern Minnesota, it is told that he "prospered well in America and was able to give each of his sons a farm before he died October 25, 1892." This family memory, like many similar ones, creates a sense of "roots" in America; the fact that the lake carries the name of one of the Norwegian families who settled there in 1852 is further concrete evidence of a historical presence. Continuity with an ancestral home may also enhance a family's self-perception of who they are. A common practice for family historians, as they trace the lineage in Norway, is to claim descent from the Old Norse kings, especially King Harald Fairhair, who is credited with uniting Norway under his dynasty shortly before 900. Such speculative claims speak to the role of the homeland in creating acceptable credentials in America.[20]

A search for roots and a celebration of family association taken together affirm a historical sense of group solidarity and of personal identity. Such pursuits surely transcend and to a great extent negate what Gans terms "symbolic"; the quest relates to a desire to establish historical continuities and a pride in being American as well as a pride in a specific personal family and ethnic heritage.

Ethnicity represents, to again be reminded of this circumstance, a voluntary association. This study assembled ample evidence for the voluntary character of middle-class Norwegian-American ethnicity. These descendants of Norwegian immigrants get much satisfaction out of their ethnic association, which of course costs them little, given the current tolerant political and cultural climate. The findings support the study by sociologist Mary Waters of how white ethnics of the third and fourth generations take pleasure in a subjective feeling of ethnic identity but usually avoid the constraints of involvement in concrete community and organizational ethnic affairs.[21] The Norwegian Americans surveyed assumed somewhat greater responsibilities in their ethnic affiliation than did those interviewed by Waters, a result likely due to the selection process for this sample of Norwegian Americans.[22] Suggestions of the voluntary nature of their ethnicity would, however, clearly have disturbed most Americans of Norwegian ancestry. There was, as with Waters's subjects, a strongly expressed and persistent notion that ethnicity is a primordial and biological condition. "I feel a common affinity when I meet other Norwegian Americans," claimed fifth-generation David G. Oihus, born in Grafton, North Dakota, in 1960 and now a resident of Tempe, Arizona. Other Nor-

wegian-American interview subjects expressed similar convictions. They simply were ethnic Norwegians and identified themselves as such.[23]

A primordial status is reinforced through family histories that document a biological link to the past, creating a sense of continuity and permanence in ethnic relations. Family history also highlights the individualistic character of the search for identity. Werner Sollors introduces the terms *consent* and *descent* to distinguish between self-made and ancestral definitions of American identity, defining *consent* as the need to show loyalty to a new culture of individualism and new political structures, and *descent* as loyalty to an ancestral heritage. He views the tension between these two concepts as the central drama in American culture. It is a tension that may never be fully resolved and is present in the quest to establish an acceptable group and individual identity when tracing ancestral lineages. John Bodnar has criticized, on the basis of historical evidence, Sollors's overemphasis on the extent to which this tension resulted from a purely personal conflict; it was also, he insists, fought on social and political ground.[24] Sollors's concept of cultural tension may, however, be useful in understanding how contemporary Norwegian Americans have fashioned their own historical memories and their own version of their past through an amalgamation of cultural traditions.

Vesterheim Genealogical Center and Naeseth Library, located in Madison, Wisconsin, was founded in 1974 by Gerhard B. Naeseth, whose name the library carries. Its purpose is to assist in preparing and collecting family histories. Its staff instills a professional approach to tracing family lines in America and through the generations in Norway. Requests for assistance have increased greatly over the years, and each year many attractive family history volumes are printed. These may, in terms used by Sollors, furnish evidence of a desire both to honor ancestral and familial ties of descent and to express their acceptance of and consent to American ideals and institutions, as the examples cited earlier show. Family histories may thus represent in some significant and easily discernible ways an effort to reconcile the tension between the two.[25]

There are other Norwegian-American family history associations and genealogical conferences, and active Internet enthusiasts will find useful genealogy sites. In Minnesota the Norwegian-American Genealogical Association, organized in 1983, operates as one of several ethnic genealogical groups under its parent organization, the Minnesota Genealogical Society, and is a subgroup of the Minnesota Scandinavian Genealogical Society. Many such family history groups carry the name "Scandinavian," such as the Scandinavian Genealogical Society, formed in Portland, Oregon, in 1991. And, naturally, Norwegian family enthusiasts join general county, regional, and state genealogical societies throughout the United States. By teaching family history research, these organizations, even if not directly Scandinavian, may

"encourage interest in Scandinavian ancestry and heritage," as publicity for the Oregon group states.[26]

The Family History Library system of the Church of Jesus Christ of the Latter-day Saints may possibly provide the most striking evidence of "the Roots phenomenon." An estimated nearly 90 percent of the 3.2 million annual visitors to the branch Family History Centers throughout the United States are not members of the Mormon Church, and although Latter-day Saints users have an added interest in genealogy from a religious standpoint, they discover the same sense of identity as others. Of the 25,000 inquiries the international floor of the Family History Library in Salt Lake City receives monthly, about 8,000 are Scandinavian.[27]

Family history enthusiasm is evident in several connections. The *bygdelag,* which began around the turn of the century among Norwegian immigrants primarily as social organizations based on Norwegian localism, now advertise their annual reunions, or *stevne,* as "a great place for genealogical research." There are thirty such national societies active at present, each bearing the name of a particular Norwegian community or district; a number of dormant *bygdelag* have been revived, and a few new ones have emerged. They are, to be sure, small, a number arranging joint reunions, but if it were not for their genealogical workshops during the reunions and emphasis on family history research, they would likely not exist at all. A transitory membership, people staying only until they have received assistance with their family histories, attests to a major motive for joining a particular society. As a historical phenomenon, the *bygdelag* reinvented themselves in the 1970s to meet a special interest within the Norwegian-American community. Their regional attachment in Norway became an obvious asset. Through their local focus, the *bygdelag* bring to bear the impact of ancestral home and hearth and the surrounding scenic wonders on the tales and records of family origins. Localism, the attachment to a romanticized vision of an ancestral home, was at the core of immigrant identity. For later generations, these same images become concrete and visible markers of kinship and familial relations and establish a historical continuity with the immigrant experience. Ethnocentric biases and loyalties are thereby reinforced.[28]

The Heartland of Norwegian Ethnicity

The analytical narrative in subsequent chapters will benefit from an overview of major concentrations of Norwegian-American populations and how they mark their presence. These were the regions surveyed and the ones that will be discussed throughout the volume (figure 8; table 3).

The 1990 census counted 757,212 first- or second-ethnicity Norwegians in Minnesota, which equals 17.3 percent of the state's population. A Norwegian ethnic presence is consequently much in evidence. The state of North Dakota is even more Norwegian, with 29.6 percent, or 189,106 individuals, identifying themselves as primarily or secondarily Norwegian. The state retains its status as the most "Norwegian" state in the union. Wisconsin reports 416,271 ethnic Norwegians, or 8.5 percent of its total population. Iowa has 152,084, equal to 5.5 percent of all Iowans. There are 106,361 Norwegians in South Dakota, which represents 15.3 percent of the state's inhabitants. These five states in the upper Midwest have within their boundaries about 42 percent of all those identifying themselves as of Norwegian ethnicity; it is a percentage that translates into 1,621,034 people. Their heavy representation in the upper Midwest is remarkable evidence of residential stability in traditional Norwegian-American regions of settlement, in spite of a pronounced geographical mobility in which Norwegian Americans have taken part.

Norwegian-American residential patterns may be extended to other midwestern states. Illinois, to the east of the five-state Norwegian core settlement area, has more Norwegians within state lines than either Iowa or South Dakota, numbering 167,003 people, which in terms of the state's total population only amounts to 1.5 percent. Michigan reported 72,261 Norwegian Americans, which although a substantial number of people, equals only 0.8 percent of all state residents. Suttons Bay and

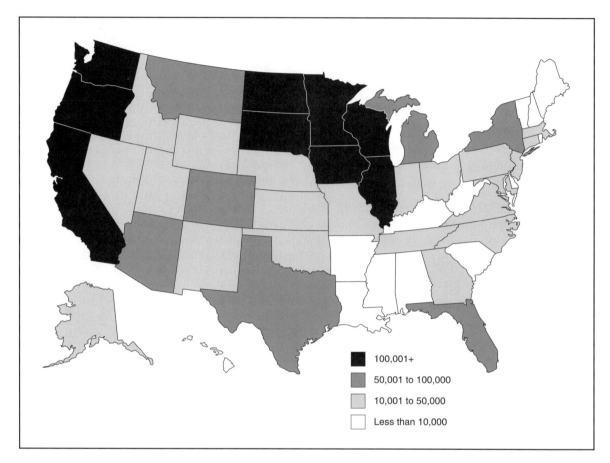

Figure 8. Geographical distribution of Norwegian Americans by state, 1990.

Northport in northwestern Michigan and other early settlements elsewhere in the state still show a Norwegian immigrant connection in their pioneer history. In Suttons Bay, for example, the Bahle's Department Store, part of an expanding family business, dates back to 1876. Its founder, Lars Bahle, came to Leelanau County from Nordmøre, Norway, in 1868; he bought a farm and built docks and warehouses on the waterfront in Suttons Bay for shipping produce. Roderic Johnson, a descendant of Lars Bahle born in 1929, recalls that "Norwegian was still spoken on the street when I grew up."[29]

Montana, adjoining the core Norwegian region to the west, boasted as many as 86,460 citizens of Norwegian ancestry, or 10.8 percent of its population, actually surpassing Iowa in

Table 3. Distribution of the Norwegian-American population by state

State	Norwegian-American population	Percentage of state population	State	Norwegian-American population	Percentage of state population
Alabama	8,489	.21	Missouri	29,531	.58
Alaska	23,087	4.19	Montana	86,460	10.82
Arizona	70,940	1.94	Nebraska	30,533	1.93
Arkansas	8,778	.37	Nevada	23,229	1.93
California	411,282	1.38	New Hampshire	8,401	.76
Colorado	75,646	2.30	New Jersey	46,991	.61
Connecticut	19,004	.58	New Mexico	13,936	.92
Delaware	3,036	.46	New York	90,158	.50
District of	2,620	.33	North Carolina	20,184	.30
Columbia			North Dakota	189,106	29.60
Florida	90,375	.70	Ohio	31,911	.29
Georgia	21,388	.33	Oklahoma	17,401	.55
Hawaii	9,054	.82	Oregon	124,216	4.37
Idaho	32,956	3.27	Pennsylvania	31,146	.26
Illinois	167,003	1.46	Rhode Island	4,010	.40
Indiana	25,978	.73	South Carolina	9,170	.26
Iowa	152,084	5.48	South Dakota	106,361	15.28
Kansas	21,878	.88	Tennessee	12,098	.25
Kentucky	7,355	.20	Texas	94,096	.55
Louisiana	9,510	.23	Utah	36,178	2.10
Maine	7,256	.59	Vermont	3,537	.63
Maryland	22,520	.47	Virginia	35,815	.58
Massachusetts	30,726	.51	Washington	333,521	6.85
Michigan	72,261	.78	West Virginia	2,598	.14
Minnesota	757,212	17.31	Wisconsin	416,271	8.51
Mississippi	4,052	.16	Wyoming	18,047	3.98

Note: The numerical strength of Norwegian Americans remains in the upper Midwest, although geographic assimilation is evident in a steady movement to other regions of the United States. In numbers Minnesota has the most Norwegians; thereafter follow Wisconsin, California, Washington, and North Dakota in that order. In percentages of state populations the ranking is North Dakota, Minnesota, South Dakota, Montana, Wisconsin, and Washington, with California in a distant eighteenth place.

percentage by a wide margin. Norwegian agricultural settlement after 1900 in the northeastern part of the state represented the northwesternmost point to which the Norwegians advanced in their march from the southern tip of Lake Michigan. The western and northwestern settlements in Montana were a part of the movement into the Far West. Darrell J. Christofferson wrote from Kallispell about the movement of his Scandinavian forebears into the Flathead Valley in northwestern Montana; one of his great-grandfathers immigrated from Stavanger, others from Sweden and Denmark. "It's my understanding," he writes, "that Norwegian and Swedish were spoken here more than English at one time, and in my mind and in my long-ago memories, the Scandinavian influence was quite strong. I can still see how the attitude of 'strong wholesome values' influences our community."[30]

Within these midwestern states Norwegians dominate in well-defined areas; the traditional regions of Norwegian settlement continue in force. It is therefore misleading to give aggregate state percentages. Some rural and small-town communities and even entire counties remain strongly Norwegian. It is in these areas that one may accept the notion developed by Kathleen Conzen of "localization of culture." Her study of Germans in Stearns County, Minnesota, leads her to conclude that German culture permeated all aspects of the local community. Speaking of the dominance of German ethnic institutions, habits, and views and how these reshaped and influenced those of the broader community, she states, "The local culture of thrift and non-ostentation . . . and the local standards by which politics were practiced, and honor and status accorded the individual, were initially molded in a German ethnic matrix, but quickly overflowed its bounds to define the county's values."[31] This process was, in other words, an adaptive one that can hardly be termed assimilation but rather involves chartering the local culture. Norwegian examples can be found in the dominance of Norwegian ethnicity in, for instance, Traill County, North Dakota, whose population in 1990 still was 64 percent first- and second-ethnicity Norwegian, or even in small towns like Spring Grove, Minnesota, and in the Pacific Northwest in Poulsbo, Washington. Localized Norwegian ethnic strength permeated many communities; Norwegian Americans shaped, as Conzen expressed it for her German subjects, the prevailing habits, worldviews, and institutions of the entire community in their own image. Although most examples are found in the Midwest, they also exist beyond the core area of Norwegian settlement. This localized cultural influence can perhaps no longer be described as an ethnic cultural hegemony, but it is still much in evidence. Contemporary Norwegian-American symbols and activities announce an ethnic presence.

There are major urban areas as well, like Chicago, Milwaukee, and Minneapolis, with substantial Norwegian-American populations even though Norwegian neighborhoods have passed into history. Within Cook County, Illinois, where Chicago is located, there were 52,679 individuals who claimed Norwegian ancestry; Milwaukee County, Wisconsin, boasted only 29,464 Norwegian-American residents; Hennepin County, Minnesota, the major metropolitan district for Minneapolis, had as many as 163,534 Norwegian Americans. There is a heavy Norwegian concentration in the adjoining and heavily urbanized counties of Anoka, with 44,188 Norwegian Americans; Ramsey—which includes St. Paul—with 53,670; and Dakota, with 42,058.[32] The Twin Cities of Minneapolis and St. Paul can thus claim the highest urban density of this particular ethnicity. Norwegian Americans from other states in the upper Midwest and from outlying areas of Minnesota have responded to the lure of the only major metropolitan area in that part of the United States and sought opportunity and diversion there. Minneapolis has retained a Scandinavian flavor and defends its position—if it ever needed to—as a Norwegian-American "capital."

The signs of a Norwegian presence are easily detected. A consequence of what Kammen called "the Roots phenomenon" is ethnic symbols and greetings at the entrances of small towns (figure 9). Strum in western Wisconsin, for instance, displays a Norwegian flag and a sign reading "Velkommen til Strum" (welcome to Strum). Similar friendly ethnic greetings may be detected on welcoming signs elsewhere where Norwegians have settled, such as Westby, also in western Wisconsin; Spring Grove, in southern Minnesota; and Story City, Iowa. The very Norwegian Canton, South Dakota, in arranging its first Scandinavian Heritage Fest in 1993, decided to make the city the "Norwegian Capital of South Dakota," and turned words into action by painting all wooden flower tubs in Norwegian motif, then decorating all garbage cans with rosemaling, and finally placing *nisser,* Norwegian good-luck elves, on light poles throughout the city. These visible ethnic symbols mark the dominant position of the Norwegian-American population.

The stability of rural communities of Norwegian Americans and their sense of ethnic domain are notable characteristics of their history. In this regard the response of Norwegian Americans to the movement into southeastern South Dakota of Dutch settlers is a case in point. As early as the 1880s, the Dutch moved from northwestern Iowa across the Big Sioux River into Lincoln County and areas farther south, as well as into Minnehaha County to the north. The spread of Dutch settlers into these Norwegian strongholds has continued to the present time. Norwegians talked critically of the invasion of the blue license plates, referring to the color of Iowa's state plates. The conservative and strongly ethnic Norwegian population in some farming communities around Canton and Hudson in Lincoln County and in the pioneer settlement of Elk Point in Union County felt overwhelmed and threatened by this "for-

Figure 9. "Welcome signs" in Norwegian are common in small-town Norwegian-American communities; here are the greetings in Strum and Westby, Wisconsin, and Milan and Spring Grove, Minnesota. Photographs by Odd S. Lovoll.

eign" invasion. A large movement of Dutch people to such solid Norwegian farming communities as Norway Township in western Lincoln County created resentment among many of the staunch Norwegian pioneer families. "You would think they are coming to plow down the Norwegian cemeteries," one informant said, claiming that "the ones who are the most threatened are second- and third-generation Norwegian Americans who never have been outside of Lincoln County." H. Allen Paulson, a fourth-generation Norwegian American born in 1928 who grew up on a farm in Norway Township, south of Canton, recalled, "My mother had strong anti-Catholic feelings and antipathies against other nationalities. She feared the Dutch invasion from Iowa, and some older people still carry these prejudices." Historian Gerald De Jong, who has studied the Dutch in Iowa and South Dakota, on the other

hand, insisted that he discovered no animosity between these two ethnic groups with much in common; both engaged in farming, were socially conservative, and religious. Nevertheless, another informant claimed that as recently as the spring of 1997 Norwegian-American farmers were outbidding Dutch buyers for acreage adjoining their property to prevent the land from falling into Dutch hands.[33]

Ethnic symbols serve to mark Norwegian

strength in many parts of the Midwest. Starbuck in western Minnesota celebrates annually the fact that the world's largest *lefse,* a rolled pancake made of dough, was baked there at a town event on July 1, 1983, and ever since Starbuck has advertised itself as the "Home of the World's Largest Lefsa," the spelling of *lefse* with a final *a* being a Norwegian-American orthographic convention. Starbuck's celebration is observed close to May 17, Norway's Constitution Day—the most prominent of all celebratory ethnic events (figure 10).

Farther south in the state the town of Madison has erected a monument to the much

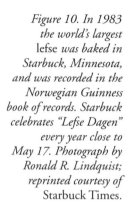

Figure 10. In 1983 the world's largest lefse was baked in Starbuck, Minnesota, and was recorded in the Norwegian Guinness book of records. Starbuck celebrates "Lefse Dagen" every year close to May 17. Photograph by Ronald R. Lindquist; reprinted courtesy of Starbuck Times.

maligned lutefisk—dried cod treated in a lye solution. The monument depicts a huge cod with a sign that advertises Madison as "Lutefisk Capital U.S.A.," supposedly to establish a dubious claim of consuming more lutefisk per capita than any other city in America (figure 11). In Norwegian-American Baltic, South Dakota, the "Uffda Burger" for some time, until new owners bought the shop, replaced the more common hamburger, and Dovray, Minnesota, even celebrates Uff-Da Days.

These symbols, then, are the superficial indicators of Norwegian-American ethnicity. For the vast majority of those who identify themselves as ethnically Norwegian, these would be the extent of their symbolic attachment and knowledge—ethnic foods of a peasant origin and an audible "uffda" now and then, used in

all kinds of connections, even in greetings, having lost much of its confined usage as an expression of unpleasant feelings (figure 12).[34] The significance of these simple manifestations of an ethnic attachment will be fully considered later.

The West Coast Experience

In Seattle, Washington, on Puget Sound, public transportation vehicles fly the Norwegian flag during the week of May 17. This may indicate that in regions with large Norwegian-American populations May 17—this prime symbol of Norwegian ethnicity—is gradually being incorporated into the array of American holidays, much like St. Patrick's Day (figure 13). This ecumenical mixing in ethnic terms is

Figure 11. A monument to cod in Madison, Minnesota, declaring the town "Lutefisk Capital U.S.A." Photograph by Charles Smith from C. Edwards Studio; reprinted courtesy of the Madison Area Chamber of Commerce.

apparent wherever the day is observed in the United States. People of many ethnicities and races march in the parade, provide entertainment, enjoy Norwegian dishes sold at stands, and line the parade route. In the 1990s ethnic traditions entered into the American mainstream with ease. Participation in these events also gives evidence, however, of a striking aspect of voluntary ethnicity. Individuals can choose their ethnic identity; for instance, they can be culturally Norwegian without having a Norwegian ancestry.[35] Many of those who are responsible for ethnic celebrations or serve in Norwegian-American organizations, as will be seen later, have no Norwegian blood. The freedom of the so-called new ethnicity to select ethnic affiliation has encouraged ethnic activi-

ties by non-Norwegians who either married into a Norwegian-American family or who in other ways developed an interest in this particular ethnicity. Because Norwegian ethnic activity remains strong and vibrant, it has a special appeal, it would appear, for individuals who belong to groups where little has been retained to mark a specific ethnicity.

The city of Seattle is located in King County, which in 1990 had 110,094 residents who claimed Norwegian ethnicity. In the state as a whole there were 333,521 first- and second-ethnicity Norwegians, or 6.9 percent of Washington's population.[36] In the protected sea lanes and bays in Puget Sound, Norwegians formed separate communities that have retained their Norwegian character. The Stillaguamish

Figure 12. A bottle of Bock Uff-da beer is an example of the widespread use of "uffda" with little attention to the term's original Norwegian meaning.

flats near Stanwood in Snohomish County and the northern part of the Kitsap peninsula, including the town of Poulsbo in Kitsap County, became strong areas of Norwegian settlement. Poulsbo marks its Norwegian identity in street names, but most of all in Norwegian greetings, themes, and decorations in Norwegian rosemaling in its small commercial district. Rosemaling, or rose painting, a folk art form that is gaining popularity among Norwegian Americans, is another expressive ethnic symbol. It

appears in all kinds of ethnic connections, on objects and signs, and as interior and exterior house decorations.

The early Norwegian settlement in Alaska represented an extension northward from the state of Washington and along the coast of British Columbia. The state currently has only 23,087 people of Norwegian ancestry, which equals 4.2 percent of all Alaskans. Major areas of concentration are in Anchorage and surrounding districts, and in Fairbanks and Juneau. Petersburg on Mitkof Island in southeast Alaska hails itself as "Little Norway" and has annually since 1958 arranged a public May 17 observance called Little Norway Festival. It is integrated into the community as, to quote from its program, a "celebration of Norway's Independence Day, America's Armed Forces Day, and the return of the local halibut fleet." The celebration is replete with displays of rosemaling, costumes worn by dancers, and Vikings in battle dress, which all relate to a persistent strong Norwegian ethnic presence in this small fishing town originally founded by Norwegian immigrants. It is another example of the integration of an ethnic event, in this case May 17, into a larger American context.[37]

Public festivals, of course, identify the ethnic composition of many communities. In the state of Washington a Scandinavian Midsummer Festival organized by the ethnic lodges attracts attention to the Nordic heritage of Astoria. Across the Columbia River in Oregon similar arrangements mark a Norwegian, and more frequently a shared Scandinavian, visibility in the state. In Junction City a Scandinavian Festival has been an annual affair since 1960, given publicity in a rather strange Norwegian "Velkommen til Forbindelsestad," the latter word supposedly intended to render the name Junction City in Norwegian. Each day of the festival celebrates a different Nordic country.[38] A Scandinavian label indicates both an effort to be inclusive and perhaps for many a feeling of interethnic assimilation, especially where the combined Scandinavian population might feel overwhelmed by much larger nationalities. It is another sign of emerging ethnic configurations and identities within an American matrix.

The state of Oregon has 124,216 citizens who claim Norwegian ethnicity, which represents 4.4. percent of all Oregonians. The Swedes have an almost identical number, with 124,620 people identifying themselves as Swedish; Danish Americans are only 47,806 strong, and Finnish Americans less than half that again, numbering 22,977. Suggestive of an emerging Scandinavian ethnic identity is the fact that as many as 28,021 residents of Oregon identified themselves in this manner. The Scandinavian identity appears in all states; in Minnesota, for instance, as many as 91,712 people gave Scandinavian as their ancestry. Still, the figures represent only a little more than 8 percent of all of Nordic background in Oregon, and in Minnesota less than 6 percent. The difference between the two regions is not

Figure 13. A public transportation vehicle marks May 17, 1997, in Seattle, Washington. Photograph courtesy of Alf Lunder Knudsen.

sufficiently significant to make firm conclusions, though one may be more likely to see oneself in a larger Scandinavian context when the individual ancestry groups are small. The figures do indicate, however, a trend toward a broader Scandinavian identification, reflecting both intermarriage and an increasing distance from the immigrant generation. A total of 678,880 persons identified themselves as ethnically Scandinavian. Individuals of mixed Scandinavian heritage are less likely, it would appear, to identify with a single nationality, that is, for example, to choose Norwegian and ignore the other Scandinavian nationality, than people whose heritage is more diverse. A Scandinavian identification is encouraged instead. "Our children Eric and Gretchen, of Swedish and Norwegian background, call themselves Scandinavian and are very jealous of their identity," Eugene S. Haugse, of Waukesha, Wisconsin, insisted; he is of Norwegian ancestry, second generation on his paternal and third on his maternal line, and his wife, Shirley Olson Haugse, is the daughter of a Swedish immigrant.[39]

Still, care must be taken not to exaggerate the extent of an inter-Scandinavian assimilation. A certain Nordic commonality has been visible from the beginnings of Scandinavian settlement in the New World; fragmentation and confrontation also held sway among Swedish, Danish, and Norwegian brethren and sisters and became a part of their American experience. They had at best a love-hate relationship. Swedish-American historian Amandus Johnson complained about the lack of Scandinavian unity in Chicago, and with a sense for the ironic in the situation, thought the cause was that the Danes only wanted to eat, the Swedes only wanted to sing, and the Norwegians only wanted to fight.[40] Mutually comprehensible spoken and written languages tied them to each other even when disagreeing, and the American environment pushed them to find and cultivate a shared Nordic heritage. Scandi-

navians were frequently assigned a common identity, which might be expressed in terms of nationality; most often all Scandinavians were designated "Swede," since Swedes were most commonly the majority nationality. Even after the language was lost among Scandinavians in America, historical and cultural commonality existed on both sides of the Atlantic. There is a natural Nordic affinity that tends to unite. Non-Nordics are regarded as different—the real foreigners.

The story is, however, more complex than simply that of a revival of Scandinavianism among the descendants of immigrants from Norway, Sweden, and Denmark during the past few decades. As in early times, a mono-ethnic celebration or society may fly a Scandinavian standard. And even at events where all three ethnic groups are represented, individual national identities are proudly proclaimed and not suppressed under a broad Scandinavian category. The situation is further complicated by the fact that a voluntary ethnicity and open Scandinavian ethnic boundaries allow people without Scandinavian descent to participate, and even to play leading roles, in ethnic life.

The main concentrations of Norwegians in Oregon in 1990 were found in Portland and surrounding counties and then south in the Willamette valley to the state capital of Salem in Marion County. Another major region of a strong Norwegian presence is in Lane County, where the university town of Eugene is located, and a third smaller concentration is in Jackson County on the southern border.[41]

Within California reside 411,282 persons of Norwegian extraction, which even though a substantial number of people, account for only 1.4 percent of California's population. The connection to the Midwest is much in evidence: more than half of the nearly 600 survey respondents in California were born in one of the midwestern states. Traditions and attitudes transplanted from Norwegian-American midwestern environments are consequently visible in the new location. San Francisco continues as a major area of ethnic activities, with societies, lodges, and festivals. Only 7,297 Norwegian Americans are listed in San Francisco County itself, but if Sonoma County to the north, Santa Clara County to the south, and Sacramento County to the east are included, the number grows to over 100,000, or nearly one-quarter of all ethnic Norwegians in the state, mainly centering on the city of San Francisco.[42]

Los Angeles boasts an urban Norwegian-American population of 78,328, but since Norwegians live dispersed in this enormous metropolitan area of nearly 9 million people, they are obviously not very visible, being found at public ethnic events or in their societies, lodges, and churches. In the suburban environment of Los Angeles, as in other major metropolitan centers, substitutes for ethnic neighborhoods exist in the automobile and the telephone, which maintain ethnic communica-

tion. These are the indispensable links of contemporary urban life, preserving ethnic association, friendships, and extended family ties. Ventura County to the north and Orange County to the south of Los Angeles have substantial Norwegian-American populations, and the relatively small Orange County has as many as 39,329. Bordering this county to the south is San Diego County including the city of San Diego, where 44,616 first- and second-ethnicity Norwegian Americans reside. The geographically large counties east of Los Angeles along the Nevada and Arizona border also contain fairly substantial populations of Norwegian Americans.[43]

As many as 75,646 people of Norwegian ethnicity have located in Arizona, representing 2.1 percent of the population. Phoenix and Maricopa County account for more than 60 percent.[44] Retirement communities in such places as Sun City, Scottsdale, and Mesa have large temporary "snow bird" populations, including many midwestern Norwegian Americans who spend their winters there. Some have moved there permanently and have reestablished social activities relating to Norwegian-American social and cultural patterns. Even an Uffda Golf Tournament, perhaps given the basic sense of the expression, an event for once accurately named, is played by transplanted Norwegian Americans. Tucson is a second center of Norwegian-American residence in the state. In a scenery that does not remind one much of Norway, or even of the Midwest, Sons of Norway lodges operate, May 17 is observed, and ethnic organizational life is conducted.

Norwegians in Utah, Colorado, and Texas

Ski sports, especially ski jumping and cross-country skiing, have been defining ethnic achievements. They are an ethnic forte that has created heroes and generated national and ethnic pride. The central mountain states of Utah and Colorado have been the site of competitions, carnivals, and heroic feats relating to these sports. Norwegian-American participation in the development of ski sports, and in making these two states centers of activity, began early. Nationwide there are twenty-five cross-country ski clubs and eighteen ski-jumping and Nordic combined clubs. Gradually, however, as skiing has become a major business enterprise, the Norwegian influence has been reduced. The expanding involvement of American commerce and an enthusiastic American public have reduced the Norwegian share.[45]

In 1990 the state of Utah had only 36,178 residents identified as Norwegian, 2.1 percent of the population. Colorado has a much more substantial number with 75,646 Norwegian Americans, representing, however, in percentage of population only 2.2, slightly more than Utah. The metropolitan areas of Denver, Boulder, and Colorado Springs have many Norwegian-American residents.[46]

In Texas the pioneer settlements of Norwegians in Bosque County remain the major Norwegian ethnic region in the state. Legislative action in 1997 at the Texas Senate and House encouraged by local chamber of commerce interests made the city of Clifton the official "Norwegian capital of Texas." The buildings of Clifton College on the Hill are striking monuments to Norwegian and Lutheran roots. As an academy and junior college, it lasted for more than half a century, closing its doors in 1954. Historical markers proudly remind people of the early Norwegian immigrants who settled in Bosque County and created a society there. Cleng Peerson Memorial Highway—so designated since 1975—runs through the county past reminders of a historical Norwegian presence. There are in the state 94,096 Texans who claim a Norwegian ethnic identity, only about 0.6 percent of the population. Consequently, outside of their heavy representation in Bosque County, they are not highly visible, except when festivals and public events attract attention to this ethnic constituency.[47] Norwegian Americans live in substantial numbers in such large metropolitan areas as Dallas–Fort Worth—Bosque County being located southwest of this urban area—and Houston. There are smaller groups of Norwegian Americans in the state capital of Austin and in San Antonio. It is in these centers that the Norwegian Society of Texas finds support and, one may say, in several respects promotes a special Norwegian-Texan ethnic identity (figure 14), perhaps most

visible in a special Texas *bunad,* or folk costume, designed in 1987. Adopted as the official *bunad* of the Norwegian Society of Texas,
this unique fantasy garment shows loyalty to a
Norwegian heritage but within a new context
and with ethnic innovations.[48]

The East Coast Tradition

Norwegian settlement in the East has had a
strong urban character. The "closeness" to the
homeland continues as a significant variable in
understanding the experience of Norwegian
Americans on the eastern seaboard. The great
ethnic and racial diversity in the population is
another variable affecting the socialization of
ethnic groups. As a consequence, ethnic boundaries are more firmly drawn than in the Midwest. It is a circumstance that is most clearly
demonstrated in Greater New York. "All who
grew up in New York always had other ethnic
groups around," Thomas Sandseth, a second-
generation Norwegian American born in 1950,
and a lieutenant on the New York police force,
explained, as he related his experience as a
young patrolman in a Jamaican community,
where "values and vocabulary were different
and people's action were not easy to understand." He did not find the diversity a problem,
although "those who grew up in the suburbs
might find it offensive." As a child growing up
in Bay Ridge, he recalled, "I always took off
school on May 17 like it was a holiday." The
New York City Police Department Viking As-

*Figure 14. The Wooden Spoon, a Scandinavian import
store in Plano, Texas, portrays the Texas Viking on a coffee
mug. Photograph courtesy of Gwen Workman.*

sociation, organized by Scandinavian police
officers within the police department in 1958,
is an example of ethnic cohesion (figure 15).
Similar societies are rare in other American
metropolitan centers. The Viking Association
is one of twenty-five ethnic, racial, and other
minority organizations. A combined Scandinavian effort is dictated by the small number of
potential members, as well as the relative numerical insignificance of Nordic populations.
"We promote pride in heritage, not intolerance," Sandseth stated further, "because in New
York there are so many ethnic groups that we
need to be tolerant, although ethnic organizations simultaneously cause ethnic polarization."

Figure 15. The Viking Association of the New York Police Department marching in the May 17 parade in Bay Ridge in 1997. Photograph by Valerie Hodgson; reprinted with permission.

Most members of the Viking Association have Norwegian ancestry, and the group is visible at events such as May 17 observances and has stood as honor guard for a number of royal visits. Another police officer and member, Gary Alan Boardman, a fourth-generation Norwegian American born on Staten Island in 1960, when asked why the New York Police Department has so many organizations, answered, "they probably look out for the rights of every individual group." How does the Viking Association look out for its members? "It is mostly to keep our heritage going." Is it difficult to be Norwegian? "No, there seems to be much hostility toward each other in this world we live in—there is the focus on nationality. But being Norwegian is kind of neutral. Nothing negative, not 'Oh, you Norwegians came and took over our country!' You don't hear that."[49]

A society calling itself Vikings unites Scandinavian-American firefighters in the New York Fire Department; its stated purpose is "to join in fellowship with members of Scandinavian heritage and make the world a better place to live." Vikings organized in 1982 "because other groups, such as Polish, Italian, Irish, and German, had their groups before," explained Donald Thorsen, born in Brooklyn of Norwegian parents in 1940.[50] The ethnic competition is obvious, though the Vikings, because of their few members, do not compete with the other societies for political favors, nor, like these larger ethnic associations, do they work for specific political causes and candidates. Boardman's and Thorsen's statements testify to the wide acceptability of a Norwegian ethnic identity, both because of reputation—the name Viking is itself a positive moniker—and perhaps even more because Norwegian numerical strength does not pose a threat to anyone.

Norwegian Americans obviously do not have a strong voice in the state of New York; in 1990 only 90,158 citizens reported being of first- or second-ethnicity Norwegian in a population of 17,990,455, or about 0.5 percent. As they have dispersed from their original areas of concentration, Norwegian Americans have become increasingly less visible. From their core region in Bay Ridge in Brooklyn, they have moved to Staten Island and Long Island, to outstate New York, and also to New Jersey and Connecticut. Greater New York has a Norwegian-American population of 56,034, according to the last decennial census, a little more than 9,000 residing in Brooklyn. The largest contingent, 16,485, however, resides in Long Island; 6,934 Norwegian Americans live on Staten Island. In New Jersey there are 46,991 people who claim Norwegian ancestry, who account for about 0.7 percent of the state's inhabitants. Connecticut has only 19,004 Norwegian Americans, about 0.6 percent of the state's residents.[51]

Several offshoots from the Norwegian community in Brooklyn exist. In the Massachusetts whaling town of New Bedford and even more so in Fairhaven just across the bay, there is a thriving community of Norwegian scallop fishermen, mainly with roots in the island of Karmøy on Norway's southwestern coast. The first Norwegian fishermen came from Brooklyn in the 1920s; during the 1930s they were mainly immigrants from the outer communities on Karmøy. Many more arrived in the 1950s and 1960s directly from Karmøy to benefit from the profitable, but surely perilous, scallop fisheries on the Georges Bank off New England. The Portuguese have gradually replaced the Norwegians as the main scallop fishermen, and a reduction in the fisheries in the mid-1960s convinced many to move to Seattle to fish in Alaska or even to return to Norway, where the discovery of oil off the southwest coast offered new employment opportunities.[52] The Fairhaven pattern of migration exemplifies the role of localism and economic motivations in migrational phenomena.

Pious Lutheranism is also a force in community formation, as it was in Norseville in Somerset County, New Jersey, founded in 1926 as an incorporated summer colony by people from the Norwegian Seamen's Church and the low-church Lutheran Brethren 59th Street Church in Brooklyn. A permanent community of some fifty families was established after World War II, when descendants of the founders returning from military service made their homes there and cultivated, as an article states, "religion, family, and a peaceful way of life."[53] Norseville gives a strong impression of being a religious community, isolated from worldly temptation, and also ethnic, because as third-generation Norwegian American and resident Hjørdis Mortensen claimed, "we want also to remember our Norwegian heritage and that we came from the Vikings."[54]

Several other Norwegian colonies exist, usually begun as vacation communities. One of these is Lake Telemark in Rockaway, New Jersey, which also has roots in the Norwegian community in Brooklyn of the 1920s. Pastor Charles Lopez, of mixed Cuban and German Russian background, who from 1978 to 1986 served Holy Trinity Lutheran Church in Rockaway, recalls a congregation of middle-class, mainly Norwegian-born—60 to 70 percent—Brooklynites. An offshoot of Trinity Lutheran in Sunset Park, the congregation was, like the 59th Street Church, a low-church congregation but in a more tolerant and liturgical Haugean tradition. "The members were warm and loving once you got beyond a cool exterior," Lopez observed. "Go any place on the east coast," a second-generation Norwegian American in Brooklyn insisted, "and you can find people who were born in or lived in Bay Ridge."[55] Even though minute in percentages of the total population, in real numbers the concentration of people of Norwegian ethnicity in this region along the Atlantic seaboard is substantial.

In Washington, D.C., and the surrounding states of Maryland and Virginia is another urban Norwegian-American population. Many reside there because of government employment and work in the District of Columbia while living outside the district itself. Connections to the Midwest are evident in Norge in James City County, Virginia, which was founded in 1896 by Norwegians from the Midwest attracted by the better climate there. Frances Hamilton, born in Norge in 1928 and a fourth-generation Norwegian American on her mother's side, related that her mother, one of seven children, had moved with her family to Norge in 1906 at age fourteen because of *her* mother's poor health. As in the Midwest, the Lutheran Church was central to community life. "I wouldn't have known I was Norwegian if it had not had the church," Frances volunteered. The influence from postwar Norway is a factor in retaining a Norwegian presence. Norwegian Americans in Norge join in the May 17 raising of the Norwegian flag and celebration at the nearby NATO headquarters in Norfolk, where Norwegian military personnel and their families are stationed.[56]

Florida is the home of many retired Norwegian Americans, many moving there from Greater New York and other regions of the Northeast. Consequently, considering the average age of those who fill the lodge halls, join singing societies, and participate in ethnic events, a general impression of Norwegian-American cultural and social activities as a "retirement culture" is reinforced there more than in any other state. Activities sponsored by Norwegian-American groups in Florida pay homage to a Norwegian heritage, even to the extent that some wear a special Florida fantasy *bunad,* adjusted, like the Texas *bunad,* to local climatic conditions and individual taste, but also showing in design some loyalty to traditional elements of the Norwegian peasant garment. A combination of the old and the invented creates a new tradition. Sons of Norway lodges are major actors in most ethnic festivities. The Suncoast Lodge has, for instance, since 1982 arranged a Viking ship regatta on Old Tampa Bay to celebrate May 17. Teams from other lodges join in the boat races, both women's and men's. The boats are Norwegian *åttrings,* an old-type ship with four pairs of oars and, in this case, a square sail. A unique Norwegian-American practice is reflected in the names given these diminutive traditional Viking Age vessels, frequently outfitted with a dragon head at the prow; "Uffda," "Tampa Viking," and "Hägar" are a few examples. The crews regularly include a majority of old-timers. "We never practice for fear of tiring ourselves out before the race," the participants may self-deprecatingly remark.[57]

There are a total of 90,375 individuals in Florida counted by the census takers as first- or second-ethnicity Norwegian, about 0.7 percent of all Floridians. They are most numerous in the West Palm Beach and Fort Lauderdale area in the southeast, and on the west coast of the state in the Tampa and Clearwater area.

There are, however, smaller and larger groups of Norwegian Americans throughout the state. Lodges of the Sons of Norway identify their main strongholds in such cities as Orlando, Tampa, West Palm Beach, and Fort Lauderdale. A movement of younger professionals into the state from Norway here—as in Houston, New York, and elsewhere—profits Norwegian visibility, though, again, they have a cultural distance from the Norwegian-American community. Norway is a large foreign investor in Florida, Norwegian companies having established themselves in the port city of Miami as a gateway to the rest of the United States and Latin America. About 1,000 Norwegians live in south Florida, most being involved in one of the Norwegian cruise lines, or in other shipping and maritime industries.[58]

Marketing Ethnicity

Marketing is an obvious dimension in any discussion of how ethnicity functions in a capitalistic American society; it regularly expresses itself as a commercial commodity. The situation in the state of Wisconsin offers a case in point. Mount Horeb, southwest of Madison, Wisconsin, has advertised itself since the mid-1980s as the "Troll Capital of the World" by featuring its Norwegian pioneer background. Its main street, lined with trolls (Norwegian goblins), is the Trollway, which stretches way beyond the town to create a tourist area that includes farmsteads and the outdoor museum "Little Norway," the latter a re-created pioneer settlement. This chamber of commerce initiative was inspired by New Glarus to the south, which became America's "Little Switzerland." Mount Horeb found another model in Stoughton farther east, where the city fathers decided to celebrate the town's Norwegian heritage through such symbols as trash cans decorated with rosemaling, Norwegian-language signs on businesses, and a large May 17 festival.

These commercial initiatives by the local business communities were dictated by a justified fear that the construction of interstate highways and the attraction of bigger cities might well leave these small towns deserted. Many small towns in Wisconsin have adopted ethnic marketing themes, a number of these Norwegian ones. Colorful ethnic symbols, exhibits, and celebrations are intended to revitalize communities by attracting business and tourism. Perhaps nowhere does the idea of an "invented" ethnicity apply more directly than in these public displays of selective and refurbished cultural symbols, a commercially re-created heritage, if you will, based, however, on the local community's history and ethnic configuration.

In Mount Horeb the troll theme was acceptable to non-Norwegians as well as to Norwegians, since even though these mythological creatures represent what Norwegian legends and folk tales are all about, they could also be safely Swiss, carved to look something like Alpine elves, and given unique American characteristics such as the tourist troll, the carp-carrying troll, the gardener, the chicken thief, the accordion player, and so on by their Irish-American wood-carving sculptor Michael Feeney (figure 16). The theme was a successful compromise. Business considerations may obviously encourage a voluntary ethnicity—the owner of the local Scandinavian import store in Mount Horeb, who also serves as president of the Sons of Norway lodge in town, is of Swiss background.[59]

Scandinavian import stores offer items of high quality, imported from Scandinavia or made in the United States. The latter items include wood carving, objects decorated with rosemaling, and clothing. Marketing possibilities have fueled some of the enthusiasm for producing folk art in wood, paint, and fiber. True artists ply their trades, some for their livelihood, and gain recognition. Their products grace many homes and give tangible evidence of the durability as well as the revival of traditional Norwegian folk crafts. These same wares are exhibited and sold at the reunions of the *bygdelag,* at May 17 observances, and at Scandinavian festivals.

There are, however, the more questionable commercial ethnic wares, which might, if one is so inclined, be categorized as "tacky Norwegian Americana," or perhaps more generously as popularized cultural expressions. Some of these representations tend to press all ethnic contingents into a uniform mold. The most visible are the mass-produced buttons, which

Figure 16. The Gardener Troll *carved by Michael J. Feeney, on the Trollway in Mount Horeb, Wisconsin. Copyright 1993 Michael J. Feeney; reprinted with permission of the artist. Photograph by Skot Weidmann.*

may claim, for example, in a humorous, ethnocentric manner, "It is hard to be humble if you are Norwegian," the nationality easily changed to suit any other ethnic appellation. These are a legacy of the ethnic revival of the 1970s. More ethnic-specific are slogans such as "Legalize Lutefisk," "Take a Liking to a Viking," and "Norwegian power, eat Lefse!" (figure 17). There are cups with the ever present Viking with a horned helmet, sprinkled with an

"Uffda" here and there, and T-shirts and sweatshirts that carry similar slogans and motifs; there are the many collections of ethnic jokes, and there are bumper stickers proclaiming pride in ethnicity. These products find a market. Most Norwegian Americans will express some levity when viewing these popular ethnic symbols, but hardly any ridicule, or any thought that they are inappropriate. "Uffda seems perfectly normal to me," a Norwegian-American

Figure 17. Buttons with typical ethnic slogans.

woman insisted in response to having the term's broad usage among Norwegian Americans lightly satirized.[60]

The Symbols of a Festive Culture

A festive and celebratory attitude toward ethnic identity has a long history. Early on, festivals and celebrations were an expression of immigrant life that found acceptance and encouragement in the host society and among the immigrants themselves. An acceptance in the nineteenth century of the notion of "immigrant contributions" to American society expressed itself in such festivals with displays of colorful national garments, dancing, and processions. These were a sanitized expression of ethnicity. Ethnic identity and its symbols were

placed on parade. Historically and down to the present time these are, then, generally expressions of cultural diversity within limits that American society approves. An encouraged safe public display of cultural loyalty to an ancestral homeland may even provide some insight into, to quote Stanley Lieberson and Mary Waters, "one of the most fundamental experiences in the creation of a nation: namely, the merger of peoples whose initial dealings with one another were characterized by antipathy, if not outright antagonism." A relative social harmony is created through an acceptable marking of ethnic pluralism—this process might even hold a key to comprehending American nation building. American society has historically demonstrated a remarkable ability to receive waves of new immigrants and to integrate them into the body politic. Seeing ethnicity in terms of a social construct, anthropologist Eugeen Roosens nevertheless views ethnic identity as a psychological reality, which gives security in a particular identification and a feeling of belonging.[61]

Ethnic identity is an ambiguous concept, which the influential Danish-American psychologist Erik H. Eriksen mainly approaches psychologically, as something located in the deep psychic structure of the individual that makes it possible "to experience one's self as something that has continuity and sameness, and act accordingly."[62] Eriksen's sense of identity is close to a primordialist ethnicity. His sense thereby differs greatly from the theory put forward by Roosens of ethnicity as a shaped, modified, and re-created relational force in contemporary society, that is, a social construct that stresses the role of ethnic leadership in mobilizing ethnic identity and collective action. Roosen's conclusion is that "ethnic groups are affirming themselves more and more [and] . . . promote their own, new cultural identity, even as their old identity is eroded" by acculturation.[63]

Some sociologists explain ethnic identity in a different way than either Eriksen or Roosens, and see it "as an artifact of interaction between the individual and society," to quote historian Philip Gleason. Of sociological assumptions about identity, he writes, "It is essentially a matter of being designated by a certain name, accepting that designation, internalizing the role requirements accompanying it, and behaving according to those descriptions." As Gleason ably demonstrates in his discourse on the term's semantic history, the concept of identity must be understood in its historical context. A psychological and a sociological perspective on identity may, however, enlighten a historical conceptual framework. Ambiguities about identity and life in America are deeply embedded in immigrant psychology. Both approaches, a psychological as well as a sociological one, may be required in analyzing sociohistorical influences.[64]

In more real terms for this study—as Norwegian-American ethnicity is linked with Norwegian-American identity—expressions and symbols that indicate a sense of belonging to and a commonality with a group designated as Norwegian-American will be viewed as an "invention" or commonalities evolving over time and in accord with the historical period under consideration. In other words, the study will consider the historical context and processes that account for how and why Norwegian Americans in the 1990s behave and feel as they do when distinguishing themselves individually and as a particular group from other segments of the American population.

Public festivals and banquets emerged in the early history of the group as significant traditions in defining Norwegian-American ethnicity. An emerging Norwegian immigrant elite in Chicago formed the Scandinavian Society in 1854. Its immediate purpose was to welcome the Norwegian violin virtuoso Ole Bull on his visit to Chicago in March of that year. A grand banquet marked the occasion. This society was short-lived and did not provide a vehicle for an ambitious Norwegian elite to gain influence, but it did create a useful model for later social activity. The formation of this society and others, although not entirely supporting Roosens's instrumentalist position on the mobilization of ethnic identity, does illustrate his theory of the basic role of ethnic leadership, generally motivated by self-interest, in the process of establishing ethnic identity and in directing the internal life of the ethnic community. A number of societies came into being in the Norwegian-American community in the following decade and after, and public celebrations occurred regularly from the 1870s. These included May 17 observances, which became the foremost public display of Norwegian ethnicity. On July 5, 1875, Norwegians in Chicago were sufficiently proud of their place in America to commemorate the fiftieth anniversary of the sailing of the sloop *Restauration* with a parade and a large open-air folk festival.[65]

This same historical event gave cause for a grand centennial celebration in 1925. The most spectacular commemoration of this milestone in the American experience of Norwegian Americans took place in the Twin Cities of Minneapolis and St. Paul. The Norse-American Centennial provided occasion for Norwegian Americans, or at least for those who arranged the festivities, to interpret and present the group's ethnic merits to the American public. It was an inspiring historical moment that at this juncture in the group's history established lasting contours of its ethnic identity. A pageant centering on the life of the Civil War hero Colonel Hans Christian Heg—"the type of all that is best and noblest in a citizen"—was a splendid production with one thousand actors in twenty-one scenes; it attested to a need to affirm a favored place in American history. Idiosyncratic qualities were made public at multiple exhibits of folk art, musical presentations, and parades of people in national costumes. The Norwegian folk character could be viewed at the thirty-seven simultaneous *bygdelag* reunions during the four-day Slooper anniversary cele-

bration. President Calvin Coolidge honored the celebration with his presence and by his endorsement of Leif Ericson as the first European discoverer of America.[66] For Norwegian Americans, the Viking image and the president's testimonial to the virility and adventurous spirit of an ethnic group with ancient Norse roots, rural values, and good American ideals became significant components of a dynamic process of self-definition. This creative and inventive process of defining the cultural and historical content of their ethnicity became essentially a question of both accommodation and resistance to assimilative forces in the historical context of the 1920s rather than a re-creation of an authentic Norwegian cultural heritage. As a festival identity was constructed and finally presented, the Norse-American Centennial created a Norway and a Norwegian-American past that in any real sense had never fully existed. As a celebratory event, it served to bestow an acceptable ethnic identity on Norwegian Americans; a reconstructed and glorious ethnic past was embraced. The event thus embodied much more than the Norwegian-American linguist Einar Haugen's assessment of the 1925 centennial; he saw it in assimilative terms mainly as "an impressive demonstration of the passing of an era."[67]

In 1975, when Norwegian Americans were aiming to celebrate the sesquicentennial of the arrival of the Sloopers, the question was posed anew if such a celebration would merely be the end of an age, especially as it came during a decade of ethnic revival and was inspired by a resulting, perhaps temporary, reawakening of a Norwegian-American consciousness, an ethnic enthusiasm that might quickly fade, it was thought, following the festivities. And, to be sure, not all Norwegian Americans desired to be defined as ethnic. "All America is discovering that it's not only all right to be ethnic . . . it's fun to be ethnic . . . and it's very American to be ethnic," a contributor to the official 1975 publication tried to convince fellow Norwegian Americans. The main events of the Norwegian American Sesquicentennial celebration, like those of the 1925 commemoration, centered on the Twin Cities of Minneapolis and St. Paul, but in conjunction with many regional arrangements across the United States. The focus was again on historical memory, "a heritage to share."[68] The intrinsic and intransigent belief in Viking ancestry, the strong individualism, integrity, and good citizenship of immigrant forebears, as well as in their descendants' positive contributions to American life was much in evidence. But augmenting this favorable ethnic self-perception was a definition of much of the Norwegian-American heritage in terms of the folk culture of immigrant ancestors. Rosemaling was being revived, and other folk arts were moving out of the museum into classrooms and community events; folk music and dancing found practitioners in later generations. Their ethnic symbolism aside, they all were emblematic expressions of Norwegian-American

ethnicity as practiced by the few rather than the many.

The various commemorative events— October 5–14, 1975—were, however, elitist, and were made more so by the presence of King Olav V of Norway at "royal banquets" and "royal receptions" and "royal visits" to institutions of a Norwegian immigrant origin. To be sure, there were luncheons honoring prominent Norwegian Americans. But even His Majesty, with his assumed lineage back to Viking kings, appeared to bequeath the heroic qualities of mythical Norse ancestors to all their descendants in America. Norwegian Americans were portrayed as a successful immigrant group, well situated and assimilated, but proud of their Norwegian immigrant roots. More attention than in 1925 was given to the Norwegian homeland; its newly found prosperity as a fledgling oil-producing nation only elevated a favorable Norwegian-American self-perception. The 1975 events, like the ones fifty years earlier, gave great visibility to Norwegian-American ethnicity.[69]

Currently, public festivals defining themselves as Scandinavian or Viking are in vogue, suggesting, as indicated earlier, an emerging Scandinavian identity alongside the more narrow nationalistic ones of Swedish, Norwegian, and Danish. May 17 celebrations, advertised as Norwegian folk festivals, are, however, common, and in recent years have gained added popularity. In a very public way, then, the new ethnicity enjoys support among latter-day

Norwegian Americans. The identifying ethnic symbols do not vary much from one event to the other.

Two of the largest community folk festivals are Norsk Høstfest in Minot, North Dakota, conducted annually in October, and Nordic Fest, in Decorah, Iowa, at the end of July. Nordic Fest has been a yearly event since 1966, attracting thousands of people to this small town in the northeastern corner of Iowa. Its inclusive name notwithstanding, the festival is publicized as a celebration of Decorah's Norwegian heritage. Vesterheim Norwegian-American Museum sponsors rosemaling and wood-carving exhibits, but also demonstrations of such folk arts as *lefse* making, figure carving, and weaving. There is storytelling, old-time fiddlers and folk dancers, and workshops in family history. Traditional Norwegian foods are served, and a lutefisk-eating contest is held. Norwegian ethnicity is on parade as a festival of arts and crafts, dance and music, troll walks and historic tours, and tales of trolls, mythology, and humorous ethnic types as well as of pioneer times in America. Participants wear Norwegian *bunads,* parade as horned Vikings, eat *lefse,* lutefisk, and Norwegian Christmas cookies, compete in Viking-type rock throwing and Norwegian-American contests in *lefse* tossing, and join in a grand procession through the main street of town, where an eclectic confusion of earnest and silly ethnic expressions and characters compete for attention. A romanticized and popularized image of Norway and a Norwegian immigrant past is conveyed during the three days of the festival. The experience for those attending must be a rewarding and festive sense of being Norwegian-American.[70]

Dating from 1978, Norsk Høstfest, in contrast to Nordic Fest, carries a narrow, nationalistic name, "norsk," that is, Norwegian, but nevertheless advertises itself in broad terms as "North America's Largest Scandinavian Festival," which the many exhibits and activities also justify. Indeed, if the program is a guide, the festival has an even wider horizon, major entertainment being provided by American stars of film and stage, like Bob Hope, Red Skelton, Tom Jones, and Tammy Wynette, some seemingly on their way down from past stardom. Norwegian-American actress Celeste Holm is a regular artist as is the "Happy Norwegian" accordionist Myron Floren, both now aging artists. "Scandinavian festivals all over the United States," Floren insisted, "are important traditions to keep alive. I think they all appreciate what I am doing and being given the name Happy Norwegian does not hurt. It has given a lot of advertising."[71]

Celeste Holm, perhaps more than any other American actress of Norwegian ancestry, has been recognized as representing the Norwegian-American ethnic group. "Well, I love them [Norwegian Americans] and they seem to love me," she explained, "In New York I am part of the Syttende mai you know."[72] In the 1990s celebrities still elicit ethnic pride.

Performers from Norway, including country-and-western singer Bjøro Håland, appear regularly. The commercialism of the five-day festival is apparent in the multitude of booths located in the large festival arena, which offer a great variety of ethnic products for sale. Less obvious is the business the thousands of people in attendance generate locally. The festival founder, Chester M. Reiten, a prominent local businessman and politician, emphasized in an interview his Norwegian heritage as a moving force in the festival. In a conservative and romantic vein, and, of course, ethnocentrically emblematic, Reiten defined his heritage "as faith in God, the work ethic, honesty, responsibility, and respect for the rights of others." These values he saw as those of his ancestors, and he hoped Norsk Høstfest and similar groups would help restore them. The initial inspiration for the festival was the local sesquicentennial celebration of Norwegian immigration in 1975. The well-known Norwegian arts and crafts as well as other ethnic identifying symbols are obvious everywhere during the festival.[73]

Scandinavian, or specifically Norwegian, community festivals are regular occurrences in all parts of the United States. Many are recently launched; a long list could be made in addition to those mentioned earlier. One example is the first Annual Scandinavian Festival in Edmonds, Washington, at which the mayor officially declared May 4, 1996, as "Troll Day" and all of Scandinavian descent as "Trolls."[74]

Contemporary Norwegians and Norwegian Americans clearly have differing visions of the nature of Norwegian-American festive ethnicity. Spokespersons for Norway obviously wish to present an image of a progressive nation of industrial and cultural growth, and national romantic notions of trolls and peasant idylls and their celebration by Norwegian Americans naturally impede their efforts. For instance, San Francisco's Norway Day Festival began in May 1993 as the result of an initiative of Norwegian diplomatic representatives in the city with the clear purpose of featuring a modern contemporary Norway. Tensions soon developed with the local Norwegian-American enclave in regard to the program. It was an unequal contest where established immigrant traditions and symbols were bound to gain the upper hand. The local Norwegian societies and organizations soon gave the festivities a traditional Norwegian-American content at the expense of program contributions from a self-confident ancestral homeland.[75]

On the other coast a Scandinavian Festival became an annual event in Atlanta, Georgia, in May 1995, organized by local Scandinavian organizations. The ethnic program content is surprisingly consistent with that described earlier—walk-about trolls, Viking reenactments, folk art, and food specialties. In Madison, Wisconsin, a Norwegian-American Fest with similar content has been arranged each year since 1994.

There are many indications that ethnicity is more and more expressed as a festive culture,

Figure 18. A diminutive Viking at the Viking Fest in Georgetown, Texas, in April 1996. Photograph by Odd S. Lovoll.

which is celebrated and accepted as an expression of ethnic identity and pride in heritage. Another example is found in the strongly Swedish-American Georgetown area of Texas, where Scandinavian Americans joined hands in April 1996 to begin a tradition of an annual Viking Fest, selecting a neutral, but easily identifiable, name that would apply to all Nordic countries (figure 18). Its Swedish bias was, however, suggested by announcing the festival as "Celebrating 150th Anniversary of Scandinavian Emigration to America," the year 1846 marking the first group migration from Sweden, which obviously ignored the sailing of the *Restauration* from Norway some twenty years earlier. A Viking longship, the *Norseman,* a copy of the Norwegian Gokstad longship from the ninth century and the property of the Leif Ericson Society in Philadelphia, was transported to central Texas (figure 19). The crew, dressed in Viking helmets and tunics, gave credibility to the name of the festival. The larger purpose of the event, as stated in the program, was to be "a step toward preserving a unique blend of Texas-Scandinavian culture." Thus, a process of inventing ethnic identity and culture is recognized and the maintenance of this created ethnicity seen as a purpose of the festival.[76]

Scandinavian festivals of greater vintage flourish. Story City, Iowa, celebrates its Scandinavian Days in May, which in this Norwegian town grew out of May 17 celebrations begun in 1966. The following year, however,

Figure 19. The Viking ship the Norseman *under full sail outside Philadelphia; the ship is owned by the Leif Ericson Society there. Photograph courtesy of the Leif Ericson Society International.*

the inclusive Scandinavian appellation was adopted, making it one of the early "Scandinavian" festivals of the "new ethnicity." Their purpose may fit into the mode of "marketing of ethnicity." Nordicfest in Libby, Montana, is an even better example of "the marketing of ethnicity" than the Story City festival. It was born out of an economic crisis in the 1980s when the local economy faltered because of the closing of local mines and a reduction in timber harvest. Logging had provided the economic base for the community. In the late 1800s employment in logging and mining had attracted many Norwegian loggers and their families from Minnesota to the Libby area. In the 1980s their descendants diversified the economy to include tourism. Nordicfest became a community effort to celebrate the heritage of the early settlers and attract people to town. Its traditional displays of crafts, ethnic food, Viking raiders, folk dancers, and *bunad* processions are enhanced by the International Fjord Horse Show, held simultaneously. These tawny draft horses associated with the fjord landscape of Norway become yet another expressive reminder of a pure and simple ancestral homeland.[77]

The acceptable symbols of a Norwegian,

and to a large extent Scandinavian, ethnicity in the 1990s show both consistency and durability. The rejection—as demonstrated in San Francisco's Norway Day Festival—of attempts to redefine Norwegian-American ethnicity by introducing elements not directly relevant to it may suggest that the significance of a Norwegian-American identity to the individual and to the group is much greater than one might judge from some of the silliness that attends festive ethnic manifestations. It may surely be inferred from the amassed evidence that ethnicity for most Norwegian Americans represents more than a symbolic expression of vestiges of an ancestral culture. Modern Norway and its culture may, however, seem strange and foreign to these same Norwegian Americans; contemporary Norwegian culture does not carry the psychological and sociological weight to inform a Norwegian-American identity. A vision of a romantic, even mythological, and pure ancestral homeland is cultivated. People attend ethnic festivities because they choose to do so, and by doing so they obviously satisfy a physical as well as a historical need for belonging. Participation in these ethnic celebrations is further evidence of the powerful ideological force—past and present—ethnicity exerts in American society.

CHAPTER 3

The Burden and the Glory

Religious Identity

The traditional dominance of Protestantism in American society has eroded in the postwar era at least in part because of large contingents of immigrants from Latin America, Southeast Asia, Africa, and the Middle East. By the early 1980s Catholics had increased over a thirty-year period from 22 to 26 percent of the population, and those practicing non–Judeo-Christian religions from 1 to 4 percent, while Protestants declined from 67 to 56 percent. By 1988, the Spanish-speaking community had become the fastest-growing minority, five times faster than the rest of the population. Hispanics numbered 20.2 million in 1990, moving up from 14.5 million in 1980. The changing ethnic and racial composition of the American population not only altered the religious landscape but increased the relative size of the groups most prone to pejorative names and subject to prejudice from the dominant socioreligious entities of the American population.[1]

In a sociological discussion in 1970 of assimilation of the several white Protestant national origin groups into the Anglo-Saxon core society, Charles H. Anderson saw a movement toward a white Protestant socioreligious community. He identified under-lying uniting similarities as a common faith, high-status national origin, "Old American" identity, a pioneering and individualistic ethos, ruralism, voluntarism, and local church organization. Anderson contended that these, and perhaps other commonalities, justify the label "white Protestant" as an acceptable self-identification. Large-scale intermarriage encouraged the process. As early as 1960 Will Herberg first suggested the notion of a collective religious group identity among white Protestants. In his perspective, in which he presented the "triple melting pot" of Catholics, Jews, and Protestants, religion was a more important factor than ethnicity as an organizing principle in American society.[2]

Ethnic and denominational diversity is, of course, still much in evidence; in fact, if anything, the United States has become much more pluralistic in its religious life. This state of affairs does not entirely refute the hypothesis of an emerging white Protestant commonality. Historically and until at least as late as the 1960s, a white Protestant identity was nearly synonymous with an American identity, but one that was divided along national origin and denominational lines. These denominational entities have not dissolved, and institutional attachment remains strong. In order to consider the strength and significance of religious self-perception and identity, it is necessary to explore such variables as church affiliation, national origin, the extent of inter-religious contact, age, gender, socioeconomic differences, geographical location, and denominational expectations.

This study does not, however, attempt to measure religious commitment. And, as Eugeen Roosens reminds his readers, there may be a hierarchy of identities for each person since everyone belongs to several social units, such as a nation, a profession, a family, an ethnic group, and a religious organization. The hierarchy of loyalties may, as Roosens explains, be inverted or changed in time, and in a given context one social identity can be more relevant.[3] Typically, a person can be first of all an American, then of Norwegian ancestry, an engineer, a Republican, and a Lutheran. Depending on external circumstances, then, the relative significance of these identities can change.

In the 1990s a postmodern relativism—however, according to Ernest Gellner, this amorphous terminology is to be understood—with its subjectivity and permissiveness in its search of the elusive truth, including the absolute truths of conscience, and an expanding secularization of society, with its emphasis on material rather than spiritual values, could in any case be thought to diminish the role of religious faith in the life of most Americans. The degree of regularity in church attendance or of membership would therefore not be of much help in determining the sincerity of individual religious conviction and identity. In many instances church participation has become little more than an expected social ritual and practice, though, certainly, many people are indeed serious about their church and faith. Whatever the case might be, it is, to point out the obvious, the active church member who makes organized religious life possible, rendering the distinction between those who are members of a congregation and those who are not a significant social factor.[4]

In a multireligious America the congregation an individual joins may, should circumstances dictate, be more a matter of convenience than of conscience, unless prejudice dissuades one from associating with a particular faith. This was the case for Norwegians with Roman Catholicism, which until a more ecumenical age, even lukewarm Norwegian Lutherans eschewed. Anti-Catholic sentiments held sway in the Norwegian community. "Norwegians where I grew up were naive and closed and tended to live in a different kind of world. They wanted to have their belief," recalls Steven Slostad, who grew up in a Norwegian-American community in southeastern Minnesota in the 1950s and 1960s. He continued, "It's kind of like my aunt at a meal with all of us together, she said, 'They're nice people, even though they are Catholic.' That's the best she could say, you know, they're nice people for being Catholic." Many Norwegian Lutherans may still not have liberated themselves from such limiting attitudes, and attendance at Catholic mass would for these Norwegian Americans not be an acceptable option. Feasible choices are generally confined to Protestant churches.[5]

The fourth-generation Norwegian American William Simonson, born in 1925 in Cameron, Wisconsin, as one of four siblings, two boys and two girls, tells of growing up in Chicago on Humboldt Boulevard. While his father was indifferent to religion, his mother, even though a Lutheran, sent the children to a Presbyterian Church located next door, but when they moved across the street, she enrolled the two girls in a Baptist Sunday school in order to avoid having them cross the very busy boulevard.[6] It is a pattern much more common than one might assume and one obvious from anecdotal evidence gathered in this investigation. The suggestion is not only of action based on convenience, or even indifference, but, more to the point, of an emerging acceptance and tolerance within a shared mainstream Protestantism. Another notable finding was the seeming ease with which many individuals within this mainstream religious tradition changed denomination, from Lutheran to Methodist or American Baptist or Presbyterian or Episcopalian, and then, not uncommonly, depending on the circumstances of their lives, returned to the Lutheran faith. These findings appear to give some credence to Herberg's thesis of a white Protestant commonality. This chapter will look at Norwegian-American ethnicity as it relates to denominational membership, and how this interaction of ethnicity and faith is experienced by persons interviewed for the study.

In American society religion has emerged as a major organizational enterprise. According to the study by Wade Clark Roof and William McKinney cited earlier, Americans continue to identify with historic religious traditions; about two-thirds were members of a local church or synagogue. People outside the formal religious structure are in some respects also touched by its broader influence and frequently profess loyalty to a religious tradition. A marketplace denominational competition tends to strengthen religious observance. The conventional historical assumption has been that in the past century about one-third of Norwegian immigrants held Lutheran Church membership, though numbers varied much between rural and urban; the figure for both perhaps increased generationally, though conventional wisdom may still not be far from the mark. Although no reliable statistics exist, it can be safely assumed that less than half of all Norwegian Americans, regardless of generation, found a formal church home in a Lutheran church. But, obviously, the church and its ethnic Lutheranism greatly influenced people far beyond the congregational bounds. Polls show distinct declines in church and synagogue memberships from the 1970s. By 1982 formal membership had sunk from roughly 75 percent in the 1960s to 67 percent, or as indicated, two-thirds of the population, and by 1990 it had fallen to a low of 55.1 percent of all Americans.[7]

At century's end Norwegian Quakers continue to have a presence in Marshall County, Iowa. The Stavanger Friends Church south of LeGrand dates back to 1864, though the first Norwegian Quakers moved to Iowa as early as 1842, when Ommund Olson built a meeting house on his farm on Sugar Creek northwest of Keokuk in Leland County. By the late 1870s, Marshall County had become the major center of Norwegian Quakers in the United States. "Even when I came here in 1948, many people spoke to each other in Norwegian," Helen Stanley Stangeland recalled. The small Stavanger

Meeting, many of its members descendants of the original Norwegian settlers, is not affiliated with any larger group of Friends. The cemetery across the road from the meeting house and the active members bear witness to the group's history. "Both sets of my grandparents came over from Norway, and since they were all Quakers, partly for religious freedom," Clarence Stangeland, born in 1923, related. "They came from Sandnes and Røldal by the city of Stavanger. My grandfather was a half brother of Andrew Stangeland, who accompanied Cleng Peerson to America in 1824." A strong sense of a common local origin in Norway, whether Quaker or not, has persisted for several generations in this farming community in central Iowa.[8]

The majority of Norwegian Americans who are members of a congregation currently belong to denominations that might be designated as moderate Protestants—Lutherans, Methodists, and American Baptists. Some are conservative Protestants, having joined fundamentalists and evangelicals in Pentecostal and Assemblies of God congregations. "The Bible is the inspired, infallible and authoritative Word of God," the Philadelphia Church in the Scandinavian Ballard section of Seattle declares in its fundamentalistic statement of faith. Its beginnings are dated to 1901, when Norwegian and Swedish Pentecostalists started having religious home meetings. It is an early example of conversion to fundamentalist and emotional Christianity by Scandinavian immigrants. The second major Norwegian center of Pentecostalism was Salem Gospel Tabernacle in Brooklyn, dating from the 1920s; it is now a multiethnic gathering. The spokesman for Philadelphia in Seattle declared, "We don't stress nationality any longer." Both are member congregations of the Fellowship of Christian Assemblies, which consists of autonomous, evangelical churches with historical roots in the modern Pentecostal movement. The Fellowship's roots are strongly Baptist, traced in part to charismatic revivals among Scandinavian Baptists in Chicago in 1906. Norwegian Americans also joined the evangelicals, however, in the rising tide of religious conservatism of the Religious Right in the 1970s, clashing with what they relentlessly termed "secular humanism" on such issues as abortion and gay rights, and crusading for greater control over the classroom in such matters as Christian morality and school prayer, and for a return to traditional family values and roles for men and women. Gerald W. Erickson, a fourth-generation descendant of Norwegian and Swedish background born in 1942, grew up in a strict Lutheran environment in Richfield, Minnesota. "My parents drifted away from the Lutheran Church and into the fundamentalist and evangelical camp," Erickson explained, "because they felt the Lutheran Church had become too liberal and accepting of secular values."[9]

Showing a higher percentage for Norwegian Mormons than anticipated and an obvious overrepresentation of Lutherans, table 4 never-

Table 4. Religious affiliation of Norwegian Americans responding to questionnaire distributed in 1995-96

Religion	Responses	Percentage
Lutheran	4,204	64.36
Baptist	95	1.45
Episcopal	102	1.56
Jewish	11	0.17
Methodist	322	4.93
Mormon	192	2.94
No affiliation	648	9.92
Non-Christian	76	1.16
Presbyterian	272	4.16
Other Protestant	301	4.61
Roman Catholic	223	3.41
United Church of Christ	86	1.32
Total non-Lutheran	2,328	35.64
Total responses	6,532	100.00

theless gives some idea of the religious diversity among Norwegian Americans in the 1990s. Lutheranism is obviously still the dominant religious affiliation. The large number of Norwegians with a formal Lutheran membership who responded may suggest the strength of ethnicity in Lutheran congregations of a Norwegian immigrant background. There are, however, an increasing number of Catholic affiliates, regularly through intermarriage. The number in the survey of 3.4 percent of Norwegian-American Catholics may seem, therefore, somewhat low, based on indications through personal interviews. A 5-percent Roman Catholic population among St. Olaf students of Norwegian ancestry may more accurately reflect current trends.

Conversion occurs regularly through marriage. Annemarie DeRoche, born in Bethesda, Maryland, in 1979, is a third-generation Catholic and a fourth-generation Norwegian American. Her grandmother Margret Solum DeRoche, born in Garretson, South Dakota, in 1911, where her father was a Lutheran minister, converted to Catholicism when she married the Catholic Charles Patrick DeRoche in 1944 after moving to Washington, D.C. While she converted to the Catholic faith, she apparently transformed her German-French-Irish husband into a "Norwegian." Granddaughter Annemarie maintained that "my grandparents on my father's side really make me feel Norwegian." Her grandfather's Norwegianness was thus what may be termed "an adopted cultural identity," a widespread experience.[10]

The Church of Jesus Christ of the Latter-day Saints (LDS) also enjoys a notable Norwegian-American following. In connection with the research for this study, Mormons made a special effort to be represented. The high percentage of Mormon responses in table 4 reflects an eagerness to be viewed as an integrated part of the Norwegian-American experience. Knute Peterson, a fourth-generation Norwegian American, was born in 1918 in the very Scandinavian Ephraim in Sanpete County, Utah. His great-grandfather Canute Peterson emigrated from Hardanger in the 1840s to the Fox River settlement in LaSalle County, Illinois, and following his conversion to Mormonism moved to Utah. Knute Peterson was brought up in a strict Mormon home, his father, Peter Peterson, holding the position of bishop, but also with a great sense of Norwegian ethnicity, much due to a strong Norwegian presence. He related the following amusing and revealing incident: "There were so many Petersons, that at a meeting where the bishop, not my father, requested Brother Peterson to stand up and offer a prayer, as many as seventeen men rose, and when the bishop corrected it to Brother Peter Peterson, only three of the seventeen sat down again."[11]

Many Norwegian Mormons came to Salt Lake City during the postwar years, many from the LDS community in Bergen, Norway. Between 1946 and 1963, 1,074 registered Norwegian Mormons emigrated. "We all thought we should join the New Jerusalem," one respondent stated. The conservative Mormon stance on women's rights and abortion aligns it with evangelicals on these issues, although the Mormon Church is outside not only orthodox Christian but all interdenominational organization. Erlend Dean Peterson, born in 1940, dean of admissions at Brigham Young University in Provo, Utah, is a fifth-generation Norwegian American; he is a direct descendant of the earliest convert in Norway to Mormonism, Svend Larsen. Larsen, a sea captain from Risør, Norway, was baptized into the Mormon faith in Aalborg, Denmark, in 1851. Peterson explained the Mormon responsibility of tracing family history and its impact: "This duty and the prescribed mission work keep alive identity specific to ancestry. It makes Mormons reach beyond the third generation. Our heritage is greatly strengthened through our family history program and mission activity." On the other hand, of course, the Latter-day Saints have not historically encouraged ethnicity since the goal is to make people blend in. "Norwegian Americans who are Mormon are more inhibited in their ethnicity because of the controlling power of the Church," explained Norwegian-born Elisabeth Lyngli, historian of the largely LDS Sons of Norway Leif Erikson Lodge in Salt Lake City, Utah.[12]

Sprinklings of Norwegian Americans exist among liberal Protestants—the Congregationalists, Presbyterians, Episcopalians, and Unitarians. In San Francisco Armand John Kreft, vicar of Holy Innocents' Episcopal Church, serves a growing congregation (figure 20). Father Kreft, born in 1948, is of Norwegian ancestry, his maternal grandparents having immigrated from Stavanger, Norway, to Edinburg, North Dakota, where they became farmers, around the turn of the century. Father Kreft is openly gay. "My sexual orientation is a non-issue in the congregation," he said. The Episcopal Church shows a greater tolerance, perhaps through a higher level of enlightenment, than most Protestant denominations. "It was the 'socially acceptable' denomination in the '50s," Kreft explained. "I grew up in California as an Episcopalian, since although my Norwegian side is Lutheran, my paternal side is Episcopalian. I have a strong relationship to my Norwegian heritage, and I am

Figure 20. The Reverend Armand John Kreft, vicar at Holy Innocents' Episcopal Church in San Francisco, California. Reprinted with permission.

proud of it. The farm in North Dakota is still in the family."[13]

Joan Lundheim Dickerson was born in Minneapolis in 1930 as the daughter of an immigrant father and a second-generation mother, and grew up in a liberal home; her father sought a rational basis rather than a religious one for belief. Following her move to Maryland and marriage to a man of British background, she became a Unitarian. She said, "Still, I enjoy Lutheran services occasionally where I might experience surprise rather than discrimination of my Unitarian confession." The Nora Unitarian Universalist Church organized in 1881 in Hanska in Brown County, Minnesota, is the only one still active of the five congregations gathered by the Norwegian author and Unitarian minister Kristofer Janson. Half or more of the 135 members in the Nora Church are Norwegian, and services in Norwegian continued into the 1940s. "People in the congregation want to retain the Norwegian heritage; as an example, every October all members, regardless of ethnic background, take part in a Norwegian *smørgåsbord*," Lorraine Becker related. Born in 1921, she grew up Unitarian as a third-generation Norwegian American.[14]

Converts to Islam and the Baha'i faith, teaching the unity of all religions, are rare among Norwegian Americans but not totally missing. They are likely to be found among highly educated individuals. Grete Roland, a third-generation Norwegian American born in Chicago in 1937 to parents described as "religiously unconventional," has had experience as an actress, taught English in Turkey, and is a multicultural educator. She belonged to the Baha'i faith, and says now, "I define myself as Socialist, Humanist, and Buddhist, but with an abiding Norwegian ethnic identity."[15]

Through marriage some Norwegian Americans have converted to Judaism. Carla H. Danziger, born in 1944 in Seattle, Washington,

to second-generation parents, relates how she met and married Israeli-born Raphael Danziger and embraced the Jewish faith, though she does not practice it. She insists that becoming involved in another culture did not cause her to depart from her ancestral Norwegian one, and at the time of the interview Danziger was serving as social director of the Sons of Norway lodge in Washington, D.C. There are also Norwegian-American Jehovah's Witnesses, a religious phenomenon in modern America that stands out because of their zeal in proclaiming their beliefs.[16]

Conversion to non-Lutheran faiths, or even a severance with organized religion, did not obliterate a historical and personal ethnic bond. In some cases it even reinforced a Norwegian-American attachment, since the change in religious conviction may have placed a childhood self-identification in some jeopardy. Still, the questionnaire survey suggests that being a member of a Lutheran church rooted in a Norwegian immigrant tradition encourages an ethnic response. On the other hand, as several of the quotations above indicate, a change in religious identity does not necessarily diminish loyalty to an ethnic identity. For Mormon converts, it became a responsibility to establish clear ancestral lineages, though not necessarily to celebrate a particular ethnic identity; even so, the quest for ancestral roots would surely encourage establishing ethnic cultural ties. Others, those practicing both conservative and liberal Christian faiths, Judaism, and religious beliefs outside the Judeo-Christian tradition, and even the many not affiliated with organized religion sought roots in a shared ethnic heritage. A conflict between loyalty to belief and to ancestry need not develop in the 1990s. The one does not neutralize the other. In their religious convictions Norwegian Americans have, then, become more pluralistic, and they are firmly integrated into an American organizational structure. Individual ethnic identities nevertheless appear to be preserved and to be a positive force in the self-perception and behavior of many Norwegian Americans. There is no longer any church body or a denominational division identifying itself as Norwegian.[17]

The Lutheran Factor

The Norwegian-American author of the classic immigrant novel *Giants in the Earth,* Ole E. Rølvaag, defined his ethnic identity in terms of the Norwegian language, Norwegian nationality, and the Lutheran faith, "The Faith of His Fathers." Lutheran and Norwegian were for most Norwegian Americans one and the same, and, even considering the point made above in regard to the current relationship between ethnic and religious identity, many latter-day Norwegian Americans retain an ethnoreligious sense of identity based in their Norwegian ancestry and the Lutheran Church. In his study of Norwegian settlements in Wisconsin around 1950, sociologist Peter A. Munch concluded that "it is virtually impossible to distinguish

'Lutheran' from 'Norwegian.'" In the Norwegian Lutheran congregations Munch studied, non-Norwegian members, mainly through marriage, were the exceptions. The statement "Norwegian and Lutheran [are] closely associated in my mind," here made by fourth-generation Norwegian American Jacqueline Lyngen Adams, born in 1946, is perhaps still a typical response, in spite of the fact that Norwegian Lutheran churches, rural as well as urban, have lost much of their ethnic exclusivity.[18]

Replicas of the uniquely Norwegian medieval stave churches are dramatic symbols of the union between the Lutheran faith and Norwegian ethnicity. Both heathen Viking motifs and the Christian symbol of the cross adorn these early Christian structures: to present-day Norwegian Americans, they may convey Viking descent as well as loyalty to a Lutheran heritage, even though medieval stave churches were erected centuries before the Reformation. The best known of these re-created wooden edifices is the model in Rapid City, South Dakota, of the famed and well-preserved Borgund stave church in Sogn from shortly after A.D. 1150. The church in South Dakota was built in 1969, and some eighty thousand people visit it annually (figure 21). In June 1998 a replica of another stave church in Sogn, the more than eight-hundred-year-old Hopperstad church in Vik, was dedicated in Moorhead, Minnesota.[19]

Church union has been a major movement within the different American Lutheran faiths; there has been an effort to unite fellow believers

Figure 21. The Chapel in the Hills near Rapid City, South Dakota, is a replica of the Borgund stave church in Sogn, Norway. Photograph by Dale A. Jensen; courtesy of Rushmore Photo & Gifts, Inc.

in ever larger organizational units. Combining forces augmented the social denominational impact of a particular faith. The Norwegian Lutheran Church (NLCA), which emerged in 1917 with in excess of four hundred thousand members, was itself a fusion of divergent Lutheran doctrinal positions. Responding to the patriotic oppressive climate of the World War I period, wanting to become an "unhyphenated" American institution loyal to the Lutheran confession, and desiring to proselytize beyond the Norwegian-American fold, the Lutheran clergy initiated motions in 1918 to drop the word "Norwegian" from the official name. An adverse reaction among the laity assumed strident and unexpected dimensions, perhaps fueled by a backlash against excessive postwar nativism, and the old name was retained. For most Norwegian Americans, the NLCA was the one point of contact with their ancestral heritage, and those taking part in the debate did indeed link orientation with label. The name did not, however, prevent the "Americanization" of the NLCA, and it moved in this direction as rapidly as the Lutheran Free Church, organized in 1897, which had not joined the merger in 1917 and never officially designated itself as Norwegian. It was an inevitable process.[20]

"Norwegian" was retained in the NLCA name until 1946, when this church body was renamed the Evangelical Lutheran Church in America (ELC). It was one of the synods that joined with German and Danish Lutherans in 1960 to form the American Lutheran Church (ALC), the Lutheran Free Church uniting with the ALC three years later. At the time of the merger in 1960, ELC reported 1,119,121 baptized congregants in 2,673 member congregations. In 1988 the ALC joined together with the Lutheran Church in America (LCA), then the largest Lutheran church in the United States, and the Association of Evangelical Lutheran Churches to form the Evangelical Lutheran Church of America (ELCA). The vast majority of church-member Norwegian Americans are currently among the 5,214,189 baptized members of the ELCA, divided among 10,914 con-

gregations, as recorded in 1995. The church body consists of several different Lutheran constituencies, and internal tensions and divisions in regard to doctrine, polity, and regional diversity are clearly visible. These conflicts reflect as well Lutheran traditions associated with a Norwegian religious heritage, most clearly the Lutheran traditions and identity of the Norwegian Synod, one of the constituent bodies of the 1917 merger creating the NLCA. Church historian Todd W. Nichol identifies these conflicts as "a lively passion for the objectivity of the truth and a participatory, democratic approach to church life."[21]

Lutheranism manifests itself among Norwegian Americans in such conservative groupings as the Evangelical Lutheran Synod, formed in 1918 by a rump constituency of the Norwegian Synod that did not merge with the NLCA, announcing its "purpose of continuing 'true Lutheranism' among Norwegians in America." With its main base in Mankato, Minnesota, it was known as the Norwegian Synod until 1958 and generally referred to as "The Little Synod." It has somewhat more than twenty-three thousand communicants at present. The synod practices a pronounced congregational autonomy and in doctrine is in harmony with the conservative German Missouri Synod's strong devotion to confessional Lutheranism, and with the orthodox confessionalism of the Wisconsin Evangelical Lutheran Synod. A doctrinal split did occur with the Missourians in the 1960s, the Norwegian group finding the Missourians moving away from their traditional Bible-based doctrine as this church entered into doctrinal negotiations with other Lutheran bodies. "I want to make it clear," George M. Orvick, its president and a second-generation Norwegian American born in Iowa in 1929, stated, "that the Evangelical Lutheran Synod stands for orthodox confessional Lutheranism which holds fast to the doctrines of verbal inspiration and inerrancy of scripture and that it rejects the historical-critical approach to Biblical interpretation." On the cover of its published doctrinal statement are the portraits of the trinity of founding fathers of the "old" Norwegian Synod—Herman Amberg Preus, Jacob Aall Ottesen, and Ulrik Vilhelm Koren—symbolizing the continuation of an unmerged church faithful to its historical legacy. The alliance with the stagnant theology of the Missouri Synod extended back to the late 1850s; it had been a fateful legacy for the "old" Norwegian Synod, strengthening conservative impulses. The long relationship with the Missourians brought Norwegian adherents directly into the large Missouri Synod church.[22]

A strong Norwegian presence in the small conservative Church of the Lutheran Brethren, headquartered in Fergus Falls, Minnesota, with only about twelve thousand members, deserves mention. In terms of pietistic low-church practices it is, of course, at the other end of the spectrum from the Evangelical Lutheran Synod. "We are pious but not pietistic," Orvick said of his group, which rejects the Haugean Lutheran direction. Lutheran Brethren, on the other hand, requires a professed personal experience of conversion in a Haugean spirit in order to be received as a communicant member. It considers itself a sister church of the Lutheran free church that came into being in Norway in 1877; the American church was founded in 1900 and continued to use Norwegian in most of its official proceedings until 1940. The president of the Lutheran Brethren, Everald H. Strom, born in 1921, is both a third-generation Norwegian American and third-generation church member. "I never rebelled against the pious religious environment of my childhood and youth, " Strom contended, "and I appreciated the language and stories of Norway, and was influenced to enter the ministry since a child by my father and grandmother." Strom attended the seminary in Fergus Falls and was ordained in 1944. Because of their geographical dispersion and active missionary work, the two small religiously conservative synods exert more influence than their size would suggest. The role of the 59th Street Church in Brooklyn in establishing the Norseville colony is an example of the national presence of Lutheran Brethren.[23]

These, then, are the current rough contours of Norwegian-American Lutheranism. There is at times striking evidence of a Norwegian, and in general Scandinavian, presence in the Lutheran Church. The Bishop of the ELCA, H. George Anderson, of Danish-Swedish extraction, speaks Norwegian fluently. In an interview he indicated that ethnic diversity as well as a firm recognition of the Scandinavian and German roots of the Lutheran Church in America continues to be a part of the vocabulary of the ELCA.[24]

The Lutefisk Meter

In the late 1940s one might still hear the following high school cheer in Scandinavia, Wisconsin: "Lutefisk og lefse—Gammelost og prim—Scandinavia High School—Basketball team." The cheer in praise of lutefisk and *lefse,* as well as of sour milk cheese and soft cheese, with all its humorous connotations, nevertheless spoke directly to loyalty to a specific ethnicity and its traditions. Authenticity was reinforced by the use of Norwegian. Such ethnic shouts emanated from the throats of American-born Norwegian youth at numerous athletic events even much later than the 1940s. References to Norwegian places of residence as a "lutefisk ghetto" or "the lutefisk belt" in Norwegian regions of settlement, and of elite Norwegian Americans as "a lutefisk aristocracy" were made in a similar lighthearted vein. That the Wisconsin State Assembly in its 1993–94 session unanimously adopted—one would hope from ignorance—in debating what constituted a "toxic substance" a tongue-in-cheek motion made by Norwegian-American assembly members establishing that "Toxic substance does not include: Lutefisk" gives evidence of the persis-

tent frivolity associated with this ethnic soul food, if not with the legislative process itself.[25]

In the years just before the Civil War, Norwegian-American wholesale firms found it profitable to import commodities for a Norwegian-American public. On August 2, 1862, the Norwegian brig *Sleipner* arrived in Chicago directly from the ocean, only the second ship to do so. It was consigned by the Norwegian-American firm of Svanøe and Synnestvedt in Chicago and carried a cargo of salted herring, dried cod, and anchovies. These Norwegian food items were offered to the Norwegian community at immigrant retail stores, such as the one opened in 1865 by the young Christian H. Jevne. Jevne expanded to become a large wholesale and import concern, importing cheese, fish, canned goods, and aquavit directly from Norway. The availability of ethnic food items made them popular at social gatherings, secular as well as religious, and they assumed an ethnic symbolic function. Elite immigrant societies set the tone. Lodges of the Order of the Knights of the White Cross, a leading Norwegian fraternity organized in Chicago in 1863, in time arranged festive lutefisk banquets. From such immigrant elites the practice spread to the entire Norwegian-American community.[26]

The traditional church "lutefisk supper" replaced the American church supper—which obviously provided the model—in Norwegian-American congregations and became emblematic of Norwegian ethnicity. It was introduced

Figure 22. Irish-American Don Foley helps himself to lutefisk at the lutefisk supper at Vang Lutheran Church in Goodhue County, Minnesota, in October 1996. Photograph by Karen Kirk; courtesy of the Red Wing Republican Eagle.

before the turn of the century but did not become commonplace until the 1920s. The supper was enriched by characteristic foods, such as the popular *lefse,* the crisp unleavened *flatbrød,* and *rømmegrøt,* a cream porridge. In 1995 the Highview Christiania Lutheran Church in rural Farmington, Minnesota, advertised its Norwegian Supper, October 14, on the Internet. "The menu consists of," it announced, "*lutefisk,* meat balls and gravy, rutabagas, boiled potatoes, sweet soup, cranberries, rolls and lots of Scandinavian goodies like *lefse* and *krumkake.*" It was a unique Norwegian-American blend of dishes hardly acceptable to the taste in Norway (figure 22). Other identifying ethnic foods are also possible. The United Kickapoo Lutheran Church in rural Soldiers Grove, Wisconsin, offered a *mølse* din-

ner, a "sweet cheese" associated with western Norway, in particular the district of Sogn, in October 1995. Congregations in the small town of Benson in western Minnesota have had church *klubb* suppers, potato dumplings, instead of the much more common lutefisk.[27]

Culinary loyalties remain significant ethnic markers for American-born whites. Ethnic experiences are linked to ethnic identity. In his study of the 1980 federal census Richard Alba found that in the single-ancestry groups about two-thirds eat ethnic food at least occasionally, and about half do so at least monthly. It is highest, as one would expect, for those who say their ethnic background is important. This conclusion is supported by the data collected for Norwegian Americans. "We have lutefisk and *lefse* for dinner, and I love lutefisk—and all our children eat lutefisk," declared Irvin Holman, born in 1925 as a third-generation Norwegian American in Hatton, North Dakota. The fourth-generation children—all with Norwegian names, Jon, Kari, and Knut—he continued, "carry on Norwegian customs and food in their homes and have a strong sense of being Norwegian." Only a quarter of those in Alba's study who say ethnicity is not important eat ethnic food. Most ethnic food is consumed as a ceremonial use, at festivities, special occasions, and holidays. This, then, becomes a valuable indicator of the role of food in maintaining a sense of ethnic tradition.[28]

The lutefisk season begins in late fall for individuals and church groups and runs into the Christmas holiday celebration. *Norway Times* in Brooklyn, for instance, announced on October 19, 1995, "Season Start for *Lutefisk* Lovers." In the questionnaire survey a larger percentage than had family histories enjoyed Norwegian-American cuisine as a part of the Yuletide observance, in fact more than 70 percent, but hardly anyone, in fact, only 12 percent, who had a recorded account of their family's time in America responded negatively when asked if they served Norwegian-American dishes. Thus, one may fairly conclude that there is a clear correlation between interest in ancestry and the consumption of ethnic food. Culinary traditions, in the terminology of anthropologists, enhance the ritual and the boundary-demarcating significance of food.[29]

Food traditions, in other words, make individuals and groups aware of their heritage and differentiate them from other social groupings. The fact that a Lutheran congregation invites the community to annual lutefisk feasts thus constitutes a fair measure of an ethnic awareness, and a decline in the serving of Norwegian-American cuisine indicates a movement away from marking a special ethnic identity. Lutefisk-soaking plants currently record a downward trend from the revival that occurred during the 1960s. St. John's Lutheran Church in Kasson, Minnesota, started lutefisk dinners in 1930 but discontinued them in 1942; the dinners were revived in 1962 and have continued annually since. Hundreds of people are served, consuming some twenty-four hundred pounds of lutefisk, five hundred dozen *lefse,* one thousand pounds of rutabagas, and one thousand pounds of potatoes. From year to year, however, a few more congregations decide to discontinue lutefisk suppers, and these may opt for culinary traditions that are more mainstream American or may offer Norwegian meatballs as an alternative to lutefisk.[30]

The smelly, gelatin-like lutefisk, as is often claimed, is an acquired taste, and in the view of some represents the "tyranny of tradition." In Norwegian rural areas soaking the dried cod in a lye solution was a simple way of making a long-preserved fish palatable (figure 23). As a bond with the past and with one's neighbors, this basic Norwegian peasant dish became holiday food in America. Mollie Croy of East

MICHAEL'S CLASSIC
LUTEFISK MEAL
Le repas Classique de Lutefisk de Michael

KEEP FROZEN   PRODUCT: U.S.A.
Garder Congele   PRODUIT: DES E.-U.A.

INGREDIENTS: COD, DEHYDRATED
POTATOES, CORN, BUTTER,
WATER.
INGREDIENTS: MORUE, POMMES DETERRE
DEHYDRATEES, MAIS, BEURRE,
EAU.

COOKING INSTRUCTIONS: MICROWAVE
* CUT A SLIT IN LOWER PORTION OF FILM APPROX. 2 INCHES LONG
* HEAT ON HIGH FOR 3 MINUTES, ROTATE TRAY
* HEAT ON HIGH AN ADDITIONAL 3 MINUTES
* LEAVE IN MICROWAVE ABOUT 1 MINUTE
* REMOVE FROM MICROWAVE WITH 2 HANDS
* DO NOT REMOVE FILM, DRAIN MOISTURE FROM LUTEFISK
  BY TIPPING UPSIDE DOWN OVER SINK BEFORE SERVING
* REMOVE FILM, SERVE WITH DRAWN BUTTER OR CREAM SAUCE,
  SALT AND PEPPER TO TASTE
* MICROWAVE OVENS VARY, HEATING TIME MAY REQUIRE ADJUSTMENT

NET WT. 367g - 13 oz

Figure 23. Mike's Fish & Seafood in Glenwood, Minnesota, has apparently carved out a niche market during the lutefisk season.

PACKED BY: MIKE'S FISH & SEAFOOD, INC., HWY 55, GLENWOOD, MN 56334

Grand Forks, Minnesota, 97 years old in 1995, recalled from her childhood the Norwegian Lutheran church near Winger, Minnesota, and the Christmas holiday food: "It was lutefisk and *lefse,* and mother always made pork roast or spareribs. The lutefisk, some of us didn't eat."[31] The surprising finding of this study is not the decline in lutefisk consumption but the reverse, the continued popularity of the lutefisk church suppers from coast to coast, more perhaps in rural congregations than in metropolitan ones. Nonetheless anyone living in areas with concentrations of Norwegian Americans, in the city as well as in the country, will be able to satisfy their taste for lutefisk and *lefse* during the holiday season, consuming in a Norwegian-American mode by rolling the fish in the *lefse,* much like a Mexican tortilla.[32]

The Wisconsin State Journal announces "lutefisk dinners abound in Wisconsin," in its September 27, 1995, issue listing upcoming dinners in eleven congregations in and around Madison. Humor prevails as the article relates how pastors Charles D. Peterson and Jerry A. Olson of Christ Lutheran Church in DeForest, Wisconsin, prepare for the lutefisk and *lefse* event in the church basement by becoming the ethnic pastors Ole and Sven, meeting with volunteers, supervising the purchase of three thousand pounds of fish and the baking of

Figure 24. Ole and Lena's homemade lefse *is made in a plant in Hatton, North Dakota.* Lefse *remains the most popular ethnic food.*

313 dozen *lefse* by the Potato Guild, and taking care of the all-important publicity (figure 24). "These men of the cloth," the article states, "become men of the napkin." The supper is "a great money-maker for the church," a consideration that promotes these ethnic feasts. The events also keep alive skills, such as *lefse* and pastry baking.[33]

Publicity attracts attention and diners. As Munch wrote in 1954, the church lutefisk suppers "are definitely American in form, contents, and purpose (as a money-making scheme)." They, of course, as stated earlier, also have a clear purpose of satisfying social needs and announcing an ethnic identity. In 1993 the *Minneapolis Star Tribune* listed under the heading "Here's where the church suppers are, from Northfield to Grey Eagle to Virginia" forty-three church suppers, of which all but a few had lutefisk as a part of the menu. Over several issues *Western Viking* in Seattle carries

notices of lutefisk suppers under its heading "Call to *Lutefisk*," and correspondents in many parts of the United States report on successful feasts. Many newspapers present stories of lutefisk suppers. These paint a unique Norwegian-American ethnic portrait. The *Cranfills Gap Record* in the heavily Norwegian Cranfills Gap in Bosque County, Texas, fills its few columns with photographs and commentary on the annual lutefisk feast, in 1995 describing it as a "Gigantic Success." The *Wisconsin State Journal* termed the event in Vermont Lutheran Church in Vermont, Dane County, "Peace, and *lutefisk* in the valley." In the deep valleys between Mount Horeb and Black Earth, the newspaper points out, the rugged hills have sheltered an old way of life associated with its pioneer settlers. These old traditions also attracted many from nearby Madison. "If you had made the trip a week ago Saturday," a local resident is quoted as saying, "you would have seen the church at the height of its social season, serving the 1,200 people who traveled up the ridge for the annual lutefisk dinner." The attraction of the dinner doubled the small town's population.[34]

Alba sees confidence in ancestry knowledge as being primarily related to food experience, and cites statistics to show that persons who are unsure of their ancestry are less likely than others to eat ethnic foods at all. It is obvious that the church lutefisk suppers, and eating Norwegian food items in general, may serve as indicators of the level of confidence in the knowledge of a Norwegian ancestry. The persistence of traditional food items should not, however, be measured only by the frequency of their use but also by their format and function within the ethnic community. Gender can be considered here as a possible variable in measuring the significance of ethnic food experiences. As the 1989 Vermont account relates, "the men wear the 'Vermont Lutefisk 89' caps, [but] the lutefisk dinner is really the church women's show." Gender's effects in general are, however, if one accepts Alba's findings, modest, and only statistically significant in comparison with other factors, as, for example, the use of ethnic foods to celebrate special occasions, but still only minimally. In other words, women may indeed be more involved than men in the celebratory role of foods as ethnic identifying indicators and cultural experiences, but the difference between the genders is small.[35]

Ethnic Transitions

Historians have emphasized the centrality of religion in forming rural communities. Jon Gjerde demonstrated how the church became an all-encompassing institution for its members in a detailed examination of Minnesota communities between 1885 and 1905. The congregation created a tight social network and touched all aspects of life—religious, social, and economic. Familial relations were strengthened through extensive in-marriage. Indeed, it was expected that when the time came, one would marry within the congregation. Even the pervasive religious controversy over Lutheran doctrine and church polity in the late nineteenth century, which caused numerous schisms in Norwegian communities, may represent, as Gjerde sees it, only a cultural conflict based on regional background in Norway, and it did not diminish the power of the Lutheran Church and clergy. The conflict merely created culturally more cohesive new congregations.[36]

Historical geographers Ann M. Legreid and David Ward, in their collaborative study of rural Norwegian communities in western Wisconsin, see the Lutheran schism simply as a transformation or reinterpretation rather than as a breakdown of the rural community. Discord increased interest in the church. The new community structures in the divisions that resulted from the controversy were more homogeneous and intense in terms of personal interaction. Thus, as a central institution, the church, even as it engaged in internal religious warfare, nurtured a sense of community by adherence to a common set of values and traditions.[37]

The extent of the role regional loyalties—perhaps somewhat overly systematized by Gjerde—played in the formation of new rural Lutheran congregations may of course be debated. There is, however, little doubt that a regional Norwegian culture reinforced congregational bonds in many Norwegian-American churches. The congregation's role as a focal point and conservative force in rural settlements in the Midwest is well established. Norwegian localism and attachment to the ancestral tongue, beliefs and values, and practices in festive as well as more mundane affairs surrounded by memories from childhood and youth of the mystical wonders of a spectacular geography clearly encouraged idiosyncratic qualities that fortified an ethnic exclusiveness and an awareness of kith and kin that in subtle ways could be passed on to American-born generations. Many church members are still much aware of the district their ancestors hailed from. The ethnic communities supporting these churches have naturally eroded, and many rural churches today stand empty, but in other cases the congregations give evidence of residential stability.

The inevitable historical process made, however, even the rural Norwegian Lutheran congregations more diverse. A gradual intermingling of people from different districts in Norway occurred early on, making regional congregational names progressively misleading, names such as Vang, Solør, Faaberg, Kviteseid, Hafslo, and Senjen, among the more than 150 Norwegian place-names of Lutheran congregations recorded by O. M. Norlie in 1916 in Minnesota alone.[38] In fact, these appellations may in many cases have identified only the origin in Norway of the majority of the founders and not an exclusive Norwegian localism. Nevertheless, the names themselves carry a message of the impact of regionalism as well as ruralism on the American adjustment of Norwegian immigrants and their descendants.

The introduction of English services at the insistence of the American-born generations and the progress made by the so-called English work brought people with no Norwegian ancestry into the individual congregations, by marriage or by pastoral recruitment. In 1917 as many as 73.1 percent of all divine services in NLCA congregations nationwide were still in Norwegian; a dramatic drop to only 61.2 percent the following year suggests the wartime pressures for cultural conformity, which hastened the adoption of English. Predictably, there were far higher percentages of Norwegian church services in rural than in urban environments. At the time of the church merger, only 37.8 percent of divine services in member congregations in Chicago were conducted in Norwegian. Especially in the cities, however, the postwar immigration came to the aid of traditionalists who supported the "Norwegian work."

Nationwide in 1925 there were about an equal number of divine services in the two languages, although resistance in the older generations kept Norwegian services alive long after attendance could justify their continued existence. A decision on discontinuance generated heated debate and opposition in a few churches into the post–World War II years. The elder generation resisted change. For a second time a postwar exodus came to the aid of the Norwegian work in some urban congregations in major centers of Norwegian settlement, such as Seattle, Minneapolis, Chicago, and Brooklyn; the renewed immigration followed a virtual break in the movement of some fifteen years beginning in the Great Depression years of the early 1930s. A few congregations retained Norwegian departments for several decades; Trinity Lutheran Church in Brooklyn, for instance, still maintains one. Outside of the Norwegian seamen's churches in the United States, whose operations are financed by the Norwegian government, only two immigrant Norwegian-language churches have survived, the Norwegian Memorial Church in Minneapolis and the Norwegian Memorial Church on Logan Square in Chicago. Even these are currently moving toward more English in their worship. The long period without new impulses from Norway had encouraged the "Americanization" of Norwegian-American religious life, a trend that postwar immigration in reality did not reverse much.[39]

Congregational and community histories convey both stability and change. The joining of non-Norwegians did not destroy a sense of Norwegian-American peoplehood, nor did this process obliterate historical congregational memories, but it did require a period of adjustment for both traditionalists and newcomers. Perhaps the greatest challenge was to those who joined. A voluntary membership led in many instances to a voluntary ethnic identity, in part or in whole, as social adjustments were being made to congregational and denominational traditions. A local multiethnic sense of solidarity may have also developed as new traditions and relations were established. It was, of course, possible to embrace the history and customs of the new religious environment without becoming one with its origin in a Norwegian immigrant culture.

A few examples will suggest the variety of patterns of adjustment to ethnic transitions. In 1988 St. Paul Lutheran Church, the first Lutheran congregation in Dakota Territory, in Elk Point, or more precisely in Brule Township, in Union County, South Dakota, celebrated its 125th anniversary, as a celebration of more than a century of "Norwegian Lutheranism in Dakota." Many of the pioneers came from Trøndelag and western Norway. It is a conservative community, all white and with deep local roots, and among those interviewed— some of them descendants of the original settlers—a strong pride in a Norwegian ancestry and in the early pioneers was abundantly evident. Another example is in Minnesota. *125 and Still Alive!* is the title of the 1995 history of

Indherred Lutheran Church in Starbuck in Pope County, Minnesota, the name identifying the regional Trøndelag origin of the founders. The first church structure was completed in 1875, five years after the congregation was organized. It joined the high-church Norwegian Synod. In 1897 a new and larger church was built. Family names of confirmants reveal a persistence of Norwegian cognomens through the generations among, naturally, many non-Norwegian surnames.

In both these congregations, it remains obvious that the indications of growth in ethnic consciousness and experiences are much more ambiguous than those that suggest a loss over time of tradition and interest in a particular ethnic background, whether strongly regional Norwegian or simply national. Migration may provide an explanation. Residential stability is regularly secured by movement into rural communities and villages, as simultaneously these give up their own youth to distant towns and cities, so that even in the St. Paul Church in the small and to some degree insular community of Elk Point, only about half of the membership was identified as Norwegian. Names on markers in the church cemetery are, however, still predominantly Norwegian. This mingling of ethnicities and traditions typifies rural and urban Lutheran congregations of a Norwegian immigrant origin alike, and a consciousness of the latter, though weakening, is still a part of congregational life. Historical developments, from first to last, included the emergence of a Norwegian-American Lutheran ethnicity, a Norwegian, Danish, and Swedish cooperation in religious affairs, and an interaction with and a recruitment of non-Scandinavians to membership in Norwegian Lutheran churches.[40]

Generally speaking, Norwegian Lutheran congregations have been better at extending membership on the basis of class rather than on the basis of ethnic or racial diversity. A white middle-class solidarity may create a new sense of a localized multiethnic loyalty, not only in religious affairs but also in secular ones, though it might be an overstatement in a congregational context to speak of the creation of a "multi-ethnic peoplehood." It is, however, a term that suggests some of the realities of community life as new local cultural and social identities emerged and as new practices and attitudes evolved based on non-ethnic commonalities. The rural character of the Elk Point Lutheran congregation served as a uniting force as this traditional farming community became ethnically more diverse. Marriage beyond the Norwegian fold occurred regularly, and customs and memory merged. This merger is one historical aspect of how new traditions and identities are created; each congregation metamorphosed into a unique social and cultural blend with a localized in-group sense of identity and belonging. It represented the creation of new commonalities through a mixture of blood and tradition. John Higham speaks of a "group consciousness on a . . . expediential basis . . . an increasing tolerance for diversity . . . permitting more and more differentiation within, outside, and across ethnic boundaries." Higham introduces the term *particularism* to explain "a heightened solidarity within any segment of the population that can define itself as somehow distinct." The term may be useful to clarify the interaction in a multiethnic society—moving a bit beyond Higham's original thought—that creates new solidarities where ethnicity constitutes only one element. In church life the process may also be seen, as Timothy L. Smith posits as a general principle, as an example of the redefinition of ethnic boundaries in religious terms, involving "a broadening of the geographic and linguistic backgrounds of persons deemed suitable for inclusion."[41]

Tradition is maintained in various fashions. The location of the present Norway Lutheran Church in "Old Muskego" has remained largely the same through the generations; its current address is in Wind Lake in Racine County, Wisconsin. The original log church—moved in 1904 to the grounds of Luther Northwestern Theological Seminary in St. Paul—was constructed on Indian Hill in the town and dedicated in 1845; a second church, also erected on the hill, was dedicated in 1871; and the third and present one, at the bottom of the hill, was dedicated in 1964. The 125th anniversary of the congregation's founding in 1843 was duly observed in 1968. It honored the Norwegian pioneer roots, and, as reported, "the women outdid themselves on the anniversary *lutefisk* dinner." In 1992 Norway

Church had its 150th anniversary observance, again with a lutefisk dinner and a Norwegian Christmas celebration, "Old Muskego" being described as a mother church of American Lutheranism; surely, it could at least claim that distinction for the NLCA. The congregation is growing, many persons of different ethnic backgrounds moving in from Milwaukee, though many of the names in the 1995 membership directory were Norwegian, some from the early days, and Scandinavian among German, Anglo-Saxon, and a few Slavic ones. What they share, if not a common ethnicity, is a pride in the pioneer past of the church and the community. On this basis, like in Elk Point, a locally expressed voluntary and multiethnic gathering around Norwegian-American traditions associated with the congregation's pioneer status takes place.[42]

The urban experience differed in fundamental ways from the rural one. A general process can be described. The creation of an ethnic community was followed by an ethnic neighborhood succession, where one ethnic group replaced another, transforming the cultural and social environment; then, as the community prospered, there occurred a suburbanization of the middle-class ethnics, leaving the ethnic enclaves largely to working-class members of the group. The old neighborhoods may for a time have served as a central ethnic district, where churches, club houses, and special events still attracted the attendance of those who had moved out to better residential locations.

By the 1880s Norwegians were well established in their second colony in Chicago, the so-called Milwaukee Avenue colony, centering on Milwaukee and Grand (then Indiana) Avenues in the West Town community. The more prosperous Norwegian Americans resided in the Wicker Park district north of the Milwaukee Avenue colony. Over a period of several decades, Norwegians moved out of this community and took their businesses with them to their new neighborhoods in the Humboldt Park and Logan Square districts. After the turn of the century, this area became "Little Norway"—the height of an active ethnic group life—and the final Norwegian concentration before dispersal to the suburbs or to the outlying areas of the city. The stability and status of the new neighborhoods were reflected in the slightly superior attitude adopted toward Norwegians who remained in the Milwaukee Avenue wards, and toward the ethnic groups that had taken over the area. As Norwegians and other Scandinavians moved away, they were replaced by Poles and by Polish and Russian Jews, who marked their presence by store signs in Polish and Yiddish as the Scandinavian ones were removed. Later Roman Catholic Italians and Slavic and Greek Orthodox Christians moved in numbers to that part of Chicago.[43]

The changing ethnic character of the area was reflected in the sale of churches to non-Lutheran faiths. Even so, religious institutions were the most resistant to change. Our Savior's Lutheran Church, the pioneer church founded within the liturgical Norwegian Synod in 1858, with its own church structure on Illinois and Orleans (then Market) Streets, did not in fact leave the Milwaukee Avenue district until the 1920s. The other early church on the West Side, Trinity Lutheran Church, an edifice erected at Grand and Peoria Streets, was organized within the low-church evangelical tradition the year before, in 1857. In 1903 an Eastern Orthodox group purchased the church, the members by then mostly having moved farther west. Visiting the church in the 1920s, Pastor K. Seehuus was disturbed, his anti-Catholic prejudices obvious, by its transformation to a Catholic place of worship and its filth and broken windows, but he thought that Lutherans might learn a lesson from the worn stairs, which suggested faithful attendance.[44]

Oak Park, a prospering western suburb, attracted especially the upwardly mobile Norwegians from the Wicker Park, Humboldt Park, and Logan Square neighborhoods. There in 1925 the United Lutheran Church of Oak Park was formed through a merger of Our Savior's, Bethlehem, and St. Paul's English Lutheran congregations. Each of the three churches represented one of the three main theological directions in Norwegian-American Lutheranism, the high-, broad-, and low-church traditions. Pastor H. P. Ausan of Our Savior's headed a separate Norwegian department within the Oak Park union, showing how strong spokesmen could embrace and promote the Norwegian work. It continued until 1943. The

1988 history celebrating the sixtieth anniversary of the church edifice in Oak Park maintains that for a generation or more, "the church was an ethnic island in the Village of Oak Park."[45]

Not until the 1950s did United recognize a need to orient itself to the community. In 1956 the congregation joined the Oak Park–River Forest Council of churches. The strong ethnic identification was thereby little by little greatly diluted, as the same history relates. In the 1990s Norwegian Americans still reside in the area, but other ethnic groups are amply represented in the community and in the congregation, though few from the black neighborhoods just to the east of the church have been admitted. Ethnic diversity is approached by the church officers, from the pastor down, by minimizing the Norwegian origin and the church's Norwegian past and traditions. "We do not want to suggest that the Norwegians are more important," a spokesperson of Norwegian background insisted. Permission was consequently denied to distribute the research questionnaire for this project since it would in fact have singled out as special one contingent of the church membership. A strong Lutheran mold fortified by social class has become the common uniting elements for ethnic diversity.[46]

Other urban congregations have followed different transitional paths. It is instructive to consider how three different Norwegian Lutheran churches in the Bay Ridge and Sunset Park area of Brooklyn have responded to a changing ethnic composition. These churches are Zion, 59th Street Lutheran Brethren Church, and Trinity. The experience of Zion Norwegian Lutheran Church, its original name, is a grim story of a congregation that waited too long to attract a non-Norwegian membership. At the Sunday service, November 26, 1995, only about thirty people were in attendance. It was an aging group, some of whom were not of Norwegian background. The congregation lacks the resources, however, to make a successful entry into the community. These signs of decline contrast sharply with the vibrancy of the earlier history of the congregation. Founded in 1908 within the Norwegian Synod, it became a thriving congregation with more than one thousand communicants by the 1930s. The loss of members through, as the congregational history states, "the great exodus to the suburbs" after World War II tapered off for a while in the late 1950s but was an inevitable development as Hispanic and Asian populations, Greek and Middle-Eastern migrants, and more recently, large Russian contingents, moved into the old Norwegian neighborhoods as the Norwegians moved elsewhere.[47]

The 59th Street Church responded to the movement into the community of large numbers of Chinese immigrants by opening a Chinese department with its own pastor; about seventy people attend the Chinese Lutheran service weekly. Lutheran converts were made among those moving into the community, and a few Chinese migrants already belonged to that faith. The congregation was formed in 1912; today most Norwegian-American members are elderly. Only in 1994 were Norwegian divine services discontinued. A complete ethnic transition, though retaining a Lutheran religious identity, is obviously in the offing.[48]

Perhaps the most successful transition was made by Trinity, a low-church congregation organized in 1890. The many Spanish-speaking people arriving convinced the congregation to introduce divine services in Spanish in 1980, in addition to those in English and Norwegian. A trilingual pastorate serves the congregation, each pastor being responsible for a separate section. The Norwegian-language section is the smallest, attracting largely elderly postwar immigrants. Norwegian was, however, prominent for a long time, with Norwegian services conducted in the main sanctuary until the early years after World War II, when these exchanged space with the English services held in the lower level. The membership was largely working-class, many being skilled dock builders, bricklayers, and carpenters. Many of the latter arrived in the 1950s. The transition has not been without difficulty or devoid of racist overtones, Robert M. Nervig, pastor in the American section explained, since many Norwegians objected to the introduction of Spanish services and the greater stress on liturgy, and the adoption of certain Catholic traditions in dress and ritual as a result. The Spanish-speaking group, on the other hand, found Norwegian religious practices evidence of true multicul-

turalism. "Many Spanish-speaking people do not learn English," Nervig explained. Consequently, religious services in their own language transcend ethnic loyalty; in fact, as the case once was for Norwegian immigrants, they make participation in organized religious life possible. By acknowledging this fact, the experience of an older immigrant group, such as the Norwegians, can create understanding of the situation of contemporary immigrants. Within the American section Korean, Danish, Swedish, German, and Italian families join the Norwegian. About one-third of the six hundred members in the congregation are Spanish-speaking. They are a growing and a younger congregational element, moving slowly into a middle-class standard of living.

Hispanic members are converts from Catholicism or Pentecostalism. Both these faiths, even though they are vastly different in doctrine, exhibit male dominance and are authoritarian in doctrine and in church discipline. The greater independence and freedom of the Lutheran Church appealed to those who sought membership there, Nervig explained. The movement toward an entirely Spanish-speaking congregation is clear, though it is some time in the future.[49]

The three congregations seem to demonstrate the conventional wisdom that the low-church Norwegian-American Lutheran posture, represented both by the 59th Street Church and Trinity, is more sensitive to community outreach than the high-church tradition with its roots in the Norwegian Synod—perhaps here exemplified in Zion—whose attitude was to wait for people to come to it. In a multicultural community, especially in New York, where ethnic consciousness is more pronounced than in the Midwest, that is not likely to occur.

Lutheran Higher Education

The legacy of the Norwegian Synod is much in evidence in Lutheran churches of North America. The influence it exercised was out of proportion to its size throughout its history, and it left its imprint as a weighty component in a succession of mergers, up to the ELCA of today. Its historical heritage as a vigorous promulgator of a search for the objective truth, its orthodoxy and penchant for ritual, as well as its democratic and participatory approach to church life is still evident at Luther Northwestern Theological Seminary in St. Paul, which now trains pastors for service in ELCA parishes. It originated as the seminary for the Norwegian Synod and in 1917 merged with the seminaries of the United Church and Hauge's Synod.

The Norwegian Synod's historical influence may also be seen in a multitude of congregations that emanated from this high-church Lutheran tradition, and even at a liberal arts institution like Luther College in Decorah, Iowa. It is one of six four-year colleges and one two-year junior college within the Evangelical Lutheran Church in America that trace their founding back to Norwegian Lutheran immigrant synods. The Norwegian-American college movement is strikingly overrepresented within the church union relative to ethnic strength. At present there are twenty-eight four- or two-year institutions of higher education in the ELCA; those of Norwegian origin thus account for an impressive one-fourth of all these colleges and, even more telling, about one-third of all full-time students.[50]

Luther College was founded in the fall of 1861, pushed through at a synodical meeting in Rock Prairie, Wisconsin, in June of that year by lay delegates disturbed over the Missouri Synod's position on slavery and the controversy it created within the Norwegian Synod itself. The school was intended to break the Missouri connection and to assume responsibility for training ministers. Such a move was beyond its resources, and the Norwegian Synod continued to train its ministers at the schools of the Missouri Synod. Only in 1876 was the beginning made for a separate theological seminary in Madison, Wisconsin. Luther College offered a preparatory course for theological training. The Lutheran clergy patterned the school after the traditional Norwegian Latin School and limited it to male students. Its first year of existence was modestly spent at the parsonage at Half Creek, near La Crosse, Wisconsin. It was moved to Decorah in the fall of 1862. The Norwegian Synod's concern for education reflected a theological point of view that required a thorough indoctrination of its membership in its beliefs and teachings. It adopted an educational rather than an evangelistic approach and held a strong conviction that secular as well as religious subjects should be taught in a Christian Lutheran atmosphere.[51]

Following the great church merger in 1917 creating the Norwegian Lutheran Church in America, Luther College was no longer alone and, as its historian David T. Nelson states, no longer "the darling of the Norwegian Synod." It then became one of two colleges to which the new church body was fully committed, the other being St. Olaf College in Northfield, Minnesota. The college began as an academy in 1874, its founder, the pastor Bernt J. Muus, dreaming of making it the second college within the Norwegian Synod. Its move toward becoming a college began in the late 1880s as a consequence of the raging religious controversies over the issue of predestination—or the Election Controversy, as the conflict generally is referred to—which split the synod. In 1890 St. Olaf became the official school of the newly formed United Church, a relationship severed by renewed conflicts for some years, until it was reestablished in 1899. This relationship brought the school into a more tolerant doctrinal environment. St. Olaf College was less influenced by classical educational ideals than Luther College and was coeducational, and its broad Christian education was accused from some quarters of being "humanistic" and "worldly." Luther College did not depart from its classical ideal and move into an American educational

mode until the 1930s, when women students were admitted. Both colleges exhibited a Lutheran piety and strict adherence by faculty and students to a Christian moral conduct.[52]

Three other schools within the NLCA union were laboriously adopting programs patterned after the American church schools in New England. Concordia College was established as an academy in 1891 in Moorhead, Minnesota, by men close to the United Church. Augustana College, which had its roots in the Scandinavian Augustana Synod, dating back to the 1860s, was located in Canton, South Dakota from 1884, and in 1918, the year after the church union, moved farther north to Sioux Falls and merged with a Lutheran normal school that had been operated by the Norwegian Synod. Pacific Lutheran College— Pacific Lutheran University since 1960—began instruction in 1894 in Parkland near Tacoma, Washington. It was founded as an academy by the Norwegian Synod. During the 1920s these three schools expanded into four-year liberal arts institutions.

Augsburg College in Minneapolis grew out of Augsburg Seminary, a training institution for pastors. The seminary's college division, introduced in 1874, was the forerunner of Augsburg College. As the school of the Lutheran Free Church from the time of the forming of this church body in 1897, Augsburg College was transformed during the years before World War I to 1922 from a department at Augsburg Seminary into a private four-year college. The only existing two-year junior college, Waldorf College in Forest City, Iowa, came out of the United Church tradition in 1903. The Norwegian-American college movement emanated from different Lutheran orientations, not infrequently hostile to each other; Lutheran denominationalism and competing educational and theological convictions may in part explain the vibrancy and endurance of this movement. It was, however, only in the years between the two world wars that the Norwegian-American colleges entered on a broad front into the mainstream of American higher education. They were small institutions; their combined enrollments in 1920, including the academy departments in some of the schools, were less than two thousand.[53]

In the post–World War II years, the six four-year colleges experienced an impressive expansion as a part of a large general growth of higher education in America. The expansion strengthened the self-respect and self-confidence of these schools. The logical question that arises is, have their educational successes in competing with established American schools diminished the appreciation of a Norwegian-American identity? As long as they were small immigrant schools of little account, plagued with an ethnic inferiority complex and tight budgets, they may have harbored a greater consciousness of their beginnings. The Norwegian background had been embraced in the earlier part of the century for the sake of, as Joseph Shaw relates, "a 'broader view' of the value of the European heritage." St. Olaf College continued until 1950 to affirm its Norwegian connection by requiring that all students of Norwegian ancestry take a year of Norwegian language, or courses in Norwegian literature in translation or in Norwegian cultural history. Sidney A. Rand, elected president of St. Olaf in 1963 and serving more than sixteen years at a critical juncture in the American transition, expressed in an interview in 1996 that keeping ties to Norway gave St. Olaf College a built-in international exposure. College bands, orchestras, and choirs regularly touring Norway serve an identical end. "St. Olaf could be a good college if it became American Lutheran and lost its Norwegian connection," Rand concluded, "but it would lose its distinctiveness."[54]

The current situation nevertheless raises the question of the extent of rhetoric and political considerations such utterances and similar ones, without questioning their sincerity, contain. A survey of the St. Olaf faculty and student body in the fall of 1996 showed a diverse population, religiously and ethnically. Still, about 22 percent of the faculty identified themselves as first- or second-ethnicity Norwegian, and 35 percent of the students did (tables 5, 6, and 8). The striking fact that 72 percent of the faculty identify themselves as Lutheran (table 7) compared to the much lower Norwegian ethnicity figure for the same group suggests a pervasive Lutheran loyalty in St. Olaf's institutional affiliation as a college of the large and ethnically diverse ELCA, and simultane-

Table 5. Ethnicity of St. Olaf College faculty, 1996

Ethnicity	Percentage
Norwegian	22.41
German	20.75
English	11.20
Swedish	7.47
Dutch	4.98
Irish	5.81
None listed	0.41
Other	19.92
Scottish	4.56
Polish	1.24
Welsh	0.41
Russian	0.83

Note: Percentages are based on first and second ethnicity combined. About 70 percent of the faculty responded to the three-part questionnaire.

Table 6. Ethnic generation of St. Olaf College faculty, 1996

Ethnic generation	Percentage
1	3.72
2	5.37
3	33.88
4	21.49
5	8.26
6	1.65
7	0.42
More than 7	3.31
Before 1800	15.29
Don't know	5.37
Does not apply	1.24

ously indicates a gradual move toward a greater Lutheran emphasis as the college's ethnic roots grow ever more distant.

On December 9–12, 1996, 1,682 students at St. Olaf were surveyed with regard to their ethnic generation, their primary and secondary ethnicity, and their religious affiliation (tables 8, 9, and 10). An increased diversity in ethnic and religious identity would alone weaken ties to the Norwegian past of the institution. Still, the fact that more than a third of the student body is first- or second-ethnicity Norwegian, and that of these more than 70 percent are Lutheran, is nevertheless revealing evidence of the strength of tradition. The high percentage of Lutherans among those of Norwegian ancestry furthermore reflects student recruitment

through Lutheran congregations. A survey sponsored by a class in psychology during the same fall semester concluded that St. Olaf College's Norwegian and Lutheran identity, both for students with Norwegian ancestry and for those without, regardless of religious faith, was important; 45 percent of the students who were surveyed reported positive effects of the college's cultural heritage in their college experience. In this respect, it appears that the student body may be more concerned about the institution's cultural traditions than the faculty or the administration are.[55]

The traditional Norwegian Christmas dinners—featuring both lutefisk and *lefse*—that are part of a celebrated Christmas choir and orchestra concert, the welcoming of Norwegian dignitaries, and even the maintenance of an academic department devoted to the teaching of Norwegian language, literature,

Table 7. Religious affiliation of St. Olaf College faculty, 1996

Affiliation	Percentage
Lutheran	
ELCA	65.69
LCMS	1.46
Other Lutheran	4.38
Non-Lutheran	
Baptist	4.38
Episcopal	8.03
Jewish	4.38
Methodist	8.03
Mormon	2.19
No affiliation	16.79
Presbyterian	7.30
Other	7.30
Other Protestant	10.22
Roman Catholic	18.98
UCC	14.60

Table 8. Ethnicity of 1,682 students surveyed at St. Olaf College, 1996

Ethnicity	Percentage
German	47.51
Norwegian	35.21
Swedish	17.99
Irish	12.31
English	10.95
Scottish	4.97
Polish	4.14
Welsh	1.72
Russian	1.07

Note: Percentages are based on first and second ethnicity combined; 592 students, representing 35.21 percent of all responses, reported Norwegian as first or second ethnicity.

and culture may on occasion appear as a polite institutional bow to the college's heritage for the sake of the college alumni. In all fairness, it must be stated that St. Olaf College maintains a larger Norwegian program than any of the other five colleges rooted in a Norwegian immigrant origin. Some of these sister colleges have a nearly negligible academic offering in Norwegian. The alumni may, even so, express a great concern for the Norwegian, and also Lutheran, heritage of St. Olaf. "The faith of my Norwegian ancestors was Lutheran," wrote Clarice Irene Anderson, whose great-grandparents immigrated from Lærdal, Norway, "and one of the highlights of my life was to see both our children, Kathryn and

Daniel, graduate from St. Olaf College, with its strong Norwegian-Lutheran connections." This perception of the college is broadly held, even in the 1990s, and many Norwegian Americans who traditionally do not attend college and only know St. Olaf by reputation also express pride and awe in the school as an ethnic institution. It affirms the value of their ethnicity. In the college's push to diversify the student body, however, this constituency is one that in the spirit of political correctness receives scant institutional attention. Earlier in the college's history this constituency represented its main mission. O. Jay Tomson, a regent of St. Olaf, and in the mid-1950s a first-generation college student there, realized that to attend St. Olaf "was an opportunity for young people with average intelligence coming out of a rural and very narrow upbringing

Table 9. Ethnic generation of 1,682 students at St. Olaf College, 1996

Ethnic generation	Percentage
1	0.51
2	1.19
3	15.08
4	38.98
5	13.90
6	5.08
7	0.68
More than 7	0.51
Before 1800	4.75
Don't know	18.21
Does not apply	1.53

Table 10. Religious affiliation of the 592 students at St. Olaf College reporting Norwegian ethnicity, 1996

Affliation	Percentage
Lutheran	
ELCA	67.28
LCMS	2.53
Other Lutheran	4.55
Non-Lutheran	
Baptist	1.01
Episcopal	1.85
Jewish	0.17
Methodist	3.04
No affiliation	5.56
Presbyterian	2.36
Other	3.54
Other Protestant	2.36
Roman Catholic	5.06
UCC	1.01

in a homogeneous community of Scandinavians to become enlightened."[56]

An analysis of the student bodies at the six four-year institutions brings to light their increased ecumenical character and ethnic diversity. In the fall semester of 1995, only about half of the combined student bodies identified themselves as Lutheran; the percentages varied from 65.7 percent at Concordia College to as low as 28.4 percent at Pacific Lutheran. There are relatively few minority students: fewer than 7 percent of the combined enrollments; 13 percent at both Pacific Lutheran and Augsburg, the two colleges located in a metropolitan area; and only 2 percent at Augustana, the smallest of the six colleges. The schools remain strongly Protestant; only a little less than 15 percent belong to the Roman Catholic Church. In spite of a greater ethnic and denominational diversity, the six colleges thus demonstrably

have their greatest appeal among Protestant Americans of a European background.[57]

Political Loyalties

Does ethnicity persist as a distinctive factor in American political life? In posing this question in the mid-1970s, Andrew M. Greeley answered in the affirmative. In political participation, Greeley points out that ethnicity rather than religion is a better guide in determining political participation. Based on his data, the highest score for political activity is registered by Irish Catholics, affirming their reputation as a highly political people, followed by Protestant Scandinavians, both significantly ahead of Anglo-Saxon voters. The lowest scores for white groups are also registered by a Catholic group, the Italians, and by a Protestant group, the Irish Protestants. German Catholics and Protestants, on the other hand, have nearly identical political participation. In regard to the Scandinavians, Greeley contends that a long tradition of political democracy in the homelands and the civic-mindedness attributed to members of the Scandinavian-American community explain high levels of political participation. Kendric Babcock claimed in 1914, considering political developments in the three homelands, that "after 1870 the average Scandinavian immigrant brought to America a fairly clear understanding of the meaning of republicanism; elections, representation, local self-government, and constitutions, are neither novel nor meaningless terms to him." Even when eliminating differences of social class and region, Greeley found in the 1970s that Scandinavian Protestants were the second most active political group in America.[58]

Norwegian Americans may express pride in such highly visible politicians of Norwegian ancestry as Hubert H. Humphrey and Walter F. Mondale, even those who have not voted for them, but the larger issue is whether Norwegian ethnicity today predisposes toward particular political convictions and affiliations. Being socially and politically active is, of course, a different matter. In a doctoral study of Norwegian-American political behavior in Wisconsin, Iowa, and Minnesota from 1880 to 1924—an era of dissidence and third-party movements—Lowell J. Soike concludes that nationality and differing Lutheran positions were at best only unpredictable determinants of political behavior. Soike's interpretation of a manifest political reformist attitude in the Norwegian-American electorate identifies a complexity of causal forces. One issue stands out. Soike identifies a strong anti-Catholicism as a central coalescing impulse of Norwegian political behavior, though this prejudice against Catholics varied in Norwegian settlements from one state to another. For a long time, however, it alienated Norwegian voters from the Democrats, who were unable to disassociate themselves from Roman Catholicism. Thus, Norwegian discontent as their traditional Republican allegiance eroded generally benefited various third-party causes. Their responses to the public issues of the day were mainly determined by local influences and specific issues. Many revolved around prevailing economic conditions.

The 1892 gubernatorial election where Knute Nelson won against his opponent, the colorful leader of the agrarian revolt, the Catholic Ignatius Donnelly, reveals the significance of local issues. Agrarian dissenters in the Norwegian northwestern counties of Minnesota resisted appeals based on religious prejudice and nationality and gave their vote to Donnelly. Their traditional agrarianism became the touchstone of political allegiance. The prosperous and politically more conservative Norwegian counties in the southeastern part of the state, however, gave Nelson large majorities. Nationality feelings here, as in the rest of the state, obviously contributed to the political success of Nelson, who was Norwegian, Lutheran, and Republican. He was throughout his illustrious career a source of much ethnic pride.[59]

The Democrats had greater success among Norwegians in Chicago, who took part, albeit in small numbers, in Democratic machine politics in the post–Civil War era. The majority were still to be found in the Republican camp. In the 1920s working-class Norwegian Americans followed a general turn toward the Democratic Party, not only in the upper Midwest but nationwide. In Minnesota the radical Farmer-Labor Party formed in 1922, an example of a successful third-party movement, had a strong and intimate relationship with Scandinavian-American voters in the state. Formed from several protest groups, its economic base lay in a dawning labor union movement in the Twin Cities and in the cooperative undertakings among farmers in the traditional areas of agrarian unrest in northwestern Minnesota. It absorbed potential Democratic voters to the extent that in Minnesota the Democratic Party remained the smallest of the three main political organizations, after both the Republicans and the Farmer-Laborites, until it merged with the Farmer-Labor Party in 1944 to become the Democratic Farmer-Labor Party (DFL). This merger and the fact that by 1930 the Farmer-Labor Party outdistanced the Republi-

cans, giving it a reign of eight years, account for much of Minnesota's tradition as a liberal state. The party represents, as Minnesota historian William E. Lass maintains, "an amalgam of culture, philosophy, and tradition that is unique to Minnesota." The Scandinavian population in the state played a significant part in shaping this political alloy.[60]

Beginning in 1905 there was with one brief exception an unbroken line of Minnesota governors who had some Scandinavian ties. Swedish historian Sten Carlsson notes the generally good relations between Swedes and Norwegians in electing Scandinavians, though party differences were more important than ethnic ones, and the candidates themselves generally avoided appealing to the electorate on ethnic grounds. Ethnic loyalties did not unite Norwegian, much less all Scandinavian, voters politically. In Minnesota one cannot really claim that the issue of nationality was a decisive factor in many elections. Nonetheless, Carlsson's striking conclusion is that outside "the Nordic countries there is nowhere in the world where the social development of a State has been determined by Scandinavian activities and ambitions as in Minnesota."[61] Norwegian Americans in Minnesota, as well as elsewhere, with their obvious reformist proclivities placed themselves in various political camps and participated broadly in formulating political cultures, ranging from reformist to conservative. The ethnic factor may have had less influence on their political conviction than did

Table 11. Political and social convictions of Norwegain Americans responding to questionnaire distributed in 1995-96

	Responses	Percentage
Conservative	2,723	40.03
Moderate	2,618	38.49
Liberal	1,055	15.51
Radical left	66	0.97
No response	340	5.00
Total	6,802	100.00

economic self-interest, regional loyalties, and political convention.

It is with this historical background that the situation in the 1990s must be considered. On the research questionnaire respondents were asked to rate themselves on a continuum of "conservative," "moderate," "liberal," or "radical left." Of the nearly seven thousand respondents, an overwhelming number rated themselves as conservative or moderate. Some who listed themselves as politically moderate indicated a conservative stance on social issues. Only 15 percent considered themselves liberal (table 11).

A strong Republican loyalty was obvious in all parts of the United States. This may again be a function of prosperity in the Norwegian-American population and thus not related to either ethnic or religious affiliation. There is a surprisingly low difference in political conviction by age, as table 12 suggests, although political conservatism, as one would expect, increases with age, and fewer individuals think of themselves as being left of center.

The percentages, as table 13 indicates, do not in fact change much even by generation, though the sixth- and seventh-generation figures are based on a relatively small sampling. Ignoring the percentages for the seventh generation, there does appear to be an increased liberalism in later generations as compared with the first three. An impression of a general conservatism in social and political convictions among Norwegian Americans remains, however, many mitigating a social conservatism with a moderate political outlook.

The ethnic factor, save for an evident active voter participation in regions of heavy Scandinavian settlement, would obviously be even more difficult to identify now than in the studies cited earlier. Indicative of this circumstance is, for instance, the fact that North Dakota, with its strongly Scandinavian electorate, has voting turnout rates 10 percentage points above the national average. Being members of an "old" and well-established ethnic population, perhaps more so than belonging to a specific ethnicity, compelled self-satisfied attitudes about the group's historical achievements to surface regularly in interviews. The interview subjects were asked to express their opinions on a series of social issues regardless of stated political affiliation: welfare, abortion, capital punishment, protected rights and affirmative action for women and minorities, gay rights, and the desirability of English as the official language of the United States. It posed a challenge to uncover any representative and

Table 12. Political and social convictions of Norwegian Americans responding to questionnaire distributed in 1995-96, by age

Age	Conservative and moderate (%)	Liberal (%)	Radical left (%)
18–29	67.09	23.11	3.80
30–39	68.83	28.25	2.91
40–49	71.07	26.45	2.48
50–59	81.39	17.51	1.09
60–69	86.51	13.06	0.43
70–79	88.24	11.36	0.41
over 80	89.22	10.50	0.28

Note: The percentages are based on a total of 6,362 responses.

consistently liberal response to social legislation in the material collected. There were, of course, a few who expressed socially radical convictions, and others who described themselves as "moderately liberal." Somewhat typical, even for people who declared themselves to be on the left politically, were the views of Geoffrey R. Wodell, a fourth-generation Norwegian American born in 1949 and a resident of Wheat Ridge, Colorado, who described himself as "very left politically," having participated in antiwar rallies during the Vietnam conflict, but who saw himself, a rather common response, as "fiscally conservative." And about the defining social issue of the death penalty, he felt that "there are people who have no right to be a part of any society."[62]

The middle-class identity of most respondents, which is where the overwhelming number of Norwegian Americans belong, may explain the dominance—in the questionnaire survey and in personal interviews—of legitimate conservative views on the social issues that they were queried about, including making English the one official language. "Well, our ancestors had to learn English," was a common and, to be sure, politically incorrect response; others stressed the unifying assimilative effect of a single official language. A representative and sincere strongly conservative position was well articulated by Arne L. Christenson, a fourth-generation Norwegian American born in 1961 in Minneapolis and brought up in a strict moral and religious family environment. His political convictions reflect those of the conservative wing of the Republican Party, and were at times expressed in terms of civic and personal morality. He was pro-life on the issue of abortion, supported no special rights "for those who choose a homosexual lifestyle," and advocated individual responsibility in matters of finance. He now resides in Fairfax, Virginia,

Table 13. Political and social convictions of Norwegian Americans responding to questionnaire distributed in 1995-96, by generation

Generation	Conservative and moderate (%)	Liberal (%)	Radical left (%)
1st	82.7	16.7	0.06
2nd	86.0	12.9	1.2
3rd	85.6	14.0	0.6
4th	76.4	21.7	1.6
5th	77.5	20.5	1.9
6th	75.5	20.4	4.1
7th	83.3	16.7	0.0

Note: The percentages are based on a total of 6,348 responses.

with his family and is the chief assistant for budget for House Speaker Newt Gingrich. "I am proud of my heritage, but perhaps more earlier then since moving to D.C.," Christenson admitted, "I find the emotional stability it gave a positive trait as long as emotions are not suppressed." A less moderating tone, and not atypical, was used about social concerns by Stanley Nesheim, a research chemist in Washington, D.C., born to Norwegian immigrant parents in 1930 in Chicago, who grew up in Bay Ridge in Brooklyn. In expressing his opposition to the American welfare system, Nesheim said, "Most Norwegians in Brooklyn are Republicans and don't like the government to get involved. They help each other."[63]

A striking number of people interviewed in regions earlier affected by the progressive Republican Nonpartisan League, both in the Red River valley of North Dakota and the northwestern counties of Minnesota, volun-

teered, however, that, oh, yes, father or grandfather had been somewhat on the left, but they distanced themselves from this aspect of their family history. Prosperous individuals everywhere tend to reject poor beginnings. Republican conservatism increases as one moves closer to the North Dakota state line, influenced by the economic interests of the big farmers in the valley. In 1973 farmers bought out a beet sugar processing company and created a growers' cooperative, the American Crystal Sugar Company, retaining the earlier name. In 1996 it owned five factories, located on both sides of the Red River. The cooperatives have no political ideological underpinning; they are based on capitalistic economic self-interest in a politically conservative community. J. Wendell Sands, born in 1938, of Alvarado, Minnesota, is a third-generation Norwegian-American beet farmer, and knows the history of this crop well. Introduced in the 1920s, sugar beets grew well in the heavy soil. The community is united through kinship: "My family has lived in here since 1873, and I am related to most people around me," Sands said. Like many operations, Sands's is mechanized, and therefore he does not have to hire the traditional migrant workers, mainly Mexican Americans.[64]

A few examples will suggest political developments in the region. Not all Norwegians, of course, ever embraced the socialist program of the Nonpartisan League. Norwegian-born state senator Ole O. Sageng, who represented Otter Tail County for several terms beginning in 1906, fought the farmer movement, partly influenced by accusations of disloyalty against the Nonpartisan League during the years of war. Sageng had joined the Populist Party in its dying years before the turn of the century and helped ease Norwegian voters into the independent progressive Republicanism. The Nonpartisan League found support where Populism had been strongest, however. Sageng's form of Republicanism gained the most votes in Norwegian precincts where the Populist urge was weaker. His daughter, Mathilda Sageng, born in 1907, relates her own strong Lutheran and Republican affiliation but admits, "I have become disillusioned with the Republican Party. Government has a responsibility to help, but people should not become dependent on government. I feel my father would have felt the same way." Ole Sageng was a staunch member of the Lutheran Free Church, and his form of progressivism likely represented well

the Protestant middle-class reform consensus of the Progressive Era. The senate district that includes Fergus Falls in Otter Tail County is currently represented by Republican Cal Larson, born in 1930. He professes great pride in his Norwegian heritage, has close ties to the Lutheran Church, and has been a regent of Concordia College. Larson describes himself as "conservative to moderate," and thus has a political conviction that reflects that of his electorate rather well.[65]

In North Dakota the state mill in Grand Forks and the state bank in Bismarck are reminders of the socialist reforms advocated by the Nonpartisan League. Clair B. Moe, born in 1948 and a fifth-generation Norwegian American on his mother's side, has worked for twenty-four years in the mill. As many as one half of the 120 workers may be of Norwegian background. When asked if the radical origin of the mill is recognized by the workers, he answered, "Some of the older ones probably know. The newer people don't have the same experience and they would not know. They simply accept that it is state owned, and it is the only state-run milling operation in the United States."

In the post–World War II years North Dakota has displayed a strong Republican color, giving Republican majorities in all presidential elections with the exception of Lyndon Johnson's candidacy in 1964. Incidents of radicalism resulting in "socialist" institutions such as the state mill were the products of external exploitation by the railroads, the grain interests, and the moneylenders. To paraphrase historian D. Jerome Tweton, the state's political climate has more often than not reflected right-wing retrenchment than left-wing experimentation. Morality issues dealing with, for example, the repeal of Prohibition, the state lottery, and blue laws regulating Sunday entertainments, have historically been placed before the electorate through either the initiative or referendum; since 1976 there has been a resurgence of referenda on morality issues in North Dakota.[66]

Mexican-American migrant sugar beet laborers have come seasonally to the Red River valley since the mid-1920s, and were joined by Mexican nationals during World War II to replace American manpower. An influx of temporary as well as more long-term Spanish-speaking minorities, not only into the valley but to the upper Midwest in general, tests local tolerance. In 1990, however, Minnesota and North Dakota still had only 53,884 and 4,665 Hispanic residents, equaling 1.2 and 0.7 percent of the population, respectively. During the 1990s additional Spanish-speaking migrants, illegal Latinos, and numerous Asian immigrants reinforced negative stereotypes. Some well-covered confrontations inflamed local prejudice. Between 1990 and 1996, Minnesota, for instance, had an increase in its Hispanic population of about 40 percent, and a growth of nearly 33 percent for African Americans, and 41 percent for Asians. It was a rapid jump in the state's minority and Hispanic populations. In 1992 the *Saint Paul Pioneer Press* reported the change under the heading, "Uff da! State hears strange, new tongues."[67]

At an earlier time, regions of agrarian revolt expressed through the Populist movement and the Nonpartisan League were not without religious and ethnic prejudice. Historian Dale Baum has argued that the Nonpartisan League tended to view the world in terms of black and white, as "an eternal struggle between God and the Devil," and contributed to isolationism, nativism, and anti-Semitism in the upper Midwest. In the 1920s even the Ku Klux Klan gained a following, some of its leaders being of Norwegian and Swedish ancestry. Most members, if Grand Forks is a representative example, belonged to the upper levels of the local business community. The compact colonies and enclaves of unassimilated Norwegians up and down the valley were, on the other hand, still viewed in the 1920s with considerable suspicion by old-stock Americans. A current suspicion of minorities, to the extent it exists, is clearly motivated more by regional and class circumstances than by ethnic proclivities. It is an area of farming, small towns, no big metropolitan centers, and a population by and large of European origin. An earlier generation of Norwegians, in a romantic ethnocentric vision of history, may even have bestowed on the Norwegian pioneers in the Red River valley the special rights and privileges associated with the settling of new land. To these earlier visionaries, the valley became the New Normandy. A statue in Fargo of Rollo, the Viking Duke of Normandy, unveiled on the occasion of the millennium of his ascendancy to the dukeship in 911, may even be said to proclaim ethnic territoriality (figure 25). The statue, a gift replica of the one unveiled in Rouen in 1911, carried the motto: "Over this land we are the lords and masters," a quote assumed to be from the Norse duke himself. The ethnic elite responsible for this and other markers of a Norwegian-American presence in the Red River valley might even have wished to claim these words as their own.[68]

Conservative Republicanism has many voices. Jens Tennefos of Fargo, North Dakota, served as Republican state senator for twenty years beginning in the mid-1970s. He is a second-generation Norwegian American, and together with a brother he owns a construction company. His conservative views—winning his first election, he thinks, on the issue of right to life—earned him the "Barefoot and Pregnant Award" from the National Organization for Women in 1978 for "his insensitivity to women's issues." Tennefos attributes his conservative values to his Norwegian-born father: "My father feared and loved the Lord and taught me respect for life and compassion for others." "Our Norwegian heritage," Tennefos felt, "is much more compassionate than the Hispanic," concluding that the newer migrants do not have the same compassion for people or respect for life. Few past or present public servants would, to be sure, express these biased

Figure 25. A statue of Rollo (or Rollon, as the name is spelled on its base), the Norse Duke of Normandy, in Fargo, North Dakota. Photograph by Ray Jackson.

beliefs as openly as here. District Court Judge Ralph Erickson in Fargo, a fourth-generation Norwegian American, nevertheless made the observation that Scandinavians who appeared in front of his bench did not commit violent crimes; such felonies were more commonly associated with other ethnicities in the community. There is little reason to question the accuracy of the judge's observation. Given the prevalent socioeconomic and demographic circumstances of the Hispanic migrants, a poorly paid, largely male population, and the discrimination they face in employment and socially, a higher-than-average crime rate might well be expected. Hispanics are, as a 1995 *Washington Post* article stated, saddled with "bad" stereotypes. In describing ethnic qualities, the Norwegian-American representatives cited above express popular Norwegian-American beliefs about their own ethnic merits, but in stating their stereotyped opinions of newcomers they are in reality exhibiting white class-based biases that are widely held.[69]

Political Voices

Even though a general conservative trend in the Norwegian-American electorate is evidenced in the political color of legislators and in expressed stances on specific issues regardless of political party in state houses and in Congress, it does not represent a hegemonic position. There are naturally differences from one state to another. Of the several Norwegian-American members of the Minnesota legislature that were interviewed, a Democrat, Senator Roger D. Moe, and a Republican, Representative Steven A. Sviggum, illustrate the political range among politicians of Norwegian ancestry. They do not necessarily reflect the political position of a Norwegian-American electorate. A successful appeal on the basis of ethnicity

can no longer be made. Senator Moe, for instance, receives his most consistent support from the Native American residents on the Red Lake Indian Reservation within his district. The two politicians represent the traditional conservatism of the prosperous southeastern counties and the Democratic Farmer-Labor stance in the poorer districts of the state. And, to be sure, a Norwegian electorate still exerts influence in both regions, though their ethnicity, like in a previous age, is less of a determinant of voting habits than is economic self-interest. At the national level, interviews with Congressman Martin Olav Sabo, a Democrat, and former Vice President Walter F. Mondale are included here. Minnesota has retained a liberal political reputation. "You are too socialistic out there," a Norwegian-American respondent in Washington, D.C., opined.[70]

Roger D. Moe, born in 1944, was elected to the Minnesota Senate in 1970 at the age of twenty-six on the Democratic Farmer-Labor ticket. He has been majority leader since 1981. Senator Moe represents the sparsely populated and vast second senate district in northwestern Minnesota, a region where farming and forestry remain the main economic base. The district is a stronghold of the Democratic Farmer-Labor Party in the state, east of the Republican districts. Moe was born within the district in Erskine in Polk County and grew up in this strongly Norwegian part of the state. All of his grandparents emigrated from Norway in the 1880s and 1890s. His American-born parents spoke Norwegian. The Lutheran church, where his Norwegian-born grandfather was a pastor, was a central part of his life, perhaps at times more social than religious, and traditional foods like lutefisk are a part of his tradition. Senator Moe revived the celebration of May 17 in the state senate as a serious holiday.

Q: How has your Norwegian heritage influenced your public service?

A: The Nonpartisan League that came from the Dakotas was a fairly aggressive movement up until World War I, and it had a great influence on the people on the prairie. We all knew that we were the servants to the bigger companies and that we were not given a fair price. This was something I was aware of relatively early. My grandfather Lars Johannes Njus, a pastor, ran for public office. He, a Norwegian Lutheran preacher, was considered the leading liberal at the time. He saw that the country needed a general pension plan. All this had a significance for how I saw the world. There were not many programs in those days, but I am the beneficiary of those programs, affordable health care and other social policies. And I believe that this is right and just.

Q: What do you see as your greatest political achievement?

A: Internally, within the office, I have opened the senate and the processes to all members. It used to be a strict hierarchy, but I gave everybody a chance to sit in various committees. I got women involved and made them

significant players on the inside. Externally, in public policy, I signed for the reorganization of the public higher education system, which I think will later prove itself to be profound. We lived on a small farm, and it was a struggle. All my father raised on the farm was a family. So he said that we ought to get an education, and he borrowed money and sent us to school.

Q: How do you feel about your Norwegian heritage?

A: I wouldn't want to be anything else! All the fun I had during the winter Olympics last year [1994]. Norway must still be on a high from that![71]

Steven A. Sviggum, born in 1951, is the Republican minority leader in the Minnesota House of Representatives, and was elected in 1978 from district 28B in southern Minnesota, which encompasses such Norwegian and historically Republican strongholds as the agriculturally prosperous Olmsted, Dodge, and Goodhue Counties. Sviggum recalls Norwegian being spoken on the streets in small towns in Goodhue County such as Wanamingo and Kenyon, where he resides, as recently as the 1960s. Norwegian foods and traditions "from eating lutefisk to celebrating May 17" were and are a part of his life. Sviggum is a third-generation Norwegian American of unmixed heritage. He is very active in the Vang Lutheran Church, founded by Norwegian immigrants in the early 1860s.

Q: Has your Norwegian background influenced your political ideology?

A: I would say yes, because my Norwegian background is a bit more conservative. It does not look for radical changes in life. The Norwegians who settled in my area tended to be fairly conservative. I don't know if that's how Norway is now, in fact, I think Norway is far more liberal than I am! But I consider my conservative sides to be my Norwegian background.

Q: How would you describe your political philosophy?

A: I would certainly be a strong conservative. I feel very strongly about individual responsibility and less government involvement. Government's role is to enhance justice, freedom, safety, thrift, and work—those are the government's responsibility. I'm not proud of the Norwegian democratic welfare state that has developed in postwar Norway. I must admit that when there is talk about health care, and my friends say that Scandinavia has done this and that, I become quite the opposite of my heritage on these [social] issues. We need to come back to a system of individual responsibility, not government dependency.

Q: What does it signify to you to be Norwegian?

A: Pride. I'm proud to tell that I'm 100 percent Norwegian.

Q: Has your interest in your heritage grown?

A: Yes, as you get older you appreciate your background more. As a young person it doesn't mean anything. I had no great interest and there was nothing that stirred my imagination. I've grown a stronger interest over the years.[72]

Martin Olav Sabo was born on a farm in Crosby, located in the northwestern corner of North Dakota, in 1938, in a heavily Norwegian area of the state. Both his parents immigrated from Norway. He learned Norwegian as his first language. He represents the Fifth District of Minnesota in the U.S. Congress—encompassing the urbanized liberal eastern Hennepin County—and was elected on the Democratic Farmer-Labor ticket the first time in 1978, following a political career in the Minnesota House of Representatives. He likes to quote the *St. Paul Pioneer Press,* which noted that Congressman Sabo "is an effective lawmaker at the center of the action to make pragmatic fiscal decisions with a liberal's compassion."

Q: What was left of Norwegian traditions when you grew up in Crosby?

A: It was, I suppose, lutefisk, lots of lutefisk, lutefisk dinners in church and in the school.

Q: How do you explain your liberal political philosophy?

A: Where I came from, the people who farmed in that area were heavily Democratic. It is more marginal farming than in the Red River valley and in southern Minnesota. In the rural townships in that part of the country the votes are twenty to one or eighteen to one.

Q: Do you see any connection between your own political concerns and your Norwegian heritage?

A: Yes, I was never quite sure how you trace that. I think the tradition of the Lutheran Free

Church had a liberal bent on politics. We attended a church in that tradition. It was strict on moral issues, even attending movies or playing cards. After graduating from high school in Alkabo [North Dakota], I went to Augsburg College, I suppose because of old Lutheran Free Church contacts, and graduated in 1959. I was heavily involved in politics all the way through college and was active with Young Democrats.

Q: What would come to your mind first if you were asked what you value most about being a Norwegian American?

A: I would say a concern for people.[73]

Walter F. Mondale was born in 1928. Both his grandfather and his great-grandfather immigrated from the farm Mundal in Sogn in the late 1850s. His distinguished political career as U.S. senator, vice president, presidential candidate, and ambassador to Japan makes him the most prominent contemporary Norwegian-American political figure. In his legislative career as a Democrat, he compiled a left-of-center voting record, particularly in the area of social legislation, in the tradition of his mentor and fellow Minnesotan Hubert H. Humphrey. His attachment to and knowledge of the ancestral home sod and family history in America may be symptomatic of latter-day ethnicity: it is individualized and passed down within the family.

Q: Do you know much about your Norwegian roots?

A: My family came from Norway with the name Mundal from a little town of the same name in Fjærland. You go up to Balestrand on the Sognefjord, then you go north on the Fjærland fjord, and then just at the end of the fjord, a spectacular, beautiful fjord. It opens out into a huge valley. And one side of it is Mundal.

Q: Where did your family settle in America?

A: They finally ended up among the first white settlers in the little town of Bricelyn, which is a Norwegian community outside of Albert Lea. My great-grandfather Frederick, I guess, got three hundred bucks and went into the Civil War. And I found his papers when I was vice president. He signed with an X, so they called him Peterson.

Q: What has been your own experience with your ethnic background?

A: My father, Theodore Mondale, spoke Norwegian fluently even though he never visited Norway. He was a Methodist farmer minister, and we moved a lot. There were always Norwegians around. My dad did not make a point of it, if you know what I mean. It was simply there. It's my generation that's more interested in the roots than they were. It came more natural to them, too, because they were still speaking the language, and they had friends they'd get together with.

Q: Did your heritage influence your life?

A: I think where the Norwegian influence came into my life was with its heavy emphasis on honesty. We were a poor family in terms of money. My dad didn't care about money, but he cared about education. All the children received higher education. My father was always reading. He was self-taught. My father was an old social gospel liberal.

Q: What made you decide to go into politics?

A: You know, I decided when I was in high school. Because I was close to my father. And I knew how important this was to him. Not politics, but the social gospel and the progressive idea. And I wanted to be a part of that.

Q: How do you experience your Norwegian background?

A: All through my life it pops up in the most unusual ways. Oh, like [Warren] Christopher and I sat down and talked one time about what it was like to grow up in a small Norwegian-American town. And you know, I understood exactly what his problem was. You know, when I grew up you got spanked for two things. One was stealing, the other was bragging. And which was the greater crime, I don't know. But in politics, basically the first thing you do is brag, see? To run for political office was hard when I first started, boy, I was so shy. And I had been taught so much not to brag or show off or, you know, to be nice and deferential. Don't be pushy and vain.

Q: Now as a prominent politician will people meeting *you* be intimidated?

A: That's very bad. If you set up a psychological elevation for yourself which is above others, you're going to lose. People will not stand for it. We're a very democratic society, and people want to know you're healthy, emotionally as well as physically, and they want to know that you've got a democratic attitude and that you're going to listen. Now they also want to see strength and character and leadership. But that is not inconsistent with democracy. I tried to be a leader. Leadership, democratic leadership, even assertive, strong leadership, is very much respected as long as there's dignity and respect connected with it.[74]

In Wisconsin interviews were conducted with seven Norwegian-American members of the Wisconsin Assembly and Senate, and with the chief justice of the Wisconsin Supreme Court. A Republican and a Democratic member are presented here.

Brian D. Rude, born in 1955, serves as the President of the Wisconsin State Senate. He was elected in 1984 on the Republican ticket from the state senate district that includes the traditionally Norwegian counties of La Crosse, Crawford, and Vernon, and resides in Coon Valley. His Norwegian ancestors were from Gudbrandsdalen, the region in Norway from which many of the original settlers originated. His ancestors immigrated in the 1850s. Senator Rude grew up surrounded by Norwegian speech and traditions. His parents were strictly Republican and Lutheran. Norwegian, Lutheran, and Republican consequently have become significant aspects of his personal involvement in church affairs, in several Norwegian-American organizations, and in public service. Senator Rude defines himself as a moderate within the Republican Party.

Q: How do you view current social issues, especially welfare?

A: I would like to bring the pendulum back to where we encourage work. It now discourages work and personal initiative. But I also see that we need a social services net for those who really can't work.

Q: Would that address problems like teenage pregnancies?

A: No, I really don't think that addresses it very much. I'm not sure government is the answer to the problems we have with a breakdown of the family structure. I am troubled by it and the increasing number of single moms.

Q: What are society's responsibilities?

A: I focus on education. One should combine educational experience and work in a way so that we can break the long-term circle of welfare dependency.

Q: How do your views relate to your Norwegian background?

A: I think my Lutheran tradition in particular moderates my views, like, for instance, on capital punishment, which I oppose because of my religious convictions. That one in particular shows my heritage. Even my pro-life voting record, which I struggle with personally, I don't see how I could come to another position because of my Lutheran background.

Q: How would you characterize a Norwegian American?

A: I see the Norwegians as very hardworking, honest and up-front people.

Q: Are there many Norwegian criminals?

A: No, when I think of it, I don't think so. I don't think we Norwegians have the crime of passion as others have, simply because of the lack of emotions!

Q: Can we be too proud of heritage?

A: It's a delicate balance. In speeches about ethnic issues, I use the quilt metaphor rather than the melting pot. We're Americans, and not shy about that. But we also understand our heritage and roots, and we bring to culture unique things about heritage, and that's part of the quilt.[75]

William Murat, born in 1957, is from Stevens Point in the early pioneer Norwegian Portage County, which is the seventy-first assembly district. He was elected by this district in 1994 as a Democrat. His family arrived from Norway in 1851 and has lived in central Wisconsin ever since. His roots in Norway are in Vestfold, Gausdal, and Kongsberg, although he has never visited these places. He is a fifth-generation Norwegian American, growing up with devout Lutheran practices and Norwegian traditions and pride in heritage. He is the fourth generation in law. Representative Murat defines himself as a moderate Democrat.

Q: How do being Lutheran and being Norwegian relate?

A: The two are very intertwined. Coming to church was the connection to other families who were of Norwegian background.

Q: Which pressing social issue in Wisconsin

would show the difference between conservative and liberal attitudes?

A: That would be issues of crime and how to solve those problems. We must invest more time and money in children, not in building more prisons. If we did that, we would not have the problems associated with significant demands on our welfare system. We must get people to build strong families and strong relations.

Q: How do we do that?

A: One thing is that we have to focus on illegitimacy and teenage pregnancies, and I think we have to try to change the moral compass around somewhat, and say that in one's teenager years that abstinence is an appropriate action to take.

Q: What about abortion?

A: I basically support the idea that there is the continuing of life from the point of conception, and that the state has an interest at a point before birth to prohibit abortion, but I'm not saying that this point is the point of conception.

Q: What do you associate with your Norwegian heritage?

A: I think there is a strong sense of family and a strong sense of community, that's perhaps the most important.

Q: What about the Viking image as an identifying ethnic symbol?

A: I actually think it's nice. It shows a rugged individualism about it and reflects the history and extraordinary challenges that the Vikings faced. Not only in terms of the voyage

in itself, but the shipbuilding and the desire to advance oneself. It required individuals with a strong direction in life and who were willing to make sacrifices on the way to achieving what they wanted.[76]

Roland B. Day, born in 1919, chief justice of the Wisconsin Supreme Court since August 1, 1995, and a justice on the high court for twenty-one years, grew up in Eau Claire. His father, Peter Oliver Day, emigrated from Fredrikstad, Norway, at age ten; he grew up as the oldest of fifteen children. His mother's roots extend back to the early colonial period. Justice Day felt he grew up in a Norwegian world in Eau Claire and thought "half the world was Norwegian." He had a lot of Lutheran friends, but his father converted to Unitarianism, and his mother did not belong to any church. Day was an only child and jokingly described himself as being of a mixed marriage, his father an agnostic and his mother an atheist. He joined a Protestant church in his early thirties, earned a law degree, and was active in Wisconsin politics in the Democratic Party. He was appointed to the bench in 1974 by Democratic governor Patrick J. Lucy and won election in 1976 in a statewide race. He now defines himself as a nonpartisan judge.

Q: What have been your political convictions, Your Honor?

A: At the university I was president of the LaFollette Progressive Club. Well, I viewed myself as liberal. I think that now liberalism has come to mean a lot of different things than it did twenty-one years ago.

Q: But surely your political convictions must affect your legal philosophy?

A: Ah, what's happened is that in recent years, liberalism on a court depends on how you are on criminal cases. If you can figure out and invent new ways to let criminals go, you're liberal. And if you stick with the law and don't, why, then they consider you conservative. So then there's a lot of people who would say I'm conservative. I consider myself moderate.

Q: Has your Norwegian heritage meant much to you?

A: I've always been proud of being part Norwegian. I've always been impressed that my dad had a large family, and I've known a lot of them. And these are always very honest, very hardworking, very intelligent people. And I think that Norwegians in this country have contributed a great deal.

Q: Do you belong to Norwegian-American organizations?

A: Yes, to Yggdrasil literary society and to the Norske Torske Klubb, but being a tee-totaler, I don't drink the aquavit.

Q: Can we be too proud of heritage?

A: Well, you know, I suppose it means different things to different people, and it depends on what their experience is. And some of them, of course, have felt that their people have gone through great persecution and have been cheated and so on. But I think the big thing is that what we ought to be concerned

Figure 26. Governor Terry E. Branstad of Iowa. Photograph courtesy of Governor Terry E. Branstad.

about, yeah, it's fun to eat lutefisk and *lefse* and to belong to these societies, but we're just part of all the other groups, too. And I think that we ought to try and get along with each other as Americans.[77]

In Iowa, a traditionally conservative state, Republican Governor Terry E. Branstad offered insights into his own political career as the dean of governors and his relationship to his mixed ethnic heritage growing up in a heavily Norwegian part of the state.

Governor Branstad from Lake Mills, Iowa, was born in 1946 to Edward and Rita Branstad (figure 26). In 1982 he was sworn in as Iowa's youngest governor in history and has been reelected ever since. He grew up on a farm in Leland, which has been in the family for about 115 years and is now operated by his brother

Monroe. His great-grandfather came over at age nineteen from the Trondheim area of Norway, together with his father. On his mother's side Governor Branstad is descended from Latvian Jews. His mother's father immigrated in 1910 from Latvia and operated a general store in Lake Mills.

Q: How did your mother and her parents adjust to the Norwegian character of Lake Mills?

A: My mother converted to Lutheranism. She still maintained a lot of Jewish heritage. My [Norwegian] grandmother made *lefse* and lutefisk and all those things, while my mother would make matzo ball soup, and she used to go to Minneapolis to buy bagels. I was raised in a Lutheran church started by Norwegian immigrants.

Q: Did you and your brother grow up feeling Norwegian or Jewish?

A: I would say Norwegian, but my mother always reminded us that we had a Jewish connection. Just about everyone was Norwegian and Lutheran. Once when I was about nine, we visited our Jewish grandmother in California, and when she asked us what our favorite food was, we answered pork chops. I think she may even have fixed them for us.

Q: What about your political convictions?

A: My family was surprisingly enough Democratic. The Norwegians were predominantly Republican in northern Iowa. But there was also a strong feeling about what I would

call Prairie Populism. And my family was very much involved in that. We became Republican in the 1960s. I considered myself a conservative Democrat but joined the Republican Party when the Democrats were moving farther and farther to the left.

Q: Do you find any Norwegian influence on your political career?

A: Oh, yes. I think that the values have had a great impact on me. We are very much family oriented and agricultural. There is a tremendous commitment to the soil and to a sense for history. There is a real pride in the Norwegian immigrants that came here and settled the area. They are honest, industrious, and hardworking people.

Q: So you think the conservative values you represent are a part of your heritage?

A: Well, I think there is no question about that. Yes, and I see that in the sense of being fiscally conservative. But maybe open-minded enough to accept change. I like to consider myself kind of a progressive conservative. I am conservative when it comes to saving the tax dollars and preserving what is good about the past, but also recognize the need to change with the times.

Q: Do you think the many ethnic enclaves and traditions in Iowa and elsewhere should be preserved?

A: Yes, I think it's great. I think it gives people a sense of identity, a sense of roots, and a sense of belonging. Iowans are a very traditional people. They are very proud of their heritage. A lot of communities and groups have done a lot to preserve it. We had Christmas programs and things like that when I was growing up. I think that gives a child a sense of identity and belonging and security. It is something that gets lost in the hustle and bustle of modern life.[78]

The Militant Norwegian American

Having traveled throughout the United States to regions of Norwegian-American settlement, a Norwegian journalist claims in a book published in 1997 that "the most vocal people of Norwegian ancestry have placed themselves on the intolerant and extreme right in America and also among many of those who are not so loud one finds many broken pots." As evidence he identifies racist language among Norwegian Americans and Norwegian-American membership in far-right groups, and gives as specific examples Rodney Skurdal, the ideologue of the infamous Freemen group in Montana in the spring of 1996, and the two militia leaders Robert Johansen in Florida and Norman Olson of Michigan, all of Norwegian ancestry. Both Johansen and Olson were interviewed for this project. Olson, though not supported by the Michigan Militia, offered to organize a relief convoy to come to the aid of the Freemen who barricaded themselves on a farm against federal agents in Jordan, Montana.[79]

It may have some merit to claim, as the Norwegian journalist does, that at a time when the American political consensus is moving right, people of Norwegian ancestry follow suit. Like most Americans, they share a certain distrust of their own government. The fieldwork and questionnaire survey support such contentions. Whether Norwegian Americans have compounded a conservative social and political agenda with a tendency to move to the extreme right of the political spectrum is more open to question. In discussing his discovery of racist language, the journalist mainly referred to Norwegian working-class people in Brooklyn. Their prejudice is more easily understood in a socioeconomic context than in an ethnic, as it may be said to reflect widespread attitudes harbored by white urbanites at the same social level. The examples given, at least, will not alone support a thesis of extremist tendencies among Norwegian Americans.

On the other hand, it may not be totally irrelevant to infer, given the group's historical experience in America, that an ethnic culture with moralistic and segregated overtones was molded that had the potential and the ability to move some individuals within the Norwegian-American matrix toward rightist beliefs and actions. There is the group's pronounced clannishness and rural isolation, its antiurban and anti-industrial agrarian revolt, the midwestern anti-Semitism associated with this revolt, an extreme form of Norwegian-American Lutheran piety, an abiding anti-Catholicism, and even the restrictive nature of many of the reform measures within the progressive political movement that Norwegian voters advocated. A careful reading of antiassimilationist statements even by such staunch Norwegian-American cultural pluralists as Waldemar Ager and Ole E. Rølvaag suggests that their anti–melting-pot rhetoric is as much concerned with the purity of "the Norwegian race" as it is a call to honor all national cultures represented in America's polyglot immigrant populations.[80]

A contemporary firmly expressed opinion—on occasion annoyingly self-satisfied—of high ethnic moral and cultural merits surely also encourages conservative ethnocentric attitudes. These convictions are, however, generally not couched in racist language; Norwegian Americans are not seen as better humans but simply as belonging to a nationality with high cultural and ethical standards. "Norwegians have a good work ethic and high morals," was the expressed opinion of Maynard O. Molstad of Canton, South Dakota, born in 1928. His grandfather emigrated from Toten, Norway. "Let's face it," he stated, "they came out here and made it go." He believed that younger Norwegian Americans have preserved the values he associates with his ethnicity. "If you go to other ethnic groups in this country, they don't seem to have them."[81] There is, as expressed by Molstad, a belief among many of those interviewed that these same sterling qualities, much in jeopardy in the old homeland, have been preserved untainted through the generations in America. They, in other words, reflect a Norway of a bygone unsullied era. It

would, however, be not only reckless but also not evidentially proven to claim Norwegian-American rightist political proclivities as an overt ethnic characteristic. The question might also become, how, if an idiosyncratic ethnic conservatism really exists, does one explain such postwar liberal Norwegian-American legends as Humphrey, Mondale, Senator Henry "Scoop" Jackson of Washington, and Chief Justice Earl Warren? There may even be a sectional difference with a more moderating political conviction in some parts of the upper Midwest than elsewhere in the United States. There are also, as examples, the La Follette tradition and the Farmer-Labor activism, both engaging many Norwegian Americans, which defined a socially compassionate and liberal political agenda.

Extremist examples are perhaps best left to speak for themselves. They may at a minimum be seen as one aspect of a general growth in conservative thought among Norwegian Americans. The Freemen, with Norwegian-American Skurdal as one of the leaders, belong to the Identity Christianity movement, know themselves as Christian and patriots, view Caucasians as the "Chosen People," express anti-Catholicism and anti-Judaism, and are racist and action oriented. Norwegian-American participation by no means, of course, gives credence to the unsubstantiated accusation made by the U.S. ambassador to Norway in the 1980s, Louis Lerner, that Norwegian Americans were among the most racist and conservative ethnic populations in America. Norwegian Americans responded with justified indignation.[82]

Not all groups to the right openly declare racist viewpoints. In fact the Florida Militia states its neutrality directly in its literature: "we will not tolerate racists."[83] Covert anti-Semitism may, however, be reflected in the many Jewish names of the listed enemies of the militia. Johansen is quoted as saying that "we envision an alliance between the different militia groups and the Christian Coalition," a rightist educational and religious group with strong political ambitions. It grew out of the unsuccessful presidential campaign of evangelist Pat Robertson in 1988. Its current executive director, Randy Tate, while representing the state of Washington in Congress in the mid-1990s, pushed to make English the official language of the United States and has been described as "a religious political extremist." Robert Johansen was born in 1929 in Brooklyn; his father immigrated from Stavanger, Norway, and his mother was born in America of Norwegian immigrant parents (figure 27). In the postwar years he received military training in the Marine Corps and later joined the National Guard and Army Reserve. Since 1971 he has been a resident of Florida, currently living in Fort Pierce; membership in the Second Regiment of the Florida State Militia is open to persons who live within thirty miles of the town.

Q: When did you join the Florida State Militia?

Figure 27. Robert Johansen of the Florida Militia. Photograph by Terje Mikael Hasle Joranger.

A: I joined in 1992 and became the spokesman for the Militia. I am the leader of about five hundred people.

Q: Are there many of Norwegian background?

A: Yes, there are some but not so many in my group.

Q: Why do you feel there is a need for paramilitary groups such as the Florida State Militia?

A: We come together to protect our rights under the American Constitution against the federal government. We want to educate people about what the government is doing to them. Through conspiracy and deceit, "One World Government" will take over our country. Jewish bankers, the Rockefellers, Carnegies, and the United Nations are behind it. Our political leaders, President Clinton, Warren Christopher, and Al Gore are conspiring with them. They want to take away our guns and make us slaves. Our Constitution says Americans can bear arms at all times. There will only be one religion, if a religion at all. The United Nations will come in and the rest of the world will follow. I imagine Norway will have no choice either.[84]

Norman Eugene Olson was born in Detroit, Michigan, in 1946. He is a third-generation Norwegian-American on his mother's side and of Swedish and German ancestry on his father's. He grew up in the Swedish Missionary Alliance Church and is himself a Baptist minister, but without having attended a seminary. "All of my education is what you call horseback education," Olson explained, "life experience and self-taught." He served in the U.S. Air Force and stayed in the military from 1964 until 1984. He is currently a pastor of a church and also a gun dealer.

Q: How did your interest in the militia begin?

A: It was probably a by-product of me serving as a pastor. Being in church, you hear many of the concerns and complaints of people. In this part of the country they were growing troubled by the loss of their control of the educational system. Government programs were taking over. And they were losing their family to the government educational system and their property because they could not repay federal loans and taxes.

Q: What are the goals of the militia?

A: The simplest explanation is that a militia represents people who come together to defend themselves against a common threat. We feel the threat of the New World Order, real or not, and the real threats of more taxes, intrusive government into our lives, permits, fees, and licenses to the point where it quenches our spirit as businessmen, fathers, and citizens. We are trying to hold that which we already have so no one will take it away from us.

Q: Are the Freemen in Montana a part of the militia?

A: Yes, in a generic sense. However, the Freemen really are outside the Constitution. Since the federal government has violated the contract embodied in the Constitution, they no longer feel bound by the contract.

Q: Why do we find Norwegians among the Freemen?

A: Well, look at the people that settled in western Minnesota, the Dakotas, and Montana. Those people are rugged, many of them Norwegian. Because only Norwegians would live in North Dakota. They came from a strong government system and with little opportunity. The Norwegians said, let's go to the Dakotas, and let's go to Minnesota, let's go to Montana where nobody else is. And we're not going to ask anything from anybody. All we want is opportunity. So, I am proud of my Norwegian heritage because of its individualistic character, not frightened of anything, not a quitter, not conquered, and willing to venture forth and to be a pioneer. That's very important.[85]

Surely, if many Norwegian Americans harbor similar intense and exaggerated ethnocentric concepts coupled with religious fundamentalism, ethnicity would go some way in explaining an attraction for the several radical-right groups by a fringe element of this population. It is, however, not a satisfactory analysis since a number of other factors seem to outweigh ethnicity. Typical of many such militia leaders, the interview subjects had military experience, were not well educated, and had ties to Christian fundamentalism. The irrationality of their reasoning is in all events difficult to explain. An explanation could be sought not in ethnic peculiarities but rather in individual life situations. No final theory has, however, been put forth to explain right-wing extremism and the irrational fear of oppressive actions by the federal government. This conspiratorial view of history reduces historical events to the conscious intent of an all-powerful and omniscient force and ultimately leads to a search for someone to blame or eliminate as the cause of social decline. A theory of social displacement has been advanced by sociologists Seymour Martin Lipset and Earl Raab. They believe that while left-wing movements are engineered by people experiencing upward mobility, the right wing attracts those whose social status is threatened, and they thus develop a preservative nostalgic and backward-looking concept of a past that may only exist in their imagination. They are not basically evil people but rather are ordinary people terrified of losing their position in the world. For Lipset and Raab, their theory is a general principle that has validity throughout American history.[86]

James Aho offers an alternative theory to status insecurity. He points to the cyclical character of rightist extremism, and to the fact that contrary to what one might assume, right-wing extremist movements increase during times of prosperity, when status anxiety would be presumed to be lessened. Aho's alternative explanation—here only alluded to—of the periodicity of the movement, a revival having occurred every thirty years since 1800, relates to the influence of fundamentalist religious movements, opportunity to access rightist structures, and generational dynamics—the formation of generational consciousness formed by Christian fundamentalism. Right-wing radicals interpret certain events as threats to their world because they are viewed from a religious point of view. This would explain the frame of reference that defines liberals, public school teachers, illicit drugs, abortion, and homosexuality, among many other issues, as wicked and harmful. Each rightist episode, Aho concludes, appears to last about a decade.[87]

Norwegian-American Bias

The questionnaire returns, interviews, and volunteered opinions on characteristic Norwegian-American traits communicate, as one would expect, strongly positive qualities. Pride in ancestry nearly dictates an affirmation of high ethnic merits, and it is a consistent factor in a Norwegian-American self-perception. The list of attributes includes such mainstream middle-class American ideals as being hardworking, given as a prominent ethnic quality by 73 percent of the respondents. Honesty was given an equal response, followed closely by being good citizens; thereafter came family commitment, rural values, and American pioneers, followed by Lutheran and Viking descent, attributes more specific to the group, and finally, by piety. Conversely, respondents consistently rejected such negative qualities as being dishonest, lazy, impoverished, or intemperate as ever typifying Norwegian Americans. Some commented on the stoicism and inability to express emotion and physical affection that they discovered in fellow Norwegian Americans, especially in those of an older generation, as limiting ethnic characteristics. "I never saw my parents hug or kiss," became a regular refrain. There were also those who admitted to having had an uncle who drank a bit much. Still, less than 3 percent of the respondents gave "intemperate" as a negative ethnic value. A positive self-image can naturally lead to prejudice against groups who are perceived not to possess such highly regarded qualities.

And, indeed, an ethnic self-definition that adopts traditional American ideals and qualities may have more to do with adjustment and conformity in a middle-class population than with strong ethnic or racial prejudices. All ethnic groups tend to view themselves in terms of

what constitutes good credentials and gains acceptance in the host society. In this regard Norwegian Americans are not unique. Mary Waters found in her study that "people described values and beliefs that are very general—in fact, held by most middle-class Americans—as being specific to their own, and not to other ethnic groups."[88]

What, then, do Norwegian Americans think about elements within the ethnic group itself that appear to threaten a traditional self-identification of what it means to be Norwegian American? This question, and the issue of gay rights that interview subjects were queried about, naturally led to a focus on prejudices in regard to sexual orientation and how these might affect gay men and lesbian women within a Norwegian-American matrix. No minority identity is more stringently assigned or through blatant prejudice has the potential of doing greater harm. A rather dramatic example of the consequences was the public outing of Congressman Steve Gunderson in March 1994 on the floor of the House of Representatives. Congressman Gunderson, born in 1951, represented the Third District in western Wisconsin, a strongly Republican area as well as one with a large Norwegian-American population. Gunderson is himself of Norwegian ancestry, and May 17 parades in such small towns as Westby and Woodville were convenient campaign events. Even though he was a popular representative in his district, his work on behalf of gays in the military generated a strong negative response from Republicans. Following the open rebuke of his sexuality and an anticipated anti-gay campaign by rightist religious and conservative social groups during the election, he pledged he would not run again for the congressional post he had held since 1980, and in doing so, he declared, "I would have loved to be in a party where your personal life doesn't matter, and you are judged by your professional conduct. But I understand that progress comes in small steps."[89]

It was precisely progress in Norwegian-American tolerance of sexual minorities that this part of the investigation considered. The St. Olaf Lesbian and Gay Alliance, or OLGA, was formed at St. Olaf, a church-related college, in 1989, and redefined to be inclusive of transgender and bisexual orientations. OLGA has a campus membership of about 250, and in addition there is a support group and a gay and lesbian alumni association. These organizations owe their existence to efforts—frequently painful ones due to overt and latent prejudicial attitudes—that began in the 1960s. A major founder of OLGA was Allison L. E. Wee, born in 1969 and a student at the college. Being the daughter of senior professor David L. Wee and a member of a family prominent in Norwegian-American Lutheranism made her mission easier, though not immediately. Eventually her father and her mother, Karen Herseth Wee, took up the cause of tolerance, even to the degree of wearing "gay" buttons and speaking out on the issue of sexual orientation.

Q: How did your parents respond initially?

A: My father never talked about it with me. I talked with my mother, and my mother talked with my dad. I know that she was supportive of gay people, but it took longer to take in the idea of her own child.

Q: How did your father respond once he learned more about it?

A: In the non-communicative Norwegian Lutheran way! I think he just took it into his political justice philosophy. What was interesting about my dad, well about my parents, is that they have both been strong feminists and have had a very socially active, social justice–oriented set of values. For my dad to find out I was lesbian was completely out of the blue. It had never crossed his mind before.

Q: How are they responding at present?

A: I think my family has taken on the gay and lesbian justice issue in a way that a lot of people took up civil rights issues in the sixties. They believe it is their duty to make a difference in the culture and not leave it to those who are already struggling with the oppression.

Q: When did you decide to begin OLGA?

A: It happened in my sophomore year in the spring of 1989. I had just come out to myself and to some student peers of mine. I had met up with a few other lesbian students on campus. At the same time there was an English professor who was lesbian. She ended up single-handedly being the sounding board and moral support for this group. She wound up choosing to give a chapel talk that spring where she came out to the community and challenged it to work harder to address gay and lesbian issues on campus. She decided not to return to campus in the fall. OLGA came out of these circumstances. I could take on the role I did because of the high profile of my parents. In the spring of 1990 we had our first gay and lesbian awareness week.[90]

Todd Rustad, the student coordinator of OLGA in 1995, explained his gay activism:

A: I came out fully to myself in October of 1994. That was right after I met my first gay friend. That was the same night that he told me he was gay. He had a sense that I was gay. After that, it was around November-December that I started to do work for OLGA. When I sort of took it over, it was in a shambles. So I brought it up to a level where it could be respected by faculty and staff.

Q: What church did you go to?

A: I grew up Catholic. My father is Methodist. He is fully Norwegian. My mother is half Norwegian, a fourth Polish, and a fourth Swedish. She was raised a Catholic. I am still very Catholic. I would like to get out of the Catholic Church. I hate the idea that someone is a sinner because of who they are.

Q: How did you yourself feel about your homosexuality?

A: Well, at first I thought it was a sin. I thought I was going to burn in hell.

Q: You would expect religion to be judgmental. What if a gay priest would say: "I'm a priest and gay. I am respected." Would that have helped you?

A: Oh my gosh. I would have been in heaven. Plus I would have been a whole new person. It would have made me think that this is a person that God selected for his work, and he's gay. That would mean that this is not such an awful thing. God would not have selected a homosexual to do His work if it was such an awful thing.

Q: You have expressed a great interest in your Norwegian heritage. Has it helped in any way?

A: No, it didn't help much. I think that the Norwegian background kind of reemphasized the standard family, the typical family. I feel that it kind of reinforced the old way of thinking.[91]

Since values associated with heritage and ethnic habits and customs are passed down in individual families, it becomes difficult for many to distinguish family idiosyncrasies from ethnicity. This reliance on family to define ethnicity is in general viewed as a positive trait. It can, on the other hand, become oppressive for people who do not conform or who feel alienated. Family and group prejudice would surely reinforce boundaries toward a homosexual subculture.[92]

Two openly lesbian sisters, Kimberly Anne Lerohl, born in 1959, and Kristin Lerohl, born in 1955, show the conflict between family values interpreted as ethnic and challenges to these values. Both women grew up in Minnesota and graduated from St. Olaf College; Kimberly is now living in Albuquerque, New Mexico, and Kristin in Portland, Oregon. They are fifth-generation Norwegian Americans on their father's side and fourth-generation on their mother's.

Q: Kimberly, did you observe any Norwegian customs growing up?

A: Oh, definitely. Ah . . . well, we were told they were Norwegian customs. Every Christmas we had lutefisk, that's Norwegian-American. Even though no one ate it, we had to have it because it was tradition. And I remember feeling that tradition was really important, and if we broke it, it was almost like we were betraying the family.

Q: What about your education?

A: Both my parents went to St. Olaf. It was the last place I really wanted to go. I went to Norway to study a year. And I really felt that the best thing about St. Olaf was I didn't have to be there, I got to leave. It was almost as if I had to leave, I had to be that far away from my family. We had been so controlled.

Q: How did you feel being a student at St. Olaf and being lesbian?

A: Horrible. It was very painful. Once I came out, it was my junior year, and I came back from Norway, I really didn't want to go back to St. Olaf. There were no other lesbians at St. Olaf who were out.

Q: You now live in a committed relationship with Anna. Did your family accept your lifestyle?

A: We have lived in Albuquerque for nine years. So I haven't lived in Minnesota for ten or eleven years. And a lot of it is because I just can't, you know, because with my family we've had to keep it a secret. I mean, I came out to them that year, my first year back at St. Olaf. I told them. And there's, you know, they never really acknowledged it. They don't talk about anything, really. And, ah, especially the difficult things. And I think pretty much the rule of the family has been, your grandmother is not to know, no one's to know.

Q: Kristin, how did you develop a sense of being Norwegian?

A: In ways that identified with being Norwegian and being Lutheran. Those two combinations were sometimes indistinguishable. As a child I internalized a tremendous amount of identity as being a Norwegian Lutheran.

Q: Did you consider your parents to be very religious?

A: Absolutely. Extremely religious. Full of doctrine and extremely, extremely rigid within their moral code.

Q: How did you experience your childhood and youth?

A: I think part of what has happened in my own experience has to do with birth order as well. I was the firstborn and also the first grandchild in the whole family. A tremendous amount of pressure was placed on that particular thing.

There was a tremendous expectation from at least two generations of how my life was to be lived, what was expected. It was sort of my role, my history, was laid out before I was aware of much of anything.

Q: Were you in touch with your own feelings?

A: Not really, because there was really nothing ever verbalized in our family. And being different in general—whether it's racial, class, or cultural—there was not a lot of toleration for differences.

Q: You were married and have three children, but are now divorced. How did your parents react?

A: There had already been a tremendous amount of fallout. It was hard to figure out which was worse, the stigma of divorce or the stigma of . . . Well, I know which was worse—homosexuality. But both of them were tremendously horrific for my parents.

Q: Is this interview difficult for you?

A: It's healing. It's always helpful in healing on my part in being able to talk to other people about it because I don't associate with the Norwegian community at all, don't associate with the Lutheran community at all.

Q: Do you still appreciate some aspects of your Norwegian heritage?

A: Yeah. There is something that is good about all of that, it's not that we can reject all of that either. So we still have our lutefisk and *lefse*.[93]

Anticlerical sentiments and indifference to church doctrine can overcome and transcend prejudice. Neal R. Holtan, born in 1947, grew up in the small town of Lake Mills, Iowa, in a strongly Norwegian district. His family has been in America since 1850, his great-great-grandfather having emigrated from Vik in Sogn. He is a successful, openly gay practicing physician in Minneapolis, where he lives together with his partner, Steve.

Q: What was it like to grow up in Lake Mills?

A: My overriding emotion is that I was very happy to leave there. I knew there was a bigger world out there.

Q: Were you aware of your Norwegian origin?

A: We definitely were aware of it. All the time! Both in the community and at home, but especially at home. My grandparents spoke Norwegian in their home, especially when they didn't want us to know what they were talking about. They got Norwegian newspapers. Everyone swore in Norwegian. And we had Norwegian food. And there were old stories.

Q: What were the stories about?

A: About old-timers. The first pioneers. My maternal grandfather had really old stories. His father was a tailor, and also a musician. He played the fiddle. And played at weddings and big events and grandpa would tell stories about those events.

Q: Did you grow up with certain expectations for behaviors that were Lutheran, Norwegian, or midwestern?

A: Well, we had an advantage because my mother's side of the family was very earthy and more peasant-type people. They made fun of those other people who were staler Norwegian Lutheran types.

Q: You indicated that you discovered a strong genetic determinant of your homosexuality by studying your family tree and discovering a large number of unmarried individuals—many bachelor uncles. When did you discover that you were gay?

A: Well, I think I heard and read other gay people say that they knew from the earliest time they had any conscious memory. And I think that was true for me too. And so it never really bothered me.

Q: Being an only son, how did your parents accept your homosexuality?

A: Well, I think they're typical of many parents. I don't know if this is a Norwegian-American thing, or just general, but they don't talk about sex. I think that's very Norwegian-American, at least from my experience. And I got a strong message from my mother, especially, and her whole extended family that they didn't really care.[94]

Concluding Remarks

While prejudice obviously can push individuals away from both family and ethnicity, this kind of experience was not an automatic or even typical response for gay and lesbian individuals. A large number of homosexual people, many more than can be included, volunteered to be interviewed; they reflected a variety of experiences with prejudice and ethnic relations. Interest expressed by their Norwegian-American relations in the research encouraged a large voluntary involvement. Many, of course, found Lutheran, and other religious affiliation, as well as ethnocentric Norwegian-American attitudes and practices, stultifying and oppressive, which is by no means limited to the gay and lesbian community. What may be termed "the bondage of tradition" related to cultural expectations obviously dictates behavior for most people. A majority of those interviewed, however, continued to treasure aspects of childhood ethnic traditions. In fact, gay and lesbian family members not infrequently become the family historians and cultivate an ancestral heritage with great passion. Psychologically, pursuing ancestral heritage obviously creates a sense of family and of belonging.

Andreas Jordahl Rhude, born in 1962, flies both the Norwegian and the gay rainbow flag in front of his house in Minneapolis as identifying markers (figure 28). He is a fourth-generation Norwegian American, serves as president of the Norwegian-American Genealogical Association, and is active in Norwegian-American affairs.

Q: How did you become interested in family history?

A: As I was growing up, our family—my

Figure 28. Norwegian flag with gay rainbow flag. Photograph by Andreas Jordahl Rhude.

parents—instilled this Norwegianness in us. We knew pretty much where the roots were in Norway, and my father's sister became interested in genealogy, I suppose at the same time when [Haley's] *Roots* came out. And so she dug into a couple of Rhude lines and wrote a couple of little books. So I became interested in that.

Q: How did your interest develop?

A: I decided to go to Norway and started taking Norwegian in college, which made me even more interested in my family history. And I decided, well, I'm going to go to Norway to live and experience what it is like and my heritage. I lived in Norway during the 1984–85 school year and started visiting some of the ancestral homes.

Q: Do you see any connection between your sexual orientation and interest in your family history?

A: I think I have run into other gay men that have this deep-set interest in learning about their families. I have experienced others who have the same type of interest as I have. I really can't explain why. And I actually have thought about that. A lot of people do family history to legitimize their existence and try to find connections with royalty or some high altruistic thing. I am simply interested in knowing my family background. We are just plain folk. Most of us are.[95]

The tension between individualism and conformity is a central theme in considering the nature of American culture and character. Even Alexis de Tocqueville noted in the 1830s this uniquely American practice of joining voluntary societies and the moderating influence of small communities on individualism: "Thus, not only does democracy make every man forget his ancestors, but it hides his descendants and separates his contemporaries from him."

Tocqueville claims, furthermore, "it throws him back forever upon himself alone, and threatens in the end to confine him entirely within the solitude of his own heart." Robert N. Bellah and his coauthors in the bestseller *Habits of the Heart* decry in the Tocquevillean tradition the passing of the strong ethnic ties that vanish as Americans move into the middle class. They invoke ethnicity as an example of community. They speak of communities of memory constituted by the past: "ethnic and racial communities, each with its own heroes and heroines." Their solution for American life is that people should belong to a community not of their choosing but one they are born into, a community of memory, where people inherit a commitment to traditional ties. If they cannot have such a community, Bellah insists, the second best thing would be for people to return to the church. The oppressive nature of automatic membership suggested above is not considered by Bellah and his coauthors. The postethnic voluntary dimension of selecting and creating one's own social networks as well as ethnic identity is here overlooked and underestimated in their discussion of "the habits of the heart that sustain individualism and commitment." They also neglect, to quote Rupert Wilkinson, "the sheer vitality of association that comes from working at it out of fear of being isolated." It is the essential contradiction in American culture between individuality and community. Kimberly Lerohl expressed the conflict: "I think we tend to surround ourselves with people who mirror us and affirm us. And I don't feel like I need to be affirmed as a Norwegian. Not in the United States."[96]

CHAPTER 4

Perspectives on the American Dream

Pilgrim's Progress

Social mobility, an improvement in the status and living conditions of the descendants of the immigrants, is the most striking fact of immigrant history. Often the progress was painfully slow, almost not visible from one generation to the next. Many children, and even grandchildren, lived in the same impoverished circumstances as their immigrant forebears had. Some immigrants became bitter because of a failure to realize the American Dream in their own lives. A disappointed immigrant of 1955 expressed that in her opinion "the first generation was sacrificed." "Very few had any dream fulfilled," she insisted, regardless of time of arrival, and she described herself as "an immigrant and second-rate citizen" who "got stuck" in America because she and her husband were too poor to return to Norway. In his classic study of social mobility, *Poverty and Progress*, Stephan Thernstrom tests the rags-to-riches theory and, indeed, concludes that in the nineteenth century there were few occupational opportunities for common laborers to attain middle-class status. Work opportunities varied over time as the character and needs of the American economy changed and as the composition of the individual immigrant groups shifted. In Boston, for instance, immigrants entered white-collar jobs in large numbers, so that by 1910 the ratio of immigrant to native—in the language of the census—middle class was 50 percent, and by 1950 it had risen to 65 percent. The immigrant middle class was, in other words, almost two-thirds as large proportionately as the native middle class. This impressive statistic does not distinguish between progress that may be attributed to the heightened level of skills and preparation over time of the individuals who comprised the foreign-born category and progress derived from the greater fluidity of the American social structure and the increased openness of economic channels.[1]

Entrance into a middle-class way of life and the security it gave are how success has been measured by most ethnic populations. Most immigrants tended to begin at the bottom, as in general they arrived with little capital and few skills with which to compete in an urban industrial society. Consequently, to chart the economic adjustment of newcomers requires a study of the rate, timing, and channels of mobility experienced by them. All ethnic groups exhibited some social mobility in time, and with pride could identify individuals among them who had attained wealth, power, and recognition in America. Progress varied greatly, however, from one nationality to another. In *The Other Bostonians,* for instance, Thernstrom documents the diverse ethnic experiences with the American myth of success between 1880 and 1970 in metropolitan Boston. In 1950 the chances were seven in ten that an immigrant in Boston held a blue-collar job. The most telling fact is, however, that the fractions of male manual laborers in the eight leading foreign-born groups actually ranged from 46 to 85 percent.

Thernstrom looked at foreign-born men aged forty-five or older. They would all be in the late stages of their careers. Less than half of the men of British or Russian Jewish origin worked as manual laborers. The Irish were at the very bottom of the occupational ladder in 1950, as they had been in 1880; Italian-born men resembled the Irish but were a bit ahead of them in occupational profile. Also strongly clustered in blue-collar occupations were Swedes, Poles, and French Canadians, but in a much stronger position than the Italians and the Irish because they had greater access to better jobs within both the blue-collar and white-collar categories. The Germans were placed between the overall immigrant average and the British and Russian pattern.

The sons of these immigrant fathers moved into the middle class at impressive rates. The differentials narrowed among the various ethnic groups in the second generation, even though differences existed. The achievements of the sons of Russian Jews were the most extraordinary. The concentration of Italian and Irish youths continued in unskilled laboring jobs, although more of the second-generation Irish than the Italian found employment in white-collar occupations. Polish youth were ahead of the Italians in white-collar jobs. Second-generation Swedish men in middle-class occupations were above the Irish, and above the Swedes again were the Germans and the English. Only among Italians and French Canadians did less than one-third of the second generation enter the middle class.

Differences in occupational achievement relate to such variables as ethnic origin and cultural idiosyncrasies, religious affiliation, and group cohesion as well as discrimination, strong families, and what Thernstrom labels "background handicaps" for those who faced the barriers of illiteracy, inability to speak English, lack of vocational skills, and ignorance of the urban way of life. Residential segregation represented another obstacle for some ethnic groups. Protestant or Jewish affiliation appeared to encourage social mobility. A relatively high educational achievement and income position for second-generation Swedish men compared to Irish youth, even though fathers in both groups had little schooling, suggests that a cultural difference entered as a second determinant.[2]

In his study of Swedish immigrants in Worcester, Massachusetts, Hans Norman looked at the rate of mobility until 1915. A large number of the Swedes worked in the iron and ceramic industries. They began arriving in 1869, when a group of ceramic workers arrived from Sweden; around 1900 the Swedes numbered some ten to twelve thousand individuals. Many of the Swedish laborers in the iron industry became foremen, and typically those who advanced had experience from iron works in Sweden. Skills learned at home worked to their advantage in the new environment. Other Swedish immigrants in the lower middle class, with experience as bookkeepers and office workers in Sweden, started their own businesses after working in jobs in Worcester for a time. Norman's study provides further evidence of the importance of resources such as training and experience that immigrants had upon ar-

rival in America. Many immigrants advanced well beyond their position at home, indicating a relationship between migration and social mobility. As a rule, migrants had a higher career mobility than those who remained in the home community. Swedish sources permit a detailed analysis of internal migrations and their relationship to career advancement. Conclusions about social mobility become somewhat more speculative and anecdotal in regard to the situation in America, however. Settling in an industrial city such as Worcester and having experience gained at home, as stated above, obviously assisted advancement that would not have occurred save for the new location. In general, like the immigrants in Boston studied by Thernstrom, Swedish workers in Worcester did well in the American labor market and were overrepresented in the category of skilled workers.

That social mobility was the result of migration is more obvious, as Norman states, in the case of penniless Swedish immigrants in rural areas in the American Midwest, who, thanks to the provisions in the Homestead Act of 1862, became owners of 160 acres of farmland practically without any cost to themselves. Their social status was greatly improved. And it is natural to assume, he continues, that taking part in building a frontier community in North America would give influence and position to immigrants that they could never have enjoyed in the homeland. Their increased status was reflected in positions of influence within religious institutions such as the immigrant church or in the political arena within the township or county governance.[3]

The Norwegian-American Farmer

Comparative social mobility studies of Norwegian immigrants and later generations of Norwegian Americans are rare. General assumptions about upward advancement are nonetheless regularly made. "By the 1970s," write Leonard Dinnerstein and David Reimers without any direct reference, "Norwegian Americans had done well and had generally moved into the middle class, with many becoming successful businessmen, skilled workers, and professionals."[4]

Information about the distribution of occupations according to nativity groups was first reported in the federal census for 1870. In the decennial occupational enumerations of the foreign stock—the immigrants and their children—that followed, reports appeared with varying detail. E. P. Hutchinson's *Immigrants and Their Children, 1850–1950* is a useful compendium of these reports. The figures for Sweden and Norway were combined in the nineteenth century. The 1900 census lists the Norwegians separately and concluded that Norwegian immigrant males were most attracted to agriculture, where they exceeded all other immigrants in relative concentration. "The sons of the immigrant farmers," the census states, "were even more strongly agricultural, but in agriculture had moved into the

farm laborer category." On a relative basis the second-generation men were even less employed in manufacturing occupations than the first generation. In the previous decade a great expansion of women employed in agriculture also occurred, principally in the laborer category. The number of agricultural laborers increased greatly as a whole in this period.[5]

Moving from farm ownership to being an agricultural laborer obviously represented a downward trend in social status in the second generation. In 1900 farm laborers comprised about a third of the farm population in the farm states. Land was becoming less available, and achieving farm ownership in the American Midwest was becoming increasingly difficult. The second generation had to reconcile itself to being tenant farmers or farmhands unless they moved to new agricultural communities or diversified agricultural production. They did both in large numbers. In these years many young people moved from the upper Midwest to join or create farming communities in the Canadian prairie provinces. "Norwegians were a mighty force in the agricultural development of the upper Mississippi Valley," Theodore Saloutos writes, "and together with Swedes, Germans, and other ethnic groups helped replenish the national larder." Members of the second generation joined the front ranks of this operation. Economic differentials did not distinguish the immigrant farmers and their sons and daughters from Americans.[6]

As recently as 1950, Norwegians were still

notably more employed as farmers compared with all foreign-born men, although they had diversified greatly occupationally, as one would expect. Also, in comparison with other female immigrants, Norwegian-born women had more employment in agriculture and less in all other occupational groups. The second generation, men and women, had the highest proportion among farmers and thereafter among farm laborers. A distinct improvement by 1950 in the occupational status of the Norwegian-American farmer in the second generation is thus indicated by the greater representation in the farm-owner category. The Norwegian stock, the first and second generations, were, therefore, still heavily involved in agricultural production and a rural way of life at mid-century.[7]

The image of the toiling wholesome farmer, of the men and women who broke the sod and made the western plains blossom, is treasured as evidence of belonging to an immigrant group that helped to build America. "Of strong and rugged physique, inured to hardship, industrious and energetic and possessing courage, will power and infinite patience they faced alike the primeval wilderness and boundless prairies and by sheer force tamed the wild nature for the permanent blessing of mankind," wrote Minnesota Railroad and Warehouse Commissioner O. P. B. Jacobson in 1921. Such was the prevailing view, cherished by later generations and given the force of accepted historical reality. This romanticized vision might under certain circumstances even

have been used against ethnic groups whose American experience came later and was urban. Their contributions and birthright to America were not as easily recognized.[8]

In 1900, 50 percent of all Norwegian-American men were listed under "agricultural pursuits"; 14 percent of Norwegian-American women fell under the same category. In both cases these percentages were ahead of all other ethnic groups by a wide margin; Danish men came closest with 42 percent, and Bohemian women with 10 percent. By 1980 men of Norwegian ancestry still were ahead of all other ethnic groups under the category "farming, forestry and fishing," 8 percent being so employed. Two percent of Norwegian-American women were classified under this category, tying with several other ethnic groups. By 1990 these figures had fallen for men who gave Norwegian as their first ethnicity to 5.8 percent. This is still a higher percentage than for the American male labor force as a whole; only 4.5 percent of all employed men were engaged in one of the primary economic pursuits of farming, forestry, or fishing. Sociologists Stanley Lieberson and Mary Waters maintain that differences in occupational patterns among specific white ethnic groups, whether "old" or "new," are interesting but rather subtle. There are, they say, continuities in the occupational concentrations that were so obvious earlier in the century. For the most part, however, socioeconomic inequalities for these population contingents are both relatively minor and unrelated to the earlier patterns of ethnic inequality. Comparative statistics for the Norwegian-American group certainly support such a conclusion. It is nevertheless of interest to note that traditions associated with farming and rural living continue in the 1990s to characterize Norwegian Americans more than they do any other white ethnic population. A perception of wholesome ruralism is, of course, an exaggeration in terms of the numbers of Norwegians currently residing outside urban areas. The notion of a special rural bond and the values and ideals associated with it is, however, a persistent legacy and a source of ethnic pride and self-identification.[9]

In the upper Midwest Norwegian-American farmers engaged in a variety of agricultural strategies. In Wisconsin, most specifically in the western part of the state, tobacco cultivation became a special ethnic activity. There existed a clear relationship between Norwegian-American identity and tobacco growing. In a 1970 study of tobacco production, Karl Raitz offered a cultural explanation for the motivation of Norwegian-American farmers in southwestern Wisconsin to produce crops since there appeared to be no direct economic link between profit and tobacco cultivation.[10]

In a later anthropological study, Robert Ibarra and Arnold Strickon expanded on and corrected some of the findings made by Raitz. They identify a farm strategy that combines tobacco growing with dairying, a viable alternative to the modern straight dairy production.

In the long run, the authors conclude, the traditionalists seemed to be better prepared to survive the farm crisis of the early 1980s than those who chose the alternative of acquiring more debt. The success of the tobacco-dairy strategy is connected, they insist, to a Norwegian-American rural culture related to the family farm and the personal and community values that surround it. The traditional Norwegian-American family farm has survived in western Wisconsin, the authors state, in a random response to environmentally selective pressures generated by both the marketplace and government policy. A loss of market and a change in price support and allotment programs by the government would, however, change the equation and bring new challenges. As a symbol of Norwegian-American identity, tobacco has in any event become part of the culture of western Wisconsin.[11]

Leland Edward Lewison was born in 1947 in western Wisconsin. He is a third-generation Norwegian American, his grandfather having arrived as a child of four in 1866, settling with his parents first in Dane County before moving on to Vernon County in the western part of the state. They hailed from the Luster district in Sogn on the west coast of Norway, where many of the people in the area have their roots. The family has owned the farm near the town of Viroqua for about one hundred years and cultivated tobacco on it. Lewison took over the farm in 1970 and operates it together with his wife, Laurie Jill, and their two sons,

Mitchell and Gregory. His experience is on a traditional Norwegian-American family farm.

Q: There is a tradition of growing tobacco back to your grandfather's time.

A: Yes, oh, yes.

Q: Did you grow up thinking that tobacco was what everyone grew?

A: Well, yah. I don't recall not growing tobacco or helping in tobacco since my early childhood.

Q: What was it like growing up on a farm where tobacco was the main cash crop?

A: Well, I guess in my childhood I remember the summers as getting out of school and helping hay and with the tobacco. When I was little, I guess there weren't quite as many opportunities for children as there are now.

Q: Do you still have a dairy operation?

A: No, we discontinued the dairy operation in 1990 and raised more tobacco.

Q: As a child, how did you help on the farm?

A: When I was little, I used to help grow tobacco plants. When I got to be ten, twelve, I used to plant tobacco on the tobacco planter.

Q: How did your responsibilities change?

A: Well, I guess that we used to help pull tobacco, which is not a lot of fun. I didn't cut tobacco until I was older, because they were always afraid you would hurt yourself. But I guess by the time I was twelve or thirteen, I was cutting tobacco. Working in the shed was my primary job as I got older. I used to hang most of the tobacco. Probably from age fourteen, I've hung tobacco.

Q: What was the next step?

A: Well, after it hung in the shed, then, since harvest, it cured. You know, they call it the curing process. It cures out. The leaves hopefully turn a nice golden brown color, and the stems dry down so that there's no moisture in the stems anymore, or very little.

Q: What happened to the leaves?

A: They were put in bales weighing approximately 45 to 50 pounds and taken to market.

Q: When did you begin to grow your own tobacco?

A: I guess probably back in the middle sixties on my own. I had some tobacco to pay my way through college.

Q: Was that a common thing for people to do?

A: Yes, if you lived on a family farm, a lot of kids had their own plot of tobacco. I may have had some even in high school, so I could buy a car. I mean tobacco paid for a lot of things.[12]

Norwegians exhibited a preference for forested parts, which were perhaps reminiscent of the homeland's scenery, and became hill farmers in great numbers in the states of Wisconsin and Minnesota. Roots were established in the family farm in the pioneering spirit of settling new land. In the heavily Norwegian Goodhue County, Lloyd Voxland, born in 1924 and a fourth-generation Norwegian American on both sides, and his wife, Geraldine Larson Voxland, born in 1923 in Mobridge, South Dakota, and a third-generation Norwegian American on her mother's side, live as retired farmers on the Voxland family homestead, the so-called old Aaby farm, the first one to be settled in the area in 1854. "It gives pride in your family," Lloyd Voxland stated, "to live on the farm of the first family." He will, however, be the last of the family to do so, since there is no son to take over the farm, and none of their three daughters has married a farmer.[13]

Possession of land was the main attraction as Norwegian farmers overcame the fear of the windswept grassland and claimed land in western Minnesota and the Dakotas. Settlement of the land created strong heroic images cherished by later generations. "It gives me great pride to know," Geraldine Voxland said, "that my ancestors were among the pioneers on the prairies of South Dakota." Because of the minor classics of Ole E. Rølvaag and even Simon Johnson's dramatic portrayal of the semiarid northern plains in *From Fjord to Prairie* (English translation, 1916), the most powerful images are of the pioneers on the great western plains, in "the giants' country," as Rølvaag's fictional accounts suggest. Even though Russian Germans may be accorded major credit for bringing the wheat culture to the region, Norwegian farmers adapted quickly to the demands of grassland spring wheat production. They succeeded, although a heavy dependence on small grains put them at the mercy of un-

certain rainfalls, and consequently they experienced fluctuating crop yields and farm incomes. From generation to generation, they displayed a remarkable staying power.[14] The following interview suggests the continuity of loyalty to an inherited way of life.

David J. Haslekaas, born in 1968, and Jan M. Bowles, born in 1973, were married October 14, 1995. They grew up on farms in the Red River valley of North Dakota and together will operate a farm south of Milton in Walsh County that was acquired by David's great-grandfather in 1887 under the Homestead Act. Continuous ownership by the same family since then was recognized in 1987 by an award designating the farm a "North Dakota Centennial Farm." Residential stability and loyalty to the family farm are highlighted in the centennial award program; numerous farms proudly display its insignia. David is a fourth-generation Norwegian American. Jan is Icelandic on her mother's side, and Irish and English on her father's. Both were raised Lutheran, and perhaps for that reason chose to become part owners of the Hitterdal church next to the farm so that it would not be torn down after services were discontinued. David's family had been a part of the church for about one hundred years. There was consequently a strong sentimental and cultural attachment to the church structure and its symbolic value as a center of a once thriving rural Norwegian-American community. Even the name, which was the community in the Telemark district of

Norway where David's grandmother came from, communicates an ethnic connection.[15]

Q: How important was the church growing up?

DAVID: When we were growing up, church was very important. Every Sunday was devoted to going to church.

Q: Are the people here still aware of the connection to Hitterdal?

DAVID: I believe not as much. We know where we have come from.

Q: Is this the kind of environment you would like your own children to grow up in?

DAVID: I think that I had a really good childhood, and I would like it carried on. Having a Scandinavian background has shaped who I am.

Q: Jan, in your home did you observe any traditions from your ethnic background?

JAN: One thing that comes to mind is the annual August 2 parade in Milton. There was one float in particular that was a Viking ship as long as I can remember.

Q: Was that Icelandic?

JAN: Yes, I believe Milton has one of the oldest Icelandic churches.

Q: What kind of values do you attach to your Lutheran upbringing?

JAN: I think what comes to mind is how hardworking and honest you have to be. You may entertain thoughts of cheating or stealing, but you never would. You are expected to show up for work and work. That was the main value instilled in us.

Q: What would a typical year be like for you growing up on a farm?

DAVID: Growing up on a farm in North Dakota, we start the farming season, the main part, in the spring, in April or May. As a kid, we had a job of picking rocks out of the field. That was the hardest job. Later you grew up and got to drive the tractor, which was the fun thing to do. In the spring we had to sow the crops. We grew basically small grains on our farm, wheat and barley, durum wheat.

JAN: I guess as far as the girls on the farm, we would always help mom. We would take the meals out to the field. When I grew up, they would come in for lunch.

Q: When did the two of you decide to go into farming?

DAVID: I think when you work on a farm, you are brought up that way.

Q: But most young people leave the farm. Why did you decide to stay?

DAVID: I just love the work.

Q: Does it concern you that the family farm is being threatened?

DAVID: Very much so.

Q: Did you feel any pressure because of tradition to operate the family farm?

DAVID: No, it was totally my choice. I am very proud of my history and tradition, but I think that there are always choices a person can make. You can't be forced into doing what you don't want. I think the tradition is there and helps us to make choices.

Q: Does the fact that your families have been here a long time help define who you are?

JAN: I believe so. Growing up in a Scandinavian country, the work ethic is better. I enjoy the people so much more, not just ours, but our neighbors. They have strong backgrounds, too.

Q: How would you feel if you had to sell the farm?

DAVID: That would be very hurtful. I don't think I could do that. It is so much a part of our family. It has been passed down from one generation to the next, and I hope that I can pass it down to a son or daughter.[16]

The Norwegian bachelor farmer is not a fictional creation of the writer and performer Garrison Keillor, but rather represents an ever increasing reality in many midwestern farming communities. David Ralph Erickstad, born in 1945, grew up on a family farm homesteaded in 1883 by his great-grandfather near the village of Starkweather in Ramsey County, North Dakota, as the oldest of seven brothers and sisters. Erickstad operates land from the original homesteaders as a bachelor farmer. He is a fourth-generation Norwegian American with roots in Jølster in the Sognefjord area of Norway. In his interview, Erickstad expressed, like David and Jan Haslekaas, representative and commonly expressed views about a rural way of life and the role of ethnic heritage. Their convictions nearly reaffirm the idealistic predictions of Paul Hjelm-Hansen, the Norwegian "discoverer" of the Red River valley in the late 1860s, that hard work on the land would prevent Norwegian immigrants from being destroyed by American materialism and would preserve the strength of the Norwegian character and develop high moral qualities.[17]

Q: Are there many single people operating farms alone in this area?

A: Yes, there are several single people that are living on farms and farming around this community.

Q: Are they also of Norwegian descent?

A: Many of them are, yes.

Q: Among the Norwegian traditions of your childhood you mention "julebukking." Can you remember that?

A: Oh, yes. People would get together during holiday time, and a bunch would drive to a home and sing Christmas carols and then maybe be invited in for lunch, and then the people from that home would join them and they would go to the next home, and they would go into the early morning hours of the night.

Q: What ethnic events are still observed in the area?

A: Well, one thing is Syttende mai up in Fairdale, North Dakota. They celebrate every year and have parades. People get together in a festive mood and have food and probably a dance and a band. I even played in and directed a band up there one time during the celebration. They have Norwegian flags and so on.

So I just know that it's Norwegian independence day, so here we are in America celebrating that.

Q: Has the Lutheran church been important to you?

A: Yes, I have been very active in church, and I've held many of the offices of the church.

Q: What are your political convictions?

A: Well, I would say I'm pretty much a conservative in a lot of areas.

Q: Do you associate specific values with your Norwegian heritage?

A: First of all I think I should say that Norwegians gave us a very stoic outlook on life. And I think it's because they had a very hard life, especially to begin with, and they struggled very much. But, ah, they had a vision, and they held to their vision, and they always strove to better themselves. So they didn't show much emotion. I never saw my father hardly ever cry or show affection much, that type of thing. But they were caring and very good people and very generous and were loving in their actions, I would say.

Q: Did you have specific material goals in life?

A: Well, I wanted to have my own farm and my own home and to be able to enjoy growing things. I grew up on a farm, and I worked for my father as a young man, and I've operated my own farm in my twenty-second year now. I would like to see the farmland continue in the family, and I have very close ties to the soil as a farmer. I feel that the land will provide for you if you care for it. I almost look at it as a heritage and almost as a birthright if you take care of it and don't think it should be given up.

Q: Can you see any direct consequence of your Norwegian heritage on the farms in the area?

A: Yes. I would say definitely there was a work ethic. And really the survival and prosperity of the farms has been based upon that.[18]

Fishing on the Pacific Coast

To assume that immigrants looked for scenery and landscapes that reminded them of their old-country home communities in their search for land in America may be a romantic concept. Economic resources and availability of property may have been greater determining factors. In his classic study *The Making of an American Community*, Merle Curti makes several observations to explain the poorer showing in the value of the farms owned by Norwegian immigrants in the Trempealeau valley in western Wisconsin than of people from other countries. Norwegians arrived with poorer resources, came after the most fertile prairie land had been taken by American- and British-born settlers, and at the start had less property. Curti does, however, concede that they may have preferred the more hilly and wooded land, of less value agriculturally, on which they settled. "Certainly," he writes, "one sees how these wooded slopes would attract a people from the narrow valleys and mountains of Norway."

And, as he suggests, their being used to small farms at home may have led them initially to choose a smaller acreage.[19]

Norwegian settlement in the Pacific Northwest and Alaska may certainly have been influenced by conditions described in 1906 by one O. H. Skotheim, then living in Albert Lea, Minnesota: "People generally have a deep longing for our wonderland around Puget Sound. . . . our wonderful west coast . . . with its multitude of resources, its constant bewitching power for the imaginative and industrious, its alluring beauty for the nature lover, and its promises of a brighter and richer future than any other part of America has offered any generation that has ever lived."[20] The large numbers of immigrants who made their home on the West Coast, moving from the Midwest or directly from Norway, hailed to a large extent from the western or northern parts of the country. They would consequently discover much that was familiar in the landscape and in modes of livelihood. It could even be claimed that they transferred a Norwegian coastal culture to the Pacific Coast.

Norwegians were active participants in several branches of the fishing industry, in particular the cod fishery in Alaska, the herring and fish oil industries, and catching salmon as trollers and trap fishermen off the coast of Washington and Alaska. They had experience as deep-sea fishermen and became the principal developers in the second phase of the evolution of the halibut fishery after the turn of the century. More than any other fishery,

halibut bestowed a special ethnic identity. "I'm just an ignorant Norwegian halibut fisherman," is a typical self-deprecating remark.

In the spring the large fleet sailed from the colorful Fishermen's Dock in Seattle to spend the season in Alaska. A fleet, consisting of fewer boats, was also stationed in Alaska. Smaller halibut schooners fished for shorter periods along the coast of Washington. By the 1920s Norwegian Americans were the dominant group in the halibut industry as fishermen and as boat owners (figure 29). A. K. Larssen estimated that 95 percent of the fishermen and even more of the owners of halibut schooners in 1920 were Norwegian immigrants. In 1940 it was estimated that of the approximately three thousand fishermen who manned the four hundred American halibut vessels, more than nine persons in ten were Norwegian, though fewer of them were Norwegian-born. The sons of the immigrant halibut fishermen were entering the industry, and in time were joined by grandsons and sons-in-law. The equipment became more sophisticated and much more expensive. Norwegian Americans are no longer dominant, however, as an ethnic group in the industry, which is declining in importance. Statistics show the downward trend in the halibut industry within the regulatory areas for commercial fishing along the coast of Alaska, British Columbia, and Washington; the total annual allotments dropped from about 74 million tons in the top year of 1988 to a little less than 44 million tons in 1995, making the

Figure 29. The halibut schooner Attu *in the 1980s at Fishermen's Dock in Seattle, Washington; the schooner was previously owned by the author's father, Alf Lowell. Photograph by Odd S. Lovoll.*

halibut season short, as the quotas were quickly filled.[21]

Norwegian Americans still participate in halibut and cod fishing, salmon trolling, and crab fishing in Alaska and elsewhere. Michael A. Ness, born in Seattle, November 26, 1941, is the son of an immigrant halibut fisherman, Andreas L. Ness, who came to Seattle from Sunnmøre, Norway, in 1930 and worked as a halibut fisherman his whole life. Michael's mother, Ingrid Widsteen, was born in Seattle of Norwegian immigrant parents. His job experience is rather typical for someone growing up in a Norwegian-American social environment where fishing was a common livelihood.

Q: Were you aware of your Norwegian background growing up?

A: Yes, very much so. I grew up in a Norwegian neighborhood in Ballard and had many Norwegian friends. At home we had all kinds of Norwegian food. I was proud of being Norwegian.

Q: How was your schooling?

A: At James Monroe Junior High School and Ballard High School there were so many Norwegians that I thought everyone was Norwegian.

Q: When did you begin fishing?

A: I began at age eighteen. My dad owned the *City of Seattle*. He also owned the *Valiant*, a sardine boat. I flew up to Alaska to fish herring. I fished herring for five seasons and two seasons crab-fished with my father. We converted the boat to crabbing in 1966 but sold it after the 1967 season.

Q: Have you fished ever since?

A: No, I had two years of military service. After that, I got a job with Pete Ness on his boat *Sylvia.* Since then I have been a halibut fisherman.

Q: Have you made a good living?

A: Fishing was poor when I began. We fished off Vancouver Island. It was meager fishing and depressed prices. So thought Alaskan halibut might be better. Got a job on a boat going to Alaska, but also there "scraggy" [poor]. I came home in October after five trips. I made more than a common laborer.

Q: How was it later?

A: Prices went up in the early seventies, and more boats came in. As a result the trips started to be shorter and shorter since the total quota was fished up fast. Now there is an individual quota for each boat. Toward the end of the 1980s, the fishing season was short.

Q: Is halibut fishing all you do?

A: No, I always have other seasonal jobs that fit into the halibut season. Money is not an overriding concern. I also fish black cod. No one fishes only halibut any longer.

Q: Is your wife Norwegian?

A: No, I married Sarah Maxwell, who is of Irish and Polish origin, in 1971. She was Catholic, and our two children, Julie and Greg, were raised Catholic.

Q: Are the children conscious of being Norwegian?

A: Oh, yes. Sarah makes *fattigmann, krumkake,* and other goodies she learned from my mom. The children are proud of being part Norwegian. Julie is a member of Sons of Norway, and they attended the Christmas service at Sunnmørslaget this year.[22]

Norwegian-American fishermen played a major part as well in the development of the king-crab fishing industry over the past several decades. Its high point was reached around 1978–80, when 150 million pounds were harvested annually. As a result, a tremendous expansion in the fleet took place. Then in the early 1980s there was a total drop in the industry. Reduced allotments made it less profitable, and a dramatic decline in the king-crab population greatly reduced the importance of this industry. The king-crab season was closed in 1994 and 1995, and a brief season of a few days in 1996 yielded only from 7 to 8 million pounds.[23]

John K. Sjong, born in 1936, is a successful recent Norwegian immigrant in the Pacific coast fishing industry. He grew up in Sykkylven in the Sunnmøre district of western Norway, a region well represented among fishermen in Seattle. Sjong emigrated in 1960 and began king-crab fishing in Alaska in 1964. Sjong became an owner of a king-crab boat for the first time in 1968 with other partners, and in 1971 he purchased another boat with his partner Konrad Uri, a second-generation Norwegian American. Together they formed Trans Pacific Industries in 1973, which experienced a phenomenal growth. The decline in the king-crab fishing made them diversify to cod fishing in 1980. The company was the most notable example of Norwegian activity in the fish-processing field as it expanded its cod operations during the 1980s, and was the first in the United States to start factory trawling. At one time the company employed six hundred people, had six factory trawlers, and did king-crab fishing in addition. The company's *Arctic Trawler* was the largest fishing vessel in the United States. It harvested cod in the Bering Sea, cleaned and filleted it immediately, and packed and froze it for the American market. In 1989 Sjong sold the factory trawlers; he retained two small crab boats.

In his interview he told about his career and family life, and related his views on Norway and Norwegian immigrants. These are representative of an immigrant who has had a successful encounter with American capitalism; they are as well expressive of Norwegian-American ethnicity in their critical attitude toward the modern Norwegian social-democratic welfare system. Many postwar immigrants justified their move to America by rejecting the prevailing political currents at home.

Q: Were most of your employees Norwegian?

A: Factory trawling got many people from Sunnmøre who came to work. There was a big influx of people.

Q: Which Norwegian organizations do you belong to?

A: I belong to the Norwegian-American Chamber of Commerce, which meets monthly, the Norwegian Commercial Club, Sons of Norway, and Sunnmørslaget.

Q: Did the people from Sunnmøre join Sunnmørslaget?

A: Sunnmørslaget is no longer so active. Not so many joined. The same people do things like they did fifty years ago and don't see any reason to change. There are no new ways of doing things. The president does what the older ladies want.

Q: What do you think of the immigrant culture?

A: Being "square-head Vikings" is a part of Norwegian-American culture. You have to be able to laugh at yourself. If not, something is lost.

Q: Is your wife Norwegian?

A: Yes. I married Berit Ingebrigtsen in 1967. She came to America from Ålesund when she was ten or eleven. I hung out with people of Norwegian descent. We met at the Norway Center, which the Sons of Norway had downtown. We have three daughters.

Q: Are you a United States citizen?

A: Yes, I became a citizen in 1965. I had to, to be a captain. By that time I thought that this is where I wanted to be.

A: What are your political views?

Q: I am conservative. I think you should do for yourself. The Norwegian welfare state is sad. The work ethic is disappearing. Scandinavians in this country are considered good workers. They were used to hard work from home and helped later immigrants. Should not give extra privileges to people who come from other countries. Norwegians here have worked hard to get where they are.[24]

In the Urban Economy

The break from the primary economic pursuits in farming, forestry, and fishing affected the rural communities in varying degrees and at different rates. The agricultural communities gave up their youth to the lure of the city. The rural young people there joined city-bred Norwegian Americans and newcomers from the old homeland. They moved from occupations such as farming, fishing, and logging. Most fishermen, of course, already resided in a built-up area and were a part of an urban economy, as was the case with men who plied the great inland lakes or were in maritime activity in American coastal waters, although they made their livelihood beyond the direct influence of the city. The economic niche that an ethnic group occupied provided a sense of identity. The Norwegian tobacco and wheat farmers are such symbolic links to the past, and, as has been seen, they still provide viable reinforcing ethnic attributes, as do the halibut fishermen and mariners of many kinds. In the Norwegian-American blue-collar urban neighborhoods, carpentry and construction served as descriptive occupational pursuits, engaged in not only by Norwegian men but Scandinavian men in general. For women, the Scandinavian domestic provided a nearly stereotypical image. These traditional Norwegian-American livelihoods define for later-generation Norwegian-American middle-class suburbanites a historical context for their ethnicity as it relates to the group's American experience. It was their parents, grandparents, and even earlier generations who in this manner through hard labor and faith in the American work ethic secured their own privileged social position. Increasingly in the 1920s, a suburban home, not an idyllic family farm, became the ideal promoted by the Norwegian-American community. The institutional and social network of the Norwegian-American urban enclaves eroded considerably during that decade. Suburbanization caused a residential scattering that made it difficult to sustain an organized ethnic community life. Its images, symbols, and historical connotations as identifying agents were, however, regularly transmitted to the new environment and to later generations.[25]

Evidence of attachment to the Norwegian-American past is found in the form of ethnic decorations, family albums, photographic portraits, and mementos that grace the homes of these latter-day suburbanites. These constitute shrines to a Norwegian-American heritage. Descriptions of displays of this kind were consistently included in the returned questionnaires from Norwegian Americans of all generations and in all parts of the country. The most mentioned items were old ancestral photographs and Bibles. For example, Pam Aakhus, a fourth-generation Norwegian American born in 1959, writes from Lakewood, Colorado: "We have pictures of old *norske* relatives, hand-carved wooden objects such as toys and a butter mold, lots of *rosemaling*, and Norwegian trunks."[26]

The larger question is whether traditional livelihoods had an impact on career and occupational choices made by later generations. In the more stable blue-collar neighborhoods, continuity was evident within the cultural entity in which people lived, as son followed father in particular trades and industries, but, obviously, no one description of an ethnic working-class community can be viewed as normative. Many variables determined the persistence of traditional ethnic modes of making a living in subsequent generations. There were great variations in rates of assimilation, in discrimination by the larger society, and in cultural and religious circumstances within the various ethnic communities. In a study of the Norwegian neighborhoods in Chicago before 1930, it was obvious that ethnic identity and community pride reinforced occupational identity.[27]

For post–World War II immigrants who arrived without professional training, the traditional immigrant trades working with wood and paint again became a common means of making a living. An identifying ethnic occupational experience gave a sense of continuity. Fellow Norwegians were still employers and might even decide who could get work through control of local unions.

Finn Gjertsen was born in 1922 in Sandefjord, Norway, then a center for the Norwegian whaling expeditions to the South Atlantic. When only seventeen, like many young men in the area, he sailed on one of the whalers. He was abroad when German forces occupied Norway in 1940. The next year he came to Brooklyn. In 1942 he joined the U.S. Army, eventually being transferred to the Norwegian-speaking Ninety-Ninth Infantry Battalion. He now resides on Staten Island.

Q: What did you do after the war?

A: It was difficult to find a job. I began painting houses. My brother and I started our own painting business.

Q: Is that how you have made a living?

A: No, in 1950 I got into the dock-builders union through a friend. It was difficult to get in if you didn't know anyone. It was then very hard work. The Norwegian foremen were tough.

Q: What organizations do you belong to?

A: I am a member of the retiree club of the United Brotherhood of Carpenters. They are mostly dock builders. We have a short meeting and a long lunch. Perhaps three-fourths of the members are Norwegian.[28]

The experience of a woman immigrant was different from that of a man coming to America in the postwar era; the opportunities for employment were restricted for those who did not have special skills. Kari Hesthag, born in 1924 in Lillesand on the southern coast of Norway, immigrated to Brooklyn in 1951. As was common in south-coast communities, her father sailed on a Norwegian ship as captain and was prevented from returning to Norway during the years of German occupation. The connections to the Brooklyn colony were well established.

Q: Why did you come to America?

A: I went over to stay for two years. These two years have become forty-four. I had an aunt here, and my thought at that time was to earn enough money for a car and for a fur coat and then go home.

Q: What work did you do?

A: I had decided to take a house job because I thought I could earn more money then and live in Manhattan. Other people in Norway who had taken house jobs in Brooklyn said you earned much more money with that. My aunt went with me to find a job, and I was there for three weeks.

Q: Why did you quit?

A: Yes, only three weeks, because the man there—the husband wasn't, wasn't . . .

Q: Did he get fresh?

A: Yes. So . . . I think that this had happened also before. They were wealthy people. So the wife gave me three weeks extra pay. And after that, I started to work in an office in a shipping firm.

Q: What was Brooklyn like when you came?

A: Everything was kind of Norwegian to me at that time . . . on Eighth Avenue. Norwegian was spoken on the streets, you know, and in the stores. And . . . it was like you were home in a way.[29]

A Socioeconomic Profile

O. M. Norlie maintained in 1925 that Norwegian Americans were integrated at all levels in the American workforce in percentages equal to the group's relative size. He assumed that Norwegians constituted 2 percent of the American population and hence would constitute 2 percent of any "line of work" listed in the census. He uses as an example the 127,270 clergymen counted in the 1920 census, of which 2 percent would be 2,545. Norlie finds support for his calculations by the fact that "Norwegian Lutherans had 1,554 clergymen in 1921, and there were many Norwegian pastors in the Reformed denominations." Using the same formula, Norlie arrived at a number of 2,900 for Norwegian-American physicians, and 1,292 for civil engineers, concluding that he could continue "down the whole list of occupations." Norlie's somewhat questionable calculations were based on the supposition that Norwegian Americans of all generations were fully assimilated into the American economic system by the 1920s. In this "American Period," as Norlie defines the years 1890–1925, he included six generations counting from 1830 to 1920, though the sixth, according to his calculations, had only twelve members. The two first generations were, of course, a matter of record; the later generations are more specula-

Table 14. Occupations of respondents to questionnaires distributed in 1995–96

Occupation	Number	Percentage
Agriculture/Fishing	383	4.92
Blue collar	398	5.11
Professional service	4,946	63.56
Retired	898	11.54
At home	820	10.54
No answer	175	2.25
Does not apply	162	2.08
Total responses	7,782	100.00

Table 15. Occupational composition of first-ethnicity American-born Norwegians in the 1990 federal census

Occupation	Men (%)	Women (%)
Managerial	14.8	12.0
Professional specialty	12.1	20.0
Technical and sales	16.5	15.9
Administrative support including clerical	5.9	27.7
Service	7.7	15.7
Farming, forestry, and fishing	6.3	1.3
Precision production, craft, and repair	17.6	1.8
Operators, fabricators, and laborers	5.7	5.3

Note: These percentages are based on the total of 1,980,796 native persons sixteen years or older who gave Norwegian as their first ethnicity. Of these, 1,275,875 (684,352 men and 591,523 women) were employed in the civilian workforce and worked at least 35 or more hours a week; 4.4 percent of the civilian workforce was unemployed.

tive, though Norlie's estimates do not appear to be completely out of line. The third generation, then the largest, numbered, according to Norlie, 989,711 persons, whereas the first two combined were 1,023,225, the immigrant generation having declined from its peak in 1910 to 362,051. If we accept Norlie's figures, in 1920 there was a total Norwegian-American population of 2,168,355. In language usually reserved for an ethnic apologist, he sets forth self-congratulatory claims of belonging to "the most independent and individualistic people that history knows about," a people "who came here to work [and] teach their children the dignity of labor in any honest calling."[30]

Table 14 presents the occupations of 6,772 survey respondents, men and women, some of whom have changed livelihood more than once; others, listed as retired, gave their occupational and professional affiliation. The category "does not apply" includes mostly students. The table's information suggests a movement into the middle class while indicating occupational diversity, and thus the respondents are generally representative of the contemporary Norwegian-American population.

Using the figures in the 1990 federal census, it is possible to paint in broad strokes a portrait showing level of income and occupational profile for both men and women of defined ethnic origins (tables 15, 16, and 17). The census categories of "blue" collar and "white" collar and "agriculture and fishing" are comparable to those employed in the questionnaire survey; the census has no listing for "at home" or "retired."

Table 16. Occupational composition of Norwegian-born persons in the 1990 federal census who immigrated before 1980

Occupation	Men (%)	Women (%)
Managerial	23.4	12.6
Professional specialty	18.5	18.6
Technical and sales	15.2	18.4
Administrative support including clerical	3.7	25.3
Service	3.9	16.6
Farming, forestry, and fishing	3.7	1.1
Precision production, craft, and repair	21.4	2.7
Operators, fabricators, and laborers	11.3	3.3

Note: These percentages are based on a total of 13,767 persons (7,408 men and 6,359 women) sixteen years or older who worked 35 hours or more in the civilian workforce.

Table 17. Occupational composition of Norwegian-born persons in the 1990 federal census who immigrated between 1980 and 1990

Occupation	Men (%)	Women (%)
Managerial	22.7	9.8
Professional specialty	25.3	21.3
Technical and sales	17.2	13.4
Administrative support including clerical	10.4	19.7
Service	7.1	30.9
Farming, forestry, and fishing	0.8	1.2
Precision production, craft, and repair	9.3	0.6
Operators, fabricators, and laborers	7.3	3.1

Note: These percentages are based on a total of 3,680 persons (2,073 men and 1,607 women) sixteen years or older who worked 35 hours or more in the civilian workforce.

All 1990 figures are for persons born in America who identify themselves as first-ethnicity Norwegians. In comparison with other Americans of European ancestry there are no significant differences save for an over-representation of Norwegian-American men in "farming, forestry, and fishing." The percentages are similar to those in the 1980 census based on ancestry. It is safe to claim, then, that by 1980, if not by 1920, Americans of Norwegian ancestry were firmly assimilated into the American economy and civilian workforce.

The postwar enumeration provides evidence of a percentage increase in the managerial and professional specialty categories, showing a greater social mobility. The special census category of post-1980 immigrants does not add statistical information that alters the picture much (table 17). Norwegian immigrants were occupied at all levels of the economy. The restrictions on immigration in legislation that became active in 1968 do, however, heavily favor skilled and professional labor, which may be reflected in the overall occupational composition of Norwegian-born workers.

Norwegian immigrants in general did better than American-born persons of Norwegian ancestry, with an average per capita income in 1989 of $21,039 as compared to $16,679 for the latter group. As many as 4.5 percent of all Norwegian-ancestry households—defined in the census as native to differentiate them from foreign-born—had an income of $100,000 or more; simultaneously, 5.1 percent, including all ages, of native Norwegian-American families had incomes below the poverty level. Selected per capita median incomes provide a comparative perspective. Those of Swedish ancestry had an average per capita income of $17,665; Danish, $17,889; Finnish, $15,514; English, $18,438; and German, $15,795. Norwegian-American levels of income are thus comparable to those of other European ethnic groups, even though they are at the lower end of the scale, but above the average native per capita income for the United States of only $14,420; 9.5 percent of all native American families lived below the poverty line. These statistics provide additional evidence of the economic assimilation of European ancestry populations in the United States.[31]

The Ethnic Commercial Elite

Historically, ethnic enterprise provided symbolic proof that the American Dream was both vital and real. To what degree immigrant entrepreneurs influenced the lives of the working class and their perceptions of social mobility is not clear, as John Bodnar cautions. In addition to the influence of immigrant capitalists, these workers were also subjected to the stimulus of unions and religious and political leaders. In Chicago, for instance, a notable social distance emerged between Norwegian-American employers and their workers. These same workers were responsible for the success of Norwegian-American businessmen and factory owners. Ethnic solidarity was, however, not lost.[32]

Entrepreneurial activity characterized Norwegian-American urban communities. The most visible commercial entities are, however, either no longer in business, incorporated into large American national and international conglomerates, or if the original Norwegian name has been retained, have lost any close ethnic affiliation. The history of the Johnson Chair Company in Chicago demonstrates the establishment and functioning of an immigrant company. Dating from 1868, it gave employment to Norwegian workers who lived close to its location in the Milwaukee Avenue colony, later relocating in the new Norwegian neighborhoods farther west on North Avenue. Many workers had already located there, and others followed. Its organizer and in time sole owner, Andrew P. Johnson, had emigrated at the age of fifteen in 1850 from Voss and learned carpentry in America before launching his successful chair production. He based his success on ethnic solidarity with his workers. Typical for his time, Johnson was a paternalistic employer, but he also appeared as a model for upward mobility, though to what extent, given the above cautionary statement, he thereby transmitted American business values and influenced worker behavior may be open to question.[33]

Another profitable Norwegian-American Chicago business endeavor is the Arthur

Andersen accounting firm, established in 1913, which has become one of the largest of its kind. Today, the Norwegian connection is slim due to changes in management and personnel. Andersen was himself an example of the Horatio Alger hero and was heavily involved in the recording of Norwegian-American history through his support of the Norwegian-American Historical Association, founded in 1925, serving as its president from 1936 to 1942. His involvement in the association could be viewed as an attempt by a successful individual to establish acceptable ethnic credentials. It was said of Andersen that "he prizes more than most men the spiritual heritage of his race."[34]

Andersen's firm was, of course, integrated into an American economic environment from the start and far removed from the world of the immigrant, but even a company as directly dependent on the immigrant community as, for instance, B. Anundsen Publishing Company in Decorah, Iowa, could be said to have forgotten its roots. In 1972 this venerable publisher discontinued the immigrant journal *Decorah-Posten,* and its current leaders, descendants of the founder, exhibit little appreciation of the company's historic role.[35] Business considerations prevail, and likely always did so from the initial issue of the newspaper in 1874, but now an appeal to ethnic heritage is no longer profitable. One can postulate that in general immigrant entrepreneurship, regardless of whether its economic base was inside or outside the ethnic community, was characterized by capitalistic free-enterprise principles and a profit motive. Altruistic rhetoric of wanting to serve the immigrant community may be viewed simply as ornamental.

The Evinrude trademark and company, founded by the Norwegian immigrant Ole Evinrude to produce the outboard motor for boats he constructed in 1901, is today consolidated with the large Outboard Marine Corporation, which in correspondence indicated no recognition of Evinrude's ancestral heritage. It had no commercial value.[36]

The three examples above typify general developments in immigrant entrepreneurship as assimilation based on economic and market considerations moved forward. A commitment to capitalist ideologies removed any ethnic consideration, not to say attachment. Industrialists, financiers, and successful professionals who cultivate a Norwegian-American identity are, on the other hand, still plentiful in the 1990s. In an era when ethnicity is celebrated, upward mobility is less of a factor in the lessening of individuals' appreciation of their origin and heritage than one might assume. Indeed, many of the most prosperous individuals of Norwegian ancestry within the American capitalist order were also those who expressed the most intense appreciation for their ethnic cultural identity, even though they cultivate exclusive social circles.

For Lee and Louise Sundet, born in 1928 and 1931, respectively—both fourth-generation

Figure 30. Eventyrhuset, built by Roe and Beverly Hatlen to celebrate their Norwegian heritage. Photograph courtesy of Roe and Beverly Hatlen.

Norwegian Americans and the prosperous owners of three companies—pride in ancestry is expressed in terms of a deep Lutheran faith and a concept of Norwegian ancestors as being stable and industrious. A more spectacular, nearly ostentatious, display of ethnic belonging is Eventyrhuset, a fairy-tale house built on a hill in Apple Valley, Minnesota, by Roe and Beverly Hatlen (figure 30). The large structure is filled with ethnic objects and decorated inside and outside with Norwegian motifs—including Viking dragon heads—in wood carving and rosemaling, and beside a large swimming pool is an artificial "Norwegian" waterfall. Roe is the chief executive officer and chairman of the large franchise of Old Country Buffet restaurants, named several years in a row by *Forbes* magazine as "one of the best 200 small companies in America." Beverly, born in 1944, is a fifth-generation Norwegian American on her

father's side, the family's roots being deep in the soil of the pioneer Valders settlement in eastern Wisconsin, and grew up as a Lutheran minister's daughter, where, as she stated, "our lives revolved around the church." Roe was born as a fourth-generation Norwegian American on his father's maternal side in 1943 in Kallispell, Montana, where his father worked in lumber mills and carpeting. "When we married," Beverly relates, "I thought our traditions would be identical since we both called them Norwegian, and it was a shock to find out there were differences, I now suppose simply because there were different family traditions." "Our house shows our pride in heritage," Roe explained. The Hatlens are typical of the Norwegian Americans who serve on the boards of ethnic institutions and who provide financial support.[37]

A large number of successful Norwegian

Americans presented themselves for interviews for this history project. It would nearly be possible to write a "Who's Who" in Norwegian-American commerce, banking, and professions based on these interviews. A representative sampling indicates the variety of enterprises nationwide among individuals who harbor a sense of ethnic belonging. Many belonged to a chapter of the Norwegian-American Chamber of Commerce (NACC). A few of the most affluent, however, chose instead more elevated social contacts outside the confines of an ethnic organizational mold. The NACC's chapters nevertheless identify a Norwegian-American elite and consist of corporate, representing both American and Norwegian companies, and individual members. The NACC was incorporated in New York, September 13, 1915, mainly to promote trade, and since 1945 has worked closely with the Norwegian Trade Council. Its first chapter outside New York, in Chicago, was not organized until 1959; there are currently nine chapters throughout the United States, in addition to the headquarters in New York. Many prominent persons not involved in business or trade with Norway join. Social activities include hosting trade missions and Norwegian dignitaries, sponsoring lectures and events, and arranging banquets and dances for chapter members, as well as Christmas luncheons and galas if the occasion dictates. These offer, as the publicity states, "excellent opportunities for member networking and for entertaining clients."[38]

The following selection of interviews includes Norwegian immigrants as well as persons born in America. Norwegian-American white-collar workers moved into bookkeeping, accounting, and banking in large numbers; in fact, the 1950 decennial census shows a concentration of second-generation Norwegian men in such positions. Some individuals advanced beyond employment to start their own accounting firms and financial institutions.[39]

Finn M. W. Caspersen, born in 1941, is chief executive officer and chairman of the board of the Beneficial Corporation in Wilmington, Delaware, a fourteen-billion-dollar financial services holding company listed on the New York Stock Exchange (figure 31). Its first office opened in Elizabeth, New Jersey, on August 6, 1914. It was maintained that the best way to rise through the ranks at Beneficial was to prepare for an executive career by starting as a stenographer or typist. This was how Caspersen's Norwegian-born father O. W. Caspersen advanced to become chief executive officer, chairman, and president of Beneficial. He had emigrated from Risør, Norway, in 1912, at the age of sixteen. O. W. Caspersen's widowed mother and two siblings had emigrated earlier while he completed his education in Norway. She ran a boarding house in Brooklyn. Finn Caspersen's mother, Freda Resika Caspersen, was born in America to Jewish immigrant parents of either Russian or Polish nationality, depending on the historical period. He and his wife, Barbara Morris

Caspersen, of old Yankee stock, have four sons, Finn Michael, Erik Michael, Samuel Michael, and Andrew Warden, all graduated from or enrolled in Ivy League institutions.

Q: After coming to America your father earned a bachelor's degree attending night school. How did he support himself?

A: First he worked in odd jobs, at a grocery store, in a stable, and then he joined the military service during the war and became an American citizen. After the war he worked as a stenographer, first in a firm owned by the Rockefellers, but didn't feel that was the way to get ahead, and then started working for Beneficial and worked his way to the top.

Q: What were the traditions of your home?

A: Most of the Norwegian traditions, some 90 percent. We had Norwegian cookies and a lot of fish, but not lutefisk, because nobody liked it. My mother learned to make Norwegian food from my father and my father's mother.

Q: Did you go to church?

A: We went to church, but not a Lutheran church. We went to the nearest one, which was a Congregational church. My mother was Jewish, but not a practicing Jew.

Q: How did your parents feel about religion?

A: My father thought it was good for a child to have a religious background. The Congregational Church was a sort of a mediating denomination. Being Protestant was important. There was a kind of anti-Catholicism in the family.

Figure 31. Finn M. W. Caspersen of the Beneficial Corporation. Photograph used with permission.

Q: What has been your own education and career?

A: I went to private school through ninth grade and switched to a boarding school in New Jersey. Later I attended the university and in 1966 graduated from Harvard Law School. In 1972 I started here when they opened a law department, then moved over to the business side and climbed up the ladder. It was a combination of luck and ability. In 1976 I became CEO of the company after four years.

Q: Does Beneficial have any Norwegian identity?

A: The chief financial officer Halvorsen is a first-generation from Grimstad.

Q: As a person in a prominent position, is there anything in attitudes, manners, values that you identify with your Norwegian or Jewish background?

A: I think it makes you very egalitarian, though that sounds funny sitting here with all this wealth. But you understand the tremendous benefits of the system and how the United States allows a person to get ahead.

Q: But has your own heritage benefited you?

A: I think so. I still go back there [Norway], and we maintain a house there. My children go there more often than I do. I think it's coming from a small country, relatively simple, that gives you a different view. As for the customs, I can't say that has had an effect on me.

Q: Were there specific values that your father passed down?

A: A tremendous work ethic. He was hardworking and believed in the family and in loyalty. They may be ethnic values.

Q: What has your sense of heritage been and has it changed?

A: My sense of being Norwegian as a child was very strong. We spent summers there from 1947 on, and I was very impressed and liked the ways. As Norway has changed and I have changed, I remain interested, but it seems that the country is much different from what it was when my father left.[40]

A persistent American image is the one of the self-made man. A contemporary American Dream may still be, both for immigrants who succeed and for successful American-born persons, that hard work will indeed be rewarded within the American capitalist system. For many prosperous individuals, the opportunity and promise of advancement heralded in nineteenth-century immigrant correspondence, the America letters, are still a part of their American ethos and reality.

Bjørn Erik Borgen, born in 1937, at Åndalsnes, Norway, is the owner of Founders Mutual Funds in Denver, Colorado (figure 32). He is considered to be one of the richest people in the state of Colorado. His company deals with mutual funds, employs over 120 people, and has assets of 3.5 billion dollars with more than 200,000 investors. Borgen immigrated to the United States together with his parents, Helene Astri and Truls Krogh Borgen, and a sister, Kari, in 1947. He grew up in Strum, Wisconsin, a small town south of Eau Claire. His interview demonstrates some of the motivations for going to America in the early postwar period, characteristics of life in a small Norwegian-American community, and how background and opportunity secured material success.

Q: How did your father make his livelihood in Åndalsnes?

A: My father was in the field of accounting, bookkeeping, office administrator, that type of work. He had a position there as a bookkeeper and office administrator in small businesses there.

Q: Did you grow up in Åndalsnes?

A: No, we were evacuated and moved to Årdal in the Stavanger area, where I grew up in the early years.

Q: What are your childhood memories in Norway?

A: Well, it is surprising that even though I was quite young, I have very vivid memories of World War II. My earliest memories as a three-year-old child in 1940 are of coming back from the mountains in Romsdalen, where my mother and I had been placed for safety. We were hiding from the Germans, who were there to repel the English, who were trying to land troops along the Romsdalsfjord.

Q: When and why did your parents decide to immigrate?

A: A lot of earlier immigrants from Årdal visited Norway when the war ended in 1945. Årdal was rich with people who had come from the United States and were returning there. And I think that my father and mother became a little bit fascinated about America and the opportunities they heard about. They had lost everything they had owned in Åndalsnes in the bombing and fire. And so they decided through connections they had with established people in America they knew, to come over and try life there.

Q: What was life like in Strum?

A: Strum, Wisconsin, had a very rich Norwegian heritage. There were lots of Norwegian immigrants from the 1800s who had lived in the area. And they were probably mostly farmers, but they were also businessmen, ran grocery stores, and they owned the local Ford automobile dealership. And that is where my father ended up, and he worked there for a long time.

Figure 32. Bjørn Erik Borgen, owner of Founders Mutual Funds. Photograph used with permission.

Q: How did you adjust?

A: Well, it was probably the best experience that I could have had. Here I was, this young boy from Norway who became an instant hit with the older generation and a source of curiosity to the young kids because I spoke Norwegian. The old-timers would gather at the local bars, and they would speak Norwegian, of course, although in many cases it was broken Norwegian or a mixture of American and Norwegian. I was fascinated at conversing with them. They thought it was a big deal. So this was a wonderful place for me to grow up and kind of gain self-confidence. The second generation were by this time the successful grocers, car dealers, or whatever they were.

Q: Were there children in Strum your age

who spoke Norwegian back in the 1950s and '60s?

A: There were very few. None of them spoke it very fluently. Those children who learned almost did not want to speak it. It was something not hip to do.

Q: Were there Norwegian traditions in Strum?

A: There was, in fact, when we first came to Strum, not every Sunday, but there was a sermon delivered in Norwegian at Strum Lutheran Church, where we belonged. Someone came periodically from the outside to deliver that sermon.

Q: Was higher education a part of your culture at home?

A: Yes, it was. I think it was always a question of whether my parents could afford it. I always worked. I think our life growing up was wonderful, but financially it was a tough life. My mother would do almost anything, cleaning, being in the fields, picking strawberries or making pickles, and taking in boarders. I started working at a very young age. I was able to save money and along with a scholarship was able to go to the University of Wisconsin. I graduated number two in my class.

Q: Your life story seems to affirm the rags-to-riches ideal of America for those who have the drive to take advantage of the opportunities they find here. How did you achieve your own success?

A: I first earned a degree in mechanical engineering at the University of Wisconsin. I felt that engineering was not what I wanted. I studied law for a year and also decided that was not what I wanted to pursue. So after a year at the law school, I left and took a job with the General Electric Company in their executive training course. While working for them, I became interested in going to business school. In 1964 I was admitted to the Harvard Business School and earned a master's degree in 1966.

Q: How did you happen to come to Denver?

A: After graduating from Harvard, I interviewed for various jobs. On my interviews in the West, in California where I interviewed with a high-tech company as a possible marketing person in the engineering field, I happened to stop in Denver. I called on an employment agency there to see if there were any opportunities. I was just fortunate enough that the head of the agency had a friend in an investment company here who had been hiring a number of young MBAs because they were building up an internal research department. The head of the investment department and I hit it off really well. He invited me to come along for a planned weekend in Vail. I fell in love with Vail and everything that it had; it was then a brand new skiing area. I wanted the job in the worst way although it was in the field of investment, which I had not specialized in. They were looking for someone who had a background in engineering and could give better security in covering the aerospace and electrical equipment industry. I received a job offer and came to Denver right after graduation.

Q: And you have been here since?

A: Yes, that was with one of our competitors. I stayed there for three years, and then there was an opportunity with this company called Founders, a tiny firm with some problems, looking for a chief investment officer. This was in 1969. In 1971 I was made president of the company. Before 1975 was over, I bought the company along with three other employees. They are no longer here since I bought them out of the business.[41]

Norwegian-American entrepreneurs began a number of businesses and became owners of factories and other commercial enterprises. A midwestern example of a man self-made through banking, a profession often chosen by Norwegian Americans, is third-generation Norwegian American O. Jay Tomson, born in 1936, who serves as chairman of the board and president of First Citizens National Bank in Mason City, Iowa, with branches in ten communities in northern Iowa. Moving from an agricultural background, Tomson attributes his success to "the old-fashioned work ethic still present among Norwegian Americans; they do not want to go to bed before they have accomplished something."[42]

The fact remains, however, that the financial and industrial magnates in the United States for the most part still bear old-stock American names. It has been a conundrum for historians of Norwegian Americans to explain why relatively few persons of Norwegian extraction have become the captains of industry or financial giants at a national level. The Norwegian American Alden W. Clausen, who served as chief financial officer of the Bank of America, established by Italian Americans, and in the World Bank, has had in recent times considerable influence in monetary matters. Clausen was born in 1923, the son of Morten Klausen, who in 1920 moved from Bø in Vesterålen to Illinois, where he made a living as a small-town newspaper editor. But there are few examples like Clausen. Historian Jon Wefald explained this state of affairs by claiming for Norwegian Americans a spirit of social cohesion and communalism that contradicted the success myth and the exploitation of the capitalist system. A spirit of progressive social reform was, Wefald insists, engendered by this ethnic heritage, reinforced by the Lutheran faith and its doctrine of justification by faith. Thus, they were not, like the Calvinists, "the elect" of God, urged on to intense economic enterprise and success as confirmation of salvation. There is, of course, reason to question Wefald's hypothesis, even though it is thought-provoking; consideration must be given as well to other explanatory factors, such as the strong rural character of the Norwegian-American group and the modest nature of the homeland's financial institutions and industrial culture as well as the occupational models that for a long time were most pronounced within the group. Outside of agriculture, these related more to people in theology, education, and public service than they did to great industrialists and financiers. In urban enclaves Norwegians were most heavily involved in carpentry and construction and as white-collar workers in accounting and as clerks, or they pursued familiar livelihoods in shipping and fishing.[43]

Religion does, naturally, affect behavior. Even the German sociologist Max Weber in his seminal *The Protestant Work Ethic and Capitalism* emphasized the effect of belief on economic behavior, rather than vice versa; for Lutherans this would mean resigned acceptance of the lot that God had assigned them. They did not pursue economic interest in the methodical manner enjoined by the Calvinists, which encouraged the development of capitalism. Other observers have considered the Norwegian folk character as lacking the required aggressiveness in business affairs that frequently typified the successful Yankee. They did not possess, these commentators claim, an adequate competitive spirit. Sociologists have eagerly pointed to a rejection of social stratification as a typical Norwegian trait. Many of the affluent Norwegian-American interview subjects insisted that they had brought up their children to show Lutheran social compassion by sharing their good fortune, to not boast about their wealth, and to appreciate the value of money. It was a nearly consistent response. In his major sociological study *Democracy in Jonesville,* W. Lloyd Warner suggests that the Norwegians there did not seek social advancement as an end in itself but instead preferred a congenial and cohesive community, and embraced a set of values that disparaged the social hierarchy and blatant commercialism of their Yankee neighbors.[44]

Commentators in Norway itself might submit what they decry as an unfortunate cultural national flaw as an alternative explanation of anti-elitism: a fear of being accused of being boastful and thus subject to ridicule. A reluctance to advertise one's own successes was more apparent among postwar immigrants who "had done well" than among the affluent American-born. It relates to an ambivalence toward the homeland and kin and friends there harbored by immigrants at all socioeconomic levels. It is compounded, as suggested above, by a strong national expectation of modesty and opposition to elitism. The term *jantelov*— the law of Jante—has been impiously introduced into the language to describe the idea "don't think you're better than anyone else," implying a petty and even tyrannical envy of those who achieve success. It is the converse of social egalitarianism.[45]

The owner of Scandia Plastics in Sheboygan, Wisconsin, Lars Graff, was born in Sør-Fron in the Gudbrandsdalen valley in 1939 and came to America in 1968 to accept a position as mechanical engineer at the Boeing Company in Everett, Washington. His successful plastic factory was begun modestly in 1979; it is now a large company that produces specialty products in plastic. "You know the way people are in Norway, I refrain from talking much about it," Graff responded to a direct question. This response was echoed by several other Norwegian immigrants who had prospered in a postwar American economy.[46]

In Salt Lake City, Utah, James LeVoy Sorenson, "An American Entrepreneur," as he described himself in his autobiographical account, in an interview insisted, "I live modestly in spite of great wealth and have taught my children to do so." Sorenson was born in 1921 as a fourth-generation Norwegian American; his Mormon faith encourages him to exercise modesty in displaying wealth. As of February 1996, he was the grandfather of forty-three children; an annual family reunion unites the large family. Growing up in near poverty, Sorenson claims that he learned hard work from his father, and communication skills as a Mormon missionary to New England, both of which prepared the ground for his spectacular financial rise in the medical device and pharmaceutical industry.[47]

Another self-made industrialist is Karsten Solheim, founder of the Ping Karsten Manufacturing Corporation, manufacturers of golf equipment in Phoenix, Arizona. Solheim was born in Bergen, Norway, in 1911, and moved to America when his parents immigrated two years later. His company developed in the 1960s, based on an ingenious golf putter and, later, on other golf clubs of exceptional quality. The company now employs some two thousand people. A substantial number of family members in three generations—obviously held together by the strong presence of the founder—

occupy administrative positions or are employed elsewhere in the company. One of Solheim's sons, Allan D. Solheim, is executive vice president, and also honorary consul of Norway, which is announced at the company's main entrance with the flying of the flag of Norway. A pious Baptist conviction furthermore dictates a religious lifestyle and donations to evangelical church groups. The postwar American capitalist system thus obviously still provides opportunity for economic advancement, even, as in the cases cited above, a move from modest beginnings to high achievement. The ethnic attachment is also clear as well as an unobtrusive attitude toward wealth. The common denominator for the three entrepreneurs interviewed may even so be a stringent belief in the rewards of the ethos of hard work, which they all attribute to their ethnic and family heritage.[48]

A unique social environment, both inside and outside the political arena, presents itself in Washington, D.C. Employment and professional opportunities attract individuals with special skills to the capital city.

Eivind A. Bjerke was born in Norway in 1943 into a large family in the farming community of Grue in Solør by the Glomma River. Since 1970 he has been a co-owner of the fashionable hair salon Lucien et Eivind Coiffure in Washington, with an exclusive clientele. He worked in a salon in Oslo before coming to the United States in 1964 to work at Per of Georgetown, owned by Norwegian-born Per Hallekjær; it enjoyed the patronage of such prominent clients as Jackie Kennedy and Lady Bird Johnson. Bjerke speaks of his White House years, when he was the regular hairdresser for President Lyndon Johnson's daughters, Lynda and Lucy, and became a good friend of First Lady Rosalynn and President Jimmy Carter. He considers his major contribution his key role in establishing the "Look Good . . . Feel Better" program, which he chairs for the Washington, D.C., Cosmetology Association. The program involves disguising hair loss following cancer treatment by the use of wigs, turbans, and other hair accessories. In 1989 Lucien et Eivind opened a wig salon. Bjerke has achieved great success, access to prominent individuals, many honors, and an affluent lifestyle. Sven Røhne, a journalist for the Norwegian newspaper *Verdens Gang,* tells of a revealing incident. "Eivind was invited to a picnic sponsored by the Norwegian Embassy," Røhne related, "where the Norwegian minister of fishery was a guest. Eivind arrived a little late, and as he entered the minister asked: 'What are you doing at an Embassy party? You are just a hair cutter.'" To which Røhne, who also was present, responded: "He is more important than *you* in *this town.*" It suggested to Røhne that "Norwegian society cut Eivind down. America built him up." His success has reinforced Bjerke's faith in the American system. "What is fantastic about this country is that you can come from a little place, a small country, and become somebody."[49]

Betty Claire Monkman, born in 1942, is associate curator in the office of the curator at the White House. Monkman has worked in Washington, D.C., since 1967. She was born in Bottineau, North Dakota, and grew up in a Norwegian-American district. Her father was half Norwegian and half Irish, and her mother Norwegian on both her father's and mother's side. Monkman is a third-generation Norwegian American on her mother's and her paternal mother's side. The interview suggests a career path and a liberating departure from and an attitude toward ethnicity not untypical for professional Norwegian-American women moving out of a confined ethnic community.

Q: How Norwegian was Bottineau when you were growing up?

A: It was very heavily not only Norwegian, but Swedish American as well. I remember visiting my mother's family church, and they were still having church services in Norwegian at that time. And several of my friends spoke Norwegian, you know, to their grandparents. I only understood certain phrases, like my grandfather would say, *fin jente,* nice girl, I think that means.

Q: Did you have Norwegian food at home?

A: Oh, very much so, yes. Always on Christmas Eve my mother would serve lutefisk and *lefse* . . . the traditional things that all the Norwegian Americans still seem to like.

Q: And you like lutefisk?

A: No, I do not like lutefisk. I do not! I never liked lutefisk. But I do like *lefse.*

Q: Were you Lutheran?

A: Oh, yes, very much so. My parents were very active in the church.

Q: Do you equate Lutheranism with being Norwegian?

A: Oh yes, oh yes. I'm not a Lutheran any more, but in fact when my mother was here a year ago, I took her to a Lutheran Norwegian service at Christmas. I still love to go to Lutheran churches just to hear the music. I have a great affinity for choral music, and I think it came from that Lutheran tradition.

Q: Do you belong to any denomination?

A: Yes, I go to the Unitarian Church.

Q: Was there anything in the Lutheran tradition that made you leave it?

A: Well, I think it was the dogma of the church. I think when I was in high school, I was very irritated by the strictness of some of the ministers. But it was perhaps mostly just growing up and growing away from things.

Q: Do you think of yourself as intellectually very independent?

A: Yes, yes, very much so, very much so. My mother couldn't understand why I rejected the Lutheran Church. She always blamed it on the university professors!

Q: How did you prepare for your present position?

A: I went to graduate school here at George Washington University because I was interested in museum work. I did a degree in American studies with the Smithsonian program they have here. Then I taught for a while. I worked in research libraries here in Washington. Because I was working, I did not complete graduate work until in 1980.

Q: How do you like living in Washington, D.C.?

A: I like it very much. I like the intellectual stimulation, the cultural activities, the sense of history, the beauty of the city, and the beauty of the surroundings.

Q: What are the main responsibilities of your office?

A: It's really for the care, the preservation, and the interpretation of the White House and its collections. We tend to work very closely with the First Ladies.

Q: Do you have any final thoughts about your life and being a Norwegian American?

A: Well, I think it's a part of my identity. It's not something I think about every day, but it is something I search out, and it's something I appreciate very much. I think my heritage is a very strong part of me.

Q: Has it influenced you in a positive way?

A: I think so. I'm not sure whether it's the Norwegian or the Lutheran or even the Midwest, or what it is, but I really think there is a combination of all these values.[50]

Tom Gjelten, born January 14, 1948, is a foreign affairs correspondent for National Public Radio in Washington, D.C. His great-grandfather on his paternal side emigrated from northern Østerdalen in Norway. On his maternal side he is a third-generation Norwegian

American, his grandfather having emigrated from Jølster in Sogn. Gjelten grew up in Forest City, Iowa, located in a heavily Norwegian district in the northern part of the state. There were Norwegian Christmas customs and foods, such as lutefisk and *lefse,* and Norwegian flags, but the use of the language was limited to phrases such as "Takk for maten" (Thank you for the food). The older generation in Forest City still spoke Norwegian in his childhood. Gjelten's career and life demonstrate the movement out of the small-town midwestern environment to greater opportunities elsewhere, in his case from a strongly Norwegian area.

Q: Did you belong to a Lutheran church?

A: Yes, religion was very important to both my parents. We had devotions every day at home. I hated it. My parents neither drank alcohol nor smoked, but tolerated that my brother and two sisters and I went to the movies and dances. They were very shy people so we did not socialize much. I was also shy. But within the family there were strong ties.

Q: Tell us about your educational experience.

A: After one year at Concordia College, I entered the University of Minnesota. In the early seventies I worked on the *Minnesota Daily,* was a part of the antiwar movement, and married a fellow student, Mary Jo Thompson, whose father was politically left-wing and an atheist. After graduation we both wanted to become schoolteachers.

Q: Did you in fact become teachers?

A: Yes, we taught for six years together on an isolated island off the coast of Maine. While there, I wrote a book about teaching in isolated communities from the point of view of a journalist. I became a specialist writer on rural education. My wife and I divorced at this time.

Q: How did you get your present position?

A: It was through a close friend of my brother, Dan, John Ydstie, who was a reporter from North Dakota of Norwegian descent. He was a promoter for National Public Radio and looked me up and got me interested. I was hired in 1983. I presented stories on radio about rural education, then joined the foreign staff and was sent as a correspondent to Central America and to Europe.

Q: How does your Norwegian heritage fit into your life?

A: I don't belong to any church. The move from Concordia College to the University of Minnesota in this regard had a symbolic significance. I was the only one in my family to leave the church. I don't belong to any Norwegian organizations, and I don't deliberately like anything Norwegian. It is not important to me. But, yet, I am profoundly affected by my Norwegian heritage. Norwegians are uncomfortable with interpersonal conflict. Arguments in the family were rare. I think I saw my mother cry only once. Norwegians are slow to show passion and affection and are easy-going—these are traits that reflect my upbringing and cultural environment because I see them in my parents and my brother and sisters.[51]

Do Norwegian Americans Commit Crimes?

Ambiguities about the value of one's ethnicity can easily arise. One respondent who described herself as "a Cheyenne woman who is part Norwegian rather than a Norwegian woman who is 'part Indian,'" found Norwegian Americans to be "drunken and stupid," and "also racist, chauvinistic, and sexist." Yet, she insisted that she is proud of and in touch with "all parts of who and what I am," speaks Norwegian, celebrates May 17, and observes Norwegian Christmas traditions, even conceding that she could associate descriptions such as "hardworking, honest, and good citizens" with Americans of Norwegian ancestry.[52]

The issue of criminality and ethnicity has historically been a sensitive one. Crime clearly represents one avenue to the American Dream. The Norwegian immigrant newspaper *Skandinaven* in Chicago throughout its history regularly countered nativist claims of immigrant criminality. People born in America, as easily demonstrated in police journals, were more prone to commit crime than the foreign-born, and yet, the newspaper editorialized in the last two decades of the nineteenth century, the "self-satisfied 'natives'" would like to lay the crimes at the doors of the immigrants." Many of the American-born criminals were, of course, the children of the immigrants. Criminal activity increased in the second generation. Organized crime has been a time-honored channel to social mobility, and ethnic networks were important in both legal and illegal enterprise. Though criminal activity based on ethnic connections can be identified in the Norwegian-American community, and Norwegian Americans were players in the illegal distribution of liquor on the coasts as well as in the urban centers in mid-America during Prohibition, Norwegians have never engaged in large-scale organized criminal enterprise. Lawbreakers were by all accounts not uncommon, however, in their midst. The majority of arrests in the nineteenth century and later appear to have been for public disorder and drunkenness; the neighborhood saloon was pervasive in all Norwegian urban centers. It was an integral part of a working-class culture with an important function as a social and charitable institution. Excessive indulgence in alcohol is the one vice some contemporary Norwegian Americans are evidently willing to acknowledge as a deplorable ethnic trait. Robert Gandrud quotes his father-in-law, a police officer in Glenwood, Minnesota, as saying: "Norwegians are the worst people to drive drunk."[53]

In 1882 the Chicago Norwegian-language newspaper *Verdens Gang* remarked in reporting the arrest of delinquent young people that "it pains us to note that many of those arrested are Americans of Scandinavian descent." The editors countered this obvious increase in criminal activity in the second generation, among "Scandinavian hoodlum youth," as *Skandinaven* had it, by claiming that "they have absorbed the spirit of lawlessness in America."[54]

Political scientist Dianne M. Pinderhughes concluded that in Chicago between 1880 and 1930 blacks and American-born whites were in that order at the top in the hierarchy of groups arrested, charged, and convicted, followed by "the southern Europeans in the middle of all groups in the city but at the top of white ethnic groups, with northern and western Europeans at the bottom." This descriptive conclusion does not, of course, address patterns of crime or the question of why these differences existed. The complexity of the latter circumstance may partly, but obviously not fully, as Pinderhughes suggests, be clarified by society's greater sensitivity to violations of social norms and values by some groups than others. Except for blacks, violation rates declined over time, which tends to support this contention. Discrimination against blacks continued while white ethnic groups gained gradual acceptance. The general historical situation has fortified a popular Norwegian, and Scandinavian, self-image of being law-abiding and reputable citizens. A consistent response by interview subjects was the honesty of fellow Norwegian Americans. Any suggestions to the contrary elicited a defensive attitude. The author has received a number of self-consciously formulated letters protesting his earlier published treatments of criminality and prostitution among urban Norwegian Americans. "It makes us look bad," one writer insisted.[55]

A concept of a relatively low rate of criminal activity and imprisonment has of course some basis in historical fact, as Pinderhughes

documents. In calculations of "nationality and criminals" for Wisconsin, where nativity for convicts was carefully recorded, in 1892, O. N. Nelson announced with ethnic exuberance that whereas the Irish had one convict for 2,328 of their population in the state, and the Germans one in 4,388, the Scandinavian-born had only one in 6,028, and that furthermore convicts from Scandinavia served on the average much less time in prison than, for instance, the German-born, indicating that their crimes had been less severe.

As of December 31, 1995, the rate of incarceration in state correctional institutions, excluding federal prisons, equaled 372 per 100,000. Posted statistics permit only a division based on race; these figures are thus not helpful in determining proportionate levels of imprisonment among white ethnic groups. For all white Americans of non-Hispanic origin, the incarceration rate in 1993 fell to 172 per 100,000, a figure that varied from 386 in Arizona to only 51 in Minnesota and 65 in North Dakota. Counting those in correctional institutions is, of course, an imperfect measure of criminal activity, and it does not address the nature of crimes committed nor the length of the sentence to be served. Different judicial cultures and practices may exhibit great variations. Texas, for instance, has a total rate of imprisonment that far exceeds the national average; in 1995 it was 659 per 100,000, whereas Minnesota with 103 prison inmates per 100,000, and North Dakota with only 90,

are considerably below. Given the social realities of the 1990s, there is little reason to assume that criminal activity would at present
vary significantly among the descendants of
European origin groups; it might be seen as
analogous to patterns of employment, which
show little ethnic variation. Measured simply
by institutional statistics, without considering
social and cultural circumstances, Hispanic
populations and African Americans give evidence of high rates of criminality compared to
Americans of European ancestry, a circumstance that naturally spawns prejudice and encourages self-righteous attitudes among white
ethnics. It reinforces ethnic self-perceptions of
a low rate of unlawful acts; several respondents
even gave the Scandinavians' lack of passion to
commit crimes as a reason. It is a belief that is
in line with adopting the mainstream ideals of
America in regard to work ethic, self-reliance,
and honesty, and internalizing these as specific
ethnic qualities. Scandinavian Americans are
by no means alone among white ethnics in this
practice. And, equally obvious, adopting mainstream ideals does not diminish or negate the
existence of a claimed culture of honesty in the
Scandinavian population.[56]

Louis A. Stender, the warden of the Minnesota Correctional Facility in Faribault, a
medium-security facility, thought a low incarceration rate for Minnesota suggested that "we
are locking up the right people." "Minnesota
has not gone down the road of just locking
people up," he stated, and insisted that the

state has one of the nation's best systems, in
terms of security, treating inmates with dignity
and respect as fellow human beings, and working on rehabilitation.[57]

Casemanager Steven J. Slostad at the Faribault facility was born in Preston, Minnesota,
in 1952, as a third-generation Norwegian
American on his paternal side and a fourth-
generation on his maternal. He was employed
at the correctional facility in Stillwater, Minnesota, in 1976, after earning an undergraduate major in criminal justice at Mankato State
University. He is currently employed at the
Faribault prison. "When I was starting," Slostad
explained, "the Minnesota prison system was
becoming more liberalized and more humane
and professional in how inmates are treated."
He agreed with Stender that "human rights
and dignity are respected, training improved
as well as the educational levels of the staff.
People like myself who have come up in the
system value offering treatment and educational opportunities to people."[58]

Two Norwegian-American inmates both
convicted of first-degree murder were interviewed at the correctional facility in Faribault.
Their attitudes toward an ethnic heritage varied greatly, which was one of the points the interviews explored. One of the inmates, Donald
Floyd Larson, was born into a large family in
Minneapolis in 1926 to Norwegian immigrant
parents. His father made a living as a house
painter. Larson was convicted in 1976 of four
first-, second-, and third-degree murders; his

sentence will expire, as his inmate record bluntly states, at "death." His occupation is listed as farmer. Larson ran away from home after completing the eighth grade.

Q: Why did you run away?

A: I didn't like it around home. My father was a drunk, and he was always punching everybody. He hit my mother, my brothers, and my sisters.

Q: How long were you on the run?

A: I hopped trains for a couple of years. After I got through running away from home, me and a couple of boyfriends robbed what was the Lake Street Liquor Store. I was seventeen years old at that time. I got ten to eighty years for that.

Q: Did this launch a criminal career?

A: Yeah, you know you go into St. Cloud Reformatory, and they don't teach you anything. I was there three years. Then I was sent to Stillwater prison. I was twenty-four when they let me out.

Q: You told me you married at age twenty-five and had four children. Did you commit crimes while you were married?

A: Yeah. I burglarized a liquor store with some other guys. One of them got into trouble and fingered me. So I went back to prison for five years. Then my wife divorced me.

Q: You decided, you said, in 1974 to go live on a farm you had purchased at Willow River. You by then had married again. Is that also when you committed the murders?

A: Well, on April 24, 1974, I come home unexpectedly. And this James Felch, our neighbor, is stealing all my power tools. Everything. We got into a big fight, and he kicked the hell out of me. And I shot him. I'm guilty. My youngest boy, Mark, and I didn't see him. He got between me and my wife, but I didn't see that. She said, "Give me the gun," and she hit my hand with the gun, and I shot my kid in the back of the neck. And I just went crazy and shot everything in sight.

Q: How many people did you kill?

A: Five.

Q: You told me that your Norwegian background did not mean anything to you. Has that changed?

A: No.

Q: How does it feel to know you will spend the rest of your life in prison?

A: Well, at first you are bitter. Honest to God, you hate everything. And then you find out this is the way the system works.[59]

Darby Jon Opsahl was born in 1968 and grew up in Young America, Minnesota. In 1992 he was convicted and given a life term for first-degree murder. He is a fourth-generation Norwegian American and was brought up in the Lutheran faith. The interview reflects his Norwegian and Lutheran upbringing. A grandmother appears as a major figure in his life. Before being arrested and charged, Opsahl was involved in an automobile accident that left him paralyzed and confined to a wheelchair.

Q: How was the relationship to your church?

A: Especially my grandparents were strict Lutherans. They encouraged us to go to church every week. I went to Bible study once a week and was involved in a youth fellowship. I didn't like it very much, but knew I had to accept.

Q: Was there a Norwegian side to your upbringing?

A: I remember my grandmother teaching me when I was like five or six years old. As a matter of fact, in summer I used to go out on the farm and stay with my grandparents. My grandmother, even though she was born in America, speaks pretty much nothing but Norwegian. I learned some phrases from my grandmother.

Q: Are you still a Lutheran?

A: Oh, yes, absolutely. The values didn't hit me until I came to prison, and I miss that. They are still there for me.

Q: Do you think of them as Norwegian ethnic values?

A: Those are the only values I know. I see other values from other people, but they don't come close to those I was taught. Like being in prison, you see people without any families or support. I think that being Norwegian we are very close-knit. Both on my father's and my mother's side we are very close-knit. They are very supportive.

Q: How did you happen to become involved in criminal activity?

A: When I was younger, I began hanging out with the wrong group. We used to drink, and we did a lot of drinking. We would spend all our money on beer and whiskey and stuff. We'd steal gas from cars. That is how it started for me. Then we broke into a school one time, dead drunk of course, and stole stuff. I spent time in the juvenile correctional facility in Sauk Center. I met all kinds of people. I was in and out of correctional facilities from when I was fourteen until I was seventeen. When I left there in 1986, I hung out with some of those same people.

Q: How did you become convicted of murder?

A: I had a lot of problems with my parents because I was out drinking and doing drugs and spending time with the wrong kind of people. They moved to Minneapolis from Young America and at first didn't want me to live with them. But I begged them, and they let me stay with them in Minneapolis. There is when my life took a bad turn. You see, October 14 of 1986 there was a burglary in Lester Prairie where a sixty-six-year-old lady was at home. Somebody kicked the door down and shot her with a .44 Magnum. I was charged with this crime. I was convicted of murder in 1992 and received a life sentence on the witness of one of the people I was hanging around with who said he was with me.

Q: You claim to be innocent of the crime you were convicted of. Would you ever kill anyone, Darby?

A: Absolutely not. I never owned a .44 Magnum.

Q: Your grandmother seems to have played an important role for you. How?

A: Matter of fact, when I was out of the juvenile facility, I would live with my grandmother out in Murdock. That would take me away from bad company. She taught me to speak Norwegian a little bit and to help out on the farm a lot. We read the Bible, and my grandparents got me involved in summer Bible camp. When you have a lot time, as I have here, you think about that and you miss it. Every Christmas and Thanksgiving we went to grandmother's house, and before we would eat our meals, we would sit around and my uncle would read the Bible, and after that we would eat and then we would play whist.[60]

The American Dream and Ethnic Identity

Does ethnicity matter? The analyzed questionnaire responses nearly spoke with one voice in the affirmative. Social mobility analyzed by comparing the occupational distribution of ethnic groups has been a widely used tool in studies of the process of assimilation. It is here that Milton Gordon's term *ethclass* applies in describing where ethnicity and occupational class convene. People tend to associate with others of the same ethnic group and social class. One may, according to Gordon, share with a person of a different ethnic group but of the same social class behavioral similarities, but not a sense of what he calls peoplehood; one shares a sense of peoplehood but not behavioral similarities with a person of the same ethnic group but different social class. Only among people of the same ethnicity and class is there, he states, a "consciousness of kind."[61] To what extent this model applies within the individualistic and privatized view of ethnic identity of the 1990s may be a moot issue, though it is obvious that Norwegian Americans generally socialize with people of their own class, if not regularly on the basis of ethnicity. When they do cultivate their ethnic heritage, class divisions can, however, be quite obvious.

This issue raises the question of whether those at the higher socioeconomic levels have a lower appreciation of their ethnicity when celebrating heritage than middle- and working-class Norwegians. Gordon's ethclass was designed to measure the strength of ethnicity as people improved their social status, the assumption being that its significance declined proportionately with upward mobility. Traditionally within the Norwegian-American community, it was held as meritorious for a person to honor his heritage even after achieving great professional or commercial success. The president of the Sons of Norway, Dennis Sorheim, spoke of the "downtown" Norwegians in Minneapolis as a category conscious of their elevated position in business and the professions and aloof to other Norwegian Americans, contrasting this social group with the historical working-class character of his organization.[62]

Respondents in both groups, however, expressed nearly identical attitudes about their historical place in America and the value they placed on their ethnic heritage.

For an "old" immigrant group like the Norwegian Americans, class may no longer be a determinant of the importance of ethnicity to the individual. In fact, people at higher social levels of education showed a greater interest in their heritage than those with less formal training. In his 1990 study, Richard Alba documented the progressive unlinking of ethnic identity from ethnic social structure. The distance to the immigrant generation has made ethnicity only one of several social identifying units Norwegian Americans belong to, arranged in individual hierarchical orders; the order of importance to the individual and how this order shifts need not be affected by the variable of social class. Other unrelated circumstances, such as age, retirement, visits to the old country, family circumstances, and special events, may be equally or more significant motivating forces in determining the importance a person attaches to ancestry and ethnic identity. Peter A. Munch's study of Norwegians in western Wisconsin around 1950 and his method of measuring interaction, or more accurately lack of interaction, with non-Norwegians by "gossip acquaintance" and "gossip circles," may not apply nearly half a century later.[63]

In a metropolitan area like Minneapolis a broad social interaction across ethnic lines is likely the norm for the majority of multigenerational Norwegian Americans regardless of level of income. A social difference as a variable is more apparent in action than in degree of articulated fervor in a search for roots and identity; as many respondents with high social status as those of working-class status insisted that knowledge of heritage served an important function in their lives. Assumptions based on class can consequently no longer be easily made in the context of determining the role of ethnicity in an "old" immigrant group like the Norwegians. The "downtown" Norwegians are simply more apt to limit their involvement in ethnic occasions to specific events, generally prestigious ones, or to those with large attendance, such as May 17 observances, and do not participate regularly. Their personal sense of ethnicity may not be in question. In this context the term *privatization of ethnicity* is clarifying in explaining the existence of ethnic identity severed from ethnic social structure. An example of an exclusive attitude may be discerned in activities surrounding the royal Norwegian visit to Minneapolis in October 1995, when a large banquet in honor of the royal couple, King Harald and Queen Sonja, excluded many prominent downtowners (figure 33). Invitations had first gone out to those active in Norwegian-American organizations and activities, in which the downtown Norwegians generally did not participate, making disappointed members of this group clamber for invitations.

Norwegian-American ethnicity can no longer be claimed to be a social structural or

Figure 33. Their Majesties King Harald V and Queen Sonja are honored at a royal banquet in Minneapolis in October 1995. Photograph by Robert Paulson; reprinted with permission of the photographer.

instrumental ethnicity in any meaningful way, but rather is a subjective and individualistic sense of ethnic identity, "a subjective belief in . . . common descent," which the German sociologist Max Weber saw as the hallmark of an ethnic group.[64] It is closely related to a unifying sense of a shared history. On Norwegian-American occasions, whether a royal visit, a May 17 observance, or a community festival, even as ethnic identity becomes privatized, a

sense of "consciousness of kind" may persist across class barriers—even if experienced only during the event and within a localized setting.

A renewed interest—even a resurgence—in the historical dimensions of ethnicity is evident among Norwegian Americans at all social levels, as the interviews cited in this chapter suggest and the study for this book in general supports. This interest relates to a passion with identification broadly visible in American society. John Holum, director of the Arms Control and Disarmament Agency, created in 1961, in Washington, D.C., is a fourth-generation Norwegian American born in 1940 in Highmore, South Dakota. He grew up on a farm in a strongly Norwegian-American community near Aberdeen. "The Lutheran faith was a big part of our social life, and I had a great sense of growing up Norwegian," Holum related. In his social life, "If the occasion arises, I am very happy to make it known that I am a Norwegian American. I genuinely feel that we should cultivate our ethnic backgrounds." Holum's belief is that "America has done an excellent job of accommodating a need for ethnic identity."[65]

The enthusiastic reception of this history project may itself be seen as evidence for a sense of historical Norwegian-American commonality; the fieldwork garnered generosity and enthusiasm among people in places of power, attained through wealth or political office, and in every other socioeconomic circumstance. It is difficult to imagine a scholarly

"JA, LENA. THEY WANT TO KNOW IF WE STILL HAVE TIES TO THE OLD COUNTRY."

Figure 34. This cartoon was printed in the Fargo-Moorhead Forum *on October 20, 1995, as a response to the fieldwork. It suggests the broad interest in the research and also the perceptions of Norwegian stereotypes. Cartoon by Trygve Olson; reprinted courtesy of the cartoonist and the Forum Publishing Company.*

endeavor that has generated more widespread interest within an entire ethnic population (figure 34). One can wonder if an extreme ethnic clannishness—so evident in the group's earlier history—persists to some extent in an altered manifestation, even keeping in mind the individualistic character of the contemporary search for ancestry and identity. If it does persist, it may offer some explanation for the enthusiastic involvement in the investigation. Later generations expressed pleasure at being included: "Finally someone is writing *our* history." It was a sentiment echoed by many Norwegian Americans with distant immigrant

roots. Some individuals went to great lengths to be included.

In "The Twilight of Ethnicity," a discussion of the resurgence of ethnicity written in 1981, Richard Alba dismisses the resurgence as a perception rather than a reality. "During the 1970s," he concludes, "ethnicity could be celebrated precisely because assimilation had proceeded far enough that ethnicity no longer seemed so threatening and divisive." In his later work in 1990, however, Alba criticizes both Gordon's theoretical concepts of assimilation and Gordon's students, who apparently see the end result of assimilation represented by "unhyphenated whites," suggesting "an obliteration of identities cast in ancestral terms." Alba emphasizes instead the significance of ethnicity in American society and its dynamic reshaping within relatively brief periods of historical time. He does this as a prelude to describing the emergence of a new ethnic group among whites, namely the European American, subsuming under that identity all descendants of European nationality groups. If such an ethnic configuration is indeed on the horizon, it appears distant from the material collected on Norwegian Americans for this study.[66]

CHAPTER 5

A Legacy of National Mutuality

The Ethnic Bond

Numerous studies, in Europe and in the United States, bear witness to the universal need of people who enter an urban industrial environment from rural circumstances to associate with each other in the new setting. People who leave their familiar social and political pattern of contacts consequently create in their new place of residence a social order of voluntary societies and organizations of many sorts. These satisfy the social and cultural needs of the migrants. The farming communities these migrants left had, of course, themselves emerged as social arrangements in response to universal human needs. A shared rural tradition formed the basis for the associations that developed among the migrants under the influence of the factory industry in the nineteenth and twentieth centuries. The move from the countryside to an industrial town had a profound effect on the way of life of the common people.[1]

The European immigrants to the United States created a new social order based on nationality, not infrequently on an old-country regional affiliation, but in many other respects shared the experience of their compatriots who were affected by industrialization and urbanization at home. For rural Norwegian Americans the Lutheran Church in its several immigrant manifestations became the focal point of and a conservative force in their life. Within the tight social network of the congregation, they found support and sustenance in spiritual and material matters and aid when need and illness made personal resources inadequate. The church did not, or could not, of course, alleviate all human suffering. Norwegian farmers sought mutual protection also outside the domain of the congregation. The two small mutual fire insurance companies with "Norwegian" in their names in the upper Midwest, one in Decorah, Iowa, and the other in Cottonwood, Minnesota, are current reminders. The Decorah company, one of some 125 similar county companies in Iowa, was founded in 1871 as the Norwegian Mutual Protective Association of Winneshiek County (Det Norske Gjensidige Beskyttelses-Selskab), currently the Norwegian Mutual Insurance Association, "to protect ourselves against loss of property caused by fire or lightning," and carried a strict nationality qualifying clause until the 1930s. The story is that this association in its earlier history may even in some arcane manner have kept non-Norwegians from moving into Norwegian-American farming communities and thus protected fellow Norwegian farmers from foreclosure and the auctioneer's hammer. It is another example of rural ethnic territoriality.[2]

The rural community was not an ideal social arrangement for everyone; it would be a grave distortion of the past to romanticize and idolize the countryside and rural living. Hardship and deprivation, as well as a lack of opportunity, were not unknown to the depressed farmer or the discouraged farm laborer. The confining circumstances of rural life were, in fact, the main motivation for farm youth to respond to the lure of the city. Yet, the urban setting was different from the rural community in some fundamental ways. Social conditions were even harsher there than those that existed down on the farm. The Danish-born journalist Jacob Riis in his nearly clinical revelations of life in the immigrant ghettos in New York in 1890, *How the Other Half Lives,* made the American public aware for the first time of the harshness of human existence in the prevailing filth, sickness, extreme crowding, and grinding poverty found there.[3]

In this uncertain and tangled environment, migrants to the city from its environs or from abroad formed a network of mutual assistance with people of a shared heritage. The Irish were the first ghetto people, crowding in their shantytowns at the outskirts of town or in dilapidated city dwellings even before the Civil War. The twentieth-century urban ghetto is associated mainly with immigrants from southern and eastern Europe. These were the Polonias, "Jewtowns," and Little Italys of great American metropolitan areas, each ghetto with a distinctive national color. In his classic novel *The Jungle,* Upton Sinclair described the clustering and frightful indigence of Chicago's Slavs employed in the bizarre and demeaning world of the stockyards, where they worked knee-deep in blood and entrails. Environmental factors, poor sanitation, and poor social services produced problematic health conditions.[4]

In urban areas such as Brooklyn and Chicago there were also little Norways alongside other ethnic clusters. In Chicago Norwegian immigrants formed urban enclaves before the Civil War, dating from the early 1830s, preceding the industrial ghetto of a later date. In the prewar years the Norwegian colony grew to number about 1,820. Health conditions were deplorable, and deadly epidemics struck the hapless immigrants. In 1849 cholera affected the Norwegian locality severely, taking the life of one in seven Norwegian immigrants, whereas only one person in every thirty-six in Chicago died during this calamitous epidemic. Such dire need required social activities by congregations. The demands on the church and its social role increased in the harsh urban environment. The religious impulse combined there with a social program to form an indispensable immigrant institution.[5]

But the ethnic ties that bound also had a secular face. To delineate mutual aid provided on the basis of ethnic commonality is not to suggest ethnic accord and harmony. To the contrary, dissension and conflict were regularly the order of the day. The many benevolent relief initiatives and mutual aid societies that came into being represented competing religious and secular interests in the Norwegian-American community. But, regardless, a sensed obligation toward those of the same people transcended inner dispute and, conversely, regularly excluded outsiders. It is telling evidence of this circumstance that the Norwegians in Chicago ceased their aid to the large public institution the Oak Forest Infirmary in the 1960s when the last Norwegian inmate died because "there was no longer anyone to give to." In other words, ethnic ties still conditioned a charitable response.[6]

In the urban colonies formed by Norwegians, the major division ran between the Lutheran Church and its social role and the many secular charitable efforts that existed. The latter were generally in the form of mutual aid societies, but in the urban setting, nearly all associations—athletic, cultural, social—functioned as mutual aid societies when need required, a major difference from the rural situation. Early secular fraternal organizations were initiated by ethnic leaders and entrepreneurs. Those who headed these gained recognition beyond the ethnic community and formed an elite among their own. The Knights of the White Cross (Ordenen af Riddere af det Hvide Kors), with a grand lodge and sublodges, which emerged among Norwegian immigrants in Chicago in 1863, is a good example of immigrant mutual assistance organizations. Begun the previous year as the Nora Society, it was founded by an emerging elite in the immigrant community. The members, all male, became *knights* and on festive occasions appeared with red capes adorned with a white cross over the left shoulder. The organization played a central role in Norwegian immigrant life.

In Chicago, Lutheran congregations felt so threatened by the appeal of secular benefit associations, which would, they claimed, bring "church people into contact with all classes of people and faiths," that they as early as the 1880s formed competing Lutheran mutual assistance societies. The several congregational societies formed the Norwegian Evangelical

Lutheran Sick and Benefit Society of Chicago, open to confirmed Lutherans from all congregations. It is remarkable that this society came into being at a time when the Lutheran Church viewed insurance as evidence of a lack of faith in God to provide for temporal wants. Such efforts were forerunners of the later Lutheran Brotherhood, which even when organized nearly forty years later encountered resistance from Norwegian Lutheran clerics. Human needs in the dire urban social environment of Chicago in the 1880s obviously required a measure of theological compromise.

But the efforts of the church left out people outside the church. These were then, if they were not members of Methodist, Baptist, or other non-Lutheran congregations, the ones who sought to protect themselves in a self-reliant manner from the consequences of unemployment and sickness by joining secular mutual assistance groups. Charitable benevolence institutions and congregational poor-relief societies as well as individual largesse came to the aid of compatriots too old or indigent to obtain membership; their only alternative was public assistance and the poor farm. The immigrant press sometimes brought individual needs to the attention of its readers. In 1897, for instance, *Skandinaven* in Chicago described in great detail the suffering and impoverishment of an aging couple, Aksel and Agathe Vingaard, who had no means of subsistence. In later issues gifts were acknowledged and a letter from the grateful couple printed.[7]

The Norwegian-American Family

Family structures are, as anthropologists and sociologists among others maintain, and obviously so, manifestations of the values of the cultural group to which the family belongs. *Ethnicity and Family Therapy* presents studies by psychotherapists in how ethnicity becomes a part of therapy; the authors, mostly therapists, take the position that ethnic difference should be considered an active dynamic in the treatment of the family. They furthermore recognize and accept in the context of therapy a set of societal distinctions; ethnic value structures are not viewed as being erased through assimilation. In their discussion, the contributors thus invade the traditional realm of social scientists in order to understand the development of dysfunction and its cure. For this study, the most intriguing aspects of their findings are the suggested ethnic distinctions rather than the psychotherapy based on them.[8]

C. F. Midelfort and H. C. Midelfort, a clinician and an anthropologist, analyze Norwegian-American families in their contribution to *Ethnicity and Family Therapy*. Their analysis emphasizes the dualistic nature of the Norwegian character as evidenced in its culture, religion contending with folklore: therapy would consequently require mediation between opposites, for instance, "the tendency toward rebellion and love of freedom contends with pressure for conformity and obedience to authority." The authors stress the preservation of ethnic values and attitudes among Norwegian Americans through the generations. The authoritarian father figure of an earlier generation is only lightly touched on to suggest that in Norwegian-American farming communities, the father retained his authoritative position, but because land was more available, children were not bound to the farm as in Norway, where the eldest son generally took over the family estate. Leaving the farm, however, created a conflict in loyalty and new sources of friction. To break away from the family caused guilt, anxiety, and even resentment, the authors claim, since individuation threatened a valued sense of belonging and community. Family unity and extended family gatherings were important and conveyed a strong feeling of continuity with the past.[9] The many signs of centennial farms, designating family ownership of one hundred years, that grace Norwegian-American agricultural communities at present strongly suggest an abiding loyalty to the idea of a family farm.

A traditional male dominance may not be entirely a circumstance of the past. In the course of our research, especially in working-class homes of Norwegian immigrants, the husband often took it upon himself to respond on behalf of his wife to questions directed to her, or even embarrassingly to correct her stated opinions on her own life situation. But this was a rare occurrence among Americans of Norwegian ancestry. No empirical research exists on patterns of child-rearing and to what extent these have been transmitted to the third generation and later. The assumption would be that they resemble middle-class American practices rather closely.

The Midelforts' study in general paints a very wholesome picture of Norwegians and Norwegian Americans, and identifies the Norwegian word *kjekk* as an ideal, meaning being courageous, positive, humorous, strong, capable, and industrious. Physical strength and endurance are prized. In America Norwegians regard social, educational, and monetary success as attainable through hard work and diligence. As one would anticipate, the study finds that emotional expression is strictly controlled, and that overt and direct aggression is rare, especially within the family.

Another characteristic is public denial of inadequacy or suffering, a stoicism that C. F. Midelfort found exemplified in the fact that Norwegians require less local anesthesia for minor surgical procedures than is common in America, and which Paul A. Qualben, a psychiatrist and neurologist with an extensive practice among Norwegian Americans in Brooklyn, extends to Norwegian Americans, claiming that "they take less anesthesia than the average Brooklynite." Qualben, himself a second-generation Norwegian American, attributes this circumstance to a cultural heritage that dictates being reserved, keeping up appearances, being performance oriented rather than introspective, and keeping feelings under control. Older Norwegian-American males in

Brooklyn, he explained, experience great problems when having to expose themselves, thereby losing dignity, and in accepting that they are sick and in need of care. "Norwegians are very slow to anger," he stated as further evidence of their stoicism, "but once they get angry will hold a grudge forever." Second-generation Patricia Patten, president of Ulabrand Lodge of Sons of Norway in San Pedro, California, describes, somewhat tongue-in-cheek, her fellow Norwegian Americans: "They are basically kind, will help each other, are usually Lutheran, make lifelong enemies, but will show up at the funeral for the food." Qualben, giving his medical opinion, saw Norwegian Americans as less depressed than other ethnic groups. They have, however, a strong sense of guilt, as members of a culture where religion plays a significant role, which results in a high rate of suicide. But Norwegians have a lower rate than Swedes do, which Qualben attributes to the ability of Norwegians to escape suicide by a rich fantasy life.[10]

The statistics available on suicide are for Scandinavia, and the issue to be resolved in this case, as in regard to some other findings, is how much of the cultural and religious causalities applies to individuals of Norwegian ancestry in the United States. The Midelforts' study of Norwegian families suggests many correlations—some seemingly speculative—between Norwegians in Norway and those of Norwegian descent in America; for instance, they identify for Norwegians in addition to a public

respect for an authoritarian national Christian church, a personal, secret, archaic pantheistic religion tied to the landscape and home, which among Norwegian Americans expresses itself, they claim, as a reverence and a sense that the church, the home farm, and the land are sacred. A second and more directly transplanted example is the historic replacement in Norway of alcohol with coffee as a social beverage in the second half of the nineteenth century, which manifests itself when visiting a Norwegian or Norwegian-American family with coffee being offered immediately as a symbol indicating the host's desire for the guests to stay. It speaks to a tradition of great hospitality, regularly expressed through the serving of food, so common in Norwegian-American homes.[11]

The extent of endogamy—intragroup marriage—provides a measure of ethnic cohesion. It also illustrates how structural assimilation relates to cultural assimilation; the degree of intermarriage is, as the sociologist Lowry Nelson maintains, the decisive test of assimilation (figure 35). Statistics for Norwegian Americans historically give evidence of a high degree of intragroup marriage; in other words, they found a Norwegian spouse, even after ethnic cultural manifestations had largely disappeared. Several studies can be cited. In Chicago in 1910 as many as 77 percent of first-generation Norwegians in selected enumeration districts had wed another Norwegian. In the second generation, as many as 46 percent of married Norwegian Americans in these same districts had found a marriage partner who was born in Norway or like themselves was of Norwegian ancestry. In Minneapolis that same year 70 percent of Norwegian-born men had wives of the same nationality. As recently as 1941, *Nordisk Tidende* found that in Brooklyn 41 percent of the second generation had married persons of Norwegian origin. These figures are very high and would be even higher in Norwegian communities outside the cities; intragroup marriage was more pronounced among Norwegians than, for instance, among rural Swedes. Not only ethnic cultural bonds but also a strong Lutheran identity and congregational social life influenced intragroup marriage, as did secular social activities and residential propinquity. A few male respondents candidly suggested that they began attending a Norwegian Lutheran church only when they began looking for a wife, because there they believed they would find a suitable life partner. "Even a smaller proportion than one-half practicing marriage within the nationality group," Nelson states in his study of rural communities in Minnesota, "would be sufficient to maintain a 'hard core' of cultural identity."[12]

The 1980 decennial census shows that 22 percent of all Norwegian-American women in their first marriage found a man who was at least partly Norwegian; in comparison 39.5 percent of Italian-American women married men of their own ancestry. Even though these statistics mean that 78 percent of Norwegian-American women and 60.5 percent of Italian-

Figure 35. One of the many silly sayings on ethnic buttons: "Some people are married to Norwegians and still go on to lead normal lives." The nationality can, of course, be changed to fit any ethnic group. The button reflects one—obviously commercially inspired—mode of celebrating diversity.

American women married outside their ethnic group, both Norwegians and Italians marry their co-ethnics more than they would be expected to based on what sociologists Stanley Lieberson and Mary Waters call a simple random choice model; in fact, according to their calculations, the odds that a Norwegian woman will marry a Norwegian man are twenty times greater than the odds that a non-Norwegian woman will marry a Norwegian man, which exceeds the odds of nineteen times greater for an Italian woman marrying an Italian man. Thus, the level of intragroup marriage for Norwegian Americans is relatively high, and strikingly so when compared to Swedish-American women, whose percentage of endogamous first unions was only 13.2; for Danish-American women the number fell even lower, to only 9 percent.[13]

In detailed interviews, it became clear that when many Norwegian Americans talk of heritage, what they frequently mean and what they wish to transmit to their children is more a sense of where ancestors came from, family memories and origin, rather than an ethnic identity of being a part of a contemporary ethnic group. Family history research in the *bygdelag*, for instance, reveals an individualistic approach to ethnic identity as do the many genealogical societies. Of course, many parents also speak glowingly of a broad Norwegian cultural heritage that they wish to pass on, not infrequently in terms of specific moral and social values they associate with being Norwegian-American. In the socialization of children, these become essential ancestral ethnic qualities.

Ethnically mixed marriages face additional challenges in how they function culturally. As a general dictum, all couples, whether of the same ethnicity or not, create new traditions as they combine and transform those from two sets of families. It is the greater cultural distance, perhaps even conflicting values, between couples of different nationalities that can pose problems of reconciliation. The process of reconciling traditions and customs, however, would be the same in all instances. Family activities are one of the most significant ways in which ethnic culture is expressed; to the extent that they are not influenced by outside forces, these activities tend to replace themselves through the generations. As an institution, the family has historically been a conservative force. Historical impulses are passed on from one generation to the next in the context of the family, which explains why ethnic food remains a basic part of ethnic identity. If traditional ethnic values are found anywhere, they are found in the family. However, as a mixing of ethnicities occurs through marriage, a construction and reconstruction of family activities may occur, perhaps one family cultural tradition being dominant or even exclusive, contingent on the general social and extended familial circumstances. This process of adjustment and invention is enriching, frequently intense, and emotion-laden. The experience is likely to leave both pleasurable and painful memories in the next generation.[14]

Who one selects as a marriage partner frequently depends on opportunity and social environment. When asked if he looked for a Norwegian spouse, one respondent answered honestly that since he did not reside in a heavily Norwegian community, none had been available to him. Among the survey respondents, Norwegians who chose to wed someone outside the group most commonly married a Protestant Scandinavian or German, but a substantial number married into a great diversity of other nationalities and differing faiths, though rarely outside European-origin groups, their choice depending on varying ethnic population mixes. In accordance with the 1980 census figures, in fact, a majority of the American-born respondents of Norwegian ancestry found a non-Norwegian spouse.

Arlene Bakke Rutuelo, born in 1964, owns the Nordic Restaurant and Delicatessen in Bay Ridge, Brooklyn, where she grew up. Both her parents are Norwegian immigrants, having emigrated as an engaged couple in 1959. Her father, Alfred Bakke, is a floor layer and carpenter. Her mother, Helene Egeland Bakke, opened the restaurant and store in March 1995 because "she did not want to lose a place where Norwegians could buy Norwegian stuff." The enterprise, in this earlier center of Norwegian-American life now rapidly changing to an Asian center, is doing very well. The neighborhood is, in fact, considered to be the third largest "China Town" in the New York area. The population transition is evidenced in the Wee Kee Restaurant, formally the Atlantic, a popular Norwegian eating establishment that currently offers both Chinese and Norwegian fare in order to retain old customers and cater to new ones. The interview reveals changes in a multicultural environment, ethnic traditions, and typical conservative Norwegian-American and Lutheran working-class attitudes.

Q: What was it like growing up in Bay Ridge?

A: We spoke Norwegian at home when I was young. There were a lot of Scandinavians here. I stayed together with a group of Nor-

wegians through high school. We knew each other from church.

Q: Did you have non-Norwegian friends?

A: Yes, a lot of non-Norwegians were moving in, and I had friends who were not Norwegian.

Q: How did you meet your husband?

A: My husband is Vincent Rutuelo. His grandparents came from Italy. He began going to my Lutheran church. He is a police officer in Manhattan.

Q: Do you have children together?

A: Yes, Danielle who is eight; Paul, five; and Vincent Jr., four.

Q: What are the traditions in your home?

A: We have Norwegian traditions and almost no Italian ones. Our children will grow up feeling Norwegian-American. Their Italian grandparents are Americanized and have few traditions from their background. They are Catholic, and we are Lutheran.

Q: Are you politically active?

A: Yes, I help local Republican politicians. The Democrats want to give everything away. I am conservative on social issues and strictly pro-life.

Q: Do you find values in bringing your children up to appreciate their Norwegian-American heritage?

A: Yes. Norwegian Americans are honest and hardworking. We should be proud of being Norwegian. Norwegians coming from Norway, however, have lost the work ethic. I will hire Norwegian Americans to work in the restaurant, but I will not hire anyone coming from Norway.[15]

The Success of Benevolence

During the last two decades of the nineteenth century, the Norwegian-American community was sufficiently mature to erect charitable and benevolent institutions. Spearheaded by the Lutheran Church, hospitals, nursing homes, orphanages, and even homes for working girls were opened to meet the social needs of the community. The competitive spirit and even hostility among the several factions in Norwegian-American Lutheranism served as motivating forces and gave rise to an inordinate number of benevolent operations; each faction pursued separate goals. In the 1920s there were, according to O. M. Norlie, no fewer than twenty-seven hospitals operated by the Norwegian Lutheran Church and one by the Norwegian Methodists. Most of the facilities that were erected, in the manner of the majority of immigrant institutions, hardly survived beyond the immigrant generation itself. Norlie does not consider the many defunct benevolent institutions. A few of those that survived have retained their identity and have even become large health care institutions; others have lost their Norwegian affiliation in a succession of mergers. The large medical facility the Lutheran General Hospital in Park Ridge, Illinois, began modestly in rented quarters on Artesian Avenue and LeMoyne Street in

Chicago in 1897 as the Lutheran Deaconess Home and Hospital. It was the third Norwegian deaconess hospital in America.[16]

The first Norwegian hospital, the Norwegian Lutheran Deaconess Home and Hospital, opened in Brooklyn in 1885 and was hailed as "the largest charitable institution founded by Norwegians in the East." The work was inaugurated by Elizabeth Fedde in 1883, the first Norwegian deaconess in America, who came to Brooklyn that year in response to a call for service to seamen and immigrants. Generally referred to as the Norwegian Hospital, it became the Lutheran Medical Center in 1968. The Sunset Park district, where it is located, had by then been separated from contiguous Bay Ridge and declared a poverty area, allowing the financially strapped institution to receive federal aid. The second Norwegian deaconess home and hospital opened in Minneapolis in 1888, relating directly to the initial mission in Brooklyn, like the later Chicago facility. The hospital became integrated into the large Fairview health care system through consolidation in 1973; the identifying Norwegian adjective in the original name had by then been long absent.[17]

The Fairview Hospital also emanated from the Norwegian community in Minneapolis. It was established by the Norwegian Lutheran Hospital Association, organized in 1906 and closely associated with the United Church, in competition with the deaconess facility to the dismay of many in the Norwegian community.

In 1916 an imposing hospital building was dedicated. The name Fairview has been retained by the divisions and large hospital units that growth and expansion dictated. Little remains of a Norwegian identity, however.

In Chicago the Norwegian-American Hospital, located in the once strongly Norwegian neighborhood by Humboldt Park, opened its doors in 1895 under the name the Norwegian Lutheran Tabitha Hospital. It was, like Fairview, the result of tensions and conflicting interests in the Norwegian community. It dropped its Lutheran connection in 1910, and in 1929 was given its current name. In the mundane world of the city, its broadly secular and ethnic appeal gained wide approval. In a nationalistic fervor it excluded non-Norwegians, save for those related by marriage, from full membership in the association that operated the hospital. Presently, the Norwegian flag flying in front of the building and the visit by King Harald and Queen Sonja of Norway in 1995 belie the fact that most patients are Hispanic and none are Norwegian; few of the physicians have any Norwegian connection. It is a community hospital, and it has clearly survived by responding to the needs of the new ethnic composition of the community.[18]

The Norwegian-American Hospital, or *Noruego Americano,* as it is rendered in Spanish, may demonstrate in some pointed ways the superficial direction ethnic identity occasionally takes. One may well ask, "what's in a name?" The hospital is hardly more ethnically Norwegian, save for the expressive symbolism, than Lutheran General in Park Ridge, and it would be closer to its ethnic affiliation, if not its roots, if it emphasized its Latino connection. Norman R. Dahl, chairman of the hospital board of trustees, is a second-generation Norwegian American, born in the Humboldt Park community in 1927; he served on the board in the mid-1960s, when the hospital was still predominantly Norwegian, and has known it all his life. Only four current members of the board are Norwegian. To a desire for greater Latino recognition expressed by Latino physicians and politicians, Dahl responds in terms that suggest his loyalty to tradition: "The hospital was founded one hundred years ago, and the Norwegians sacrificed and put their sweat and money into building it—today it is here to serve the community. And the Norwegian king and queen and prime minister honor us by their visits. See what we have provided you, I tell the Latino community."[19]

Some clinics and hospitals started as individual or family enterprises still carry the original names. Examples are the Quisling Clinic in Madison, founded in the late 1920s by Sver Quisling and joined by four brothers, all medical doctors; the Midelfort Clinic in Eau Claire, which was founded in the late 1920s as a private group medical practice, although it dates back to 1892, when Hans Christian Midelfart opened his medical practice there; and the Gundersen Clinic in La Crosse, all in Wisconsin. Originally staffed by physicians trained in

Norway, these small medical facilities enjoyed the confidence of the Norwegian immigrant community. In the same manner as the larger hospitals, they have gradually become integrated into other medical groups by merger, sale, or collaboration. Adolf Gundersen arrived in the small river town of La Crosse in the spring of 1891 with a medical degree in surgery from the university in Oslo. He remained in America, it has been suggested, because the hierarchical medical system in Norway prevented rapid career progress for young doctors. His socialistic convictions were not uncommon among Norwegian immigrant medical doctors in the nineteenth century. The clinic, currently with more than 260 physicians, began modestly as a small group practice above a drugstore in downtown La Crosse. "Group practice was a pioneer midwestern invention and endeavor," Sigurd B. Gundersen Jr., a grandson of the founder and a surgeon at the clinic, explained. Operating as a family partnership, a dynasty of medically trained sons and grandchildren eventually made it one of the best-known group practices in the nation. Nepotism was abandoned in 1964, Sigurd Gundersen related, when the clinic became a corporation. An ethnic origin is still in evidence. "There is great pride in the Norwegian identity within the family," Gundersen concluded.[20]

Nursing homes naturally do better than hospitals in preserving a Norwegian milieu. The residents of Norwegian ancestry retain an ethnic emphasis. The passing older generation

that is being housed has memories of a functioning ethnic subgroup in speech and social interaction. Even nursing homes with no ethnic ties in Norwegian areas of settlement may serve lutefisk and other traditional Norwegian-American fare on some occasions. Other facilities cater directly to the ethnicity of the local population. An example of the latter, the privately founded Sannes Skogdalen nursing home in Soldiers Grove in western Wisconsin hoists the Norwegian flag and displays the overt symbols of Norwegian ethnicity, not of earlier times but as contemporaneously interpreted, from rosemaling, trolls, and Vikings, down to the silly make-believe Uffda Club membership certificate in the administrator's office. The Norwegian-American atmosphere is clearly a source of comfort to the largely Norwegian residents as well as an obvious marketing advantage. The one-hundred-year-old American-born Ole K. Helgerson, born in 1896, assured everyone of his satisfaction with life in the home and that "it is good to be here" in an authentic local Sogning vernacular learned from immigrant parents.[21]

On the East Coast the Eger Lutheran Homes on Staten Island was founded in 1916 in Brooklyn through a bequest from Carl Michael Eger, and ten years later moved across to Staten Island. Norlie listed twenty "homes for the aged" operated by the Norwegian Lutheran Church in America in that decade. The Eger Homes are, then, as a matter of course presently affiliated with the Evangelical

Lutheran Church in America. It has an ethnically diverse resident population, though the Norwegian background is still apparent in staff and in resident services. More of the Norwegian background is preserved in the Norwegian Christian Home and Health Center, still located at its 1903 location in Brooklyn. May 17 is observed, and residents and staff march in the annual May 17 parade. The most apparent influence is, however, here as in other Norwegian-founded homes for the aged, as they were originally called, a pervasive Lutheran piety in word and practice.[22]

In Chicago the Norwood Park Home, opened in 1896, and Bethesda Home for the Aged, dating from 1911 and intended solely for indigent and destitute Norwegians, still communicate their Norwegian immigrant origins. Visitors walking the halls can still hear Norwegian spoken among the residents. The same would be the case, and even more so, at the Norse Home on Phinney Ridge, overlooking the old Norwegian residential areas below in Ballard in Seattle. Sponsored by Norwegian-American organizations and erected by the Wick Construction Company, founded by a Norwegian immigrant, the home opened its doors in 1957 to serve Norwegian residents. Its charitable intent allowed for forty-four free rooms for "deserving Norwegians." The Norse Home relates directly to an earlier effort to meet the needs of the Norwegian-American community, the Norwegian Hospital Association, formed in 1913. This group was able to

operate a hospital only for a brief period of time, from 1923 to 1926, where, as *Washington Posten* announced, "the sick boy's message will be understood and sent back home to an old mother." Even today, then, in a setting with more recent immigration from Norway, the building and operation of the Norse Home demonstrate that an appeal on the basis of nationality elicits a charitable response.[23]

Lutheran Brotherhood

A Common Bond is the title of the voluminous commissioned history of Lutheran Brotherhood of 1989, suggesting, of course, a common Lutheran faith as the tie that binds. At its inception in 1917 there were also the bonds of a shared ethnic heritage. Its founding related directly to the events that created the Norwegian Evangelical Lutheran Church in America that year. The official history reverently refers to the pre-1917 situation as "Faith and Vision." The articles of incorporation were signed at the convention that in June 1917 formed the new church body, the name indicating the influence of such fraternal groups and mutual aid societies as the Sons of Norway, with which it would compete to sell insurance, the one sacred, the other profane.

Antagonism toward the Sons of Norway as a worldly secret order was still strong among devout Lutherans. But the alternative suggested by a Lutheran mutual aid organization was also anathema to conservative Lutheran pastors, who from their pulpits vehemently attacked the very concept of life insurance as an offense to their faith in God's providence. Thus, the organization represented the progressive faction within Norwegian-American Lutheranism, evidenced by the strong involvement in designing the new aid society of Herman Ekern, a follower of the Wisconsin Progressive leader Robert La Follette and a champion of his cause. As insurance commissioner in Wisconsin from 1911 to 1915, Ekern encouraged major reforms in the state's insurance industry. He knew how the various types of insurance organizations—stock companies, mutual companies, and fraternal benefit societies—operated, and drew on this knowledge in shaping the Lutheran insurance organization along the lines of a fraternity. To overcome the suspicion of church leaders about secular fraternities, Ekern looked to religious fraternal insurance groups as a model and sanctioned alternatives to secular lodges, such as the Aid Association for Lutherans, organized by laypeople of the Wisconsin Synod in 1902.

Lutheran Brotherhood, whose original name was Luther Union, was organized for the mutual benefit of its members: any baptized Lutheran who was a member of a Norwegian Lutheran congregation was entitled to join. Opposition to insurance within the Norwegian Lutheran Church in America cooled the relationship, and official ties weakened and faded entirely away after 1919, so that in 1920 the Norwegian qualification disappeared, and the brotherhood was open to "any man or woman between the ages of sixteen and sixty who is a Lutheran or is affiliated with any Lutheran organization." It aimed to be for the Lutheran Church what the Knights of Columbus was for the Catholic Church.[24]

Lutheran Brotherhood is currently one of the largest and most successful fraternal benefit societies in the United States, in 1988 operating some 740 branches and about 1,600 agents throughout the country, and in 1996 having 41.5 billion dollars in life insurance alone in force and a membership of 1.2 million. Its history is, however, fraught with tension, bitter internal power struggles, and adjustments to a series of Lutheran Church mergers. In one of the major power rivalries beginning in 1958, which eventually spread beyond the home office, the issue arose as to the precise relationship between the fraternity and the American Lutheran Church (ALC) formed through mergers in 1960. The ALC passed a resolution stating that "Whereas the Church does not own or control the Lutheran Brotherhood, neither does the Lutheran Brotherhood have any voice in the affairs of the Church." Just as the ALC was becoming less Norwegian following the merger, Lutheran Brotherhood as an independent fraternal benefit society was also becoming less ethnically oriented. Its official journal, *Bond*, stated in 1996 that Lutheran Brotherhood's purpose was "to provide financial security for members and to serve Lutherans, their congregations, institutions and communities."

In this broad statement of purpose, the church body that is a natural extension of its initial Norwegian-American parent church in 1917, the Evangelical Lutheran Church in America, is not mentioned; neither is any other specific Lutheran synod. Its inclusive Lutheran identity, regardless of ethnicity or theological position, is well established.[25]

The Norwegian connection is, however, still visible in many of Lutheran Brotherhood's recent and current leading figures. Robert P. Gandrud, born in 1943, in Glenwood, Minnesota, has served as president since 1987 and chief executive officer from the following year. He is a fourth-generation Norwegian American with roots in Hallingdal, his great-grandfather having emigrated in 1867. His interview reveals a strong sense of a Norwegian background typical of many who grew up in Norwegian-American communities.

Q: Growing up in a Norwegian area of the state, did you attend a Norwegian Lutheran church?

A: Yes, I was brought up Lutheran, and we were members of a congregation that came out of the old Norwegian Synod. My father was confirmed in the Norwegian language, and he and my mother spoke Norwegian, especially when they did not want us children to know what they were talking about.

Q: Did you feel Norwegian growing up?

A: I felt Norwegian, but not until I visited Hallingdal did I gain a sense of being Halling.

I will likely attend the Hallinglag meeting in Brooten this summer.

Q: What about Lutheran Brotherhood and its Norwegian background?

A: The Norwegian background has been played down. Members of the board of directors think the future is with the Lutheran Church and not in the Norwegian background. The Norwegian background is not stressed at our banquets, but I hate to think that this is a denial of it. We do serve lutefisk at our Christmas party.

Q: What is your own personal relationship with your heritage?

A: I am very proud of it. I think of my ancestors leaving the homeland with such high hopes and strength. Glenwood, Minnesota, was not a friendly place in 1867. I am very proud of how strong and driven they were. It was a feeling that was fortified when I visited Norway.

Q: What about Norwegian Americans today?

A: I do business with Norwegian Americans every day. They are trustworthy people.[26]

A Retirement Culture

American fraternalism provided a fruitful organizational model for the many immigrant nationalities that sought security and social order in America's great cities. Organizational structures and ritualistic practices in secret societies and voluntary associations, as well as their social and cultural objectives, emulated such

American fraternities and systems of lodges as Freemasonry, Odd Fellows, and Knights of the Maccabees. The Knights of the White Cross in Chicago is another early fraternity. Fraternities were immigrant expressions of what the social theorist Anthony Oberschall has called the associational mode of solidarity. In the late nineteenth century they replaced the traditional communal benevolence of rural life and the support and bonds that the extended family had provided earlier. Members did not generally belong to the classes that would have taken part in Masonic practices before emigrating, and consequently fraternalism became a part of their American experience. The emphasis was on mutuality, benefit functions, and, of course, male camaraderie. "Lodge night" in the immigrant community satisfied social needs and a desire to rise above the mundane demands of everyday life.[27]

Material benefits, however, represented the greater reality of the various brotherhoods, as these were responses to the needs, uncertainties, and demands people encountered in an unfamiliar and perilous urban and industrialized environment. Sons of Norway, with headquarters in Minneapolis, remains the most successful entrance into Norwegian immigrant fraternalism. Organized modestly among a group of common workers in north Minneapolis during the hard 1890s on January 16, 1895, it was, in fact, a latecomer to the movement; its roots can be traced back to earlier mutual assistance efforts in Chicago. The idea

for a mutual aid society had likely come from the Independent Scandinavian Workers Association in Eau Claire, Wisconsin, organized in 1893. It had begun in 1889 as a local lodge of the Scandinavian Workers Association, a group organized in Chicago in June 1870. The two organizations with their individual lodge systems followed the trend in American fraternalism during the final quarter of the nineteenth century and became fraternal benefit societies, providing life insurance for their members in large predetermined amounts.[28]

Replicating existing and earlier models, in 1898 the Sons of Norway became an incorporated order in the state of Minnesota, as the Independent Order of Sons of Norway. With the addition of new lodges the following year, the parent lodge became Nidaros Lodge No. 1; thereafter the familiar arrangement of a supreme lodge with an expanding number of sublodges ensued. In the course of the decade following 1905, the order became a nationwide fraternal organization. Just before World War I it had 153 lodges with a total membership of nearly 11,000 and 2.3 million dollars of life insurance in force. As the Sons of Norway celebrated the centennial year in 1995, it reported 360 lodges in the United States, 39 in Canada, and 21 in Norway. Its membership in the United States was then 66,903, and it had 733 million dollars of life insurance in force.[29]

The commissioned history of the Sons of Norway, *An American Saga* by Sverre Norborg, published in 1970, neglects the significance of the human emotions and social activities sheltered in numerous local lodges, and the historical narrative thereby assumes the appearance of a laudatory position paper on fiscal growth with a running commentary extolling leading figures within the fraternity. The introduction of Carl G. O. Hansen, the editor of the order's magazine, *Sons of Norway,* now the *Viking,* is an example of the generally effusive and uncritical language of the account. "Steeped in the cultural traditions of Norway, this noble American was a central figure in the fascinating transition era," Norborg writes, "when American 'Norwegianism' was transplanted to the rich soil of American civilization." Be this as it may—the excessive use of glowing adjectives notwithstanding—the most poignant and revealing aspects of fraternal life are lost, as is, of course, any realistic evaluation of the order and its historic role.[30]

The Sons of Norway has a high percentage of social members, a category of noninsured members established when the order was incorporated, again taking its cue from other fraternal benefit societies. In 1995 a striking 71 percent of the members fell into the social membership category, the noninsured obviously joining for social and cultural reasons. Social members were initially defined as those "who are above the age limit" of fifty to be insured, or "rejected by the medical officer," but "who otherwise are qualified for membership and socially acceptable." The former referred to the Norwegian nationality and male qualifications

for membership, and the latter to the morally uplifting character of the fraternal movement reflecting the moralistic attitudes of urban reformers of that day. Applicants had to provide proof of moral worthiness. Encouraged by the consolidation with an independent Pacific Coast lodge movement and the ethnic fervor of the prewar period, in the years 1910–12 the order discontinued compulsory insurance requirements, and the number of purely social members grew steadily.

Gender and nationality restrictions on membership were gradually removed, though only non-Norwegian spouses who understood the Norwegian language could join after 1918. Not until its new set of articles of incorporation were adopted in 1946 did the order grant membership on the broad basis of "Norwegian affiliation," in addition to birth or descent. Women were admitted after 1916 as social members "in places where there is no lodge of the Daughters of Norway," and in 1950 this sister benefit society, organized as the Daughters of Norway in Minneapolis in 1897, merged with the Sons of Norway. At the time of its merger the Daughters had 3,500 members. The official name of the Sons of Norway, however, remained unchanged and in spite of heated discussions never reflected the fact that in time the "daughters" surpassed the "sons" in sheer numbers. Of the lodges responding to the survey, 54 percent of the members were women; they surpassed men in numbers in all age categories.[31]

The conventions of the Sons of Norway for some time rejected the formation of English-speaking lodges. Only the hysterical advocacy for cultural conformity during World War I and the immediate postwar years, as well as the wishes of American-born members, convinced the order to authorize English-speaking lodges in principle in 1918, the first one formed being Progress 204 in Chicago in 1920, though the order resisted pressures to designate English as its official language. That did not occur until 1942. An idealistic concern for Norwegian cultural heritage characterized the early history of an order predominantly consisting of laboring people. Stated aims included making "the members good and loyal citizens of their adopted country, by the promotion of their social, moral and intellectual development." Its moral concern, typical of the era of progressive reform in general and the fraternal moral climate of that time in particular, affirmed itself in a strict policy of temperance; in 1905 the fraternity adopted a strict provision prohibiting the use of intoxicants "in any form whatever" at any events sponsored by the supreme lodge or by any sublodge of the order. Persons engaged in "the liquor traffic" were barred from membership, a provision reaffirmed in the 1930s, even after the end of Prohibition.[32]

From a sociohistorical perspective, the post–World War II years brought striking, though not unexpected, changes in the membership and program of the order. A reorganization occurred, reflecting the increased strength of urban Norwegian Americans compared to the rural population; many rural lodges discontinued due to a drop in membership in the years following the war. There was as well a decline in the number of Norwegian-born Americans to a low of about a quarter million in 1940, the majority of whom would have been too old to be included in the order's insurance program. The existing quota laws would prevent a large postwar immigration. Urbanization and the passing of the immigrant generation thus affected later developments. Still, in 1946, when the order adopted a new set of articles of incorporation, the Norwegian impulse and a fear of the loss of organizational unity based on a common ethnicity kindled considerable opposition to the proposal to admit people of other than Norwegian nationality. Central leaders emphasized instead of ethnic commonality the communal bonds of fraternal benefit insurance.[33]

The order moved from one with a working-class vision and identity to one of the middle class, as the second-generation membership achieved the American Dream through higher social status. The percentage of members in professional occupations shown in Table 18 reflects the trend that took place as the American-born generations joined the Sons of Norway.

The greater efficiency of the creation of a new system of field staff in the insurance operations indicated an increased business approach centrally. The model for the officers and agents, or so it appears, became the successful American entrepreneur. The departure from past practice became evident in the order's new headquarters in Minneapolis, opened in 1962; a bar with private liquor lockers could be said to symbolize a dramatic shift in values. In fact, especially during that decade, the Sons of Norway earned a reputation for heavy alcohol consumption at its social functions. A growing indifference in many members to established rituals and ceremonies, considered nearly sacred at an earlier age, advances further the impression of a departure from tradition.[34]

Beyond the Minneapolis headquarters, the picture is vastly more varied. Indeed, each of the many lodges and the communities in which they exist present unique identities and practices. John Higham's salient notion of a "new particularism" applies in the sense that it defines distinct group solidarities as these differentiate themselves from a larger norm. "District Happenings" reported by individual lodges, appearing in the *Sons of Norway Viking* magazine and lodge newsletters, highlight these differences. There is even a certain resentment in some lodges of the dictates from the headquarters about how to celebrate heritage, but others maintain that the influence on lodge activities from the Minneapolis office is minimal; a localized sense of identity and tradition is visible. A fading sense of a national, ethnic community encourages this localized and particularistic celebration of Norwegianness. Nevertheless, "heritage week" at the Sons of Norway head-

Table 18. Occupation of 11,619 members of the Sons of Norway

Occupation	Percentage
Agriculture/Fishing	4.42
Blue-collar	12.43
Professional	25.19
Retired	57.96

Note: Questionnaires were sent in 1995 to all of the 360 American lodges of the Sons of Norway; 98 lodges answered for a response rate of 27.2 percent.

quarters reflects a common set of symbols, all associated with a romanticized vision of an ethnic identity—Viking images, folk dancing, *bunads,* and peasant crafts—that is embraced by all lodges; they all in one manner or another mark May 17 and Leif Ericson Day in October. In addition to a traditional annual *"Lutefisk, Lefse* and Meatball Dinner," often preceded by a "working *lefse*-baking party" for the lutefisk—as noted by Solbakken Lodge in North Orange County, California—there are many "American" activities listed in lodge publications, for instance, "Western Night," "Crab Feed," "Hawaiian Luau," "Valentine's Dinner and All-Male Fashion Show," not to forget the all-American favorite standby, the "Potluck Dinner." The entertainment and events are limited only by imagination and leadership as well as by local circumstances, but in general they reflect the tastes and preferences of an aging group of people. "It gets to be like a coffee klatch with deadly business meetings," complains Kenneth Holberg Ducat, on his paternal

Table 19. Ages and gender of Sons of Norway members

Age by gender	Percentage
Male < 30	4.36
Female < 30	5.37
Male 30–39	2.69
Female 30–39	3.01
Male 40–49	4.44
Female 40–49	4.89
Male 50–59	6.09
Female 50–59	7.40
Male 60–69	11.73
Female 60–69	13.40
Male > 69	16.62
Female > 69	20.00

Note: The 98 lodges that responded listed 17,087 members, or 25.6 percent of the total membership in the United States. Of these, 54 percent were women.

side a third-generation Norwegian American born in 1919, about the Sol Byer Lodge in the retirement community of Sun City, Arizona. It is not an uncommon complaint. As with most vintage practices, there is reluctance to change. Keeping a society unchanged, in spite of talk about attracting the younger generation, becomes for many its main appeal. Explaining how she generated new life in the Ulabrand Lodge in San Pedro, California, Patricia Patten claimed that "I've got many enemies who resisted change. People now like to come. It was the fifty-year-olds who saved the lodge."[35]

In spite of sociocultural variations from lodge to lodge, there is a general graying of the membership, a development most service and fraternal organizations exhibit (table 19). In the context of the Norwegian-American community, the aging character of its members is symptomatic of the "hard core" of Norwegian-American organizational and cultural life in general. To quote Sherrill Swenson, president of Solbakken Lodge, on its Western theme dinner: "The members are too old to dance, so we just eat and go home." Norwegian-American activities represent what may fairly be described as a "retirement culture." It is retirees that give content and direction to the creation and promotion of a Norwegian-American cultural identity. This state of affairs is obvious in the statistics on active Sons of Norway members; in fact, nearly 60 percent of the members in lodges that responded were retired. It is also the impression of most of those active in lodge work. Some responses simply stated, "Oh, we're mostly retired people." Impressionistic evidence following visits to numerous lodge meetings with few exceptions surely reinforces this opinion.[36]

The age composition of the membership may simply be a question of recruitment. People in retirement are more apt to seek an organizational outlet for their social impulses. The large number of noninsured members suggests that such considerations, as well as a reawakened interest in family background, move people to join. The situation need not herald the end of the organization or of Norwegian-American culture, merely a new state of affairs. Many expressed great regret at not discovering ethnicity and developing an interest in their ancestry before those who could inform them were dead. The Sons of Norway, in the manner of other ethnic organizations, plays a part in this discovery. It is frequently the only "Norwegian" show in town. When the lodges gather people in typical retirement communities in, for instance, Florida or Arizona, they, perhaps paradoxically, in some respects act like an extended family, reviving the order's original spirit of mutual support and concern in social matters and when sickness strikes. These lodges provide further evidence of a genuine retirement culture.

Lodge life serves a variety of purposes for individual members. Personal disagreement or differences about program preferences have been known to cause internal splits and give rise to the formation of new lodges. In Denver, for example, Fjelldalen Lodge resulted from a departure of dissatisfied members from Trollheim Lodge in the early 1990s. Both are thriving enterprises; the conflict itself may have created added lodge loyalty. "We are getting a lot of new members in their late forties and in their fifties," suggested George R. Holte, an officer and charter member of Trollheim Lodge. In other centers of Norwegian settlement, lodges are unable to attract members of any age. Snorre Lodge in Thief River Falls, Minnesota, located in an extensive Norwegian region, has atrophied to a surprising degree given the potential for growth. The officers in Snorre Lodge that were interviewed were elderly women. A feminization of both membership and leaders

in this instance and in many similar ones becomes an index of decline. Fewer than ten members come to Snorre's monthly gatherings. Obviously this and other lodges in similar circumstances have not found a purpose, or a dynamic leadership, that will attract and satisfy the social needs of a local membership.[37]

Gender is the primary force in maintaining the small Daughters of Norway organization on the Pacific Coast. The first lodge, Valkyrian, was organized in 1905. It never merged with the Sons of Norway like the midwestern women's order did; the grand lodge office travels with the president. There are currently eighteen lodges, most of which are in the state of Washington, but some are also in California, Nevada, and Montana. They are all small, from fifty to one hundred members, and consist mostly of older women, though interest in crafts has attracted some younger members. Ruth G. Durham, born in Halsa, Norway, in 1920, came to Seattle in 1958 and is active in the Daughters of Norway. She explained that the Daughters of Norway is purely a social and cultural organization for women. As the following interview suggests, it promotes traditional women's values and activities:

Q: Why do you think there is a need for a women's organization?

A: Women are more comfortable with each other. We meet to do women's things. And here women can speak.

Q: What kind of things do you do?

A: We do Norwegian crafts, Hardanger embroidery, knitting, bead work, and rosemaling. Almost every lodge has good rosemalers. We also do cooking and baking of such items as *rømmegrøt* and *lefse*. We even have unisex folk dancing.

Q: Is the organization growing?

A: A new lodge, the Solveig Lodge, was organized on Whidbey Island on February 24, 1996. It was a result of crafts interest.[38]

In a social and cultural context the Norwegian Society of Texas (NST) may in some sense be viewed as a competitor to the Sons of Norway lodges in that state, though part of the reason for its founding on March 8, 1975, was reluctance by the Sons of Norway to establish itself in Texas due to the relatively small number of Norwegians there. Today Nordtex Lodge in Dallas and Ensom Stjerne Lodge in Houston represent the order in the state. As of spring 1996, NST had six chapters in various cities in Texas, all bearing Norwegian names: Midnattsolen, Solhjem, Snorre, Viddhjem, Trollhjem, and, of course, Viking. A popular Leikarring, a folk dance group, came into being in the founding year. The chapters assemble jointly at the Althing—the name of the historic Norse legislative assembly—the governing body, three times annually. Save for Snorre in Houston, which has a predominance of younger Norwegian-born members, this social and cultural organization is made up largely of retirees.

Wayne A. Rohne, born in 1931 in Cranfills Gap in Bosque County, Texas, was one of the incorporators of NST and is an attorney-at-law. He is a third-generation Norwegian American on his father's side and a fourth-generation on his mother's.

Q: What is the purpose of the Norwegian Society of Texas?

A: Its purpose is to protect Norwegian heritage. We all observe May 17, Midsummer Night's Eve, and have a Christmas party. Most chapters meet twice a month with different kinds of programs. We also have other than Norwegian programs, as an example, Western ballads as a part of our American culture.

Q: Do you have to be Norwegian to join?

A: No, the NST has 480 members. You don't have to be of Norwegian background to join. Anyone who is interested can become a member.

Q: How do you feel about being Norwegian?

A: I am proud because I think of all the good things Norwegians have done in the Bosque County area, especially of my family, who came as immigrants and became good citizens.[39]

Cod and Aquavit

Immigrant elites were prominent in the early fraternal movements, exemplified among the Norwegians in Chicago in the Order of the Knights of the White Cross. Male elite societies flourished in many urban settings and created a refined high life among the more prosperous members of the immigrant community. These societies replicated customs at the same social level in the homeland. A uniquely immigrant organizational manifestation is the male luncheon club. Male camaraderie is cultivated by eating boiled fresh cod and potatoes washed down with golden aquavit and beer. In social status this menu greatly surpasses the lowly lutefisk with its roots in peasant culture, and reflects the standing of the members. The most common name of these social entities became *torskeklubben,* that is, "the cod club." Food here assumes the double role of identifying both ethnicity and class.

The mutual aid aspect at this level of the Norwegian-American community became evident in the timing and composition of the original "cod club," Torske Klubben, organized in 1933 as a social club in Minneapolis during the Great Depression; the Norwegian-American men in business and the professions who organized the club may have found mutual support in this fellowship in the harsh commercial climate of that decade. Its social function was also clear, as well as its desire to cultivate language and heritage. Most of the founders were born in Norway.[40]

In Seattle the Norwegian Commercial Club organized for the same purpose in 1932, announcing even in its name the livelihoods of its members; networking within the ethnic fold gave advantages in business ventures and commercial deals. Even though both these pioneer groups currently function mainly as social clubs,

this dimension has not disappeared. Within the prominent circle of successful men in business, commercial agreements may be negotiated and employment secured for ambitious sons of members.

The Minneapolis Torske Klubben has retained a strict male Norwegian membership qualification, while other similar groups have permitted women to join. The Norwegian Commercial Club in Seattle admitted women members beginning in the early 1990s. Rumblings of legal action by some Norwegian-American women in business preceded their formal admission, the idea being that they were discriminated against in their conduct of business. The venerable Fish Club of San Francisco, founded in 1914, has in recent years also admitted women to its fish luncheons. It dubbed these successful and not-always-so-young female professionals "mermaids" in keeping with the unusual nomenclature of these societies in general, the president holding the title "Rex Sole." Trygve G. Morkemo, born in Åfjord in South Trøndelag, Norway, 1931, occupied this position in 1997. Like many of the members, Morkemo is a prosperous immigrant, serving as president of a shipping service company he started in San Francisco. "It is not geared into business," Morkemo explained about the Fish Club, "but it is convenient for them to join." The main membership has historically been shipping and business professionals, but people outside shipping also have joined. Having a low visibility and profile, to quote from the 1996 anniversary history, the club "always had constituents who knew the right person, who could establish contact, communicate, understand and act accordingly." Ethnic networking functioned well in the promotion of individual as well as cultural agendas. Hosting prominent visitors, including royalty from Norway, elevated the club's standing and influence. The men who meet at the Fish Club luncheons, with their orientation often toward Norway—many retaining Norwegian citizenship—feel, one assumes, that they are socially above the members of lodges of the Sons of Norway, with their historical working-class composition, but they may even feel they have a social edge on the respected Norwegian Club of San Francisco, founded in 1898, with its own club house on 1900 Fell Street. Its interest and membership are more Norwegian-American than the Fish Club's; furthermore, it democratically declares that it is open "to all Norwegian men of good repute, regardless of rank or station." Even so, this male social club also exudes a certain elitist attitude.[41]

The Minneapolis cod luncheon club decided on "boss" as an appropriate title for its chief officer, and this title has been adopted by many similar clubs. The practice suggests an effort to bridge the ethnic and the American commercial and cultural worlds. The model was the prosperous and efficient American man of business.

The ethnic revival of the last few decades has produced a large number of cod luncheon clubs in many parts of the United States organized along the same lines as the older ones, though many have more liberal membership qualifications in regard to gender, social standing, and purity of nationality. People with no Norwegian standing are drawn into a Norwegian-American social environment, reflecting the process of assimilation as well as the voluntary aspect of ethnic affiliation. There are, however, great local variations. The Chicago Torske Klub came into being in 1960, and emulating the Minneapolis group, called its president "boss." Open only to men, it nevertheless welcomes persons of all occupational and professional backgrounds and those not of Norwegian ancestry, though no black American has yet been inducted into membership. The Norwegian Fish Club of San Diego, organized only in 1995, consists of an affluent group of Norwegian-American men. In Mormon Salt Lake City the all-male Norwegian fish luncheon club—Fiskeklubben, organized in the early 1990s and modeled after the San Francisco group—serves cod and other types of fish with boiled potatoes but without alcoholic accouterments. It consists mainly of postwar immigrants, and mastery of Norwegian is required in order to join, the purpose being "to eat fish and talk Norwegian" while enjoying male camaraderie. The stress on language replicates the original intent of Torske Klubben in Minneapolis and current practice in the San Francisco Fish Club.[42]

Several cod luncheon clubs have emerged in Minneapolis and St. Paul and other places in Minnesota. None of these has gained the prestige of the original Torske Klubben, even though in the pioneer group a greater democracy in who is admitted has become more noticeable in recent years. This is an inevitable development; the gradual dissolution of a functioning Norwegian-American community makes a sense of elitism ever more difficult to maintain. Many of the members are also active in more prestigious American societies and social activities. For these Norwegian Americans, Torske Klubben may simply represent their modest bow to heritage. At one point this club boasted half the Minnesota Supreme Court as members, and there were long waiting lists of people eager to join.

The current "boss" of Torske Klubben is Donald Omodt, born in St. Paul, Minnesota, in 1927, and long-time, now retired, sheriff of Hennepin County. His grandfather Bernt Omodt emigrated from Norway in 1893 when seventeen years old. In America he married Maggie Mulligan of Irish descent and converted to Catholicism. Boss Omodt's father, Hugh Omodt, became a police detective in the St. Paul police department. He was the first in his family to leave farming. He married Lillian Becker, a second-generation German American. Don Omodt was brought up as a Catholic and with a mixed ethnic heritage. He thinks of himself as a Norwegian American. The interview provides insight into ethnic identity and how an elite ethnic social organization functions and views itself in the 1990s.

Q: Considering your mixed ethnic heritage, how do you explain your sense of being Norwegian?

A: It was to begin with through my grandfather, who after he and grandmother separated, came to live with us. He talked Norwegian with my father. I became very close to my grandfather, who told me about Norway and our relatives there. In 1935, when I was about eight, he bought me a pair of skis and taught me how to ski even though he by then was close to sixty. I knew, of course, that my name was Norwegian. Later in life a family reunion in 1969 established contact with my kin; a visit to Norway, where I saw the family farm in 1971, and a book about our family in America came together at about the same time and became a turning point in my life. Roots and heritage are very important to me. I had joined Torske Klubben in 1968.

Q: How do you see the purpose of an elite ethnic men's club in the 1990s?

A: Its main purpose is to enjoy good fellowship with other people who have a special feeling for roots. We want people who are proud of their heritage. I don't think a pride in belonging to an elite is important, but people are proud of being Torske Klubben members. I am at times a bit concerned that too many members with mixed ethnic backgrounds will weaken the Norwegian attachment. I therefore encourage more full-blooded Norwegians to join.[43]

The Academic World of Norwegian Culture

In a now-classic study of the American middle class in the twentieth century, C. Wright Mills considers the discontent that ambitious individuals may experience in academic life. The profession carries little status, he claims, in relation to the pecuniary sacrifices it exacts and the meager pay and lifestyle it offers. And, he continues, "the discontent of some scholars is heightened by their awareness that their intelligence far exceeds that of men who have attained power and prestige in other fields."[44]

Mills does not consider the immigrant experience. What he overlooks in his equation is the opportunity for rapid social advancement that an academic career offered children of immigrants, moving as they did from working-class to middle-class status in one generation. The ethnic community itself provided employment in its institutions of learning. Those in the field of Norwegian literature and language show how an ethnic heritage is transmuted into an academic career. Within the ethnic fold, it quite clearly bestowed social standing if not great pecuniary rewards. The teaching of the Norwegian—or more properly Dano-Norwegian—language began as instruction in the mother tongue, in congregational schools, academies, and colleges. It grew out of the needs and wishes of the immigrant community itself. The prominent Norwegian-American linguist Einar Haugen traced the teaching of Norwegian at the college and university level from the founding of Luther College in 1861, whose catalogs were printed in Norwegian, and a portion of them as late as 1906. Most of the students went out as pastors to serve in Norwegian-language congregations and needed a thorough linguistic training. Even after Luther College and the other immigrant institutions of higher learning became predominantly English in their language of instruction, they retained a faculty of Norwegian.[45]

Efforts to establish Scandinavian professorships began as early as 1869 with the pioneer Norwegian-American scholar Rasmus B. Anderson as a prime mover. In 1870 as an instructor at the University of Wisconsin, he introduced Norwegian into the curriculum. In 1875 he was made professor of Scandinavian languages. There is great family pride in his pioneer position; the "Ship Andersonian," a round-robin circulating within the family, continues its year-long travels, creating family unity. Al Stensby, a great-grandson, claimed: "If I didn't have a great-grandfather who was a celebrity, I would probably not have been interested in my Norwegian background."[46]

As a result of state legislative resolutions, the universities of Minnesota and North Dakota offered Norwegian instruction beginning in 1883 and 1891, respectively. The political clout of the Norwegian-American constituency is reflected in these actions. The University of Washington has offered courses in Norwegian regularly since 1912. These are historically the universities with the longest continuous teaching of Norwegian. The 1989 directory of Scandinavian studies in North America lists twenty-four institutions in the United States that offer at least some instruction in Norwegian, with a total enrollment in the first year of less than one thousand students. The universities of Wisconsin, Minnesota, and Washington and Luther and St. Olaf Colleges had the largest enrollments.

Most faculty with advanced degrees in Scandinavian studies, language, literature, history, and social sciences received their degrees from one of ten American universities; few have graduated from universities in Scandinavia. Twenty-six individuals of the 530 included in the directory with Scandinavian teaching and research interests considered themselves as primarily Norwegian language teachers.[47]

The very form of what is correct Norwegian—its orthography—has posed a problem for the instruction in Norwegian. In few instances—highlighted by the peculiarity of the Norwegian situation—is the concept of two cultures, one Norwegian, the other Norwegian-American, more clearly in evidence than in the discussion of what constitutes a literary Norwegian language. The common Dano-Norwegian literary language of Danish and Norwegian immigrants attained a nearly sacred quality. It was the language of their institutions, secular and religious, and of sacred and profane literature. The written Dano-Norwegian and the corresponding spoken forms continued in Norwegian Lutheran congregations beyond the transition to English in many immigrant homes. It was elevated as a formal spoken medium to a position far above the lowly old-country local peasant vernaculars. An elderly woman in Wisconsin who grew up in a home where English was the main language of communication but attended a church where services in Norwegian were common insisted that "as a child, I felt that Norwegian must be very special, since it was the language we used when we addressed God."

Norwegians in America clung to the cherished Dano-Norwegian as a literary expression of their heritage. The series of nationalistic orthographic changes in the homeland to make the literary language conform better to Norwegian speech habits, especially notable after the 1890s, and the specific legislated orthographic reforms in 1907, 1917, and 1938 were viewed by many Norwegian Americans as a betrayal of a common linguistic heritage. Still, around 1900, changes in Norwegian orthography could no longer be ignored in the immigrant community. The minor reforms of 1907 simplified the task of instruction for teachers of Norwegian. They worked with young people born in America whose loyalty to a specific spelling was not ingrained.[48]

Publications directed at older Norwegian Americans and people born in Norway, newspapers like *Decorah-Posten* and the church magazine *Lutheraneren*, resisted even minor changes that their readers would find troublesome. In 1926 the editor of *Decorah-Posten* wrote:

> We recently looked through the first volume of *Decorah-Posten* and found that the newspaper's linguistic form in 1874 was almost exactly the same as in 1926. And all other Norwegian journals in the Northwest are the same. But this has put us in the strange position that our newspapers have a dress that no longer exists either in the language of Norway or Denmark. We have become something for ourselves between the two.

A Norwegian-American orthographic tradition had emerged. Not until 1939 did the newspaper introduce the modest spelling reforms adopted in Norway in 1907, and only modest linguistic changes occurred thereafter until *Decorah-Posten*'s demise in 1972.[49]

The traditional language spoke to a primordial sense of identity and was endowed with an emotional aura that neither the reformed orthography and modernized linguistic usage of Dano-Norwegian, *bokmål*, as this predominant literary form was defined, or the competing official New Norse written standard, *nynorsk*, could bestow. Norwegian Americans rejected New Norse, a constructed nationalistic written form asserted to be a synthesis of rural dialects that had most faithfully retained the forms of Old Norse, as it had no place in their self-perception of who they were, and no

identifying emotional content. The confusion that the radical 1938 spelling reforms caused could not be ignored, however, by those who made a living teaching Norwegian. They made a decision in principle to follow the literary forms established by law in Norway and abandon the traditional standards employed by Norwegian-American publishers. Textbooks in the new spelling were ready in 1940, and Norwegian, one can claim, became an academic subject in American schools alongside other foreign languages.[50]

Norwegian studies in the United States thus obviously grew out of a Norwegian-American cultural world. It underwent a shift from the lower to the higher levels of learning, as one would expect, as Norwegian-speaking communities vanished. In the post–World War II era, Norwegian language instruction has mostly disappeared from high schools, and even earlier, in the 1930s, parochial instruction in Norwegian in the congregation ceased but continued in colleges and universities. This historic fact is easily lost sight of by those who view the situation from the homeland. A disrespectful attitude toward an immigrant culture may be the consequence. One example is revealing. With great effort, the Norwegian community in Chicago and commercial groups in Norway funded an endowed position in Norwegian literature and language at the University of Chicago in 1961. Guest professors from Norway regularly occupied the chair. In the early 1980s, to the dismay of Norwegian Americans aware of the situation, the current guest scholar suddenly decided that "real" Norwegian was the minority and rural-based New Norse, and resolutely abandoned the predominant Dano-Norwegian, or *bokmål,* hitherto taught, in favor of this less-known literary standard. Thus, out of ignorance of the Norwegian-American community the professor introduced a language conflict foreign to most Norwegian Americans based in sociocultural and political circumstances in Norway.[51]

The traditional immigrant vision of a national romantic Norway is even today perpetuated in Norwegian language instruction, especially at undergraduate institutions, and often reinforced with student folk dance groups, rosemaling decorations, and the serving of ethnic food items. The most evocative images persist. Those of a contemporary Norway frequently revolve around striking scenery from the land of the midnight sun and winter sporting events.

Like many small literature departments at both undergraduate and graduate levels, Scandinavian and Germanic departments, by which Norwegian language and literature are generally taught, struggle to maintain acceptable academic standards in granting advanced degrees and in the research agendas of their faculties.[52] From the perspective of national Scandinavian graduate institutions, there may be much to question. As early as 1911, professional students of Scandinavian formed their own organization, the Society for the Advancement of Scandinavian Study. Its history is one of struggle and modest achievements. Its annual meetings, though they currently have impressive attendance, reflect in the uncertain quality of many of the scholarly presentations the challenges that a lack of resources and institutional appreciation pose in maintaining standards in small and narrowly focused academic fields. Even so, Scandinavian studies have moved beyond their initial parochial limitations to become integrated into the American system of higher education.

The Choral Tradition

Male a cappella singing is a common Nordic and German cultural tradition. It has proven to be one of the most enduring cultural transplants and has been augmented with women's singing groups, but these were relatively few compared to the large number of men's groups. The Grieg Ladies' Singing Society in Chicago, the first women's choir there, was organized in 1915, some forty-five years after the all-male Normennenes Singing Society emerged as a purely Norwegian chorus in 1870 (figure 36). Although male choruses existed earlier, the male singing movement evolved in the 1870s. Some 275 male choruses were organized nationwide, the greatest period of growth falling between 1880 and 1920. Some of these, of course, functioned only briefly. Male choruses were a major movement in the Norwegian-American community, though it would be a

Figure 36. The Grieg Ladies' Chorus in Chicago. This women's chorus was formed in 1915 as the first Norwegian women's choir in Chicago. Photograph courtesy of Irene M. Bjorvik and the Grieg Ladies' Singing Society.

gross misconception to claim, as a journalist for the Chicago newspaper *Vinland* did in 1982, that in the nineteenth century "the first two things they [Norwegian immigrants] did when they formed a new community were build a church and start a men's chorus. Then they built their home." No new group has been formed since the 1970s, when only one new male singing society emerged. These singing groups have observed a strict male-only policy, even to the extent of forcing out of the Norwegian Singers' Association of America, formed in 1910, male choruses who have admitted women.[53]

In their repertoire and traditions the Norwegian-American singing societies are rooted in a national-romantic nineteenth-century Norway. They have thereby evinced the early Masonic connection in the homelands with fraternal practices and the general nationalistic nature of the male chorus movement. In America the Norwegian singing societies perpetuated a romantic preindustrial vision of Norway and perhaps thereby soothed nostalgic longings. The Grieg Ladies' Singing Society adopted the Norwegian Hardanger peasant costume (*bunad*), the one favored by national romantics, as its official dress when performing. Some of the early choruses, such as Normennenes, were elitist as well as nationalistic, gathering men at the upper strata of immigrant society. The Singing Society Bjørgvin, organized in Chicago 1882, revealed other forces at work in how associations were made. The strength of localism and an urbane exclusiveness barred from membership men who were not from the city of Bergen or its environs. Contrary to other Norwegian-American institutions and societies, choruses have maintained the use of the Norwegian language.

The Norwegian Singers' Association of America was a successor to the Danish, Norwegian, and Swedish singing society the United Scandinavian Singers' Association, formed in 1886. In 1892 the political conflict between Sweden and Norway caused the Swedish singers to withdraw; Danish and Norwegian singers had a formal cooperation until 1910, when the Norwegian national association came into being. Regional associations of male choruses organized both on the East Coast and the West Coast. Any ethnic restrictions that may have applied in the past are in the 1990s relaxed to the point where membership is open to anyone with an interest in Scandinavian song, music, and culture. Consequently, there has been a rebirth of a Nordic composition; other nationalities with traditions of male singing, such as German and Swiss, are well represented, but by no means exclusively. Cultural activities encourage a voluntary affiliation. Singing in Norwegian is a matter of rote learning, even for men of Norwegian ancestry, since most members are of the second or third generation and later. In many cases chorus membership has become a family tradition, illustrating how cultural traditions are passed on within individual families.

The large singing festivals, or *sangerfest,* remain the most expressive and grand events of the movement. Large spectacular festivals have been arranged every other year. The first one with Norwegian-American male choruses was held in Philadelphia in 1887, the second one two years later in Chicago. In 1962 in Salt Lake City and again in 1989 in Seattle, choruses from all over the United States convened for a *sangerfest.* Otherwise, regional festivals have been the norm. In the manner of other immigrant cultural activities, the choruses increasingly belong in the category of a "retirement culture," and the size and number of choruses are declining.[54]

Alf Lunder Knudsen was born in 1934 in Brooklyn, New York, to Alf and Hjørdis Lunder Knudsen, both immigrants from Stavanger, Norway. In addition to directing the Norwegian Male Chorus of Seattle and being active in the Pacific Coast Norwegian Singers Association, Knudsen has since 1990 owned and published *Western Viking* in Seattle, one of the two surviving Norwegian immigrant journals, and thus interacts with the Norwegian-American community in the final period of a linguistic transition (figure 37). He explained that the old-timers complained that there was too much English, and others that there was too much Norwegian. A logical solution was bilingual columns. As a local ethnic subculture declines, publications seek a national audience. *Western*

Figure 37. Alf Lunder Knudsen directing a male chorus in Seattle. Photograph courtesy of Alf Lunder Knudsen.

Viking has subscribers in all fifty states and, to quote Knudsen, "creates a semi-historical record of what is occurring in Norwegian America in the 1990s."

Q: How many members does the Seattle Norwegian male chorus have?

A: The chorus today has fifty singers. I brought the membership up to one hundred. It was at one time down to only thirty. It is tough to keep up.

Q: What are the ages of the members?

A: There are half a dozen in their thirties. Then the ages jump up to fifty, sixty, seventy, and eighty. They are not all Norwegian.

Q: How much of the repertoire is Norwegian?

A: At song festivals about two-thirds of the selections are in Norwegian and the remainder English. There are high school choirs that sing better in English, and on the other hand, some of the singers don't know Norwegian. The standard old repertoire remains the romantic nationalistic songs.

Q: What is the purpose for existing in the 1990s?

A: It is a dilemma. There are ten Norwegian male choruses on the West Coast. In Seattle there is the Norwegian Ladies Chorus, and there are women's singing groups elsewhere as well. They all, of course, preserve, promote, and perpetuate Norwegian music. At the U.S. bicentennial in 1976 I arranged the European Ethnic Song Festival. Since then, Norwegian men's and women's choruses have sung together. Earlier there was only rivalry and no cooperation. It is a social and cultural part of the Norwegian-American community.[55]

A Voluntary Ethnicity

In their study on Norwegian families, C. F. Midelfort and H. C. Midelfort stress the preservation of ethnic values and attitudes among Norwegian Americans through the generations. The findings of this study agree with theirs. Nevertheless, the question remains as to how many of the nearly four million first- and second-ethnicity Norwegian Americans in what David Hollinger describes as a postethnic America have any real sense, not to say active appreciation, of a special ethnic ancestry and identity. Even in heavily Norwegian Spring Grove, Minnesota, research efforts were rebuffed by a woman bartender with no Norwegian ancestry, who claimed that her Norwegian-American husband "doesn't give a d—— about being Norwegian"; the fact of his Norwegian background could not be denied. No conversation was arranged with the husband, though a pile of questionnaires was left in the local bar, and a number of these were completed and returned.[56]

Robert Hughes, himself an immigrant from Australia, in his *Culture of Complaint* (1993) defends a non-ideological multiculturalism as an educational concept, "learning to see through borders," and as an antidote to America's difficulty in imagining the rest of the world and other Americans. The future composition of American elites, he posits, "will lie with people who can think and act with informed grace across ethnic, cultural, and linguistic lines." Since differences in race, ethnicity, and culture will endure globally and within the United States, Hughes contends, and one big world family does not exist and will never likely emerge, the structures ethnic groups create are "eminently worth knowing about for their own sake."[57]

Those who cultivate a personal ethnic identity will not likely do so on a non-ideological basis or view multiculturalism in the pure light of education. Ethnocentricity becomes a much more compelling force; it does not automatically—although it may—invite tolerance or even interest in other ethnic and racial cultures. It is, however, for Americans of European extraction a matter of voluntarism. The decision to be ethnic or not is consequently an individual choice, as is the particular ethnicity. As the intermingling of nationalities proceeds over the generations, it furthermore poses a problem for many individuals to maintain information on multiple ancestral heritages, and one particular line may be favored. One may accept Hollinger's contention that this circumstance represents a step beyond multiculturalism. An awakened fascination with heritage is a common occurrence, as is a latent, but unconscious, feeling for roots and ancestry. Numerous Norwegian Americans claiming no particular interest in their background, on further questioning, revealed that a number of ethnic traditions are part of their family life. Interest may even be as amorphous as that of third-generation Norwegian-American Robert J. Engelstad, born in 1952 and currently employed in a large financial mortgage investment company in Washington, D.C., who stated: "We have no ethnic traditions, but I have a desire for such things." His father's seventy-fifth birthday in 1995 was observed with a Norwegian theme.[58] Even more common were the many interview subjects who enthusiastically related a rediscovered, or simply discovered, ethnicity cultivated with some passion. Interest was frequently triggered by altered family and social circumstances or by specific events relating to heritage.

Dianne Buttrick Sawyer, born in 1951 and now residing in Plano, Texas, is of English heritage on her father's side and English and Norwegian on her mother's. Dianne's grandmother was a second-generation Norwegian American. Dianne related how she began wondering about certain family traditions and where they came from, such as opening gifts on Christmas Eve, and why her Norwegian heritage had been suppressed. Her joining a Sons of Norway lodge in 1973, and her introduction through a new friend there to the Norwegian-American Harvard linguist Einar Haugen, who encouraged her to research her Norwegian family line, "opened a new door for me," Dianne insisted. Another route of discovery was experienced by Diana Fitzgerald, born in Brooklyn in 1924 and of Swedish and Norwegian descent on her father's side. She grew up in her Scandinavian grandparents' home with numerous ethnic traditions. Her 42-year marriage to an alcoholic and abusive man of Irish-Indian descent ended in 1989. Their two children think of themselves as Irish. Diana, a resident of Washington, D.C., rediscovered her Norwegian heritage in 1994, when the Winter Olympics in Norway served as a catalyst, creating pride in heritage, and encouraging her to become active in several ethnic organizations, though as she opined, "I wish Norwegians were a bit more fun."[59]

Marriage remains a significant avenue for "converting" to a new ethnic culture. Several telephone calls from women of no Norwegian background encouraged interviews with "super-Norwegian mothers-in-law." These daughters-in-law insisted that to be accepted, they had striven to become the best *lefse* bakers in the world and to acquire a taste for lutefisk. These women were placed in a facetious category of "ethnic survivors," and interviews were conducted with them rather than the in-laws. On later reflection, this category appeared in some cases as an appropriate description of both the joy and the adversity endured by these women who tried to become one with their husband's ethnicity. Likely due to ethnicity being identified with food, an immersion in a Norwegian-American cultural environment was more common for women than men. Catherine Egenberger, the initial "survivor," in Byron, Minnesota, explained about her marriage to Paul Halverson in 1982: "Paul's older brother, John, married a sensible 100-percent Norwegian Lutheran woman. I am from mixed background and was raised Catholic. Mary and Palmer [in-laws] were always nice to me, but I also was always aware that I was somewhat of an outsider." About their children, she stated that they "take for granted that we are Norwegian and have been raised on *lefse,* know the smell of lutefisk, and know all the troll stories."[60]

A different take on adopting a new ethnicity was offered by Nancy B. Thurson of Scituate, Massachusetts, born in 1935, who, as she wrote, was of very mixed European background, and "although my surname, Schlag, was German, I did not grow up with a tug to that culture or any other." In 1956 she married Andrew Roy Thurson, a Norwegian postwar immigrant from Flekkefjord, who upon becoming a naturalized American citizen three years earlier had Americanized his name, Arnfinn Torkildsen, to signal his intent "to put the Old Country behind him." "His young American wife," Thurson relates about herself, "was *very* interested in the very culture he was trying to put into the background." "I really thought," she recalls, "that it was great to have a name to put to oneself, to 'be Norwegian' instead of all-American." "My husband now says that I am more Norwegian than he," Thurson concludes. Clearly, her experience illustrates the attraction of unique cultural traditions and how these relate to ethnic identity in American society. As a child in school, Thurson recalled, "how much I 'envied' children . . . who 'were something'—perhaps Irish or German, or the one Jewish girl whose background and religion were unlike most of the rest of ours."[61]

Another example of a fascination with the idea of ethnicity, and the esoteric experience it might provide, was related by Patricia Barret Klove, born in 1924, a resident of Falls Church, Virginia, who is of old Yankee stock. Her mother belonged to the Daughters of the American Revolution. Now divorced from a Norwegian-American man, she related how when their children were in their teens, she developed an interest in genealogy and Norwegian traditions, eventually joining the Wash-ington Lodge of the Sons of Norway and the Norwegian Society, thereby also making her children aware of their Norwegian heritage. "My grandchildren are even more aware of being Norwegian," Klove explained, "because the grandparents on the other side do nothing about their Welsh and Irish heritage. I have introduced them to their Norwegian heritage."[62]

Norwegian-American community events and open ethnic boundaries, to be sure, create interest among individuals of Norwegian extraction, but they also invite people of any other ethnic background into a Norwegian-American fellowship. In the 1990s, the very ethnocentricity and vibrancy of Norwegian-American ethnicity as it is expressed on celebratory and festive occasions appeal to individuals whose ethnic background is not as clear or is not celebrated. It might be clarifying at this point to introduce two new terms: an *enlisting ethnicity* to categorize an ethnicity that regularly attracts converts or recruits, and a *contributing ethnicity* for a less active ethnicity. The assembled data make it obvious that as an identifying force Norwegian-American ethnicity enlists individuals on a voluntary basis. Fourth-generation Norwegian American Geneva Allen Finstad, born in 1935, tells how the annual church lutefisk supper of the St. Olaf Lutheran Church in Cranfills Gap, Texas, evolved from being the responsibility of the church women to a popular community project. The dried cod is purchased from the Olsen Fish Company in Minneapolis and soaked in lye by her son, Gary Finstad. "Many who are involved have no Norwegian background," she explained, "and a number of the some eight hundred who are served come from Waco, Dallas, and Fort Worth." Organizational life, as has been exemplified earlier, enlists many non-Norwegians in leading as well as supporting capacities. Mary Keller Lovdahl, born in 1924 of mixed German and British ancestry, of Appleton, Wisconsin, relates how after marrying Harold M. Lovdahl, a third-generation Norwegian American, she developed an interest in his background to the extent that she has served for many years on the district board of the Sons of Norway. "My first experience with Norwegian customs," Mary Lovdahl recalled, "was the first Christmas when we went to his mother's and she was cooking lutefisk! And I was pregnant—it was horrible." "But we never discussed whether or not our children should grow up being Norwegian, it was simply accepted."[63]

Given the multitude of experiences affecting the human condition, generalizing about any one of the forces that shape individual lives represents at best an assertion with numerous exceptions. Ethnicity becomes a fluctuating and fluid variable whether considered from an "enlisting" or "contributing" perspective. Its voluntary nature dictates dramatic individual differences in the importance it is accorded. Aside from broader social and political factors, ethnicity's role in an individual's life is determined by a large array of personal circumstances, as suggested in the cited examples, and by how these circumstances change during a person's lifetime. The broad thrust of demographic change, as Richard Alba states, may certainly be toward a weakening of ethnic identities. Yet, the United States will remain an ethnically dynamic society. Older ethnic groups may even be said, as Alba further suggests, to have been given new vitality by the surge beginning in the mid-1960s of immigration from Asia, Latin America, and the Caribbean. These new arrivals are reminders of the cultural pluralism that has historically characterized the United States, and encourage other Americans in some cases to establish ethnic boundaries, but more significantly to seek a satisfying and empowering ethnic identity. It is a quest, not to diminish its importance, that in contemporary American society is encouraged by a currently fashionable voicing of ethnic identity and pride in heritage.[64]

CHAPTER 6

The Norwegian-American Matrix

Preserving a Heritage

How do Norwegian Americans of the 1990s define their ethnic heritage? Why do they consider it worth preserving? These are the basic issues in any discussion of the generational adjustment of an ethnic group with a long history in the United States. One may quote Andrew Greeley, who in his 1974 work maintained that "certain aspects of the immigrant heritage are emphasized and developed in response to the challenge of American society," so that, he insisted, "an ethnic group has a cultural system that is a combination of traits shared with other groups and traits that are distinctive to its own."[1] In the 1990s this statement has the appearance of a truism.

In the waxing and waning of ethnic consciousness throughout American history, Norwegian Americans have as a group and as individuals combined accommodation with resistance to assimilative forces to invent, if you will, an expressive ethnic cultural identity. It is how this identity is manifested today within a largely middle-class Norwegian-American matrix that the preceding chapters have attempted to delineate and interpret.

The linguistic situation perhaps better than other indicators betrays the distance in time from the initial impulse. It is not only the audible "uffda" that defines linguistic limitations but also strange uses and misrepresentations of Norwegian words and expressions; these suggest an attitude that if it somehow sounds Norwegian, it must be all right. Also at the professional level, among mainly American-born academic instructors of Norwegian—evidenced even in the group's published communications—a stilted and idiomatically problematic usage of Norwegian may appear. Native fluency would naturally be an unrealistic expectation. But even at this level, language may be said to play a symbolic cultural role in addition to being an academic discipline. Norwegian language courses are offered outside academic institutions. Grandparents and parents conscious of a linguistic heritage may foot the bill to send offspring to a summer language camp that offers Norwegian. The best known is likely Concordia Language Villages, sponsored by Concordia College in Moorhead, Minnesota.[2]

Numerous local lodges of the Sons of Norway also give some rudimentary instruction in Norwegian, mostly taught by people not trained as teachers. The names of some of these same lodges are strange creations, for example, Ensom Stjerne Lodge in Texas, which in translation is "lonely star," not "lone star" as certainly was intended. Others are impossible neologisms, like Vannland, perhaps to render "lake country"; Skjønndal, for, one might assume, "beautiful valley"; and Epledalen, which though literally translated is "the apple valley," is a hopeless compound in Norwegian. They are all truly Norwegian-American inventions. In Arizona one finds such incongruous combinations as Desert Fjord and Overtro Fjell, the latter a strange rendering into Norwegian of Superstition Mountain. Lodge names with ethnic symbolism such as "Viking," "Leif Ericson," and "troll" are common, as well as the names of Norwegian historical persons, events,

and places. Startling linguistic constructs are, of course, found elsewhere, for instance, in Story City, Iowa, where a large sign decorated with rosemaling invites people as they leave town to "*Komme igjen*," for "come back," employing the Norwegian dictionary infinitive form for "come" rather than the correct imperative "*kom*" (figure 38). The expression also presents a problem of idiom, since a more common greeting would be "*velkommen igjen*" or even "*velkommen tilbake*," for "welcome back." In Norwegian-American settings of the 1990s, the use of any kind of Norwegian at all, rather than its accuracy, is obviously the paramount concern.[3] Few Norwegian Americans viewing these hapless linguistic efforts know much about Norwegian. The Norwegian language, or approximations of it, suggests, on the other hand, a primordial ethnic identity and provides acceptable cultural symbols of a Norwegian heritage, much like old-country food items, folk arts, and folk music.

The 1990 federal census reported about eighty thousand speakers of Norwegian in the United States. Anecdotal evidence makes this figure seem somewhat high, even though about one-third of the questionnaire respondents claimed to know some Norwegian. Minnesota alone had sixteen thousand individuals who spoke the language, making Norwegian the second most common European tongue in the state after German. The postwar immigrants probably represent a substantial part of the whole.

The Norwegian vernacular passed down through the generations in America has not entirely disappeared. Maurice Aslakson, born on a farm in Hoff Township in Pope County, Minnesota, in 1931, grew up in a Norwegian-speaking community. His grandfather, Haldor Aslakson, immigrated from Sør-Aurdal in Valdres in 1871 at the age of seventeen, more than 125 years ago; in 1875 he married seventeen-year-old Inga Halvorson, also from Valdres, and homesteaded as a lowly cotter son—a landless peasant—in Hoff Township alongside farmers' sons from the same district in Norway. Haldor brought his parents to America when they were in their sixties. He and Inga had eleven children, many of whom continued to live in the area. In such an ethnic family environment the local speech can be transferred. Maurice has never visited Norway, and now operates his grandparents' homestead, but he speaks an authentic dialect learned as a child interspersed with a few Americanisms. He claims, however, that there are very few who now master it: "I practice speaking Norwegian to myself in the barn." His children and grandchildren have not learned Norwegian.[4]

Farther north in the state, in the little town of Rothsay in Trondhjem Township in Otter Tail County, a truck stop off the busy interstate serves as a breakfast meeting place for twelve or more old-timers who get together to practice the Norwegian vernaculars learned in an immigrant home as children, where the language was passed down from parents, grandparents, and

Figure 38. Sign in Story City, Iowa, thanking visitors and welcoming their return. Its incorrect grammatical and idiomatic usage is symptomatic of the representation of the Norwegian language in the Norwegian-American community. Photograph by Odd S. Lovoll.

Figure 39. Two lifelong residents of Rothsay, Minnesota, and grandsons of Norwegian immigrant homesteaders Nanton Raw and Alf Honrud, enjoy their morning coffee at the local truck stop and café while practicing the Norwegian peasant vernacular they learned as children. Photograph by Odd S. Lovoll.

in two cases even from great-grandparents (figure 39). Many have ancestral roots in Hadeland but also in other districts mainly in eastern Norway, and they master the hybrid dialect forms of the old language as they had heard them. "We Norwegians around here like other Norwegians, and we enjoy getting together," someone at the truck stop volunteered. Viewed superficially, then, the language situation currently reflects the cultural vestiges of a once flourishing Norwegian-American community. The significance and nature of heritage, however, transcends external manifestations.[5]

In a certain sense a Norwegian-American heritage represents an identity through shared as well as individual historical memories, real and imagined; these are not associated with a

particular language. This sense of identity frequently rests in an individualistic and personal feeling for family and ancestry. In his poetic and perceptive 1988 novel, *An American Memory,* Eric Larsen, himself of Norwegian immigrant background, views three generations of a Norwegian-American family, descendants of Norwegian pioneers, on the midwestern plains. They are seen through the eyes of the fourth generation. "My father's father was born in the year 1882 on the tall-grass prairies of Iowa," the novel reads. "From his own distinguished and Norwegian immigrant father he inherited extremely long bones, a towering brow, deep-set eyes, and an intense, deeply unquestioning faith in Christ that sequestered him effectively from the mainstream of the changing world into which he was born," the text concludes. The narrator's memories and search for identity are imbued with sadness, the loneliness of growing up, but also with the fabric of real living as experienced on a nearly abandoned farmstead. His quest to understand himself eventually leads him to two trunks in the attic containing his father's possessions, "the remnants of his father." "Here indeed," he concluded, "I came upon my true heritage." His heritage is expressive of his family's history in America, and is a subtle transfer from one generation to the next of certain values, behavior, and attitudes. He discovers this heritage in memories of the past beginning with his great-grandfather, "who came from Europe . . . [and] his numerous children born on the nineteenth-century prairies of Iowa."[6]

The collective symbols of the group, displayed at celebratory events of many kinds, connote the superficial trappings of a Norwegian-American identity. As elements in a larger feeling for heritage, however, they carry significant symbolic strength. In defining heritage, most Norwegian Americans of the 1990s would seek a deeper and less concretely symbolized explanation in a generational transfer of moral and ethical standards. The evidence in the material collected for this study is overwhelming in its listing of positive traits associated with an ethnic heritage. Converging with this perception is the pride expressed in pioneer forebears. Their history frequently commences at the water's edge with the first of their ancestors landing on the American shore. Family histories, reunions, traditions—new and old, invented and transplanted—speak to a unique concept of a Norwegian-American heritage and why it is deserving of being passed on to later, American-born generations. Whether expressed in public space or harbored without fanfare in private, ethnicity persists as a defining component for individuals who identify with historical memories of a Norwegian-American presence.

Ethnic Humor

Pervasive stereotyping of immigrant nationalities and racial groups is an integral part of America's mass culture. The designated ethnic image of Scandinavians has never been as pronounced or as vicious as that of many other ethnicities. For example, by 1920, James S. Pula has determined, "the image of the crude, mentally deficient 'dumb' Polack was fixed in American stereotypy." For the Polish Americans, a long period of negative stereotyping by the host society promoted poor self-esteem and a rejection of heritage. The ethnic image furthermore discouraged economic advancement and thus assimilation into American society. Pula concludes that Polish Americans still suffer from a lack of social acceptance and full equality in hiring and promotion. Scandinavians may be designated "dumb Swedes," regardless of Nordic nationality, or "herring chokers," the term originating in herring gill netting but also carrying the idea that Scandinavians eat herring until they choke. In cartoons Scandinavians were generally portrayed as blond, blue-eyed, naive, and gullible; they were not, however—even though as an immigrant people they surely experienced negative attitudes—subject to the intense prejudice or systematic discrimination that became the lot of Slavic, Italian, and Jewish European populations. By 1920, most Scandinavians even placed themselves on the side of the Anglo-Saxon culture, joining in its negative imaging of "new" immigrant groups. To quote John Higham, the "Scandinavians showed their undiluted Americanism by joining in the cry for higher bars against the new immigration." In-group caricaturing of familiar stereotypes may thus be more acceptable to Scandinavians than to immigrant groups subject to ridicule and overt prejudice.[7]

Humor contributes to cultural awareness, and thus may be said to have a conservative function by retaining an ethnic identity. Simultaneously humor contributes to the process of acculturation. One may speculate that the popularity of the 1996 film *Fargo,* with its exaggerated regional speech habits, even among those it portrayed as slow-witted Scandinavians, speaks to the broad appeal of stereotypes as identifying figures. Jokes about stupidity are the most widespread of ethnic jokes. Stereotypes may, as in this case, even be more regional than ethnic, though the two frequently merge, and they obviously contain an element of anti-intellectualism. This portrayal of the funny-sounding Midwesterner is echoed in nu-

merous publications, from the 1987 book and tape *How to Talk Minnesotan* by Howard Mohr to the legion of compendiums and collections of Norwegian-American humorists. A phrase collection shows Scandinavian influence with examples like "Is it too windy back there then?" and Mrs. Axel Olson explaining to her grandson why the hired man died, saying "Well, when your time's up, your time's up." The collection carries a recommendation that it should be read aloud "preferably by one with a genuine, rural Scandinavian-American brogue!" The collection has its roots in the ethnic dialect humor that flourished until the end of the 1920s.[8]

Norwegian-American humor has long traditions. It was not basically different from other ethnic humor. The urban immigrant found entertainment in local theater groups and at social events where stereotypes were regularly presented. In this setting a Scandinavian commonality often prevailed. The Swedish-American vaudeville performer Hjalmar Peterson, alias "Olle i Skratthult," gained great popularity among all Scandinavians. His brand of ethnic humor, presented in Swedish vernacular in an American vaudevillian tradition, earned him great fame; his rendering of the popular ballad "Nikolina" sold thousands of records coast to coast. Scandinavian theater performances regularly concluded with dancing, making attendance a major social event. An example of the many performers of ethnic humor in the years after World War I, two sisters,

Eleonora and Ethel, performed as the "Olson Sisters" within the Norwegian ethnic community and won fame beyond it for their Norwegian dialect stories, mixed Norwegian and English dialogue, and their portrayal of the difficulty of immigrant adjustment. "Isn't it funny vit people here in America," a Norwegian immigrant woman said in one of their comic monologues, "dey don't talk Norwegian and dey don't talk English."[9]

The contemporary equivalents, having lost a Norwegian-speaking audience, may be said to have also lost the intimate context that made ethnic humor exude warmth and familiarity and on occasion even lifted it to a universal and eloquent exposition of the human condition. Much of contemporary Norwegian-American humor has its locale in a midwestern setting. Norwegian Americans in the East, especially, are less in tune with the most prevalent Norwegian-American humor than those in the Midwest, or even on the Pacific Coast, with its ties to Norwegian-American midwestern culture. Bill Kristian Jakobsen, growing up in Brooklyn in the 1950s and 1960s, recalls the self-deprecating stories told by Jewish and Italian playmates in the neighborhood and felt left out because "there were no good Norwegian jokes." He only heard "Ole and Lena jokes" in the 1980s, when he lived for a time in Oklahoma.[10]

In a series of publications, E. C. "Red" Stangeland of Sioux Falls, South Dakota, spread his "Ole and Lena Jokes" and his "Uff Da Jokes"

throughout the United States. His humor is crude, regularly making fun of ignorant Norwegian immigrants. The question-and-answer joke is popular: "What do you get when you cross a Norwegian with a flower? A blooming idiot." Another joke deals with confronting the new society and caricatures both newcomer and established immigrant: "When Ole came to America from Norway, he was extremely nervous when it came time to apply for citizenship. He approached the judge who gave the exam and confessed, 'Yudge . . . I don't speak Englesk so purty good . . . I am yust a poor uneducated Norwegian. I'm afraid about taking da citizen testing.' 'Don't you vorry, Ole . . . ve going make you a citizen of Junited States sure as my name is Yudge Bjorn Torvaldson.'"[11]

Stangeland appeared in stand-up comic acts with "Uncle Torvald," alias Robert L. Johnson, for twenty-three years until his death in August 1995. Johnson as Uncle Torvald removes his dentures and puts on a red stocking cap and an outfit to match to play the part of a slow-witted fall guy in this comedy pair (figure 40). Johnson, born in 1923, grew up in Sioux Falls, a third-generation Norwegian American on his mother's side and second-generation on his father's. His father operated a restaurant and saloon. Robert's upbringing was rather typical.

Q: Did you attend church as a child?

A: We belonged to the First Lutheran Church and never missed a Sunday service.

Figure 40. "Uncle Torvald," alias Robert L. Johnson, with E. C. "Red" Stangeland. Johnson's stereotyping of the Norwegian American typifies current ethnic humor, especially in the Midwest. Photograph courtesy of Robert L. Johnson.

Q: What was your father like?

A: My father was a good teller of stories. People liked him, and he liked people.

Q: How did you make a living?

A: I worked for the John Morrell Company in Sioux Falls. In later years in the hog butchering plant, which had a capacity in 1988 when I retired of killing and processing 1,000 hogs an hour.

Q: How did you become Uncle Torvald?

A: About thirty years ago I started doing

pantomimes like Stan Boreson in Seattle. I used some of his recordings and entertained in homes. Then in 1975 at the first Nordland Fest I started a joke-telling contest with "Red" Stangeland. Then I as Uncle Torvald and Red began entertaining several groups with forty-five-minute shows.

Q: Did you make much money?

A: We made from two hundred to a thousand dollars a show.

Q: Doesn't the kind of humor you represent give a less-than-flattering picture of Norwegian Americans?

A: Norwegians can take a joke on themselves. Not all groups can do that. They see beyond the joke. Being able to accept jokes has made people like Norwegians.[12]

Most Norwegian Americans apparently agree. There was a near 100-percent consensus on this point by those interviewed; Norwegians are able to jest about their American experience. Other practitioners of ethnic humor seem to agree. "Granny That Funny Old Lady," Dorothy Stager of Pipestone, Minnesota, appears on stage at state and county fairs and sells videos of her performances, where she "pokes fun at 'Pa,' her Norwegian roots and day-to-day events people of all ages can recognize." Her father was of German ancestry and her mother Norwegian. When asked why she chose to identify with her Norwegian side, she responded, "My Norwegian-American grandmother lived with us, and I decided early to be

Norwegian. I use her accent in my comedy shows. My sister decided to be German. I enjoyed the humor of the Norwegians. I never heard that the Germans made fun of themselves. The Dutch are an even worse audience as they don't think they should laugh at all."[13]

When asked about the nature of ethnic, specifically Norwegian-American, humor, the Norwegian-American television personality Stan Boreson, "The King of Scandinavian Humor," on KING Television in Seattle, responded, "Norwegian Americans have a lot of confidence and can therefore make fun of their heritage." The idea expressed was, of course, that other ethnic groups may not possess such self-confidence. In reality in-group ethnic stereotypes exist broadly in American culture. For example, in spite of the impression "Granny That Funny Old Lady" has of contemporary German Americans, German—referred to as Dutch, an approximation of *Deutsch*—dialect humor became a popular genre in the nineteenth century. There are other theories than the one held by Boreson and others about the nature of ethnic humor. It is important to bear in mind that it is the stereotypes that are consistently seen as laughable, and the person who believes stereotypes to be accurate and truthful. Boreson created many characters, such as "Aunt Lena," where he dressed up as a woman; "Uncle Torvald," later adopted by Robert Johnson; and even a Japanese cook who served "sweet and sour lutefisk" and "wanton pickled herring," crossing ethnic lines to caricature Norwegian-American cuisine. Thus, by telling ethnic jokes on his own group, the Norwegian-American individual is not accepting his ethnic identity as the object of ridicule; quite to the contrary, humor becomes a vehicle to assert a positive ethnic identity, whether told to an in-group audience or to an out-group listener. As Lois Leveen explains, by carrying stereotypes to the extreme—for instance, "What is two miles long and has an IQ of 6? A Sons of Norway parade"—humor reveals how ridiculous these extremes are, and makes "both the stereotype and its proponents the true butt of the joke."[14]

Self-irony was present among Norwegian Americans as well as among other ethnic populations from the earliest years of immigration. Ethnic humor appeared before the individual ethnic group had entered "a community of laughter" with the host society, and may then, as has been theorized, represent a means of earning acceptance of one's group through collective identity within the established culture. The contemporary exponents of Norwegian-American humor are not atypical of the majority of Norwegian Americans. Both Boreson and Johnson, for instance, are like many of the interviewed Norwegian Americans: Lutheran church-going persons with conservative political views who grew up in strongly Norwegian-American environments. By ridiculing the Norwegian-American stereotype, they affirm their own perceived ethnic merits, which naturally would not ever be the object of biased ridicule. Yet, they

Figure 41. A plaque decorated with rosemaling shows its Norwegian-American origin in the use of the inescapable ethnic term "uff da."

were, in fact, making fun of themselves; it is an unwritten law in ethnic humor that jokes are only told on one's own group. Humor thereby establishes and promotes ethnic boundaries. If indeed, as an apparent consensus within the group seems to hold, Norwegian Americans to an unusual degree enjoy derogatory and mocking jokes about in-group stereotypes, this characteristic may be further evidence of persistent ethnocentric forces.

Reinventing Folk Culture

The most distinctive folk arts and peasant crafts were produced in districts located in the central highland region of Norway, which experienced emigration early on. Immigrants from these mountain valleys and upland communities, joined by immigrants from the inner fjord districts of western Norway, were the main shapers of the pioneer Norwegian immigrant community in the American Midwest.

Nevertheless, not many immigrants had an opportunity to ply familiar rural crafts and art in America. During the early years of settlement, the demands of getting established and the availability of inexpensive mass-produced goods severely reduced the amount of hand craftsmanship. Goods from the peasant community, objects of artistic and cultural worth, made their way across the Atlantic with the immigrants. These are now proudly displayed in the homes of descendants of the immigrants as reminders of the early years of settlement and provide unique evidence of ethnic belonging. They attain high prices at auctions and sales. This continuity with the past has in recent times encouraged a revival of Norwegian folk arts and crafts.[15]

The folk art of rosemaling is the most emblematic of a Norwegian-American identity and the most popular expression of a transplanted and, if you will, reinvented folk tradition. In grossly corrupted versions as well as in highly skilled artistic forms, rosemaling appears on objects of many kinds, such as chests, boxes, plates, bowls, and farm and town signs; even on trash cans located on street corners; on programs for events; in serving establishments and on their printed menus; on store fronts; and as decorations in private homes, on cupboards and other pieces of furniture, to announce a Norwegian connection (figure 41). The objects are often artificial, created to be decorated rather than for practical use. They are, to quote from a history of Norwegian folk art, objects that show "respect of the Norwegian-American for relics of an ancestral past."[16] They become artifacts of an ethnic heritage. At times the most simple and perjured imitation of this venerable folk art serves as an ethnic symbol.

The revival of rosemaling in the Norwegian-American community is largely associated with the name of Per Lysne, although there were other contemporaneous practitioners of this art form. A line of continuity to the past and to the immigrant community is, however, difficult to establish. In the late nineteenth century, rosemaling was even a dying tradition in the homeland. Lysne emigrated from Lærdal in Sogn in 1907, the son of a painter who was associated with the revival of this art in Norway. Lysne practiced his art in America, his best works being in the one living art tradition in Os in Hordaland, with which he was intimately familiar. In America Lysne developed a following beginning in the 1940s and became the mentor of such influential Norwegian-American rosemaling artists as Ethel Kvalheim. Although interest was awakened in that decade, a flourishing of rosemaling in America occurred later, in the late 1960s and 1970s.[17]

All of Lysne's students were women. In Norway rosemaling had been a traditional male activity. A commentator on the subject explains female domination in the latter-day rosemaling movement by the fact that the art came to be seen as a free-time activity and hobby craft, and was presented in women's columns in local newspapers or in women's publications. It became an ethnic artistic expression and a pastime. Its genuine Norwegian character made it more attractive than other folk arts and crafts. It became a craft for their Norwegian background, as one artist insisted. Ethel Kvalheim's experiences with rosemaling illustrate how it was transformed in America from a male-dominated art to one practiced almost solely by women. Kvalheim was born in Stoughton, Wisconsin, in 1912. Three of Kvalheim's grandparents were born in Norway, and one in America of Norwegian parents.

Q: When did you meet Per Lysne?
A: After I married Arthur Kvalheim, I lived one block from Lysne. My interest in rosemaling started about 1940 when I saw what Per Lysne could do. I visited him in his studio.
Q: What was Lysne's role in the art movement?
A: Rosemaling was done in several parts of the country, but Per Lysne must be credited with bringing this art from Norway.
Q: What did you paint?
A: I painted mostly in the Telemark style and until 1967 painted and sold artifacts. I didn't know any other painter until I met Vi Thode at an art show in Madison.

Vi Thode, born in 1917, is of old-stock American background. She grew up sixty miles west of Hannibal, Missouri, and moved to Stoughton in the 1960s. She exemplifies the many practitioners with no Norwegian background who took an interest in rosemaling.

Figure 42. Wall cupboard decorated by Vi Thode in American Rogaland rosemaling style. Photograph courtesy of Vesterheim Norwegian-American Museum.

Her experience represents a stage in making ethnic cultures mainstream American. Thode has authored five books on this folk art.

Q: Where did you learn rosemaling?

A: I took classes from nearly "everybody" but without instructional material after coming to Wisconsin. I learned little by little and practiced mostly the Rogaland style. This painting tradition is the only one that developed in a special American Rogaland style (figure 42). The Halling style, for instance, has not changed much, although a few painters like Dorothy Peterson [artist in Cashton, Wisconsin] have done something different in this style.

Q: How long did you yourself teach?

A: I have taught rosemaling for thirty years.

Q: Who were your students?

A: I usually had from fifteen to twenty students. They were of all kinds of nationalities. Not all had any artistic skills.

Q: Do you think interest in rosemaling will continue?

A: Interest will last into the next century, but it will obviously die out like in Norway. It is more popular here than over there. The Wisconsin State Rosemaling Association, founded in Stoughton, has perhaps two hundred to three hundred members, mostly women, but a few men. Some are very commercially inspired and just look for something to sell. These are not the real artists.[18]

The blossoming of American rosemaling may be dated to the first National Rosemaling Exhibition sponsored by Vesterheim Norwegian-American Museum in Decorah, Iowa, in 1967, as a part of the first Nordic Fest. Artists from the upper Midwest and elsewhere in the United States exhibited. The Norwegian rosemaling artist Sigmund Aarseth was invited to conduct the first class. What followed were annual instruction sessions by Norwegian artists. These stressed historical regional accuracy in style and were critical of the departures from the regional traditions of the early revival pioneered by Per Lysne and his followers. The careful study of regional styles has continued, though both the Rogaland and the Halling styles have developed American traditions, thus suggesting an ethnic reinvention in addition to an ethnic revival. "I would say my style might be something called Minnesota American Rosemaling," Millie Jacobson claims. In Plano, Texas, Suzanne Gary Katz, of English background, teaches the American Rogaland style learned from Vi Thode, and explains that "the Rogaland style is natural in this country because of its similarity to the Pennsylvania Dutch tradition."[19]

Sigmund Aarseth, born in 1936 in Hjørundfjord in Sunnmøre in western Norway, studied painting in Oslo, and became a master painter in the German craft tradition. He learned rosemaling styles in Telemark and Valdres before visiting the United States and becoming a regular instructor in the art for American students.

Q: What is the position of rosemaling in Norway compared to America?

A: There is absolutely no comparison. In Norway there are three words you should not say: *nisselue, graut* [pixie-cap, porridge], *rosemaling*. They are considered very romantic and very country. There are no schools or even a place to exhibit and no competitions in the same way as in America.

Q: How would you explain the interest among Norwegian Americans and also among Americans of other nationalities?

A: In America there is a strong interest not only in folk art but in decorative painting. Good painters have picked up the rosemaling techniques quickly even though they only heard about it in my classes. This interest has broken all ethnic boundaries. I have had Native American students and many Japanese.

Q: Are the regional traditions confined to certain localities in America?

A: In America styles are more tied to painters than to areas. I would say that there are nine or ten good painters with their own personal style who have formed different schools of rosemaling in America.

Q: What about the different styles?

A: The Rogaland style, for instance, became nearly the "Vi Thode style," because she worked on it with such talent and got many followers. There is perhaps a little jealousy be-tween different styles; one who paints Halling-dal might think that is best. And, frankly, some people talk down a little on the Rogaland style, but I think it is decorative and has come to stay in America. On one of the American rosemaling tours to Rogaland, there they had a display of old Rogaland painting. The American artists were all more or less surprised to see the real difference from what they call "Rogaland" in America. It is an example of how a style rooted in Norwegian tradition can make new roots in America and become an American style.[20]

A phenomenal growth in interest in rosemaling is evidenced in the numerous local and regional societies from coast to coast that cultivate this art form: these range from the California Rosemaling Association and Western Rosemalers' Association in the Seattle area to the New England Rosemalers' Society and the Mid-Atlantic Rosemaling Society, with many large and small groups existing in between; groups such as Illinois Norsk Rosemalers' Association, South Dakota Rosemaling Association, and Wisconsin State Rosemaling Society as well as smaller groups, like the Fox River Valley Rosemalers in Illinois, and the Coulee Region Rosemalers and the Twin Ports Rosemaling Association, both in Wisconsin, and the Rosemalers of New Mexico in Albuquerque. About fifteen hundred subscribers receive the Vesterheim *Rosemaling Newsletter,* published in Decorah. These organizational developments reflect an explosive flourishing since the 1970s of a traditional art form that cannot be understood unless ethnicity is considered as a major force. Even given the appeal of rosemaling on purely aesthetic and decorative grounds to Norwegians and non-Norwegians alike, its striking visible call to a unique heritage, in its artistic as well as in its more spurious presentations, speaks to an individual search for roots and identity with the past that is evident in many areas of Norwegian-American life. Functioning in this capacity, the revival in America of this folk art represents a Norwegian-American reinvention and reinterpretation of tradition. Rosemaling, even on caskets and grave markers, discloses a deep emotional component in ethnic identity.[21]

The carved *kubbestol* constitutes an ethnic icon of another folk art, wood carving, either decorated with rosemaling or preserved in a wood finish. This traditional Norwegian piece of folk furniture, a log chair, is carved from a single log, or *kubbe*. Like other wooden objects, whether painted or not, the *kubbestol* reveals the purely decorative and symbolic role of ethnic folk art. Wood-carvers produce the variety of items decorated by rosemalers, and the art has remained largely a male activity. In Norway the carved acanthus and the *kubbestol* combined at the turn of the century to become strong Norwegian national symbols. Tarkjel Landsverk, emigrating from Seljord in Telemark to Minnesota in 1883, became the best-known exponent in America of the combination of acanthus carving and the *kubbestol*.[22]

Decorative wood carving was the art most commonly continued among Norwegian-American artists. The revival in this art form beginning in the 1970s, nearly a decade after the beginning of the rosemaling revival, had strong links to the past because artists like Halvor Landsverk—the son of Tarkjel, born in 1909—have continued the older tradition and remained active into old age. Their works overlapped the broader revival in wood carving. Halvor, still active in 1997, has carved over three hundred log chairs, and in his designs gives a more prominent place than his father did to Viking motifs and scenes from Norway, but he continues with acanthus, giving it "a bolder, more agitated character." Again, ancient skills are preserved and new traditions created based on the old models. Between 1983 and 1994 nine American craftsmen gained gold medal status through repeated awards in the annual national competitions sponsored by Vesterheim Norwegian-American Museum.[23]

Harley Refsal of Decorah, Iowa, born in 1944, with all his grandparents immigrants from Norway, has a level of accomplishment in the Scandinavian national style of freestanding figure carving that has made him a teacher and a revivalist in this technique in Norway as well as in America. In fact, when he taught his first class in the late 1980s in Norway, the venerable art of figure carving was dead there. National romantic skills and sentiments are thus traveling back to the homeland. They are, as folk artist Sigmund Aarseth insisted, much more

Figure 43. Wood-carver Phillip Odden sitting in a kubbestol, *or log chair, he carved. Photograph by Odd S. Lovoll.*

prized in America than in Norway. These immigrant influences with their roots back to the nineteenth-century emigration era are also evident in the currently common group visits by members of the *bygdelag* societies. Receptions for American kin, as when the Telelag conducts its annual *stevne* in Telemark—in the heart of traditional Norwegian folk culture—become celebrations of an idealized vision of the ancestral district. Such events are replicated elsewhere in Norway and confront modern-day Norwegians with the reality of a Norwegian-American concept of a shared heritage.[24]

Else J. Bigton, an immigrant from Norway, and Phillip Odden, a third-generation Norwegian American, are accomplished wood-carving artists. They have operated Norsk Wood Works in Barronett, Wisconsin, since 1979, and carve and sell beds, cupboards, plates, and other objects (figure 43). Odden carves log chairs, about eight to ten annually, and, to quote an art historian, has "during the past few years moved toward a rougher [acanthus] style and introduced some of the playfulness and fantasy found in some early folk material." The historian goes on to predict that it is a direction that the revival may take, "now that the original sources have been quite well explored and many of the techniques mastered."[25] Bigton and Odden have jointly authored a manual in the techniques of wood carving in Norwegian, again giving evidence of a tradition actively pursued in America that has fueled interest back in Norway.

Q: Who purchases carved objects?

A: They are all ordered, and not everyone who places an order is Norwegian. They are people fascinated by Norwegian folk art and have an interest in advance. They are in general interested in heritage. Wood carving sells well.

Q: What about your Norwegian customers?

A: They have a romantic view of Norway. They interpret Norway as a rural country with mountains and fjords and request romantic carved scenes with a stabbur [traditional storehouse on pillars], for instance. They create a "Norwegian Room" in their homes like a shrine to their heritage.

Q: Why do you think they need such a room?

A: It is important to have a sense of place, where you or your ancestry came from.[26]

Folk art in all its variations as it exists in the United States satisfies the specific needs of identity and belonging, but it also has a deep individualistic quality, and it develops unique interpretations. Folk art attracts the interest and participation of people outside the ethnic group, and in this way, to express these developments in traditional terms, represents immigrant contributions to American culture. In fact, the folk art expressions as interpreted in America are simply becoming a part of a common American cultural heritage. This is as true in folk music and folk dancing as in other popular art forms; the revival of these Norwegian folk expressions has followed the same

pattern as the revival of painting and wood carving.

The venerable Hardanger fiddle, or *hardingfele,* is the most unique and expressive of the Norwegian folk instruments. Its four additional lower sympathetic strings resound to the vibration of the four upper strings as these are being stroked, giving the instrument a sound similar to the Scottish bagpipe. On June 18, 1983, a small group of American Hardanger fiddle enthusiasts meeting in Mount Horeb, Wisconsin, launched the Hardanger Fiddle Association of America. This group succeeded another society, Spelemanns Laget af Amerika (The Fiddlers' Society of America), organized in Ellsworth, Wisconsin, in 1914, at a time when there were many players. In traditional style they arranged fiddle competitions to promote "the old music heritage from father's and mother's land." Its activity subsided around World War II, and an attempt to revive it by arranging a competition in 1952 failed. Beginning in the early 1920s, there was a revival of interest in the homeland that since has renewed the popularity of this national folk instrument. The more recent American effort draws on this reawakening, and folk music remains a living tradition with many accomplished musicians. In America, however, there are few fiddlers among the several hundred people who have joined the new society. Rather uniquely, St. Olaf College offers instruction in the Hardanger fiddle by Andrea Een, who competes in the contests in Norway

Figure 44. Andrea Een, professor in the department of music at St. Olaf College, gives instruction on the venerable Hardanger fiddle. She actively works to revive interest in this national folk instrument through the Hardanger Fiddle Association of America. Photograph courtesy of Andrea Een.

and is an active participant in the Hardanger Fiddle Association of America (figure 44). Its stated goal is "to help preserve and promote the music of the Hardanger fiddle, the regular fiddle and Scandinavian dance in America."[27]

The stated intent of the fiddle association, "to acquaint Americans of Scandinavian descent with these elements of their ancestral heritage," does not limit participation to an extended Scandinavian category, which is open to anyone interested regardless of ethnic background. This situation is even more evident in dancing than it is among Hardanger fiddle enthusiasts. Many of the numerous Norwegian or Scandinavian folk dance groups, organized independently or as interest groups in lodges, societies, and educational institutions, frequently attract dancers without any ancestral ties to Scandinavia. In the Seattle area, for instance, the Skandia Folkdance Society, founded in 1949, is one of the several popular Nordic folk dance groups in the area. Only about half of the active members, musicians as well as dancers, are of Scandinavian heritage, and even the large Asian population is represented among the dancers. Dances taught go beyond the Swedish, Danish, and Norwegian traditions in hambo, schottische, and waltz to include more intricate local dances, such as the telespringar and other regional variants. Music and dance become universal languages. The Leif Erikson Lodge of Sons of Norway in Seattle sponsors Leikarringen, formed in 1960. It is a purely Norwegian ethnic folk dance group,

Figure 45. The Stoughton High School Norwegian Dancers. Photograph courtesy of Jean Reek.

and the dancers perform in their Norwegian folk costumes, or *bunad*, at community and Norwegian-American functions.[28]

The Stoughton High School Norwegian Dancers cultivate another type of Norwegian folk dancing (figure 45). The group began in the spring of 1953 as part of the physical education program, inspired by the reintroduction of May 17 festivities the year before, and has become a touring folk dance group of high school students. The founder, Jean Reek, of English ancestry, exemplifies the "Norwegian by choice" ethnicity, symbolized in her home, which is entirely decorated with wood carving and rosemaling by such artists as Per Lysne. By incorporating Norwegian folk dancing in a high school curriculum, Reek became a part of a revival, which made her "Anderson, Johnson, and Swanson students aware of their heritage," interpreted as folk art and popular dancing.[29]

Skoal, Y'all

Figure 46. The Texas bunad *of the Norwegian Society of Texas, modeled by Phil and Maroline Megard. Its swirled symbols of Texas incorporated into a Norwegian festive peasant garment suggest the adaptation and reinvention of Norwegian cultural expressions in the American environment. Photograph courtesy of Phil and Maroline Megard.*

Dancing as a way of identifying with a specific ethnicity, and one which attracts people of varied ancestries, is promoted by many bands throughout the country. Such musical groups as Skål Klubb Spelmannslag, organized around 1990, are indicative of a growing audience. They perform at festivals, fairs, and other events, sell tapes, and create interest in old-time Scandinavian music.[30] In 1988 the Norwegian Society of Texas adopted as its official *bunad* a special Texas fantasy pattern, originally designed for Leikarringen, its dance group, but worn by everyone, men and women. As described in chapter 2, few creations can be said to symbolize more firmly the adaptation and reinvention of a Norwegian peasant tradition to suit an American environment: cotton and polyester have been substituted for wool, and the design includes "Texas bluebonnets and Indian blankets, a mockingbird tail, oil derrick, and lone star all put together in a pattern of rosemaling swirls" (figure 46). These are the symbols of a Norwegian Texas identity, a visible two-culture concept, if you will, a reinvented, transplanted tradition displayed with pride to announce ethnic belonging.

At a national level in the ethnic community, the *bunad* worn by women in the Sons of Norway—the official dress of the earlier Daughters of Norway—may be regarded as a pure Norwegian-American costume. Its design was inspired by the festive peasant *bunad* from the Hardanger region in western Norway. This isolated and rugged coastal district with its unique folk life appealed to nineteenth-century national romantics; depicted by artists and praised by poets, it symbolized the essence of the visionary national impulse. The persistent annual reenactment at the *stevne* of Hardanger-laget—the regional society representing that district—of the wedding scene in the famed national-romantic painting *The Bridal Procession in Hardanger,* by Adolph Tidemand and Hans Gude, perhaps more than any other event reveals the idealized and romanticized notions of Norway present in the Norwegian-American psyche.

Winter Sport as an Ethnic Symbol

The formative years of skiing in the United States toward the end of the nineteenth century reflect one aspect of the reorientation of American culture during the decades on either side of 1900. The development of skiing can be seen as one way in which antimodernism expressed itself in the pre–World War I generation. Skiing provided both a healthy and a moral outlet for individuals who wished to escape from a materialistic and urban society without abandoning its comforts and advantages. As E. John B. Allen explains in *From Skisport to Skiing,* published in 1993, the privileged American college students who took to skiing as a recreation and sport "kept its Norse foundation but modified it to suit their leisure-oriented, romantically inclined youth."[31]

Urbanization affected Norwegian Ameri-cans on their scattered farmsteads as well as those who lived in towns and large metropolitan centers. As they attained a middle-class economic position, Norwegian Americans wherever they resided imitated urban patterns of behavior in housing, dress, household amenities, and the like, inhibited only by their cultural background and the pietistic influence of the Lutheran Church. The *bygdelag,* which emerged at that time, with a largely rural membership but not infrequently led by urbanized successful Norwegian Americans, may be viewed as another kind of reaction against the constrictions and conformities of an industrial and materialistic America, and as a desire to return to the freshness and openness of nature. The renewed passion for skiing among Norwegian Americans was, then, another side of a strong antimodernism in American society. But, perhaps, even more clearly, skiing became for Norwegians in America as well as in the homeland a quintessential ethnic activity that embodied many of the most treasured mythologies of the group.[32]

Norwegian immigrants introduced the sport of skiing to America. Its genesis and history may be traced from its utilitarian function in 1841, when American neighbors in Wisconsin discovered the ski tracks of Gullick Laugen from Numedal, who had gone on skis to Beloit to buy flour, and wondered what animals had left the strange marks in the snow; to the legendary "Snowshoe" Thompson, or Jon Thoresen from Telemark, who for nearly twenty years beginning in 1856 carried the mail on skis across the wild Sierra Nevada mountains; to the sport's recreational and competitive developments in the 1880s. Cross-country and ski-jumping competitions then became an ethnic transplanted winter culture. Until the 1850s, skiing in Norway had served mainly a utilitarian function as a means of transportation, though it had deep mythological roots in the nation's history and was linked closely to the creation of a Norwegian identity. In that decade a revolution in ski design and bindings occurred in mountainous Telemark, making skiing a recreational and competitive sport, and giving rise to later romantic claims of Telemark being "the cradle of modern skiing." These developments all occurred during a period of high romanticism and striving for national identity. The sport inspired patriotic sentiments and became a true expression of Norwegian national aspirations.[33]

The first actual ski competition took place in an urban setting in Oslo in 1866, when "the Telemark Skiers Came to the Capital." Symbolizing the transfer of tradition, Sondre Norheim himself, credited with pioneering modern skiing, moved from Telemark in Norway to North Dakota in 1884, when he was nearly sixty years old. Family pride and a persistence of myth and tradition remain as cherished legacies. Two of his great-great-great grandchildren, both in working-class circumstances, Bonnie Pine Haven, born in 1942, and Jack Pine, born in 1949, who live in Portland, Oregon, recall tales of Sondre's exploits passed down through the generations to children and grandchildren on the family farm in North Dakota, and how "Sondre got in trouble from his father because he jumped from the top of the roof."[34]

In the thirty years after 1880, during the period of heaviest Norwegian immigration, local clubs promoted skiing sports, laying the foundation for modern skiing. Modern skiing represents a transformation and a process of modernization of this sport as it adjusted to the American consumer society. In 1905 the National Ski Association (NSA) was formed on the initiative of the Norwegian-American skier Carl Tellefsen in Ishpeming, Michigan, and as many as twenty-eight clubs joined in the next ten years. The NSA's role was to regulate club activities in order to assure equality in competitions. The many local clubs became cults with strong nationalistic tones and in the early period had ethnic membership qualifications. As Allen explains, the sport retained the ideals and ethnic exclusiveness associated with the term *Ski-Idræt,* embodying both heroic qualities and a goal of achieving purity of mind and body. The Norwegian explorer Fridtjof Nansen became an archetypal representative of the *Idræt* ideal in 1888, when he and his party crossed the Greenland continental ice shelf on skis. This was an unheard of and sensational deed that for the first time made skiing known to the world; it provided an international hero for Norwegians everywhere.[35]

Aurora Ski Club, organized in Red Wing, Minnesota, in 1886, was the first ski club in America of note, though the year before clubs had been organized both in St. Paul, Minnesota, and in Altoona, Pennsylvania. The two brothers Mikkel and Torjus Hemmestvedt, Norwegian champions, introduced ski jumping to the American public at Aurora's first tournament on February 8, 1887. As new clubs were formed, ski jumping became closely associated with Norwegians; it conveyed a male winter rite while creating a new set of ethnic heroes. The daring competitive flight from takeoff to landing affirmed the Viking spirit and masculinity of the participants. Indeed, "ski jumper" acquired frequent usage as a nickname for all Norwegians, not only for those who displayed fearless feats of bravery on the many ski-jumping scaffolds that were built; these announced an ethnic presence of some magnitude.[36]

Norge Ski Club was organized by a group of eighteen young Norwegian-born men in Chicago in the banner year of 1905, when Norway unilaterally declared the union with Sweden dissolved, its name "Norge" (Norway) proclaiming a patriotic ethnicity. A distinguishing characteristic of modern sport, as argued by Allen Guttmann, is the principle of equality and achievement; there is no exclusion on the basis of class, and a democratic spirit is thereby encouraged. This circumstance was much in evidence at ski competitions. Norge Ski Club arranged its first competition at Fox River Grove in 1907. There on Cary Hill the club eventually built a large steel scaffold. Norge Ski Club emerged at a time of a gradual Americanization, as well as of a revival, of skiing following a period of declining interest in the 1890s. It was, in fact, the acceptance of the sport by the American public that produced the really large attendance of the 1920s. Norway had, the Chicago newspaper *Norden* explained, its famous Holmenkollen Day, while Chicago had its Norge Day at Fox River Grove. It became a celebratory ethnic event alongside May 17, with the same enthusiastic crowds as at meets in Norway, "with lunch packages, and coffee, warm sausages, orange crates [to sit on], and a bottle of spirits in the back pocket."[37]

A transition occurred in the 1920s and 1930s as the sporting activities of downhill and slalom skiing in the alpine countries were carried to America by a wave of immigrants from that region of Europe. In the interwar years, skiing became mechanized, manifested in new skiing venues, in the technical attributes and fashions of the sport, and in their marketing. By 1940 skiing was ready to take off as a major industry; it was a development that heralded the enormous flourishing of the sport in the postwar decades.

The alpine activities—daring slalom combinations and downhill events—are by far the dominant competitions. Currently both men and women compete. In 1995 more than fifty thousand people belonged to the United States

Ski Association in Park City, Utah, divided among 369 member clubs, the vast majority in the alpine branches. Actually, only eighteen member clubs are listed specifically in the Nordic category, but many of the other clubs also sponsor Nordic events. The transition to alpine disciplines thus did not eradicate the Norwegian, and, to be sure, Nordic heritage is still expressed competitively in cross-country racing and ski-jumping meets. For easily understood reasons, cross-country skiing is the most commonly practiced sport and increasing in popularity. But even though ethnic practices are carried on, the disciplines attract an ever more ethnically mixed participation. While family traditions, with several generations of the same family joining a particular ski club, may maintain a visible Norwegian-American presence in the membership, many younger members, as much as 70 percent, for instance, in the Norge Ski Club, mainly people from the community, do not have a Norwegian ancestry. Even so, as the Norwegian-American veteran ski jumper LeRoy Ruud stated, ski-jumping is still "an identifying symbol for Norwegian Americans."[38]

Nordic combined events, jumping and cross-country, find participants in many clubs. The Nordic Minneapolis Ski Club, incorporated in 1926, attracts young skiers. Fourth-generation Norwegian-American on his mother's side and champion ski jumper Mark Hammel, born in 1965, knew very little about his ethnic heritage, ski jumping as a family tra-

dition being the only reminder (figure 47). Older Norwegian friends in north Minneapolis with stronger ethnic ties than he became his role models in ski jumping when he was only eight. A successful competitive career in ski jumping was in time launched. Many skiers have a general interest in the activity, but for others it embodies an ethnic heritage, and both may be found in the jumping and Nordic-combined clubs and in the many other clubs not specifically dedicated to the Nordic heritage. Its ethnic symbolism is naturally most evident in clubs in heavily Norwegian areas, such as in the Eau Claire Ski Club, founded in 1887, and in the Snowflake Ski Club, founded in Westby in 1923, both in western Wisconsin. A high percentage of the jumpers there are of Norwegian ancestry. Individual and groups of Sons of Norway lodges own skiing and other recreational facilities. The Leif Erikson Lodge in Seattle, as one example, owns Trollhaugen Ski Lodge in the Snoqualmie Pass in Washington.[39]

Skiing encourages close contacts with the Norwegian homeland, and more recent impulses from there express themselves in organizational events such as the Birkebeiner competitions and Ski for Light. Cross-country skiing is a Nordic discipline that has grown in popularity. A health-conscious American public has discovered, as did collegiates and urbanites in the earlier history of the sport, physical and emotional wellness in skiing. The American Birkebeiner, known as the Birkie, is an annual Nordic ski festival in Hayward, Wisconsin,

Figure 47. Mark Hammel of Minneapolis wins first place in the North American Championships in Ishpeming, Michigan, in 1988. Photograph courtesy of Jeff and Fran Hammel.

begun in 1973 and patterned after the one in Lillehammer, Norway, which commemorates a historic event during Norway's civil war in the thirteenth century.[40] Two Norse warriors wearing birch-bark leggings for protection, thus called "birkebeiner," or "birch leg," saved the infant heir to Norway's throne, the later King Håkon Håkonson, from being captured by his enemies by escaping on skis, carrying the royal child for fifty-five kilometers to safety. This considerable marathon distance is raced by competitors from all over the United States and from foreign countries, who assemble in Wisconsin for the Birkebeiner competitions. There is the "korteloppet," or "short race," of twenty-five kilometers for the less intransigent

competitor, and there is the Barnebirkie, or children's Birkie, introduced by the Sons of Norway in 1987 (figure 48). The latter is the largest children's race in the country; children between the ages of three and thirteen ski down Hayward's main street. Some twenty-five thousand skiers and spectators assemble annually for this winter event. The fame of the American Birkebeiner ski race, its Norwegian linguistic references, and its celebration of the splendor of the Norwegian Middle Ages again communicate the sport's ancient Norse roots and immigrant foundations.[41]

The Ski for Light ski races are more reflective of a social-democratic contemporary Norway than they are of a heroic past, though

Figure 48. The Barnebirkie races for young skiers in Hayward, Wisconsin. Photograph courtesy of Sons of Norway.

like the Birkebeiner race, they promote cross-country skiing, albeit specifically for blind and visually impaired athletes. The event emulates Ridderrennet, "The Knight's Race," in Beitostølen, Norway, arranged for the first time in 1964, indicative of the social-democratic inclusiveness of the Norwegian welfare state. The name refers to the saga age, a constant source of inspiration, and the story of Sigvat from Valdres, who saved himself and his bride by a desperate leap on horseback over a dangerous waterfall while being pursued by his enemies. A

romantic vision of an army of knights is conjured up at the ski races for blind competitors, each one accompanied by a sighted guide on the racing course. The first national Ski for Light tournament took place in 1975 in Summit County, Colorado, and since has been arranged at various points throughout the United States, augmented by local competitions.[42]

The Norwegian ski instructor Olav Pedersen, born in Voss, Norway, in 1917, encouraged by the blind Norwegian entertainer and director of a health sports center for the disabled, Erling Stordahl, became the recognized "father of Ski for Light" (figure 49). In 1964 he moved from Norway to Breckenridge, Colorado, to teach alpine skiing. Pedersen resides in the skiing mecca of Colorado, among such main skiing venues as Breckenridge, Vail, and Steamboat Springs. Both Nordic and alpine branches are practiced, Steamboat Springs being the main "Nordic town," renowned for jumping, cross-country, and combined Nordic events. Recreational skiing was brought to Steamboat Springs by "The Flying Norseman," Carl Howelsen, who earned this name in 1907 jumping on skis for the Barnum and Bailey Circus for packed audiences at Madison Square in New York, given publicity as "ski sailing." The sport was brought to an American public in many ways. In January 1914, Howelsen announced the first ski tournament in Steamboat Springs. The main ski hill in Steamboat Springs, described as "the world's best ski course," was in 1917 at the fourth annual winter carnival there given the name Howelsen Hill. The Colorado Ski Museum and Ski Hall of Fame in Vail give evidence of the early participation by Norwegian skiers as well as the sport's influence on the state's cultural and social development.

Q: Olav Pedersen, how many students have you taught?

A: I have taught about eighteen thousand Americans how to ski by now, at all ages. I would say up to ages seventy to seventy-five.

Figure 49. Olav Pedersen, cofounder of Ski for Light, by his home in Breckenridge, Colorado, in February 1996. He was then seventy-nine years old and still an active ski instructor. Photograph by Odd S. Lovoll.

Q: What techniques did you teach?

A: Mostly alpine skiing. And we used to think that we had a special alpine skiing method that we called the American method. It's very much the same as in Europe of course. It's not that much different. But it has developed very well here in the United States.

Q: What about the Nordic branches?

A: When I came in 1964, it was difficult to find anybody who would like to talk about cross-country. Nordic skiing wasn't skiing. Skiing was downhill. And, of course, that is typical American. They like this easy thing coming up and coming down without any big effort.

Q: How is it now?

A: In the thirty years since I came here, the negative attitude to cross-country has changed a lot.

Q: Do you teach Nordic skiing?

A: I am teaching Nordic now. My experience in Norway as ski jumper and at championship meets is probably why the Nordic Ski Center in Breckenridge wanted me to help develop cross-country and Nordic skiing here. And in that respect I must say that the most important things I've done is coaching seniors in Colorado, people over fifty-five. This year we had, I think, the fifteenth senior games. When people see that, they also understand how beneficial Nordic skiing can be for people who are older.

Q: Are there many Norwegian ski instructors?

A: When I first came, we were six born in Norway, and I knew some American-born Norwegians. But you know the Americans have taken over more and more of the positions.

Q: How would you assess Norwegian contributions to teaching skiing?

A: I would assess them as very, very important for the development of skiing in the United States. Absolutely. I think that without boasting I can say that the Norwegians have always been very, very highly respected and looked at as the best people to help them [Americans] learn to ski.[43]

The Homeland and Images of Norwegian Ethnicity

What is the role of the homeland in the Norwegian-American community? Later-generation Norwegian Americans frequently relate before-and-after experiences following a visit to the ancestral sod. But even those who have never visited the birthplace of a distant ancestor may reveal a sense of "homeland" outside the United States. There are, to be sure, levels of interest in heritage in those who identify with a Norwegian-American ethnicity. The wood-carving artists Else Bigton and Phillip Odden identified three categories in their relations with fellow Norwegian Americans: "Many Norwegian Americans only have ethnic jokes, which is their only tie to the old country. They have not come any farther. Then you have a group that has come so far as to want to go back to Norway and find where the family came from. Then finally there are those who live it. It is their lifestyle, and they create Norwegian surroundings in America. They are serious." But Bigton and Odden also maintain about the second category that "many who have been on a tour of Norway see only the facade, the mountains, fjords, and don't look any farther. It is a sanitized view of the ancestral homeland."[44]

Obviously, shifting emotions prevail. And, of course, everything from ethnic jokes to a sanitized romantic view of the old homeland can be variously interpreted. They cannot in any case be automatically dismissed as simply superficial. Categorizing degrees of ethnic self-identification is further complicated by the obvious fact that all three manifestations identified above may quite regularly be seen in one and the same individual. Ignorance of one's ethnicity and the culture of the homeland amplified by artless American conventions of behavior can perhaps more accurately explain how many Norwegian Americans articulate their sense of ethnicity. It cannot be taken at face value. Still, to state the obvious, attitudes about ethnicity can assuredly move in a real sense from indifference to passion for heritage; but, on the other hand, to emphasize the point, a trivializing public display may not always indicate ridicule or an absence of an emotional attachment to heritage and ancestry. It may just as well be regarded as a mode of expression concerning ethnic identity in a well-established and self-confident population. Thus, a visit to the "old" homeland may in later generations simply reinforce romantic immigrant visions or, conversely, provide new insights—in all instances one can anticipate an emotional experience and a renewed fascination with family roots. For many Norwegian Americans, a visit

to the ancestral haunts commonly satisfies identity needs.

Many respondents spoke in glowing terms of their meeting with the ancestral haunts. As an example, Ted Ahre of Woodburn, Oregon, born in 1944, relates how through a visit in 1990 to the farm in Boknefjord, Norway, which his great-grandfather had left in 1874, the first in his family to do so, he rediscovered his Norwegian heritage to the extent that he and his wife, Marla, a second-generation Norwegian American on her father's side, are both taking Norwegian evening classes. Knowledge of the language may thus frequently provide a meaningful search for identity. As Ahre said, "I enjoy being in contact with Norway, and our children have picked up involvement in being Norwegian, and it will continue as they are surrounded by it."[45]

A different experience has been had by Shauna Sandner Chance, born in 1971 in Sacramento, California, as a fifth-generation Norwegian American on her mother's side and mainly German on her father's. She discovered her ethnicity as a member of the youth group of the local Sons of Norway lodge, skiing with the lodge members, and participating in ethnic festivals in her hometown, where she represented the Norwegian heritage wearing a *bunad* and giving talks about Norway. Shauna learned rosemaling, Norwegian dances, and *lefse* baking, all a part of a traditional ethnic symbolism that was introduced into her home life. She spent a year at a Norwegian high school in 1989–90 and learned to speak Norwegian fluently. This appears as a seminal event in her life. "After I had been in Norway," Shauna related, "I learned to know who I was through a strong sense of identity and knowledge of where I came from."[46]

The positive images of the homeland far surpass negative ones, the latter currently mainly associated with Norwegian whaling and seal-hunting activities along its coast, which generate protests from animal-rights groups and produce harmful media attention. As Liv Aannestad—with Norwegian immigrant parents—of Tempe, Arizona, responded in the questionnaire survey in 1996, when she was fifteen years old, "I am proud that I have a Norwegian background, so I hope that others will appreciate it and not look down on Norwegians because of issues such as whaling." An ethnic group's status in America is contingent on a favorable reputation of the homeland. And the connection is always back to life in America: the ancestral homeland plays a part to the extent it enhances acceptance in the new society. "The more I read about my ancestors," Lois Mickelson in Stevens Point, Wisconsin, born in 1924, explained, "the more I admire them tremendously for their courage, and they were hardworking people and they served our country well." Her great-great-great grandparents Peter and Anna Indreli came to America in 1848 with most of their children. "Many of them were in the Civil War," she continued, "and one of my ancestors was taken prisoner.

. . . Probably the most touching thing that happened to me was coming to Norway in 1988 and feeling that I had come home and visiting the church where my grandfather was baptized. It was an overwhelming experience. I found that we still have the same values as they have." The latter referred to the Lutheran tradition. She said, "I see the relationship between Lutheran and Norwegian even more with people who are Norwegian but not Lutheran—there seems to be this kind of gap."[47]

The Olympic Winter Games in Lillehammer, Norway, in February 1994, which enjoyed rave reviews for how the games were organized, enjoyed spectacular seasonal weather, and awarded Norway an impressive record of medals. The games became a source of great pride for Norwegian Americans, regardless of distance from the immigrant generation. The sight of Norwegian champion athletes in traditional winter sporting events reinforced cherished heroic images of their ethnicity. No single aspect of contemporary Norway was mentioned more frequently by respondents in describing their attitude toward a Norwegian "homeland"; all were interviewed a year or two or even longer after the games had taken place, which made interest more than a passing response. Giving voice to the ethnic pride generated by the winter games, Lois Mickelson said, "I was extremely proud of the Olympics and how beautiful it was," a sentiment consistently expressed.[48]

Sister Cities International in Alexandria, Virginia, founded in 1956, promotes, as its literature states, "citizen diplomacy" by developing "municipal partnerships between United States towns, cities, counties, states, and similar jurisdictions in other nations." It enjoys a high profile, with the president of the United States serving as honorary chairman. Seventeen Norwegian municipalities had by 1996 found "sister cities" in the United States. These are in general communities with substantial Norwegian-American populations. An interesting example is the little town of Elbow Lake, Minnesota, which announces its Norwegian heritage by permanently flying the Norwegian flag alongside the American one at the city hall. It was assigned Flekkefjord in 1970 as its Norwegian affiliated city, though few of the Norwegians in the area have kinship ties to that part of Norway.[49]

The consequences of establishing links to Flekkefjord were notable. The former Worm Lake was renamed Lake Flekkefjord, and every year the town celebrates Flekkefest, with a parade and floats, a festival king and queen, special hats and T-shirts, all in the spirit of an American small-town festival. Ethnic symbols in rosemaling and food are on display. Mayoral exchanges and visitors symbolize the trans-Atlantic relationship. "Our emphasis on Norway has strengthened the community's sense of its history and revived old customs," Lowell Smith, a fourth-generation Norwegian American born in 1946, relates, "so that we between

Christmas and New Year go *julebukking*. We visit people at various places and are given a bit to eat and perhaps do a little singing and drink acquavit. Many of our older citizens recall this old custom. Then they covered their faces so as not to be recognized, but now we don't." Smith rediscovered his own Norwegian roots through residing in Elbow Lake, but also by marriage to Virginia Strand, who had been brought up in a Norwegian-American family environment. Norwegian traditions and food became a part of family life. "Modern-day Norwegian Americans need to learn from the older generation how to have a good time," reflects Smith's general feelings toward ancestry and heritage.[50]

In any conversation or exchange of views with Norwegian Americans the topic consistently reverts to the ancestral American experience. The images of modern Norway evoke less interest save for spectacular events that affirm ethnic merits. By transforming the homeland into a symbol of ethnicity, Herbert Gans theorizes, American ethnics can leave out "those domestic or foreign problems that could become sources of conflicts for Americans." The American-born generations instead look to the time when grandparents or great-grandparents left Norway, always viewed in heroic terms, to create a new life for themselves and their posterity in America. The small farm, notwithstanding its message of poverty and narrow horizons, represents the essence of their roots. Vice President Walter Mondale commented that Mundal in Sogn, the little farm on the

Sognefjord, bore great family import after several visits. He hoped to introduce his grandchildren to this ancestral spot.[51]

One may obviously accept the idea posited by Gans that the symbolic function of the old country is facilitated by a historical interest in "the old countries as they were during or before the time of ancestral departure," without dismissing this interest, as Gans does, as merely symbolic and thus not of major substantive significance in later generations. The identifying value of a gloried past, which both immigrants and nation-states celebrate, is further advanced if historical space is increased, for instance, for the Greeks, back to antiquity. Their status in American society was thereby enhanced. When on February 12, 1911, President Theodore Roosevelt visited the famous Hull House settlement in Chicago, a major center for Greek immigrants, he stated that the Greeks, "unlike other ethnic groups who were expected to abandon old-world loyalties and look toward a new life in America, were exempt because of their own illustrious history."[52]

Nordic immigrants focused on the Age of the Vikings, the first significant historical age in northern Europe, to establish similar acceptable ethnic credentials. No other symbolism is more pronounced, from the syndicated cartoon series "Hägar the Horrible" by Chris Browne to more serious ethnic enterprise and institutions, religious and secular. The Viking appellation adorns commercial and recreational establishments of all kinds; in Minnesota

even its professional football team's helmets are decorated with fictional Viking horns. The Norwegian-American Ninety-Ninth Infantry Battalion of World War II adopted a Viking ship as its emblem; the annual reunions of surviving veterans are ethnic reminders of a patriotic Viking spirit.[53]

In the 1870s the pioneer Norwegian-American scholar Rasmus B. Anderson in his *America Not Discovered by Columbus* raised the claim of European discovery of America by Leif Ericson. All Nordic nationalities in America claim a common ancestry with this famed Norse explorer; it gives credibility to an assertion of a birthright in America. Norwegian Americans appear, however, in many instances to have appropriated the discovery and heroism of the Vikings as specifically Norwegian distinguishing ethnic historical attributes. And again, the serious and the frivolous mingle to give comic relief and to communicate the more earnest strivings of the champions of the recognition of Norse discovery. Silly T-shirts and posters proclaim "Leif Landed First." On the more sober side are the many statues of the great Norse discoverer that were raised to remind later generations of his prowess and achievement. Boston had the first statue, unveiled in 1887, and since then Chicago, St. Paul, Duluth, Seattle, Minot, and other places have raised their own sculptured representations of the Norse hero (figure 50). Only in Minot, North Dakota, is Leif Ericson specifically described on the base of the statue as an

"Icelandic explorer," disclosing some inter-Nordic tension in regard to nationality.[54]

Monuments and statues to honor memorable compatriots, both those emanating from the immigrant community itself and heroic national Norwegian figures, are intended to show coming generations, as it might have been expressed in an earlier age, "the strength of the Norwegian race." Herman O. Fjelde, a prominent Norwegian-born physician described as "the father of Norwegian monuments in the Red River valley," in 1912 at the unveiling of the statue of Rollo, the heroic Norse duke of Normandy, justified his zeal to erect memorials thus: "In our work to show that we or Norwegian descendants will be thought of as being among the most advanced in the world . . . much effort has been devoted to monumental works that will inspire our future situation." The raising of monuments fell under the domain of leaders who wished to create unifying ethnic symbols. This activity can obviously be claimed to present an elite manipulation in which the group's past was employed to foster unity and pride in heritage. In this manner it is analogous to the creation of public memory through commemorative monuments in a national context; these also represent a manipulative product of a leadership to encourage patriotism and civic duty. The specific agendas of the ethnic elite are reflected in the persons and events that are selected for statuary honors. "We Norwegians," *Skandinaven* of Chicago wrote as plans were being made to raise a statue

Figure 50. The Leif Ericson statue in Seattle, Washington. Photograph by Odd S. Lovoll.

of Leif Ericson for the World's Columbian Exposition in 1893, "also wish [like other nationalities] to merit honor through the means of a monument." Leif Ericson became the main monumental figure, but his statue in Chicago was not unveiled until October 1901. Impetus and support for the bronze nine-and-one-half-foot statue of the Norse explorer came from prominent Norwegian-American businessmen. The effort itself gave visibility and promoted social acceptance for this immigrant commercial elite. At the unveiling in Humboldt Park, the banker Paul Stensland declared in a high-flying oration, "Leif Ericson in America is now and forever a fact, not only in his old Vinland, but in busy Chicago, in our very midst."[55]

In an ethnically diverse setting, a competitive spirit among the many ethnic populations was obvious in most cases, and it encouraged the erection of numerous markers of ethnic greatness—to such nationalistic poets as Bjørnstjerne Bjørnson and Henrik Wergeland and to the lay preacher and religious icon of Norwegian-American Lutheranism Hans Nielsen Hauge, but also to Norwegian-American legends on skis like Sondre Norheim and Snowshoe Thompson, and to the valiant hero Colonel Hans Christian Heg of Civil War fame. In placing ethnic heroes within the historical progress of the nation, these statuary symbols become, perhaps ironically, assimilationist in nature; they show as well, in Werner Sollors's terminology, consent and loyalty to new cultures and political structures. There is also a manifest loyalty to an ancestral culture of descent. Even though the tension between these two conflicting desires remains, one may agree with historian John Bodnar that a mediating ethnic culture has evolved that attempts to reconcile this double loyalty.[56]

Ethnic commemorative activities continue to encourage common historical memories and a reconciliation of loyalty to Norwegian ancestors and to the cultural and political pressures of America. By the little town of Norway in the Fox River valley of Illinois—claiming to be the first permanent Norwegian settlement in America—there are on the Cleng Peerson Memorial Highway, which runs from Yorkville to Ottawa, monuments to the centennial in 1934 of the settlement's founding and to the Slooper sesquicentennial celebrations in 1975, both monuments honoring "the pathfinder of Norwegian immigration." It was here Peerson supposedly had his famed dream. Falling asleep on the hill under an oak tree after great fatigue and hunger from many days of wandering, he in his dream saw "the wild prairie changed into a cultivated region teeming with all kinds of grain and fruits, beautiful to behold that splendid houses, barns stood all over the land occupied by rich, prosperous and happy people." There are numerous elaborate accounts of "Cleng Peerson's dream," one of the historical mythologies of Norwegian-American history. Peerson's own thoughts, as he related, turned to Moses and the Promised Land.[57]

Leif Ericson has remained the icon and quintessential hero of the Norwegian-American experience. His name graces parks, squares, streets, and drives. In 1997, when Trondheim observed its one-thousand anniversary, the Leif Ericson Society of the Northwest in Seattle donated a ten-foot-tall replica of the Leif Ericson statue that overlooks the Seattle harbor. In the year 2000 the assumed millennium of Norse discovery will be celebrated; observances are spearheaded by the Sons of Norway and Leif

Ericson societies and include heavy involvement of all the Nordic governments.

The Leif Ericson Society International in Philadelphia, "Honoring America's First Hero," owns a Viking ship, the *Norseman,* which is sailed on the Schuylkill River near downtown. Annually since 1964, primarily as a result of the work of such groups as the one in Philadelphia, the president of the United States has proclaimed October 9 as an official Leif Ericson Day. The proclamation itself is a self-congratulatory ethnic document in which the Nordic-Americans, as the group is identified, are said to share with Americans certain values, among these, "democratic ideals, an abiding faith in the value of ingenuity and hard work, and a deep belief in the sanctity of the individual." Leif Ericson embodied, as did his descendants in America, the document suggests, these sterling qualities; in America his kin became "brave pioneers . . . [and] helped push the American frontier to the west, building communities and farms and enriching American life and culture." Greater accolades could not be heaped on any single ethnic group. The proclamation reiterates a deep self-perception of the group's American experience; descent and consent discover a mediating and reconciling vision of past and present in exalted ethnic merits.[58]

The Viking Image Gone Astray

Not all Viking Age societies are primarily devoted to the promotion of Leif Ericson. The Viking Age Club in Minneapolis, for instance, was organized in 1986 to study Viking history and to reenact it. "The Viking image is one of many images to portray yourself," Gary Anderson, a third-generation Norwegian American born in 1947 stated. "You don't have to be Scandinavian to look at a Viking ship and say: 'That takes guts!'" His son Eric, born in 1969, explained that men join because of the Viking romance, while women members more gradually develop an interest. The club criticizes misrepresentations of Viking helmets and weapons that are exhibited widely in Norwegian-American circles. "Norwegians are better at showing the Viking Age as their own than are other Scandinavians," fourth-generation Dennis Rusinko, born in 1946, thinks, because of "Snorre, who wrote about the Norwegian kings and their lineages. This gave Norwegians many tales about their history."[59]

Such organizations as the Viking Age Club in Minneapolis pride themselves on their educational and historical integrity and abhor extremist groups that use Viking images. There are many of these. The Ásatrú Alliance, its main office in Payson, Arizona, is an association of so-called kindreds, or local societies, that practice "the ethnic religion of the Northern European peoples." It sponsors national assemblies, or "things," and publishes the magazine *Vor Tru* to promote its cause, which is stated as "the restoration of that Faith as epitomized during the pre-Christian era in Europe" (figure 51). The Heathen Way, with its quarterly *Yggdrasil,*

Fall/Winter
Issue #55
$5

Figure 51. Vor Trú, *published by the Ásatrú Alliance. Cover reprinted with permission of* Vor Trú.

published in San Francisco, and international Odinist groups all hold the pagan religious beliefs of "our ancestral religion known as Odinism or Asatru," and "preach and practice courage, honor, the importance of family and ancestral bonds, strength, freedom, and joyful, vigorous life."[60]

Fringe pagan worship societies exist, such as the Loki Cult, which limits its worship to the infamous Norse god Loki. Even Odinists compare this cult to Satanists and criticize its sacrifice, or *blot,* to the evil Loki. Racist overtones, though not always overtly expressed in such groups, are stated in several ways, and not only by members of these Viking societies. For example, an article under the pseudonym Thor Sannhet sent to *Norway Times* said, "Norway . . . represents the 'idea' of a Nordic homeland. It embodies the 'Viking' spirit of the Nordic people, just like Israel embodies the spirit of Judaism or Japan embodies the spirit of Shinto." Consequently, it should close its borders to foreign population elements. Serving as spokesman for a Viking Day Festival in Portland, Oregon, in July, 1993, which attracted some 350 people, William Fox, alias Thor Sannhet, of Norwegian descent, defended the right to celebrate "the Nordic heritage and cultural revivalism," against accusations by human rights groups that the festival "might be a subtle effort to promote the views of white supremacists." The local media alleged that ties indeed existed to such intolerant groups among the organizers, and monitoring the event, the Coalition for Human Dignity recognized "upward of ten racist skinheads."[61]

Overtly racist neo-Nazi groups with international organizational connections—also in Norway—are exemplified in National Vanguard Books, the publication arm of the National Alliance, organized in 1974 in Hillsboro, West Virginia, with William Pierce as its ideologue. "Any White person (a non-Jewish person of wholly European ancestry) of good character" is eligible for membership if he embraces the goals of the Alliance; "homosexuals and bi-sexuals" are specifically excluded regardless of race. The group declares itself an Aryan society whose publications, which are regularly on the Vikings and the Middle Ages, assist, as the catalog explains, in understanding "the common racial, linguistic, and cultural roots of all our Aryan ancestors." The literature is reminiscent of the exploitation of Viking images by Norwegian collaborators and the German occupying forces during World War II and of the racist political ideology of the national socialists. Thereafter these national symbols from the Age of the Vikings and their unifying function were for decades compromised. Obviously, promoted by self-serving Nordic nationalists, these artifacts of the homeland's past may indeed suffer a similar fate in America. Norwegian Americans would then be deprived of a prime and evocative symbol of their ethnicity.[62]

Constructing Historical Memory

What is the portrait that emerges of contemporary Norwegian Americans? Their history in America has been well told, and the artifacts of that history may be viewed in local and national museums. Still, it is clear that as an ethnic group Norwegian Americans have not surrendered their historical memories to the custodians of these institutions. Norwegian-American ethnicity remains a vital and progressively changing factor of American life.

The Norwegian-American Historical Association (NAHA) emerged from one of the group's historical moments. The Norse-American Centennial celebrations in 1925 in the Twin Cities stimulated great ethnic pride. Following the festivities, a meeting was called at St. Olaf College on October 6, 1925, where organizational work for the new learned society was concluded. It evinced a move toward professionalism by ethnic historical societies and a maturing of American historiography. Theodore C. Blegen, born in 1891 to immigrant parents, was then a young professor of history; as editor for thirty-five years he established procedures and standards of selection, writing, and editing that gained recognition in the scholarly community.

Blegen was typical of several young historians of non-English background, many of Scandinavian origin, who developed an interest in immigration as a significant field of study. The young historians who investigated the Scandinavian-American experience could do so knowing that by the 1920s they were studying nationalities that were held to be "desirable" by American society. Other newer immigrant groups suffered the intolerance of that decade. Norwegian ethnic leaders of the 1920s faced the challenges to ethnic unity caused by demands for patriotic conformity, consumerism, and suburbanization by celebrating the rural immigrant past. Ignoring the city, even when not harboring antiurban sentiments, these leaders presented the group's history to the next generation and to other Americans by describing its rural roots. They engaged in what amounts to a construction of ethnic memory. These wholesome images of independent god-fearing and hardworking immigrant farmers were fortified by NAHA's publications during the first years of its existence; of high professional merit, these works of scholarship favored the colorful saga of pioneers settling on the farms of the Midwest and the reminiscent immigrant lore of diarists, letter writers, and chroniclers. The popularity of Ole E. Rølvaag's epic novel *Giants in the Earth* (1927) demonstrated the appeal of a rural past and accounts of homesteading Norwegian-American farmers to people struggling with the complexities, dangers, confusion, and biases of a rapidly changing modern America. It has been a lasting legacy.[63]

The protection and preservation of vernacular culture had long roots in the Norwegian-American community. Inspired by the Norse-

American Centennial, the acquisition and safe-keeping of objects brought over from Norway and from the immigrant community gained an institutional base through the founding of the museum that since 1969 has carried the name Vesterheim Norwegian-American Museum, in Decorah, Iowa. It is a large ethnic museum funded mainly by the Norwegian-American community. Its beginnings date to 1877, when professors at Luther College began collecting immigrant artifacts. The two institutions, NAHA and Vesterheim, were carried forward on the same wave of enthusiasm, with the co-operation of basically the same group of individuals and with a clear division of responsibility. The museum presents in visual form the lives and circumstances of Norwegian-American pioneers, whereas NAHA preserves the books, periodicals, newspapers, manuscripts, and other archival material relevant to its publication program.

Even as a highly professional enterprise, the Decorah museum, in its educational program, its outdoor assemblage of log cabins and other structures, and its extensive collection of pioneer immigrant objects, has from first to last reinforced nineteenth-century notions of Norwegian-American life. In fact, the museum defines for the twenty thousand or more annual visitors and its eight thousand members what constitutes the basis for a Norwegian-American identity. "We are the interpreter and home for the masses," director Darrell D. Henning explained, "and not elitist like some public insti-

tutions might be. People from the whole socio-economic spectrum can relate to the collections of material and the social history behind them representing all class levels in the immigrant community." For most people, a sense of a unique past and the construction of ethnic historical memories are more easily acquired through viewing museum objects, buildings, and monuments than by perusing the interpretive works of scholarship.[64]

Concrete evidence of a historical presence may be viewed in the Nordic Museum, located in the old Scandinavian Ballard section of Seattle. The museum was founded on a broad Scandinavian basis in 1980 but confines itself to "the Nordic heritage in the Pacific Northwest." The upper Midwest is naturally best positioned to preserve artifacts from the pioneer era. Nestled in one of the numerous coulees of western Wisconsin is the open-air museum Norskedalen, literally Norwegian Valley, in Coon Prairie, dedicated in 1983. Its stated purpose is to preserve nature and honor the cultural heritage of the Norwegian immigrants who began arriving in the area in the 1850s. A renewed enthusiasm for the vernacular evidence of a pioneer culture manifests itself—each in a very different setting—in these two recent museum projects.

Museums with lower professional standards but with great public appeal function with success within a Norwegian-American matrix. Little Norway, or Nissedahle—valley of the elves—beneath the imposing Blue

Mounds west of Mount Horeb, Wisconsin, is a privately owned outdoor museum that opened for public visits in 1937. Numerous visitors are attracted to this museum, which provides a romantic interpretation of a Norwegian-American heritage, and even displays the Victorian recreation of a stave church—Norway House—that housed Norway's exhibit at the Columbian Exposition of 1893. Scholars will find much that is disturbing in the museum's historical presentation of the pioneer period, which is, to quote, "as much a product of mind and imagination as it was reality." It represents the personal mythology and concept of ethnicity shaped by its founder, Isak Dahle, and consequently, a concept that corresponds to that of most Norwegian Americans, "especially," as Marion J. Nelson points out, "those who rediscover their cultural heritage after once having been Americanized." Little Norway's acceptability to the public rests on this imaginative representation of ethnicity. While documenting how later generations of Norwegian Americans perceive their past, Little Norway with all its ambiguity of interpretation furthermore allows for a progressive invention and reinvention of ethnic identity based on its eclectic collection of the props of a material culture.[65]

Hjemkomst Heritage Center in Moorhead, Clay County, in western Minnesota, demonstrates how a dominant ethnic symbol is superimposed on a vernacular presentation of pioneer life. The replica of the Gokstad Viking ship, given the name *Hjemkomst*, built by Robert Asp in Hawley, Minnesota, and in May of 1982 sailed to Norway, is the feature attraction of a new building uniquely designed to accommodate the ship. In the lower level of the same structure, Clay County Historical Society exhibits objects, many of them Norwegian, from the pioneer era in the Red River valley. Placing a Viking ship in this prairie landscape—in this case literally surmounting the vernacular displays—in the midst of a pioneer Norwegian agricultural region rich in artifacts of a continuous ethnic presence may truly be viewed as the ultimate in historical symbolism, re-creation, and inventiveness. Norwegian Americans here become, at least symbolically, the new Vikings of the West in the guise of brave nineteenth-century pioneer settlers as two major images of a Norwegian-American identity merge in an incongruous and confusing construction of historical memory. A Scandinavian Hjemkomst Festival annually attracts attention to the ship's existence.[66]

The Descendants of the Sloopers

As Norwegian-American history approaches the 175th anniversary on October 9, 2000, of the arrival of the sloop *Restauration,* an appropriate starting point for some concluding observations is the Norwegian Slooper Society of America. Its organization in 1925 was yet another example of activities inspired by the immigration centennial. It is the Mayflower Society of Norwegian Americans; the notion to emulate this prestigious Yankee group gave evidence of a striving for exclusivity within the Norwegian-American community, on the one hand, and of a desire to establish honored credentials beyond ethnic bounds, on the other. Only individuals who can trace their lineal descent to one of the Sloopers of 1825 and their spouses qualify for membership. The society's purpose is to honor the pioneer immigrants and "to perpetuate to a remote posterity the story of their spirit and deeds." Its main social event is an annual banquet on the Sunday closest to October 9. The historian of the Sloopers, J. Hart Rosdail, in his compendium of 1961, presented a roster of 7,130 living Slooper descendants—approximately 2,050 families—of the fifty-three voyagers of 1825. As many as 15 percent were by then of the seventh generation. Even as late as the 1960s, 25 percent of people of Slooper ancestry still lived within a radius of seventy miles of the original Fox River settlement in LaSalle County, Illinois.[67]

At commemorative Norwegian-American events the Sloopers and those of Slooper descent have been recognized and honored. Yet the Slooper Society has never gained the elite position its founders envisioned. In the individualistic search for roots of the "new ethnicity," the ethnic revival has not come to the aid of many of the older organizational efforts. Ethnic elitism is, as stated in regard to other exclusive groups, in any case difficult to maintain as assimilation moves forward. Most of those attending the annual dinner have been

people in ordinary circumstances. As is the case with many Norwegian-American organizations, its membership is aging, and an active leadership cannot easily be created. In keeping with general developments, a feminization of those in charge unfortunately gives further evidence of a general decline in status.

The increased number of women involved in ethnic organizational life does, on the other hand, also highlight a clear finding of the fieldwork. To some extent ethnicity proved itself to be gender-related. Women attached more significance than men to their ethnic relations. Nearly 60 percent of all questionnaire respondents were women, and women surpassed men in numbers at all age levels. In the questionnaire four options in answer to the question on the importance of Norwegian heritage were given: great, some, little, and none. Women were more likely than men to choose "great" to indicate the influence ethnicity had in their lives. The current president of the Slooper Society, Patricia Ainsley Hayes, was born in 1946 and is a sixth-generation Slooper. "I just went to the meeting in 1988 and was elected president at once," Hayes explained, "and I think we are pretty proud that the Sloopers' ship was the first to make the trip." In her family seventh- and eighth-generation Sloopers are in place.[68]

Patricia Peterson, born in 1965, is a sixth-generation Slooper. Her father, Silas Peterson, born in 1942, who is fifth-generation, has achieved through land ownership and a long family history in the pioneer community of

Figure 52. The "Velkommen til Norway" sign declaring Norway, Illinois, "the first permanent Norwegian settlement in America" inspires pride among local Norwegian Americans and in those with roots in this pioneer community. Photograph by Odd S. Lovoll.

Norway, Illinois, a prestigious position in the local community and among people of Slooper descent (figure 52). The Norwegians in the area are still to a great extent engaged in farming, and a working-class social environment is evident. The Peterson family donated the land on which the Lutheran church is built. Norway is a conservative community with strong religious values and conscious of its Norwegian origin.

Q: Silas, what was it like to grow up in the Norway community?

SILAS: I grew up on my grandfather's farm right here in Norway. His name was also Silas, and he had a three-story brick house. And of course we were farmers and had milch cows and did everything by hand. Most of the farm

work was done by horses. It was kind of a family thing, you know.

Q: Were you conscious of your Norwegian heritage?

SILAS: Yes, very much so. I think I was in second or third grade before I realized that Norwegians were not the only people in the world. There are so many people here who are Sloopers and related. I've been an officer of the Sloopers. I felt an obligation not only to my family, but the Slooper Society to get younger people to come. I was proud to have my family there.

Q: Patricia, when you were young, was there still a sense of a Norwegian community?

PATRICIA: Yes, very much. The emphasis was on the family and family traditions. The food was a big part. I started going to the Slooper dance when I returned after about five years in Texas. I was married and older then, and I think therefore I appreciated more my family and who we were.

Q: Silas, when you think of heritage, is it America or Norway?

SILAS: The big thing for me is here in America. Here I can make a statement. My grandchildren are the sixth generation to be members of the oldest Norwegian Lutheran church in North America. They are the seventh generation of the first Norwegian immigrants.

Q: Were you brought up in a pious environment?

SILAS: Oh, yes, very much. Dancing, playing was sinful. We didn't listen to music or take out a deck of cards. I rebelled for a while, but the roots were so embedded in me that I came back to where I should be.

PATRICIA: I don't think Norwegian and Lutheran are identical. But I was glad that my husband, Keith, who is of German background, was also Lutheran. He was my only boyfriend. I was eighteen when we got married.

Q: How do you feel about your Norwegian ancestry?

PATRICIA: I am very grateful for it. And I hope that I can pass it on to my children.

SILAS: I always say I'm an American because I was born in America. But my heritage is Norwegian, and I'm proud of that.[69]

Most statements by Norwegian Americans reflecting on "the promise of America," as viewed by later generations, give evidence of a strong conviction that they had benefited greatly from the actions of immigrant forebears who had the courage to pursue a promise that was fulfilled, if not in their time, then by their American-born descendants. Statistics reveal a solid occupational assimilation within a clear middle-class socioeconomic environment. A political conservatism may in part arise from improved economic circumstances, though it is clear that, as is the case for most contemporary Americans, there is an intrinsic distrust of politics and politicians in general. Political conviction is in any event more a product of class and region than ancestry. Ethnic affiliation is of greater importance to most Norwegian Americans. They may discover and cultivate it within the medium of John Higham's "new particularism," which he sees as superseding pluralism. Applied to ethnicity, particularism may be insightful in understanding the localized expressions of Norwegian ethnicity in organizations, clubs, community festivals, and religious congregational life. A sense of a Norwegian-American national community is clearly weakening, and ethnicity is consequently increasingly expressed as distinct group and community interpretations of a specific cultural identity. As Norwegian-American organizations and societies continue a visible downward trend in membership and activity, celebratory festive events are becoming the main public manifestations of an ethnic attachment, even when fueled by local chamber of commerce agendas. They are also reflections of the fact that many Norwegian ethnic activities in folk arts, music, and dancing are entering an American mainstream cultural community; even ethnic symbols like May 17 observations have in some regions been transformed into local community celebrations. The special bonds of farming and Slooper descent in Norway, Illinois, illustrate components of ethnic community-building seen in many traditional areas of Norwegian settlement. A Norwegian community identity may, however, in the 1990s be as much a state of mind for individuals of Norwegian ancestry as it is a reflection of a social reality. The situation nevertheless speaks to a quest for roots and self-identification by those who are involved.

Individuals of unmixed Norwegian heritage, those with weak Norwegian ancestral links, or those with none may join in the particularism of ethnic affiliation. Paralleling the fellowship sought on the basis of a shared ethnicity is the individualistic and privatized quest for roots and personal identity. A feeling for ethnic identity by no means requires an active display. And there are the many who may have little concern for their heritage, some even having become what Higham has termed "non-ethnics." It is nevertheless a revealing fact that

to the question on ethnic ancestry in the 1990 federal census, an impressive 90 percent or more subjectively reported at least one specific ancestry. This figure does not, of course, separate individuals for whom ethnic ancestry is still a strong identity from those for whom ancestry is merely a label or a distant genealogical memory. Yet, it is still evidence of how most Americans continue to view themselves and their fellow Americans in terms of ethnicity.

What is clear from this study is that a combination of overt and subtle forces in the late 1960s and in the 1970s triggered a revival—a new ethnicity—among large segments of the many generations of Norwegian Americans. It may even be seen in part as a reaction against the assimilation and loss of cultural idioms that had occurred by then. This urge remains strong toward the end of the century. No one can remain totally indifferent to the many and varied tributes to ethnicity. Norwegian Americans are not participating in a balkanization of American society but, to the contrary, in a mobilization to affirm the historical and social position of Americans of Norwegian ancestry within the American republic. Norwegian Americans are, obviously, not "strangers in a strange land" but an intrinsic component of a continuous process of nation building. It is in that context that they become reminiscent of their past as an immigrant people.[70]

Notes

1. THE SHIFTING FACE OF NORWEGIAN AMERICA

1. John O. Evjen, *Scandinavian Immigrants in New York, 1630–1674* (Minneapolis: K.C. Holter, 1916); pages 19–139 have biographical sketches of fifty-five Norwegian colonists between 1630 and 1674.

2. U.S. Bureau of the Census, *Detailed Ancestry Groups by States, 1990* (Washington, D.C.: Economic and Statistics Administration, Bureau of the Census, October 1992), 3.

3. U.S. Bureau of the Census, *Ancestry of the Population of the United States, 1990* (Washington, D.C.: Economic and Statistics Administration, Bureau of the Census, August 1993), 57; Stanley Lieberson and Mary C. Waters, *From Many Strands: Ethnic and Racial Groups in Contemporary America* (New York: Russell Sage Foundation, 1988), 43–45.

4. U.S. Bureau of the Census, *Detailed Ancestry Groups by States, 1990,* 4–5.

5. Olivier Zunz, ed., *Reliving the Past: The Worlds of Social History* (Chapel Hill: University of North Carolina Press, 1985), 63.

6. John Higham, *Send These to Me: Jews and Other Immigrants in Urban America* (New York: Atheneum, 1975), 231–46.

7. Ottar Dahl, *Norsk historieforskning i 19. og 20. århundre* (Oslo: Universitetsforlaget, 1970), 37.

8. See the discussion of pan-Scandinavianism by Odd S. Lovoll, "A Scandinavian Melting Pot in Chicago," in Philip J. Anderson and Dag Blanck, eds., *Swedish-American Life in Chicago: Cultural and Urban Aspects of an Immigrant People, 1850–1930* (Urbana: University of Illinois Press, 1992), 60–67.

9. August B. Hollingshead, *Elmtown's Youth and Elmtown Revisited* (New York: John Wiley and Sons, 1975), 194–95, 346.

10. Interview with H. George Anderson, Bishop of the Evangelical Lutheran Church in America, by Odd S. Lovoll, Northfield, Minnesota, April 14, 1997.

11. Michael Kammen, *Mystic Chords of Memory: The Transformation of Tradition in American Culture* (New York: Vintage Books, 1993), 234–39; Kallen is quoted on 236; Philip Gleason, "American Identity and Americanization," in Stephan Thernstrom, ed., *Harvard Encyclopedia of American Ethnic Groups* (Cambridge, Mass.: Harvard University Press, 1980), 42–44, summarizes Horace Kallen's major publications.

12. An interview about the research with staff writer Chuck Haga, published in the *Minneapolis Star Tribune,* May 17, 1996, was interpreted by some Norwegian Americans as offensive to their ethnicity. The interview was, among other points, understood to say that Norwegian Americans were becoming more conservative and even a bit racist toward newer Americans. A radio talk-show host described the author as "the man who destroyed Syttende mai." James Johnson from Willmar, Minnesota, in a letter dated May 18, 1996, to the Sons of Norway, stated: "I find this article to be defamatory towards Norwegian-Americans and an attack on their ethnic and cultural identity and legitimate political views." Beverly A. Webster, also from Willmar, commented in a letter to the author dated May 21, 1996: "Your referring to near-racist attitudes among Norwegian-Americans, I believe to be too strong language. You must be referring to the emigrants from Mexico. This prejudice certainly is understandable. Norwegian-Americans do not like it, when those who can work, collect welfare, which we pay for."

13. Rolf M. Nilsestuen, *The Kensington Runestone Vindicated* (Lanham, Md.: University Press of America, 1994), xiii. The two main scholarly works are Erik Wahlgren, *The Kensington Stone: A Mystery Solved* (Madison: University of Wisconsin Press, 1958); and Theodore C. Blegen, *The Kensington Stone: New Light on an Old Riddle* (St. Paul: Minnesota Historical

Society, 1968). In chapter 5, pages 92–125, Blegen discusses Sven Folgelblad, an itinerant Swedish schoolteacher, and Ole Eriksson Hagen, a retired Norwegian professor, as possible perpetrators of the hoax. Nilsestuen attacks Wahlgren in particular. The amateur Norwegian-American historian Hjalmar Rued Holand (1872–1963) made proving the authenticity of the Kensington Stone a life mission. He remains the authority for many believers in regard to the genuineness of the runic inscriptions and the notion of Viking mooring holes.

14. Interview with Doris Engen Burkey by Lovoll, Alexandria, Minnesota, March 4, 1996.

15. U.S. Bureau of the Census, *Detailed Ancestry Groups by States, 1990,* 4. The statistics and the two tables are computer-generated analyses of collected data.

16. For an account of how Norwegian prisoners of war in England between 1807 and 1814 became converted to Quakerism and formed societies of Friends in Stavanger and Oslo, see Berit Eide Johnsen, *"Han sad i prisonen . . ." Sjøfolk i engelsk fangenskap 1807–1814* (Oslo: Universitetsforlaget, 1993). A number of works give overviews of Norwegian migration and settlement. See Odd S. Lovoll, *The Promise of America: A History of the Norwegian-American People* (Minneapolis: University of Minnesota Press, 1984); Ingrid Semmingsen, *Norway to America: A History of the Migration* (Minneapolis: University of Minnesota Press, 1978); and Arlow W. Andersen, *The Norwegian-Americans* (Boston: Twayne, 1975).

17. The most influential of the early guidebooks is Ole Rynning, *Sandfærdig beretning om Amerika til oplysning og nytte for bonde og menigmand* (True Account of America) in 1838.

18. Odd S. Lovoll, "From Norway to America: A Tradition of Immigration Fades," in Dennis Laurence Cuddy, ed., *Contemporary American Immigration: Interpretive Essays* (Boston: Twayne, 1982), 86–107.

19. For a detailed description of Norwegian settlement up to the 1920s, see Carlton C. Qualey, *Norwegian Settlement in the United States* (Northfield, Minn.: Norwegian-American Historical Association, 1938). See also Odd S. Lovoll, *Norwegians on the Land. Address for the Society for the Study of Local and Regional History* (Marshall, Minn.: Department of History, Southwest State University, 1992).

20. T. A. Hoverstad, *The Norwegian Farmers in the United States* (Fargo, N.Dak.: Hans Jervell Publishing Co., 1915), 11–13, 29; O. M. Norlie, *History of the Norwegian People in America* (Minneapolis: Augsburg Publishing House, 1925), 349.

21. Robert P. Swierenga, "Ethnicity and American Agriculture," *Ohio History,* summer 1980: 323–44.

22. Lowell J. Soike, *Norwegian Americans and the Politics of Dissent, 1880–1924* (Northfield, Minn.: Norwegian-American Historical Association, 1991), 71–74; John C. Hudson, "Migration to an American Frontier," *Annals of the Association of American Geographers,* June 1976: 242–65.

23. See Odd S. Lovoll, *A Century of Urban Life: The Norwegians in Chicago before 1930* (Northfield, Minn.: Norwegian-American Historical Association, 1988).

24. For a detailed description of ethnic life in Minneapolis, see Carl G. O. Hansen, *My Minneapolis* (Minneapolis: privately printed, 1956).

25. David C. Mauk, *The Colony That Rose from the Sea: Norwegian Maritime Migration and Community in Brooklyn, 1850–1910* (Northfield, Minn.: Norwegian-American Historical Association, 1997).

26. Knut Gjerset, *Norwegian Sailors in American Waters: A Study in the History of Maritime Activity on the Eastern Seaboard* (Northfield, Minn.: Norwegian-American Historical Association, 1933); Knight Hoover, "Norwegians in New York," *Norwegian-American Studies* (Northfield, Minn.) 24 (1970): 221–34.

27. Kenneth O. Bjork, *West of the Great Divide: Norwegian Migration to the Pacific Coast, 1847–1893* (Northfield, Minn.: Norwegian-American Historical Association, 1958), 74–134, 135–77.

28. See Sverre Arestad, "The Norwegians in the Pacific Coast Fisheries," *Pacific Northwest Quarterly,* January 1943. See the discussion about Polish Americans in Neil C. Sandberg, *Ethnic Identity and Assimilation: The Polish-American Community. Case Study of Metropolitan Los Angeles* (New York: Praeger Publishers, 1974), 73.

29. The main works on Norwegian-American Lutheranism are the two volumes by Clifford E. Nelson and Eugene L. Fevold, *The Lutheran Church among Norwegian-Americans* (Minneapolis: Augsburg Publishing House, 1960). See also Mag-

nus J. Rohne, *Norwegian-American Lutheranism up to 1872* (New York: Macmillan, 1926); and Eugene L. Fevold, "The Norwegian Immigrant and His Church," *Norwegian-American Studies* (Northfield, Minn.) 23 (1967): 3–16.

30. See S. S. Gjerde and P. Ljostvedt, *The Hauge Movement in America* (Minneapolis: Augsburg Publishing House, 1941); Marcus Lee Hansen, "Immigration and Puritanism," *Norwegian-American Studies* (Northfield, Minn.) 9 (1936): 1–28.

31. H. F. Swansen, "The Quakers of Marshall County, Iowa," *Norwegian-American Studies and Records* (Northfield, Minn.) 10 (1938): 127–34.

32. Roald Kverndal, "Bethelship 'John Wesley': A New York Ship Saga from the Mid-1800's with Reverberations on Both Sides of the Atlantic Ocean," *Methodist History,* July 1977.

33. Arlow W. Andersen, *The Salt of the Earth: A History of Norwegian-Danish Methodism in America* (Nashville: Norwegian-Danish Methodist Historical Society, 1962).

34. P. Stiansen, *History of the Norwegian Baptists in America* (Wheaton, Ill.: Norwegian Baptist Conference in America and American Baptist Publication Society, 1939).

35. Arlow W. Andersen, *The Immigrant Takes His Stand: The Norwegian-American Press and Public Affairs, 1847–1872* (Northfield, Minn.: Norwegian-American Historical Association, 1953).

36. Odd S. Lovoll, "*Decorah-Posten:* The Story of an Immigrant Newspaper," *Norwegian-American Studies* (Northfield, Minn.) 27 (1977): 77–100; Odd S. Lovoll, "The Norwegian Press in North Dakota," *Norwegian-American Studies* (Northfield, Minn.) 24 (1970): 78–101.

37. Odd. S Lovoll, "*Washington Posten:* A Window on a Norwegian-American Urban Community," *Norwegian-American Studies* (Northfield, Minn.) 31 (1986): 163–86.

38. Millard L. Gieske and Steven J. Keillor, *Norwegian Yankee: Knute Nelson and the Failure of American Politics, 1860–1923* (Northfield, Minn.: Norwegian-American Historical Association, 1995).

39. Lovoll, *A Century of Urban Life,* 179–81, 265, 290–95; Theodore C. Blegen, *Norwegian Migration to America: The American Transition* (Northfield, Minn.: Norwegian-American Historical Association, 1940), 300–30, 547–56.

40. Duane R. Lindberg, *Men of the Cloth and the Social Cultural Fabric of the Norwegian Ethnic Community in North Dakota* (New York: Arno Press, 1980).

41. Soike, *Norwegian Americans and the Politics of Dissent,* 119–52; Carl H. Chrislock, *The Progressive Era in Minnesota, 1899–1918* (St. Paul: Minnesota Historical Society, 1971); Paul Kleppner, *The Cross of Culture: A Social Analysis of Midwestern Politics, 1850–1900* (New York: Free Press, 1970); Elwyn B. Robinson, *History of North Dakota* (Lincoln: University of Nebraska Press, 1966), 187–90.

42. Soike, *Norwegian Americans and the Politics of Dissent,* 156–69; Odd S. Lovoll, "*Gaa Paa:* A Scandinavian Voice of Dissent," *Minnesota History,* fall 1990: 86–99.

43. *Thirteenth Census of the United States, 1910: Population,* 1: 963.

44. Herbert J. Gans, "Symbolic Ethnicity: The Future of Ethnic Groups and Cultures in America," in Herbert J. Gans, Nathan Glazer, Joseph R. Gusfield, and Christopher Jencks, eds., *On the Making of Americans: Essays in Honor of David Riesman* (Philadelphia: University of Pennsylvania Press, 1979), 206–7.

45. Lovoll, *A Century of Urban Life,* 249–53; E. John B. Allen, *From Skisport to Skiing: One Hundred Years of an American Sport, 1840–1940* (Amherst: University of Massachusetts Press, 1993), 3–12, 47–74.

46. For a comprehensive statement about immigrant literary art, see Orm Øverland, *The Western Home: A Literary History of Norwegian America* (Northfield, Minn.: Norwegian-American Historical Association, 1996).

47. Odd S. Lovoll, *A Folk Epic: The* Bygdelag *in America* (Boston: Twayne Publishers for Norwegian-American Historical Association, 1975).

48. See C. Sverre Norborg, *An American Saga* (Minneapolis: Sons of Norway, 1970).

49. Jon Gjerde, "The Effect of Community on Migration: Three Minnesota Townships 1885–1905," *Journal of Historical Geography,* October 1979: 403–22; Jon Gjerde, "Conflict and Community: A Case Study of the Immigrant

Church in the United States," *Journal of Social History,* summer 1986: 681–97; Ann M. Legreid and David Ward, "Religious Schism and the Development of Rural Immigrant Communities: Norwegian Lutherans in Western Wisconsin, 1880–1905," *Upper Midwest History* 2 (1982): 13–29.

50. In *History of the Norwegian People in America* Norlie lists Norwegian-American benevolent institutions (426–33). For 1922, he lists, including Lutheran and other denominations, four deaconess homes, fourteen children's homes, one home finding society, three rescue homes for girls, twenty hospices and inns, twenty-eight hospitals, and twenty homes for the aged located throughout the United States. Extinct institutions are not included in his listing.

51. U.S. Bureau of the Census, *Ancestry of the Population of the United States, 1990,* 159, 363–64, 465–66.

52. A number of scholars are reconsidering the process of identity formation and the character of multiculturalism. See, as examples, Werner Sollors, ed., *The Invention of Ethnicity* (New York: Oxford University Press, 1989); David A. Hollinger, *Postethnic America: Beyond Multiculturalism* (New York: Basic Books, 1995); Ernest Gellner, *Postmodernism, Reason and Religion* (New York: Routledge, 1992); and Robert Hughes, *The Culture of Complaint: The Fraying of America* (New York: Oxford University Press, 1993).

2. IN THE AMERICAN MOSAIC

1. Werner Sollors, *The Invention of Ethnicity* (New York: Oxford University Press, 1989), ix-xx. For a critique and amplification of the theory of invention, see Kathleen Neils Conzen, David A. Gerber, Ewa Morawska, George E. Pozzetta, and Rudolph J. Vecoli, "The Invention of Ethnicity: A Perspective from the U.S.A.," *Journal of American Ethnic History* 12 (fall 1992): 3–41; see also Elliott R. Barkan, "Race, Religion, and Nationality in American Society: A Model of Ethnicity—From Contact to Assimilation," *Journal of American Ethnic History* 14 (winter 1995): 38–75; William Petersen, "Concepts of Ethnicity," in William Petersen, Michael Novak, and Philip Gleason, eds., *Concepts of Ethnicity* (Cambridge, Mass.: Belknap Press of Harvard University Press, 1980), 1–26.

2. Eric Hobsbawm, "Introduction: Inventing Traditions," in Eric Hobsbawm and Terence Ranger, eds., *The Invention of Tradition* (Cambridge: Cambridge University Press, 1984), 1–14. See also Richard H. Thompson, *Theories of Ethnicity: A Critical Appraisal* (New York: Greenwood Press, 1989).

3. Thomas J. Archdeacon, *Becoming American: An Ethnic History* (New York: The Free Press, 1983), 232.

4. For an excellent study of a two-culture concept, see H. Arnold Barton, *A Folk Divided: Homeland Swedes and Swedish-Americans, 1840–1940* (Carbondale, Ill.: Southern Illinois University Press, 1994).

5. Since persons who reported two ancestries were included in more than one ancestry group, the sum of responses will be greater than the total population. Of the total American population in 1990 of 248,709,973, as many as 90.4 percent reported at least one specific ancestry.

6. U.S. Bureau of the Census, *Detailed Ancestry Groups by States, 1990* (Washington, D.C.: Economic and Statistics Administration, Bureau of the Census, October 1992), III-4–III-6, 3.

7. Interview with Lila Oftenæs Larsen by Terje Mikael Hasle Joranger, Camas, Washington, January 16, 1996.

8. *Norway Times,* May 9, 23, 1996; interview with Gail Petersen by Odd S. Lovoll, Brooklyn, New York, November 27, 1995; interview with Victor Samuelsen by Lovoll, New York City, November 21, 1995.

9. Interview with G. Joanne Ashland by Lovoll, Houston, Texas, April 25, 1996.

10. U.S. Bureau of the Census, *Ancestry of the Population of the United States, 1990* (Washington, D.C.: Economic and Statistics Administration, Bureau of the Census, August 1993), 57.

11. Interview with Richard Berhow by Joranger, Vancouver, Washington, January 17, 1997.

12. Interview with Karin Lier Brevig and Ola Brevig by Lovoll, Balboa Park, San Diego, California, February 9, 1996.

13. Interview with Jan H. Henricksen by Lovoll, San Diego, California, February 9, 1996.

14. Odd S. Lovoll, "From Norway to America: A Tradition of Immigration Fades," in Dennis Laurence Cuddy, ed., *Contemporary American Immigration: Interpretive Essays* (Boston: Twayne, 1982), 94–95, 96.

15. Herbert J. Gans, "Symbolic Ethnicity: The Future of Ethnic Groups and Cultures in America," in Herbert J. Gans, Nathan Glazer, Joseph R. Gusfield, and Christopher Jencks, eds., *On the Making of Americans: Essays in Honor of David Riesman* (Philadelphia: University of Pennsylvania Press, 1979), 203–4.

16. Michael Kammen, *Mystic Chords of Memory: The Transformation of Tradition in American Culture* (New York: Vintage Books, 1993), 641–45.

17. *The Aaker Paper,* 1985.

18. A great number of family histories were donated to the Contemporary History Project. These will be permanently stored in the archives of the Norwegian-American Historical Association, Northfield, Minnesota.

19. Sanford K. Fosholt, *The Charcoal Burner's Legacy: A History of the Goplerud Family* (Muscatine, Iowa: by the author, 1990), xxxll, ixl–xlii, 719–99 list descendants; letter to the author from Sanford Fosholt, dated September 28, 1995.

20. *125th Anniversary of the Omsrud-Thordson-Torgrimson Emigration from Norway Celebrated This 13th Day of August, 1978* (n.p., n.d) , 70–71.

21. Mary Waters, *Ethnic Options: Choosing Identities in America* (Berkeley: University of California Press, 1990), 147, 150–55.

22. Many of the interview subjects were found in Norwegian-American organizations. An effort was made to find as many Norwegian Americans as possible who were not actively involved in ethnic social and cultural groups.

23. Interview with David G. Oihus by Lovoll, Phoenix, Arizona, February 5, 1996. The influential anthropologist Clifford Geertz in *The Interpretation of Cultures: Selected Essays* (New York: Basic Books, 1973) emphasizes a primordial character of ethnicity, originating in the basic group identity of human beings. In his view, people have an essential need for belonging that is satisfied by groups based on shared ancestry and culture.

24. Werner Sollors, *Beyond Ethnicity: Consent and Descent in American Culture* (New York: Oxford University Press, 1986), 5–6; John Bodnar, *Remaking America: Public Memory, Commemoration, and Patriotism in the Twentieth Century* (Princeton, N.J.: Princeton University Press, 1992), 42–43.

25. See publications by Vesterheim Genealogical Center, *Norwegian Tracks,* especially July 1975, July 1993, July 1994, and April 1996; see also *Avisen,* May 1993, August 1994, published by the Norwegian-American Genealogical Association; interview with Blaine Hedberg, director of Vesterheim, by Lovoll and Joranger, Madison, Wisconsin, July 18, 1996.

26. Membership application form for the Scandinavian Genealogical Society, formed October 23, 1991, Portland, Oregon.

27. Letter from Marit H. Lucy, Family History Library, Salt Lake City, Utah, October 29, 1996. The Genealogical Society of Utah was founded in 1894 to gather genealogical information and assist in tracing family histories.

28. See Odd S. Lovoll, *A Folk Epic: The* Bygdelag *in America* (Boston: Twayne Publishers for Norwegian-American Historical Association, 1975), on the history of the *bygdelag* until about the 1970s. On page 218 Lovoll predicts: "If trends have been accurately assessed, it would seem that changed conditions and circumstances leave little room in the future for the *bygdelag.*" This statement preceded the movement's rebirth through its involvement in genealogy. Information from Marilyn Somdahl, president of the Council of Bygdelags, in conversation with Lovoll, Minneapolis, May 17, 1997.

29. U.S. Bureau of the Census, *Ancestry of the Population,* 12–27; interview with Roderic Johnson by Joranger, Suttons Bay, Michigan, May 8, 1996.

30. U.S. Bureau of the Census, *Ancestry of the Population,* 12–27; Darrell J. Christofferson, electronic letter, February 28, 1995; *Traverse, the Magazine,* April 1988; Carlton C. Qualey, *Norwegian Settlement in the United States* (Northfield, Minn.: Norwegian-American Historical Association, 1938), 170–71, 193–94.

31. Kathleen Conzen, "Mainstreams and Side Channels: The Localization of Immigrant Cultures," *Journal of American Ethnic History,* fall 1991: 5–20, quote page 13.

32. U.S. Bureau of the Census, *1990 Census of Population. Social and Economic Characteristics. Wisconsin* (Washington, D.C.: Economic and Statistics Administration, 1993), 214; *Illinois,* 101; *Minnesota,* 205, 207, 211.

33. Some of the respondents wished to be anonymous; interview with H. Allen Paulson by Lovoll, Canton, South

Dakota, May 24, 1996; Gerald De Jong, "The Coming of the Dutch to the Dakotas," *South Dakota History*, winter 1974: 20–51; telephone interview with Gerald De Jong, June 30, 1997; several other interviews with Norwegian Americans in Canton, Hudson, and Elk Point, South Dakota; "Scandinavian Spring, Canton, S.D., May 21, 1994."

34. The *Tracy Headlight-Herald*, April 26, 1995, in Tracy, Minnesota, for instance, announced the research project with a large "Uffda," no doubt to make the research team feel welcome.

35. Waters, *Ethnic Options*, shows how choosing ethnic identity is an option only for white Americans, leaving black Americans outside voluntary ethnicity. For a discussion of a shared Scandinavian-American identity, see J. R. Christianson, "Scandinavian-Americans," in John D. Buenker and Lorman A. Ratner, eds., *Multiculturalism in the United States: A Comparative Guide to Acculturation and Ethnicity* (New York: Greenwood Press, 1992), 103–29.

36. U.S. Bureau of the Census, *Ancestry of the Population*, 27; U.S. Bureau of the Census, *1990 Census of Population. Washington* (CD-ROM).

37. U.S. Bureau of the Census, *Ancestry of the Population*, 12; U.S. Bureau of the Census, *1990 Census of Population. Alaska* (CD-ROM); *The 1996 Viking Visitor Guide, Petersburg, Alaska;* "Velkommen to Petersburg Little Norway Festival" (brochure); "Little Norway Festival 1996. Schedule of Events and Map of Event Locations" (program).

38. "Junction City Scandinavian Festival" (program); letters to the author from Beverly Hackleman, dated February 1, May 7, 1996; *Western Viking*, May 10, 1996.

39. U.S. Bureau of the Census, *Ancestry of the Population*, 18, 25; Christianson, "Scandinavian-Americans," 120–22; interview with Eugene S. Haugse by Lovoll, Brookfield, Wisconsin, April 4, 1996.

40. Odd S. Lovoll, "A Scandinavian Melting Pot in Chicago," in Philip J. Anderson and Dag Blanck, eds., *Swedish-American Life in Chicago: Cultural and Urban Aspects of an Immigrant People, 1850–1930* (Urbana: University of Illinois Press, 1992), 66.

41. U.S. Bureau of the Census, *1990 Census of Population. Oregon* (CD-ROM).

42. U.S. Bureau of the Census, *1990 Census of Population. California* (CD-ROM).

43. Ibid.

44. U.S. Bureau of the Census, *1990 Census of Population. Arizona* (CD-ROM).

45. E. John B. Allen, *From Skisport to Skiing: One Hundred Years of an American Sport, 1840–1940* (Amherst: University of Massachusetts Press, 1993), 139–44, 145–70; *1995–1996 U.S. Skiing Cross-Country Competition Guide,* compiled and published by the United States Ski Association, Park City, Utah; *1995–1996 U.S. Skiing Jumping/Nordic Combined Competition Guide,* compiled and published by the United States Ski Association, Park City, Utah. See also Sureva Towler, *The History of Skiing at Steamboat Springs* (Steamboat Spring, Colo.: n.p., n.d.).

46. U.S. Bureau of the Census, *1990 Census of Population. Colorado* (CD-ROM); U.S. Bureau of the Census, *Ancestry of the Population*, 12, 27.

47. Dorothy Ann Brown, *We Sing to Thee: A Story about Clifton College* (Waco, Tex.: by author, 1974); interview with Dorothy Ann Brown by Lovoll, Clifton, Texas, April 23, 1996; U.S. Bureau of the Census, *1990 Census of Population. Texas* (CD-ROM); U.S. Bureau of the Census, *Ancestry of the Population*, 27.

48. Letter from Eudoris Dahl, director of Dallas/Arlington Leikarringen and state coordinator for the Norwegian Society of Texas, dated September 17, 1996.

49. Letter from Thomas B. Sandseth, Second Vice President, N.Y.P.D. Viking Association, dated December 11, 1995; interview with Sandseth by Lovoll, New York, November 17, 1995; *Viking News,* September 1995; interview with Gary Alan Boardman by Joranger and Lovoll, Staten Island, November 20, 1995.

50. *F.D.N.Y. Vikings Newsletter,* January 1996; interview with Donald R. Thorsen, Brooklyn, New York, November 27, 1995.

51. U.S. Bureau of the Census, *1990 Census of Population. New York* (CD-ROM); U.S. Bureau of the Census, *Ancestry of the Population*, 12, 21.

52. Interview with Ellen Skaar by Joranger and Lovoll, Fairhaven, Massachusetts, November 29, 1995; *Haugesunds Avis,* November 25, 1975; *Karmsund,* October 25, 1995.

53. *Christian Science Monitor,* June 16, 1959; *Franklin News-Record,* February 25, 1988, October 11, 1990; Adolph Johansen, "Reminiscences," September 24, 1966, typescript.

54. Interview with Hjørdis Mortensen by Joranger, Norseville, New Jersey, December 1, 1995.

55. Interview with Charles J. Lopez Jr. by Lovoll, Los Angeles, February 2, 1996; *Grand Opening. The B.U.L. Cabin, Nor-Bu Lodge No. 427 Sons of Norway, Lake Telemark, New Jersey, November 22, 1991; Holy Trinity Lutheran Church, Fiftieth Anniversary, 1941–1991,* special publication.

56. U.S. Bureau of the Census, *Ancestry of the Population,* 18, 27; newspaper clipping from 1928; interviews with Berit Mesarick and Frances H. Hamilton by Lovoll, Norge, Virginia, November 10, 1995.

57. Notes from a visit to the Regatta in Old Tampa Bay, Florida, May 13–14, 1995; Einar Bredland, *Sons of Norway Third District Lodge History* (Minneapolis: Sons of Norway, 1995), 262.

58. U.S. Bureau of the Census, *Ancestry of the Population,* 15; U.S. Bureau of the Census, *1990 Census of Population. Florida* (CD-ROM); "Booming Norwegian Business in Florida," *News of Norway,* May 1997.

59. *Southwest Wisconsin's Uplands 1995 Free Visitors Guide,* 36; *New Glarus Wisconsin: America's Little Switzerland since 1845* (New Glarus Chamber of Commerce, 1995), 4–14; *Norway Times,* December 14, 1995; *Mount Horeb Mail,* November 14, 1996; *The Journal,* May 27, 1992; interview with Ardis Gyland by Lovoll, Stoughton, Wisconsin, September 24, 1995; visit to Stoughton and several interviews, September 25, 1995; interview with Phil Martin by Lovoll, Mount Horeb, Wisconsin, September 30, 1995.

60. Following a speech to a Norwegian-American gathering October 26, 1996, concerning Norwegian-American ethnicity, the author was confronted by a woman who accused him of thinking like a "Norwegian" and not a "Norwegian American," because the author did not seem to understand how natural a term like "Uffda" was in all aspects of Norwegian-American life. It was simply an ethnic identifying utterance and not limited to expressing criticism or ill feelings.

61. Stanley Lieberson and Mary Waters, *From Many Strands: Ethnic and Racial Groups in Contemporary America* (New York: Russell Sage Foundation, 1988), 5; Eugeen E. Roosens, *Creating Ethnicity: The Process of Ethnogenesis* (Newbury Park, Calif.: Sage Publications, 1989), 15–16.

62. Philip Gleason, "Identifying Identity: A Semantic History," in *Speaking of Diversity: Language and Ethnicity in Twentieth-Century America* (Baltimore: Johns Hopkins University Press, 1992), 123–49; Eriksen quoted on pages 131, 143.

63. Roosens, *Creating Ethnicity,* 9.

64. Gleason, "Identifying Identity: A Semantic History," 123–49. See also John Higham, "Ethnic Pluralism in Modern American Thought," in *Send These to Me: Jews and Other Immigrants in Urban America* (New York: Atheneum, 1975), 196–230; and Elliott R. Barkan, "Reflections on the Roots of American Ethnicity," in Øyvind T. Gulliksen, David C. Mauk, and Dina Tolfsby, eds., *Norwegian-American Essays* (Oslo: NAHA-Norway, 1996), 31–60.

65. Odd S. Lovoll, *A Century of Urban Life: The Norwegians in Chicago before 1930* (Northfield, Minn.: Norwegian-American Historical Association, 1988), 65–67, 130.

66. U.S. Congressman O. J. Kvale of Minnesota was likely President Coolidge's authority on Norse discovery.

67. Carl H. Chrislock, "The First Two Centennials 1914 and 1925," in Paul E. Foss, ed., *Norwegian American Sesquicentennial 1825–1925* (Minneapolis: Norwegian American 1975 Sesquicentennial Association, 1975), Haugen quoted on page 37.

68. Paul D. Rusten, "A Heritage to Share," in Foss, ed., *Norwegian American Sesquicentennial,* 8–9.

69. Chrislock, "The First Two Centennials 1914 and 1925," 34-37; Lovoll, *A Folk Epic,* 166–73. April R. Schultz in her doctoral dissertation, published in an abbreviated form as *Ethnicity on Parade: Inventing the Norwegian American through Celebration* (Amherst: University of Massachusetts Press, 1994), discusses the invention of Norwegian-American ethnicity as expressed in public celebration. Her concluding discussion on "Historical Memory and Ethnicity," pages 123–33, places the Centennial in an insightful theoretical framework.

70. Several programs of Nordic Fest, publicity flyers, and several visits; interview with Marilyn Haugen Roverud by Lovoll, Decorah, Iowa, May 14, 1996; interview with Donald Olsen by Joranger, Decorah, Iowa, May 14, 1996; interview with Darrell D. Henning, Director of Vesterheim, by Lovoll and Joranger, May 15, 1996.

71. Interview with Myron Floren by Lovoll, Minot, North Dakota, October 11, 1995.

72. Interview with Celeste Holm, by Lovoll, Minot, North Dakota, October 11, 1995.

73. Interview with Chester M. Reiten by Lovoll, Minot, North Dakota, October 11, 1995; Lori and Jim Olson, *Norsk Høstfest: Heritage Comes Alive* (Helena, Mont.: American and World Geographic Publishing, 1995), 7, 15–24; several publicity mailings, newsletters, programs, and impressions from visit October 10–12, 1995, and interviews with a number of participants, performers, arts and crafts people, operators of sales booths, and people attending the festival.

74. *Western Viking,* April 26, 1996.

75. Bob Hendrickson, letter dated April 10, 1995; history of "Norway Day Festival"; *News of Norway,* March 1996; *Norway Times,* May 16, 1996.

76. *Viking Fest. Immigration Celebration 1846–1996* (Georgetown, Tex.: Viking Fest Committee, 1996); visit to Viking Fest, Georgetown, Texas, April 27, 1996.

77. Information on Story City supplied by Kay Jacobson Munsen, Story City, Iowa; *The Des Moines Register Datebook,* May 23, 1996; "A Scandinavian Festival in Beautiful Kootenai Country, Libby, Montana, Every Year in Mid-September, Sept. 12, 13 & 14, 1996," World Wide Web www.libby.org.

3. THE BURDEN AND THE GLORY

1. U.S. Bureau of the Census, *Detailed Ancestry Groups by States, 1990* (Washington, D.C.: Economic and Statistics Administration, Bureau of the Census, October 1992), III-5; Wade Clark Roof and William McKinney, "Denominational America and the New Religious Pluralism," *Annals of the American Academy of Political and Social Sciences,* July 1985: 24–38; Philip Perlmutter, *Divided We Fall: A History of Ethnic, Religious, and Racial Prejudice in America* (Ames: Iowa State University Press, 1992), 3–11.

2. Charles H. Anderson, *White Protestant Americans: From National Origins to Religious Group* (Englewood Cliffs, N.J.: Prentice-Hall, 1970), 7, 119, 124–25, 131–33, 173–77; Will Herberg, *Protestant-Catholic-Jew* (Garden City, N.Y.: Doubleday and Company, 1960), 234.

3. Eugeen Roosens, *Creating Ethnicity: The Process of Ethnogenesis* (Newbury Park, Calif.: Sage Publications, 1989), 16.

4. Ernest Gellner, *Postmodernism, Reason, and Religion* (New York: Routledge, 1992), 22–40; Martin E. Marty, "Ethnicity: The Skeleton of Religion in America," *Church History* 41, 1 (March 1972): 227–28.

5. Interview with Steven J. Slostad by Odd S. Lovoll, Faribault, Minnesota, April 23, 1997.

6. Interview with William Charles Simonson by Lovoll, Washington, D.C., November 6, 1995.

7. Roof and McKinney, "Denominational America and the New Religious Pluralism," 25–26; see, for instance, Martin B. Bradley et al., *Churches and Church Membership in the United States 1990: An Enumeration by Region, State, and County Based on Data Reported for 133 Church Groupings* (Atlanta, Ga.: Glenary Research Center, 1992), 4; Gibson Winter, *Religious Identity: The Formal Organization and Informal Power Structure of the Major Faiths in the United States Today* (New York: Macmillan Company, 1968).

8. Helen Stangeland, *Stavanger Friends Yesterday and Today* (Marshalltown, Iowa: Stavanger Friends Church, 1985); interviews with Clarence and Helen Stanley Stangeland, Dunbar, Iowa, October 22, 1995, by Terje Mikael Hasle Joranger, and on June 6, 1996, by Joranger and Lovoll.

9. Henry Jauhiainen, *Fellowship of Christian Assemblies: United States Handbook* (Madison, Wis.: Fellowship Press, 1992); *Philadelphia Church 85 Anniversary: A Brief History* (Seattle, Wash.: Philadelphia Press, 1986); interview with Gerald W. Erickson by Lovoll, Washington, D.C., November 12, 1995.

10. Interviews with Margret Solum DeRoche, William Henry DeRoche, and Annemarie DeRoche by Joranger and Lovoll, Bethesda, Maryland, November 5, 1995.

11. Interview with Knute Peterson by Lovoll, Salt Lake City, Utah, February 24, 1996.

12. Interview with Erlend Dean Peterson, Provo, Utah, February 23, 1996. Conversations with several members of the Leif Erikson Lodge of Sons of Norway, Salt Lake City, almost all of whom were Norwegian-born Mormons, February 24, 1996; Elisabeth Lyngli, historian of the lodge was interviewed at this event. See also Gerald Myron Haslam, *Clash of Cultures: The Norwegian Experience with Mormonism, 1842–1920* (New York: Peter Lang, 1984); and Helge Seljaas, "The Mormon Migration from Norway" (master's thesis, University of Utah, 1973), 290.

13. Interview with Father Armand John Kreft by Lovoll, San Francisco, April 18, 1997.

14. Interview with Joan Lundheim Dickerson by Lovoll, Washington, D.C., November 5, 1995; interviews with Pastor Dennis Preston and Yvonne Torgrimson Blomquist by Joranger, Hanska, Minnesota, June 19, 1996; "Annual Meeting Nora Unitarian Universalist Church, June 2, 1996"; interview with Lorraine Becker by Joranger, Hanska, Minnesota, June 19, 1996.

15. Interview with Grete Roland by Joranger and Lovoll, Chicago, April 3, 1996.

16. Interview with Carla H. Danziger by Lovoll, Washington, D.C., November 14, 1995.

17. Roof and McKinney, "Denominational America and the New Religious Pluralism," 26–27, 30–31; see also Frank S. Mead, *Handbook of Denominations in the United States,* rev. ed. by Samuel S. Hill (Nashville, Tenn.: Abingdon Press, 1985).

18. Einar Haugen, *Ole Edvart Rölvaag* (Boston: Twayne Publishers, 1983), 38–40; Peter A. Munch, "Segregation and Assimilation of Norwegian Settlements in Wisconsin," *Norwegian-American Studies and Records* (Northfield, Minn.) 18: 136; interview with Jacqueline Lyngen Adams by Lovoll, Balboa Park, San Diego, California, February 10, 1996.

19. Ola Storsletten, *En arv i tre. De norske stavkirkene* (Oslo: H. Aschehoug and Co., 1993), 164, 182; *Minneapolis Tribune Picture Magazine,* August 3, 1969; *Sogn Avis,* January 25, 1997. Replicas of other stave churches exist in Minnesota, Wisconsin, Florida, and perhaps elsewhere.

20. Carl H. Chrislock, "Name Change and the Church, 1918–1920," *Norwegian-American Studies* (Northfield, Minn.) 27 (1977): 194–223.

21. O. H. Hove, *The Evangelical Lutheran Church, Annual Report, Twenty-Fourth General Convention Central Lutheran Church, Minneapolis, Minnesota, April 19–21, 1960* (Minneapolis: Augsburg Publishing House, 1960), 9; Office of the Secretary, Department for Rosters and Statistics, Evangelical Lutheran Church in America (March 1996); Todd W. Nichol, introduction to *Vivacious Daughter: Seven Lectures on the Religious Situation among Norwegians in America,* by Herman Amberg Preus, trans. and ed. Todd W. Nichol (Northfield, Minn.: Norwegian-American Historical Association, 1990), 30.

22. Mead, *Handbook of Denominations,* 148–49, 151–52; Clifford E. Nelson and Eugene L. Fevold, *The Lutheran Church among Norwegian-Americans* (Minneapolis: Augsburg Publishing House, 1960), I: 161–63, II: 210–22, quotation on II: 220; *A Concise Doctrinal Statement of the Evangelical Lutheran Synod: We Believe Teach and Confess;* J. Herbert Larson and Juul B. Madson, *Built on the Rock: In Commemoration of the Seventy-Fifth Anniversary of the Evangelical Lutheran Synod 1918–1993* (Mankato, Minn.: Evangelical Lutheran Synod, 1992); interview with George M. Orvick by Lovoll, Northfield, Minnesota, May 24, 1997.

23. Interview with George M. Orvick; interview with Everald H. Strom by Joranger and Lovoll, Fergus Falls, Minnesota, March 5, 1996. See Joseph H. Levang, *The Church of the Lutheran Brethren 1900–1975: A Believers' Fellowship— A Lutheran Alternative* (Fergus Falls, Minn.: Lutheran Brethren Publishing Company, 1980).

24. Interview with Bishop George Anderson by Lovoll, Chicago, March 27, 1996.

25. Art Lee, *Leftover Lutefisk: More Stories from the Lutefisk Ghetto* (Staples, Minn.: Adventure Publications, 1984), 176–77; *Wisconsin Statutes and Annotations, 1993–94* (Madison, Wis.: Revisor of Statutes Bureau, 1994), 2151.

26. Odd S. Lovoll, *A Century of Urban Life: The Norwegians in Chicago before 1930* (Northfield, Minn.: Norwegian-American Historical Association, 1988), 74–83, 89, 206.

27. Internet message from Phyllis Stuckmayer to St. Olaf College faculty, October 12, 1995; information received from Jacob and Arvalene Vedvik, Ferryville, Wisconsin; interview with Clara Swingseth by Joranger and Lovoll, Benson, Minnesota, August 15, 1995. In his "The Lutefisk Dinner Directory," pages 173–204, Gary Legwold, *The Last Word on Lutefisk: True Tales of Cod and Tradition* (Minneapolis: Conrad Henry Press, 1996), lists 258 places throughout the United States, including churches, lodges, and restaurants, where this ethnic dish is served.

28. Richard D. Alba, *Ethnic Identity: The Transformation of White America* (New Haven, Conn.: Yale University Press, 1990), 85–91; interview with Irvin C. Holman by Lovoll, Fargo, North Dakota, March 11, 1996.

29. *Nordic Times,* October 19, 1995; Judith G. Goode, Karen Curtis, and Janet Theophano, "Meal Formats, Meal Cycles, and Menu Negotiation in the Maintenance of an Italian-American Community," in Mary Douglas, ed., *Food in the Social Order: Studies of Food and Festivities in Three American Communities* (New York: Russell Sage Foundation, 1984), 143–218.

30. Interview with Richard (Mike) Field, proprietor Mike's Fish and Seafood, by Lovoll, Glenwood, Minnesota, March 13, 1996; interview with W. B. "Bill" Andresen, Olsen Fish Company, by Lovoll, Minneapolis, April 17, 1996; *Wisconsin State Journal,* September 27, 1995; "*Lutefisk* Supper Statistics," St. John's Lutheran Church, Kasson, Minnesota.

31. Quoted in *Grand Forks Herald,* December 17, 1995.

32. In some districts in eastern Norway the tradition of eating lutefisk rolled inside a *lefse* is not uncommon.

33. *Wisconsin State Journal,* September 27, 1995.

34. Munch, "Segregation and Assimilation," 105; *Minneapolis Star Tribune,* October 16, 1993; *Western Viking,* January 5, 1996; *Cranfills Gap Record,* December 13, 1995; *Wisconsin State Journal,* October 29, 1989.

35. Alba, *Ethnic Identity,* 114–15; Goode, Curtis, and Theophano, "Meal Formats, Meal Cycles, and Menu Negotiation," 211–13.

36. Jon Gjerde, "The Effect of Community on Migration: Three Minnesota Townships 1885–1905," *Journal of Historical Geography,* October 1979: 403–22; Jon Gjerde, "Conflict and Community: A Case Study of the Immigrant Church in the United States," *Journal of Social History* (1986): 681–97.

37. Ann M. Legreid and David Ward, "Religious Schism and the Development of Rural Immigrant Communities: Norwegian Lutherans in Western Wisconsin, 1880–1905," *Upper Midwest History* 2 (1982): 13–29.

38. O. M. Norlie, *Norsk lutherske menigheter i Amerika 1843–1916* (Minneapolis, Minn.: Augsburg Publishing House, 1916), 437–840.

39. Lovoll, *A Century of Urban Life,* 119–20, 276–77; Einar Haugen, *The Norwegian Language in America: A Study in Bilingual Behavior,* 2 vols. (Bloomington: Indiana University Press, 1969), 257.

40. Interviews with Doris Hanson, Donald Hanson, Raymond Wennblom, Wilma Ellis Wennblom, Opal Johnson Noble, Thelma Kalstad, and Darlene Adam Michelson by Lovoll and Joranger, Elk Point, South Dakota, May 25, 1996; David P. Grant, *125 and Still Alive! Indherred Lutheran Church, Starbuck, Minnesota* (Starbuck, Minn.: Indherred Lutheran Church, 1995).

41. Peter T. Alter, "The Creation of Multi-Ethnic Peoplehood: The Wilkerson Washington Experience," *Journal of American Ethnic History,* spring 1996: 3–21; John Higham, *Send These to Me: Jews and Other Immigrants in Urban America* (New York: Atheneum, 1975), 196–230; Timothy L. Smith, "Religion and Ethnicity in America," *American Historical Review* 83 (December 1978): 1168.

42. Karen Hanson, *In Jesus' Name Shall All Our Work Be Done* (Wind Lake, Wis.: Norway Evangelical Lutheran Church, 1992), 111–15, 126–27; Barbara Palmer and Jim Pederson, *The Town of Norway Then and Now: A Bicentennial Project* (Norway, Wis.: Bicentennial Committee, 1983), 37–42; *Norway Evangelical Lutheran Church Membership Directory,* August 1995; interview with Karen Hanson by Joranger, Minneapolis, September 19, 1995.

43. Lovoll, *A Century of Urban Life,* 139–49, 284–90.

44. Ibid., 62, 63–64, 68, 145.

45. Lovoll, *A Century of Urban Life,* 276, 312; *60 Years in Oak Park, United Lutheran Church, 1928–1988.*

46. *60 Years in Oak Park, United Lutheran Church, 1928–1988;* interviews with several church officials and members by Joranger and Lovoll, United Lutheran Church of Oak Park, Oak Park, Illinois, March 28, 1996.

47. *Norway Times,* October 17, 1996; visit to Zion Lutheran Church, Brooklyn, November 26, 1995; interview with Diane Wildow, pastor of Zion Lutheran Church, by Lovoll, November 26, 1995; *Yesterday, Today, Tomorrow: Zion Lutheran Church Golden Jubilee Year* (Brooklyn, N.Y.: Zion Lutheran Church, 1958).

48. Interview with church office by telephone by Lovoll, 59th Street Church, November 18, 1996.

49. Interview with Robert M. Nervig, senior pastor Trinity Lutheran Church, by Joranger and Lovoll, November 26, 1995; interview with Per W. Larsen, pastor Norwegian section of Trinity Lutheran Church, by Lovoll, November 26, 1995; *Trinity through the Years, 1890–1965* (Brooklyn, N.Y.: Trinity Lutheran Church, 1965); *Trinity through the Years, 1966–1990* (Brooklyn, N.Y.: Trinity Lutheran Church, 1990). The trilingual names of the church are Trinity Lutheran Church, Iglesia Luterana de la Trinidad, and Trefoldighetskirken.

50. Nichol, introduction to *Vivacious Daughter,* 30; Nelson and Fevold, *Lutheran Church among Norwegian-Americans,* I: 184, 187; *Higher Education Trends Analysis,* 1996 ed., prepared and published by the Division of Higher Education and Schools of the ELCA, Chicago, Illinois. In the fall term of 1995, 14,301 of the 44,036 full-time students at the twenty-eight ELCA institutions were enrolled in colleges of a Norwegian immigrant origin, equal to 32.4 percent.

51. David T. Nelson, *Luther College, 1861–1961* (Decorah, Iowa: Luther College Press, 1961), 45–60; Nelson and Fevold, *Lutheran Church among Norwegian-Americans,* I: 151–90.

52. Nelson, *Luther College,* 169; Joseph M. Shaw, *History of St. Olaf College 1874–1974* (Northfield, Minn.: St. Olaf College Press, 1974), 59–83, 90, 98, 108–11; Odd S. Lovoll, *The Promise of America: A History of the Norwegian-American People* (Minneapolis: University of Minnesota Press, 1984), 110–12.

53. See Erling Nicolai Rolfsrud, *Cobber Chronicle: An Informal History of Concordia College* (Moorhead, Minn.: Concordia College, 1966); Walter C. Schnackenberg, *The Lamp and the Cross: Sagas of Pacific Lutheran University from 1890 to 1965* (Tacoma, Wash.: Pacific Lutheran University Press, 1965); Carl H. Chrislock, *From Fjord to Freeway: 100 Years, Augsburg College* (Minneapolis: Augsburg College, 1969); Emil Erpestad, "A History of Augustana College" (Sioux Falls, S.Dak.: typescript, 1955); Odd S. Lovoll, *Det løfterike landet. En norskamerikansk historie,* rev. ed. (Oslo: Universitetsforlaget, 1997), 130–32.

54. Shaw, *History of St. Olaf College,* 241–45, 396–97; interview with Sidney A. Rand and Lois Rand by Joranger and Lovoll, Minneapolis, May 1, 1996.

55. St. Olaf College, student and faculty survey, fall 1996.

56. An appeal to St. Olaf College alumni in the April-May 1995 issue of the *St. Olaf Magazine* to respond to questions concerning ethnic and religious issues of their college experience produced a number of lengthy responses. One of these was a letter from Clarice Irene Anderson, May 31, 1995, of Minneapolis. Research for this book involved a large number of informal interviews in the states of the upper Midwest with people of Norwegian background, which frequently included references to St. Olaf College and other colleges of a Norwegian immigrant origin. Interview with O. Jay Tomson by Lovoll, Clear Lake, Iowa, June 9, 1996.

57. *Higher Education Trends Analysis,* 1996.

58. Andrew M. Greeley, *Ethnicity in the United States: A Preliminary Reconnaissance* (New York: John Wiley and Sons, 1974), 125–35, 187–91; Kendric Charles Babcock, *The Scandinavian Element in the United States* (Urbana: University of Illinois Press, 1914), 142.

59. Lowell J. Soike, *Norwegian Americans and the Politics of Dissent, 1880–1924* (Northfield, Minn.: Norwegian-American Historical Association, 1991), 47–52, 56–62, 79–83. See Millard L. Gieske and Steven J. Keillor, *Norwegian Yankee: Knute Nelson and the Failure of American Politics, 1860–1923* (Northfield, Minn.: Norwegian-American Historical Association, 1995).

60. Lovoll, *The Promise of America,* 120, 130–31; Millard L. Gieske, *Minnesota Farmer-Laborism: The Third-Party Alternative* (Minneapolis: University of Minnesota Press, 1979), 45, 61, 81, 320–32; William E. Lass, *Minnesota: A Bicentennial History* (New York: W. W. Norton and Company, 1977), 22.

61. Sten Carlsson, "Scandinavian Politicians in Minnesota around the Turn of the Century: A Study of the Role of the Ethnic Factor in an Immigrant State," in Harald S. Naess and Sigmund Skard, eds., *Americana Norvegica,* vol. 3 (Oslo: Universitetsforlaget, 1971), 263-67.

62. Theodore B. Pedeliski, *Interest Groups in North Dakota: Constituency Coupling in a Moralistic Political Culture* (Grand Forks, N.Dak.: Bureau of Government Affairs, University of North Dakota, 1987), 47 n. 9; interview with Geoffrey R. Wodell by Lovoll, Denver, Colorado, February 16, 1996.

63. Interview with Arne L. Christenson by Lovoll, Washington, D.C., May 7, 1996; interview with Stanley Nesheim by Lovoll, Washington, D.C., November 6, 1995.

64. Interview with J. Wendell Sands by Lovoll, Alvarado, Minnesota, March 9, 1996.

65. Interview with Mathilda Sageng by Lovoll, Fergus Falls, Minnesota, March 5, 1996; telephone interview with Cal Larson by Lovoll, February 26, 1998.

66. Interview with Clair B. Moe by Lovoll, North Dakota Mill and Elevator, Grand Forks, North Dakota, October 12, 1995; Soike, *Norwegian Americans and the Politics of Dissent,* 115, 162–63, 168; Elwyn B. Robinson, *History of North Dakota* (Lincoln: University of Nebraska Press, 1966), 218, 221–26, 288, 330–34. See Richard M. Scammon and Alice V. McGillivray, *America Votes 21: A Handbook of Contemporary American Election Statistics* (Washington, D.C.: Elections Research Center, 1995).

67. *Saint Paul Pioneer Press,* September 20, 1992; annual population estimates by the census bureau as reported in *Minneapolis Star Tribune,* December 19, 1997; and on the bureau's World Wide Web site.

68. Dale Baum, "The New Day in North Dakota: The Nonpartisan League and the Politics of Negative Revolution," *North Dakota History,* spring 1973: 4–19; see *North Dakota Quarterly,* autumn 1981: 82; Odd S. Lovoll, "Simon Johnson and the Ku Klux Klan in Grand Forks," *North Dakota Quarterly,* autumn 1981: 9–20; William L. Harwood, "The Ku Klux Klan in Grand Forks, North Dakota," *South Dakota History,* fall 1971: 301–35; Pedeliski, *Interest Groups in North Dakota,* 2, 23; see, for instance, Peter Thoresen Reite, ed., *Fra det amerikanske Normandi* (Moorhead, Minn.: privately published, 1912), 18–23; i.e., from the American Normandy. The statue of Rollo was unveiled July 19, 1912, at a grand celebration in Fargo. The Rouen citizens had offered a replica of the statue, a symbol of their mixed French and Viking ancestry, as a gift to the people of the United States. Through the efforts of Dr. Herman O. Fjelde, Fargo secured the statue. As the main speaker at the Fargo ceremonies, Professor Julius Olson of the University of Wisconsin deeply offended the French by extolling the virtues of the Germanic race over the Latin and all Catholics by calling out the name of Martin Luther.

69. Interview with Jens Tennefos by Lovoll, Fargo, North Dakota, March 12, 1996; interview with District Court Judge Ralph Erickson by Joranger and Lovoll, Fargo, North Dakota, March 11, 1996. The article by Pamela Constable in the *Washington Post National Weekly Edition,* October 23–29, 1995, was reprinted in the seventh edition of *Race and Ethnic Relations* (Guilford, Conn.: Dushkin/McGraw Hill, 1997), 166–68.

70. Interview with Stanley Nesheim by Lovoll, Washington, D.C., November 6, 1995.

71. Interview with Senator Roger D. Moe by Joranger and Lovoll, State Capitol Building, St. Paul, Minnesota, August 30, 1995.

72. Interview with Steven A. Sviggum by Joranger, State Capitol Building, St. Paul, Minnesota, August 29, 1995.

73. Interview with Congressman Martin Sabo by Joranger and Lovoll, Minneapolis, October 6, 1995; biographical sketch provided by Sabo's congressional office.

74. Interview with Vice President Walter F. Mondale by Lovoll, Minneapolis, January 29, 1997.

75. Interview with Senator Brian D. Rude by Lovoll, Wisconsin State House, Madison, September 26, 1995.

76. Interview with Representative William Murat by Joranger and Lovoll, Wisconsin State House, Madison, September 26, 1995.

77. Interview with Chief Justice Roland B. Day by Lovoll, Wisconsin State House, September 26, 1995.

78. Interview with Governor Terry Branstad by Joranger and Lovoll, Des Moines, Iowa, June 5, 1996.

79. John Arne Markussen, *Frihet og frykt. Nærbilder fra USA* (Oslo: Gyldendal Norsk Forlag, 1997), 128–33, 135.

80. See, for instance, Waldemar Ager, "The Melting Pot," in Odd S. Lovoll, ed., *Cultural Pluralism versus Assimilation: The Views of Waldemar Ager* (Northfield, Minn.: Norwegian-American Historical Association, 1977), 77–86; and O. E. Rølvaag, *Omkring fædrearven* (Northfield, Minn.: St. Olaf College Press, 1922).

81. Interview with Maynard O. Molstad by Lovoll, Canton, South Dakota, May 24, 1996.

82. *USA Today,* April 3, 1996; James A. Aho, *The Politics of Righteousness: Idaho Christian Patriotism* (Seattle: University of Washington Press, 1990), 13, 18, 24, 52; Markussen, *Frihet og frykt,* 132.

83. "The Florida State Militia Statement of Purpose."

84. Interview with Robert Johansen by Joranger, Fort Pierce, Florida, November 13, 1995. *Dagbladet* (Oslo), June 11, 1995; *The Resister: The Official Publication of the Special Forces Underground,* autumn 1994. The *Minneapolis Star Tribune,* June 5, 1997, carried a report about the Christian Coalition's support of Oliver North, the hero of the right-wing movement, in the 1994 U.S. Senate campaign. *Minneapolis Star Tribune,* June 12, 1997.

85. Interview with Norman Olson by Joranger, Alanson, Michigan, May 9, 1996.

86. Seymour Martin Lipset and Earl Raab, *The Politics of Unreason: Right-Wing Extremism in America, 1790–1970* (New York: Harper and Row, 1970), 484–87, 508–15.

87. Aho, *Politics of Righteousness,* pages 212–26, contains an insightful discussion of theories of right-wing extremism and Aho's alternative theory.

88. Mary Waters, *Ethnic Options: Choosing Identities in America* (Berkeley: University of California Press, 1990), 134.

89. Steve Gunderson and Rob Morris with Bruce Bawer, *House and Home* (New York: Dutton Book, 1996), 268, 271–72; *USA Today,* August 1, 1996.

90. Interview with Allison L. E. Wee by Lovoll, Northfield, Minnesota, December 16, 1996.

91. Interview with Todd Rustad by Lovoll, St. Olaf College, July 18, 1995.

92. Waters, *Ethnic Options,* 131–38. See also Edwin H. Friedman, "The Myth of the Shiksa," in Monica McGoldrick, John K. Pearce, and Joseph Giordano, eds., *Ethnicity and Family Therapy* (New York: Guilford Press, 1982), 499–526.

93. Interview with Kimberly Anne Lerohl by Joranger, Albuquerque, New Mexico, February 6, 1996; interview with Kristin Lerohl by Lovoll, Portland, Oregon, January 17, 1996.

94. Interview with Neal R. Holtan by Lovoll, Minneapolis, October 17, 1995.

95. Interview with Andreas Jordahl Rhude by Lovoll, Minneapolis, August 27, 1996.

96. Alexis de Tocqueville, *Democracy in America,* ed. Richard D. Heffner (New York: Mentor Book, 1956), 194; Robert N. Bellah et al., *Habits of the Heart: Individuals and Commitments in American Life,* updated ed. (Berkeley: University of California Press, 1996), 153, 157–58, 163; Waters, *Ethnic Options,* 148–50, 153, Rupert Wilkinson quoted on page 153; interview with Kimberly Lerohl.

4. PERSPECTIVES ON THE AMERICAN DREAM

1. Ellen Tvetenstrand, letter to author, October 3, 1995; Stephan Thernstrom, *Poverty and Progress: Social Mobility in a Nineteenth-Century City* (Cambridge: Harvard University Press, 1964); Leonard Dinnerstein and David M. Reimers, *Ethnic Americans: A History of Immigration and Assimilation* (New York: Dodd, Mead and Company, 1975), 117–38; Stephan Thernstrom, *The Other Bostonians: Poverty and Progress in the American Metropolis* (Cambridge: Harvard University Press, 1973), 114–15.

2. Thernstrom, *The Other Bostonians,* 111–12, 138–42, 160–75; Alice Kessler-Harris and Virginia Yans-McLaughlin, "European Immigrant Groups," in Thomas Sowell, ed., *American Ethnic Groups* (New York: Urban Institute, 1978), 107–37.

3. Hans Norman, *Från Bergslagen till Nordamerika. Studier i migrationsmönster, social rörlighet och demografisk struktur*

med utgångspunkt från Örebro län, 1851–1915 (Uppsala: Acta Universitatis Upsaliensis, 1974), 237–40, 252–59, 261–70, 292–93. For an overview of theories of assimilation, see Milton M. Gordon, *Assimilation in American Life: The Role of Race, Religion, and National Origins* (New York: Oxford University Press, 1964).

4. Dinnerstein and Reimers, *Ethnic Americans,* 124.

5. E. P. Hutchinson, *Immigrants and Their Children, 1850–1950* (New York: Russell and Russell, 1956), 163, 167–68, 171–75, 179.

6. Robert Swierenga, "Ethnicity and American Agriculture," *Ohio History,* summer 1980: 323–44; Kenneth O. Bjork, "Scandinavian Migration to the Canadian Prairie Provinces, 1893–1914," *Norwegian-American Studies* (Northfield, Minn.) 26 (1974): 3–6; Odd S. Lovoll, "Bardo in Norway and in Canada and the 'Canada Fever' in the Upper Midwest," in Hans Storhaug, ed., *Norwegian Immigration to Canada* (Oslo: Universitetsforlaget), forthcoming; Theodore Saloutos, "The Immigrant Contribution to American Agriculture," *Agricultural History* 50, 1 (January 1976): 54–55.

7. Hutchinson, *Immigrants and Their Children,* 224–39, 241–42.

8. O. P. B. Jacobson, "Contributions to Agriculture," in Harry Sundby-Hansen, ed., *Norwegian Immigrant Contributions to America's Making* (New York: International Press, 1921), 30.

9. U.S. Bureau of the Census, *Ancestry of the Population of the United States, 1990* (Washington, D.C.: Economic and Statistics Administration, Bureau of the Census, August 1993), 363; U.S. Department of Labor, *Handbook of Labor Statistics* (August 1989), 78; Stanley Lieberson and Mary C. Waters, *From Many Strands: Ethnic and Racial Groups in Contemporary America* (New York: Russell Sage Foundation, 1988), 121, 155–61.

10. Karl B. Raitz, "The Location of Tobacco Production in Western Wisconsin" (Ph.D. diss., University of Wisconsin, 1970).

11. Arnold Strickon and Robert A. Ibarra, "The Changing Dynamics of Ethnicity: Norwegians and Tobacco in Wisconsin," *Ethnic and Racial Studies* 6, 2 (1983): 174–97; Arnold Strickon and Robert A. Ibarra, "The Norwegian-American Dairy-Tobacco Strategy in Southwestern Wisconsin," *Norwegian-American Studies* (Northfield, Minn.) 32 (1989): 3–29.

12. Interview with Leland Edward Lewison by Odd S. Lovoll, on his farm near Viroqua, Wisconsin, September 8, 1995.

13. Interview with Lloyd Howard Voxland and Geraldine Bernette Larson Voxland by Terje Mikael Hasle Joranger and Lovoll, Wanamingo, Minnesota, July 3, 1996.

14. Interview with Lloyd Howard Voxland and Geraldine Bernette Larson Voxland; John C. Hudson, "Migration to an American Frontier," *Annals of the Association of American Geographers,* June 1976: 243–65; Odd S. Lovoll, *The Promise of America: A History of the Norwegian-American People* (Minneapolis: University of Minnesota Press, 1984), 146.

15. *Haslekaas Family 1887–1987* (Grafton, N.Dak.: July 1987).

16. Interview with David J. Haslekaas and Jan M. Bowles Haslekaas by Lovoll, Grand Forks, North Dakota, October 8, 1995.

17. Peter A. Scholl, *Garrison Keillor* (Iowa City: University of Iowa Press, 1993), 126; See also Garrison Keillor, *Lake Wobegon Days* (New York: Viking, 1985); Odd S. Lovoll, "Paul Hjelm-Hansen: Norwegian 'Discoverer' of the Red River Valley of Minnesota and Settlement Promoter," in Vidar Pedersen and Zeljka Svrljuga, *Performances in American Literature: Essays in Honor of Professor Orm Øverland on His 60th Birthday* (Bergen, Norway: University of Bergen, 1995), 161–78.

18. Interview with David Ralph Erickstad by Joranger, Starkweather, North Dakota, October 9, 1995.

19. Merle Curti, *The Making of an American Community: A Case Study of Democracy in a Frontier Community* (Stanford, Calif.: Stanford University Press, 1959), 186–92.

20. O. H. Skotheim, quoted in *Washington Posten,* August 17, 1906.

21. The author's father, Alf Lowell, made his livelihood as a halibut fisherman in Seattle and owned a small schooner, the *Attu.* The author is therefore well acquainted with the social environment of Norwegian-American halibut fishermen. Sverre Arestad, "Norwegians in the Pacific Coast Fisheries," *Norwegian-American Studies* (Northfield, Minn.) 30 (1985): 96–129; Ralph W. Andrews and A. K. Larssen, *Fish and Ships* (New York: Bonanza Books, 1959); International Pacific

Halibut Commission, *Report of Assessment and Research Activities 1993* (Seattle: 1994); telephone interview with Greg Bargmann of the Washington State Department of Fish and Wildlife, Olympia, Washington, December 12, 1996.

22. Interview with Michael A. Ness by Lovoll, Seattle, January 13, 1996; interview with Andreas L. Ness by Joranger, January 13, 1996.

23. Arestad, "Norwegians in the Pacific Coast Fisheries," 111–16.

24. Interview with John K. Sjong by Lovoll and Joranger, Seattle, January 9, 1996; telephone interview by Lovoll, December 12, 1996.

25. See, for instance, John R. Jenswold, "Becoming American, Becoming Suburban," *Norwegian-American Studies* (Northfield, Minn.) 33 (1992): 3–26.

26. Questionnaire response from Pam Aakhus, dated February 2, 1996.

27. Milton Cantor, "Ethnicity and the World of Work," in M. Mark Stolarik and Murray Friedman, eds., *Making It in America: The Role of Ethnicity in Business Enterprise, Education, and Work Choices* (Lewisburg, Penn.: Bucknell University Press, 1986), 98–115; Odd S. Lovoll, *A Century of Urban Life: The Norwegians in Chicago before 1930* (Northfield, Minn.: Norwegian-American Historical Association, 1988), 20–25, 37–38, 72–73, 80–83, 153, 231–35.

28. Gerd Nyquist, *Bataljon 99* (Oslo: Aschehoug, 1981); interview with Finn Gjertsen by Lovoll, Gjøa Sporting Club, Brooklyn, New York, November 19, 1995.

29. Interview with Kari Hesthag by Joranger and David Mauk, Brooklyn, New York, November 16, 1995.

30. O. M. Norlie, *History of the Norwegian People in America* (Minneapolis: Augsburg Publishing House, 1925), 349.

31. Lieberson and Waters, *From Many Strands,* 158–59; U.S. Bureau of the Census, *Ancestry of the Population, 1990,* 363–64, 409, 438–39, 441, 444, 447–48, 487–88.

32. John E. Bodnar, *The Transplanted: A History of Immigrants in Urban America* (Bloomington: Indiana University Press, 1985), 138–39; Lovoll, *A Century of Urban Life,* 159–61; Lovoll, *The Promise of America,* 123–24, 202, 204.

33. Lovoll, *A Century of Urban Life,* 159–61.

34. Lovoll, *A Century of Urban Life,* 281.

35. Interview with Jack Anundsen and Erick Anundsen by Lovoll, Decorah, Iowa, August 25, 1995.

36. Correspondence with the Outboard Marine Corporation dated August 11 and 28, 1995, and a response dated August 16, 1995.

37. Interview with Louise and Lee Sundet by Joranger and Lovoll, Minneapolis, Minnesota, April 10, 1996; interview with Beverly and Roe Hatlen by Lovoll, Apple Valley, Minnesota, December 14, 1996.

38. In addition to the international headquarters in New York, there are NACC chapters in Chicago, Minneapolis, Seattle, Portland, San Francisco, Los Angeles, Houston, New Orleans, and Miami, as well as a chapter in Oslo, Norway. Together with the Norwegian Trade Council, NACC publishes the *Norwegian Trade Bulletin.* See membership directories for individual chapters. For typical activities, see reports on NACC in *Norway Times,* January 11, May 23, and June 6, 27, 1996.

39. Lovoll, *The Promise of America,* 204.

40. *Beneficial Corporation, Wilmington, Delaware, 3rd Quarter Report 1995; Seventy-Five Years and Good for More: Beneficial* (Peapack, N.J.: Beneficial, 1989); interview with Finn M. W. Caspersen by Lovoll, Beneficial Center, Peapack, New Jersey, November 20, 1995.

41. *The Denver Post,* June 13, 1996; "Bjørn Borgen, Årdal og Denver: Trekvart miliardær—hittil," *Kapital* 21, 1 (January 1994): 38–45; *News of Norway,* March 1996; interview with Bjørn Erik Borgen by Lovoll, Denver, Colorado, February 13, 1996; and December 27, 1996, by telephone.

42. Interview with O. Jay Tomson by Joranger and Lovoll, Mason City, Iowa, June 9, 1996.

43. Jon Wefald, *A Voice of Protest: Norwegians in American Politics, 1890–1917* (Northfield, Minn.: Norwegian-American Historical Association, 1971), 3–4, 8–17.

44. Johan Fr. Heyerdahl, "Husmorsøkonomi på verdensplan," *The Norseman,* November 1990: 40–41; Evon Z. Vogt Jr., "Social Stratification in the Rural Middlewest: A Structural Analysis," *Rural Sociology* 12 (December 1947): 365; Max

Weber, *The Protestant Work Ethic and Capitalism,* trans. Talcott Parsons (New York: Charles Scribner's Sons, 1958), 118–21; W. Lloyd Warner, *Democracy in Jonesville: A Study of Quality and Inequality* (New York: Harper and Row, 1949), 168–92; Richard Weiss, *The American Myth of Success: From Horatio Alger to Norman Vincent Peale* (Urbana: University of Illinois Press, 1988), 18–23.

45. The notion of the *jantelov* was developed by the Danish-Norwegian author Aksel Sandemose (1899–1965) in his 1933 novel *En flyktning krysser sitt spor* (A Fugitive Crosses His Track), after the town of Jante, where the novel's protagonist grew up.

46. Interview with Lars Graff by Joranger and Lovoll, Kahler, Wisconsin, September 24, 1995.

47. James LeVoy Sorenson, *Finding the Better Way: The Life and Outlook of James LeVoy Sorenson, An American Entrepreneur* (Salt Lake City, Utah: n.p., 1992); interview with James LeVoy Sorenson by Lovoll, Salt Lake City, Utah, February 24, 1996.

48. Interview with Karsten Solheim by Joranger, Phoenix, Arizona, February 7, 1996; interview with Allan D. Solheim by Lovoll, Phoenix, Arizona, February 7, 1996.

49. Interviews with Eivind Bjerke by Lovoll, Washington, D.C., November 11, 1995, and May 6, 1996; John A. Markussen, "Eivind Erobret det Hvite Hus," *Dagbladet,* February 21, 1993; interview with Sven Røhne by Lovoll, Washington, D.C., May 6, 1996; Mary Finch Hoyt, "A Remarkable Woman's Inspiring Story: 'Why I Kept My Cancer a Secret,'" *Good Housekeeping,* June 1989, 154–55; "What's Beauty?" *Washingtonian,* July 1994, 71, 107, 110.

50. Interview with Betty Claire Monkman by Lovoll, the White House, Washington, D.C., November 13, 1995.

51. Interview with Tom Gjelten by Joranger and Lovoll, Washington, D.C., November 7, 1995.

52. Questionnaire response by Viktoria R. Y. Medicine Elk, Littleton, Colorado, February 14, 1996.

53. Lovoll, *A Century of Urban Life,* 28–29, 120–21, 128–29; *Skandinaven,* March 8, 1881; October 6, 1907; *Skandinaven* (daily), January 28, 1884; March 14, 1897; interview with Robert Gandrud by Lovoll and Joranger, Minneapolis, April 8, 1996.

54. *Verdens Gang* (Chicago), April 26, 1882; *Skandinaven* (daily), January 28, 1884; March 14, 1897.

55. Dianne M. Pinderhughes, *Race and Ethnicity in Chicago Politics: A Reexamination of Pluralist Theory* (Urbana: University of Illinois Press, 1987), 154–55, 160, 180.

56. O. N. Nelson, "The Nationality of Criminal and Insane Persons in the United States," in O. N. Nelson, ed., *History of the Scandinavians and Successful Scandinavians in the United States,* vol. 2, rev. ed. (Minneapolis: O. N. Nelson and Co., 1900), 1–11; Kathleen O'Leary Morgan, Scott Morgan, and Beal Quitno, eds., *Crime State Rankings 1996: Crime in the 50 United States* (Lawrence, Kans.: Morgan Quitno Press, 1996), 115; Kathleen O'Leary Morgan, Scott Morgan, and Beal Quitno, *State Rankings 1996: A Statistical View of the 50 United States* (Lawrence, Kans.: Morgan Quitno Press, 1996), 65; U.S. Bureau of the Census, *1990 Census of the Population, General Population Characteristics* (1990 CP-1-1), 53, 66, 141, 227.

57. Interview with Louis A. Stender, warden, Minnesota Correctional Facility, by Lovoll, Faribault, Minnesota, April 23, 1997.

58. Interview with Steven J. Slostad by Lovoll, Minnesota Correctional Facility, Faribault, Minnesota, April 23, 1997.

59. Interview with Donald F. Larson by Lovoll, Minnesota Correctional Facility, Faribault, Minnesota, April 23, 1997.

60. Interview with Darby Jon Opsahl by Lovoll, Minnesota Correctional Facility, Faribault, Minnesota, April 9, 1997.

61. Gordon, *Assimilation in American Life,* 51–54.

62. Interview with Dennis Sorheim by Lovoll, Minneapolis, May 29, 1996.

63. Richard D. Alba, *Ethnic Identity: The Transformation of White America* (New Haven, Conn.: Yale University Press, 1990); Peter A. Munch, "Segregation and Assimilation of Norwegian Settlements in Wisconsin," *Norwegian-American Studies and Records* (Northfield, Minn.) 18: 131–35.

64. Max Weber, quoted in Alba, *Ethnic Identity,* 313.

65. Interview with John Holum by Lovoll, State Department Building, Washington, D.C., November 14, 1995.

66. Richard Alba, "The Twilight of Ethnicity among American Catholics of European Ancestry," *Annals of the American Academy of Political and Social Science* 454 (March 1981): 86–97; Alba, *Ethnic Identity,* 310–19.

5. A LEGACY OF NATIONAL MUTUALITY

1. See, for instance, for the situation in Europe the classic social study on the effect of industrialization on the life of common people, Rudolf Braun, *Industrialisation and Everyday Life,* trans. Sarah Hanbury Tenison (Cambridge: Cambridge University Press, 1990). Studies of the emergence of ethnic subcultures in the United States are legion; consult references in Richard Kolm, *Bibliography of Ethnicity and Ethnic Groups* (Rockville, Md.: National Institutes for Mental Health, Center for Studies of Metropolitan Problems, 1973); and Wayne Charles Miller, *A Comprehensive Bibliography for the Study of American Minorities* (New York: New York University Press, 1976). A more recent reference work is David L. Brye, ed., *European Immigration and Ethnicity in the United States and Canada: An Historical Bibliography* (Santa Barbara, Calif.: ABC-Clio Information Services, 1983).

2. Interviews with Lester Korsness, Walter E. Hove, and Ron Borsheim, board members, Norwegian Mutual Insurance Association, by Odd S. Lovoll, Decorah, Iowa, May 14, 1996; documents relating to the history of the Norwegian Mutual Insurance Association in the Norwegian-American Historical Association archives.

3. Jacob A. Riis, *How the Other Half Lives: Studies among the Tenements of New York* (1890; reprint, Cambridge, Mass.: Belknap Press of the Harvard University Press, 1970).

4. Andrew M. Greeley, *That Most Distressful Nation: The Taming of the American Irish* (Chicago: Quadrangle Books, 1972); William Shannon, *The American Irish* (New York: Macmillan, 1963); Upton Sinclair, *The Jungle* (1906; reprint, Urbana: University of Illinois Press, 1988); David Ward, *Cities and Immigrants: A Geography of Change in the Nineteenth Century* (New York: Oxford University Press, 1971); Herbert J. Gans, *The Urban Villagers: Group and Class in the Life of Italian-Americans* (New York: Free Press, 1965); Gerald D. Suttles, *The Social Order of the Slum: Ethnicity and Territory in the Inner City* (Chicago: University of Chicago Press, 1968).

5. Odd S. Lovoll, *A Century of Urban Life: The Norwegians in Chicago before 1930* (Northfield, Minn.: Norwegian-American Historical Association, 1988), 38–42, 60–61, 69.

6. Lovoll, *A Century of Urban Life,* 313; Odd S. Lovoll, "Norwegian-American Mutuality in the Iron Decade: 'Nordlyset' of Chicago," in Faith Ingwersen and Mary Kay Norseng, eds., *Fin(s) de Siècle in Scandinavian Perspective: Studies in Honor of Harald Naess* (Columbia, S.C.: Camden House, 1993), 179–91.

7. Lovoll, *A Century of Urban Life,* 86–89, 202–3, 205–10, 210–11, 212–21; John E. Bodnar, *The Transplanted: A History of Immigrants in Urban America* (Bloomington: Indiana University Press, 1985), 120–30; Carl G. O. Hansen, *My Minneapolis* (Minneapolis: privately printed, 1956), 111, 254–59.

8. Harry Aponte, foreword to *Ethnicity and Family Therapy,* ed. Monica McGoldrick, John K. Pearce, and Joseph Giordano (New York: Guilford Press, 1982), xiii-xiv.

9. C. F. Midelfort and H. C. Midelfort, "Norwegian Families," in McGoldrick, Pearce, and Giordano, *Ethnicity and Family Therapy,* 438–56.

10. Midelfort and Midelfort, "Norwegian Families," 438–56; interview with Paul A. Qualben by Lovoll, Brooklyn, New York, November 17, 1995; interview with Patricia Patten by Lovoll, San Pedro, California, February 1, 1996; Herbert Hedin, *Suicide in Scandinavia: A Psychological Study of Culture and Character* (New York: Grune and Stratton, 1964).

11. Midelfort and Midelfort, "Norwegian Families," 444, 445–46.

12. Lowry Nelson, *The Minnesota Community: Country and Town in Transition* (Minneapolis: University of Minnesota Press, 1960), 45–53; Lovoll, *A Century of Urban Life,* 231; Odd S. Lovoll, *The Promise of America: A History of the Norwegian-American People* (Minneapolis: University of Minnesota Press, 1984), 213–14; Albert Jenks, "Ethnic Census in Minneapolis," *American Journal of Sociology,* May 1912: 776–82; Lowry Nelson, "Intermarriage among Nationality Groups in a Rural Area of Minnesota," *American Journal of Sociology* 48 (March 1943): 591.

13. Stanley Lieberson and Mary C. Waters, *From Many Strands: Ethnic and Racial Groups in Contemporary America* (New York: Russell Sage Foundation, 1988), 172–73.

14. Charles H. Mindel and Robert W. Habenstein, *Ethnic Families in America: Patterns and Variations* (New York: Elsevier, 1976), 1–11. See also Bernard Farber, *Family Organization and Interaction* (San Francisco: Chandler, 1964).

15. Interview with Arlene Bakke Rutuelo by Lovoll, Bay Ridge, Brooklyn, November 21, 1995.

16. O. M. Norlie, *History of the Norwegian People in America* (Minneapolis: Augsburg Publishing House, 1925), 432; Lovoll, *A Century of Urban Life,* 212–15.

17. A. N. Rygg, *Norwegians in New York 1825–1925* (Brooklyn, N.Y.: Norwegian News Company, 1941), 88–89; Hansen, *My Minneapolis,* 111, 255.

18. Lovoll, *A Century of Urban Life,* 213.

19. Interview with Norman R. Dahl by Lovoll and Terje Mikael Hasle Joranger, Norwegian-American Hospital, Chicago, March 29, 1996.

20. *Staff Edition: A Newsletter for the Staff Members of Physicians Plus,* April/May, 1997; "The Midelfort Story," copy provided by Luther Midelfort Mayo Health System, Eau Claire, Wisconsin; Susan T. Hessel, *Medicine: The Gundersen Experience 1891–1991* (La Crosse, Wis.: Gundersen Clinic, 1991), 1–8, 11, 89–90; interview with Sigurd Gundersen Jr. by Joranger and Lovoll, La Crosse, Wisconsin, September 11, 1995.

21. The Three Links nursing facility, founded by the Odd Fellows, in Northfield, Minnesota, for instance, serves lutefisk dinners for residents, family, and friends annually during the Christmas holidays. Interviews with Donald Sannes, administrator, and Ole K. Helgerson, resident, by Joranger and Lovoll, Sannes Skogdalen, Soldiers Grove, Wisconsin, September 6, 1995.

22. Norlie, *History of the Norwegian People,* 433; Paul A. Qualben, *Eger Cares: Yesterday, Today, and Tomorrow: A 75th Anniversary Retrospective* (Staten Island, N.Y.: Eger Lutheran Homes, 1991); *Norwegian Christian Home and Health Center 90th Anniversary,* booklet; visits to the different institutions in Brooklyn and Staten Island in November 1995.

23. Research in Chicago, 1985–88, by Lovoll, and interviews with residents of the two nursing homes; Lovoll, *A Century of Urban Life,* 218–21; report, "15th Anniversary Hospital Association Norse Home, March 15, 1988," typescript; Thor Bjornstad, "Norse Home—Early History," typescript; *Norse Home Retirement Center News,* December 1955; Odd S. Lovoll, "*Washington Posten:* A Window on a Norwegian-American Urban Community," *Norwegian-American Studies* (Northfield, Minn.), 31 (1986): 172–73; visit to the Norse Home by Joranger and Lovoll, Seattle, January 1996, interviewing a number of staff and residents.

24. William T. Hakala, *A Common Bond: The Story of Lutheran Brotherhood* (Minneapolis: Lutheran Brotherhood, 1989), 13–35, 46–47; Lowell J. Soike, *Norwegian Americans and the Politics of Dissent, 1880–1924* (Northfield, Minn.: Norwegian-American Historical Association, 1991), 122, 127–28, 191.

25. Hakala, *A Common Bond,* 106–9, 141–45; *Lutheran Brotherhood Bond,* spring 1996.

26. Interview with Robert Gandrud by Lovoll and Joranger, Lutheran Brotherhood headquarters, Minneapolis, April 8, 1996.

27. Anthony Oberschall, *Social Conflict and Social Movements* (Englewood Cliffs, N.J.: Prentice-Hall, 1973), 119; Mary Ann Clawson, *Constructing Brotherhood: Class, Gender, and Fraternalism* (Princeton, N.J.: Princeton University Press, 1989), 21–42; Lovoll, "Norwegian-American Mutuality in the Iron Decade," 179, 185, 187–88; Lovoll, *A Century of Urban Life,* 89.

28. Clawson, *Constructing Brotherhood,* 221; Lovoll, *A Century of Urban Life,* 208–10; Carl G. O. Hansen, *History of Sons of Norway: An American Fraternal Organization of Men and Women of Norwegian Birth or Extraction* (Minneapolis: Sons of Norway Supreme Lodge, 1944), 10–25.

29. C. Sverre Norborg, *An American Saga* (Minneapolis: Sons of Norway, 1970), 77–78, 159; Kelly Mundell, manager, Member and Lodge Services, Sons of Norway, provided the 1995 statistics.

30. Norborg, *An American Saga,* 159. The order's magazine began February 1, 1904, as *Sønner af Norge.* In 1944 the

name became *Sons of Norway,* reflecting the transition to English, and in November 1993, was changed to the *Viking,* per- haps indicating the enhanced ethnic value of the Viking imagery as an identifying symbol.

31. Norborg, *An American Saga,* 43–49, 147; Hansen, *History of Sons of Norway,* 22–25, 77–78, 137, 150.

32. Norborg, *An American Saga,* 92, 126; Hansen, *History of Sons of Norway,* 25, 43, 52, 123–24, 137–38, 168, 285, 301; Carl H. Chrislock, *Ethnicity Challenged: The Upper Midwest Norwegian-American Experience in World War I* (Northfield, Minn.: Norwegian-American Historical Association, 1981), 61–62, 132.

33. Norborg, *An American Saga,* 142–43, 151–52, 165.

34. Bent Vanberg, *Sons of Norway* (Minneapolis: Sons of Norway, n.d.), 24–25; 1995 survey of Sons of Norway lodges; interview with Dennis Sorheim by Lovoll, Minneapolis, May 29, 1996.

35. John Higham, *Send These to Me: Jews and Other Immigrants in Urban America* (New York: Atheneum, 1975), 229; interview with Kenneth Holberg Ducat by Lovoll, Sun City, Arizona, February 4, 1996; interview with Patricia Patten by Lovoll, San Pedro, California, February 1, 1996.

36. Interview with Sherrill Swenson by Lovoll, Los Angeles, California, January 31, 1996.

37. Interviews with Beverly and Robert King by Joranger and Lovoll, Denver, Colorado, February 16, 1996; interview with George R. Holte by Lovoll, Denver, Colorado, February 16, 1996; interviews with Jim and Sonja Hillestad, Northfield, Minnesota, July 30, 1995.

38. Interview with Ruth G. Durham by Lovoll, Seattle, Washington, January 13, 1996, and by telephone, June 19, 1997.

39. Interview with Wayne A. Rohne by Lovoll, Clifton, Texas, April 23, 1996; *Snorre Posten,* September 1995.

40. Paul E. Foss, ed., *Torske Klubben. The Norwegian Luncheon Club of Minneapolis, Minnesota, Celebrates Its Golden Anniversary, 1922–1983* (Souvenir Book, 1983), 8, 12–15.

41. Olaf T. Engvig, *Shipping and Culture: The Fish Club of San Francisco 1914–1994* (San Francisco: Fish Club, 1996), 15–26; interview with Trygve G. Morkemo, San Francisco, California, January 23, 1996. The Fish Club has no formal membership. Jean Labadie, "The Norwegian Club of San Francisco," typescript; *Articles of Incorporation, Bylaws, and Mem- bership of the Norwegian Club,* published in January 1993.

42. Written statement about the Chicago Fish Club by David Cornwell, secretary, Chicago Torske Klub, January 28, 1997; Joranger, notes and several brief interviews after attending the Norwegian Fish Club of San Diego, February 9, 1996; Terje I. Leiren, information provided electronically, March 25, 1997; telephone interview with Kjell Winger by Lovoll, Fiskeklubben, Salt Lake City, Utah, June 30, 1997.

43. Interview with Donald J. Omodt by Lovoll and Joranger, Minneapolis, April 17, 1996; interviews with Omodt by Lovoll, April 5 and July 7, 1997.

44. C. Wright Mills, *White Collar: The American Middle Class* (New York: Oxford University Press, 1951; reprint, 1974), 132.

45. Einar Haugen, *The Norwegian Language in America: A Study in Bilingual Behavior,* 2 vols., 2d ed. (Bloomington: In- diana University Press, 1969), 1: 137–40.

46. Interviews with Robert C. Anderson, a grandson of Rasmus C. Anderson, and Al Stensby, a great-grandson, by Lovoll, in San Gabriel, California, February 3, 1996.

47. Robert B. Kvavik, ed., *Directory of Scandinavian Studies in North America* (Madison, Wis.: Society for the Advance- ment of Scandinavian Study, 1989), 9–11, 20–21, 54–55.

48. Haugen, *The Norwegian Language in America,* 1: 141–49.

49. Odd S. Lovoll, "*Decorah-Posten:* The Story of an Immigrant Newspaper," *Norwegian-American Studies* (Northfield, Minn.) 27 (1977): 98.

50. Joshua A. Fishman et al., *Language Loyalty in the United States: The Maintenance and Perpetuation of Non-English Mother Tongues by American Ethnic and Religious Groups* (The Hague: Mouton and Co., 1966), 343–52.

51. Hedin Bronner, "A Centenary of Norwegian Studies in American Institutions of Learning," in *Norwegian-American Studies and Records* (Northfield, Minn.) 20 (1959): 158–69. Information in Irving Highland Papers, Norwegian-American

Historical Association Archives, Northfield, Minnesota. Mr. Highland headed the Society for Preservation of Norwegian Culture, Inc., which raised the money for the chair at the University of Chicago. Electronic correspondence with Professor Jan Terje Faarlund at Norway's University of Science and Technology, Dragvoll, April 3, 1997. To the question why he "changed over to" New Norse, Professor Faarlund defensively responded: "I did not 'CHANGE OVER TO New Norse.' New Norse is one of two co-equal official languages in Norway and I chose one, the one that is the least offered in the United States."

52. St. Olaf College maintains the only foreign-language department in the United States designated Norwegian.

53. Alf Lunder Knudsen, "The Norwegian Male Chorus Movement in America: A Study," (Ph.D. diss., University of Washington, 1989), 3–4, 18, 22, 60, 70–71, 180, quote on page 51.

54. Knudsen, "The Norwegian Male Chorus Movement in America," 3–4, 18, 22, 60, 70–71, 180; Lovoll, *A Century of Urban Life,* 88, 135, 255, 257.

55. Interview with Alf Lunder Knudsen by Joranger and Lovoll, Seattle, January 9, 1996.

56. Midelfort and Midelfort, "Norwegian Families," 438–56; David A. Hollinger, *Postethnic America: Beyond Multiculturalism* (New York: Basic Books, 1995), 1–17.

57. Robert Hughes, *The Culture of Complaint: The Fraying of America* (New York: Oxford University Press, 1993), 96.

58. Interview with Robert J. Engelstad by Lovoll, Washington, D.C., May 6, 1996.

59. Interview with Dianne Buttrick Sawyer by Lovoll, Plano, Texas, April 21, 1996; interview with Diana Fitzgerald by Lovoll, Washington, D.C., November 12, 1995.

60. Telephone conversation with Catherine Egenberger, September 5, 1995, and letter to author dated the same day.

61. Letter from Nancy B. Thurson, Scituate, Massachusetts, dated March 18, 1996.

62. Interview with Patricia Barrett Klove by Lovoll, Washington, D.C., November 12, 1995.

63. Interview with Geneva Allen Finstad by Joranger and Lovoll, Cranfills Gap, Texas, April 23, 1996; interview with Mary Keller Lovdahl and Harold M. Lovdahl by Lovoll, Green Bay, Wisconsin, September 22, 1995. Harold Lovdahl, born in 1917 in Iola, Wisconsin, relates how his American-born father insisted that the children speak Norwegian to him. "One day I came home from school and told my father: 'I don't want to speak Norwegian because I am an American.' My father responded: 'You must be proud that you are an American, but if you want anything to eat you will have to speak Norwegian.'" This exchange was conducted in Norwegian and also related to the author in 1995 in authentic dialect Norwegian.

64. Richard D. Alba, *Ethnic Identity: The Transformation of White America* (New Haven, Conn.: Yale University Press, 1990), 312; Neil C. Sandberg, *Ethnic Identity and Assimilation: The Polish-American Community. Case Study of Metropolitan Los Angeles* (New York: Praeger Publishers, 1974), 70–75.

6. THE NORWEGIAN-AMERICAN MATRIX

1. Andrew M. Greeley, *Ethnicity in the United States: A Preliminary Reconnaissance* (New York: John Wiley and Sons, 1974), 308–9.

2. Odd S. Lovoll, "The Norwegian-Americans," in Judy Galens, Anna Sheets, and Robyn V. Young, eds., *Gale Encyclopedia of Multicultural America,* vol. 2 (New York: Gale Research, Inc., 1995), 1007–8; publicity material for Concordia Language Villages.

3. In doing fieldwork, a long list of strange usages of Norwegian was assembled. When these were pointed out, they elicited only humor and no apology or intent to change.

4. Interview with Maurice Aslakson by Terje Mikael Hasle Joranger and Odd S. Lovoll, Hoff Township, Pope County, Minnesota, August 15, 1995; *Pope County Tribune,* January 23, 1989.

5. Interview with Joyce Bruns by Lovoll and Joranger, Rothsay, Minnesota, March 6, 1996. Interviews were conducted March 6, 1996, with all of those who met for breakfast at the Rothsay Truck Stop and Café. John J. Peterson, a fourth-generation Norwegian American, is quoted. Don Carlsrud, born in 1923, related that his grandparents came from Norway,

and although his older sister knew only Norwegian when she began school, he, in fact, knew only English and actually learned Norwegian from the other children in the small rural school he attended so he would not feel left out. English was enforced in the classroom, but "as soon as the bell rang," Carlsrud explained, "just like that, it was Norwegian."

6. Eric Larsen, *An American Memory* (Chapel Hill, N.C.: Algonquin Books, 1988), 23, 141, 225.

7. James S. Pula, "Image, Status, Mobility and Integration in American Society: The Polish Experience," *Journal of American Ethnic History,* fall 1996: 74–95, quote on page 91; Dag Blanck, "Constructing an Ethnic Identity: The Case of the Swedish-Americans," in Peter J. Kivisto, ed., *The Ethnic Enigma: The Salience of Ethnicity for European-Origin Groups* (Philadelphia: Balch Institute Press, 1989), 134–52; John Higham, *Strangers in the Land: Patterns of American Nativism, 1860–1925* (New Brunswick, N.J.: Rutgers University Press, 1994), 304.

8. Lawrence E. Mintz, "Humor and Ethnic Stereotypes in Vaudeville and Burlesque," *MELUS,* winter 1996: 25–26; Christie Davies, *Ethnic Humor around the World: A Comparative Analysis* (Bloomington: Indiana University Press, 1990), 82, 309, 310–14; Howard Mohr, *How to Talk Minnesotan: A Visitor's Guide* (New York: Penguin Books, 1987); Janet Letnes Martin and Suzanne (Johnson) Nelson, *Is It Too Windy Back There, Then?* (Hastings, Minn.: Caragana Press, 1996), xii, 236.

9. Odd S. Lovoll, *A Century of Urban Life: The Norwegians in Chicago before 1930* (Northfield, Minn.: Norwegian-American Historical Association, 1988), 97–100, 137–38, 260–63.

10. Interview with Bill Kristian Jakobsen by Lovoll, Brooklyn, November 18, 1995.

11. Red Stangeland, *Ole and Lena Jokes—Book III* (Sioux Falls, S.Dak.: Norse Press, 1988), 34; Red Stangeland, *Norwegian Home Companion* (New York: Barnes and Noble, 1987), 2.

12. Interview with Robert "Uncle Torvald" L. Johnson by Lovoll, Sioux Falls, South Dakota, May 23, 1996.

13. Telephone interview with Dorothy "Old Granny" Stager by Lovoll, April 4, 1997.

14. Holger Kersten, "Using the Immigrant's Voice: Humor and Pathos in Nineteenth-Century 'Dutch' Dialect Texts," *MELUS,* winter 1996: 3–17; Lois Leveen, "Only When I Laugh: Textual Dynamics of Ethnic Humor," *MELUS,* winter 1996: 29–55, quotes on pages 42, 43; Stangeland, *Norwegian Home Companion,* 13.

15. Odd S. Lovoll, "Emigration and Settlement Patterns as They Relate to the Migration of Norwegian Folk Art," in Marion Nelson, ed., *Norwegian Folk Art: The Migration of a Tradition* (New York: Abbeville Press, 1995), 125–32.

16. Nelson, "Norwegian Folk Art in America," in Nelson, *Norwegian Folk Art,* 92–93.

17. Nelson, "Norwegian Folk Art in America," 92–93; Philip Martin, *Rosemaling in the Upper Midwest: A Story of Region and Revival* (Mount Horeb, Wis.: Wisconsin Folk Museum, 1989), 58.

18. Martin, *Rosemaling in the Upper Midwest,* 30–31; interview with Ethel Kvalheim and Vi (Vivian) Thode by Lovoll and Joranger, Stoughton, Wisconsin, July 17, 1996. Of Vi Thode's five instructional books, four are almost totally devoted to the Rogaland style. The so-called American Rogaland has been attributed to her work and has many practitioners in Dane County, Wisconsin. An American Telemark style is in particular found in Milan, Minnesota, with such artists as Karen Jenson and Nancy Schneck. In St. Paul Addie Pittelkow practices this style, although in St. Paul and Minneapolis the Hallingdal style is most prominent, with such artists as Judith Nelson and John Gundersen.

19. Martin, *Rosemaling in the Upper Midwest,* 44–47; undated letter from Millie Jacobson in folder of information on rosemaling provided by Gladys J. Shelley, herself an accomplished rosemaling artist in Cambridge, Minnesota; interview with Suzanne Gary Katz by Joranger and Lovoll, Plano, Texas, April 21, 1996.

20. Interview with Sigmund Aarseth by Joranger, Volbu in Valdres, Norway, November 30, 1996.

21. Archival material in Vesterheim Norwegian-American Museum, including newsletters, newspaper clippings, brochures, lists of gold medal winners in rosemaling, and correspondence; interview with Gail Peterson by Lovoll, Brooklyn, New York, November 27, 1995. Rosemaling artist Elvera Bisbee in Tracy, Minnesota, displays her own lavishly decorated marker to be placed on her grave. Sunhild Muldbakken in Sioux Falls, South Dakota, decorated some fifty caskets in rosemaling for the Miller's Funeral Home in Sioux Falls from about 1982 until 1990. Telephone interview with Sunhild Muldbakken by Lovoll, April 11, 1997, and letter containing additional information dated April 21, 1997. Her husband, Odd

Muldbakken, is a wood-carver; Sunhild decorates the objects he makes in rosemaling and has won the gold medal in the Vesterheim competition for her art.

22. Nelson, *Norwegian Folk Art,* 76–77.

23. Nelson, "Norwegian Folk Art," 90–93, 96, 267; interview with Frida Mindrum Nowland and Ronald Nowland by Joranger and Lovoll, La Crosse, Wisconsin, September 9, 1995. Frida Nowland is related to the Landsverk family.

24. Telephone interview with Harley Refsal by Lovoll, July 24, 1997.

25. Nelson, "Norwegian Folk Art," 96.

26. Nelson, "Norwegian Folk Art," 96. Interviews with Else J. Bigton and Phillip Odden by Joranger and Lovoll, Barronett, Wisconsin, July 16, 1996; brochure titled "Norsk Wood Works, Ltd. Established 1979. Else Bigton and Phillip Odden, Designers and Builders of Quality Norwegian Furniture." See their coauthored, *Treskjærerkunsten. Innføring i flatskurd, drakestil, akantus, relieff og figurskjæring* (Oslo: Universitetsforlaget, 1996). Many hobby wood-carvers as well as many who sell their carvings are active in America.

27. Carl T. Narvestad, *A History of the Hardanger Fiddle Association of America, 1983–1993* (Granite Falls, Minn.: Hardanger Fiddle Association of America, 1993); Odd S. Lovoll, *A Folk Epic: The* Bygdelag *in America* (Boston: Twayne Publishers for Norwegian-American Historical Association, 1975), 208, 223–24; membership brochure of the 1983 society.

28. Interview with Elizabeth Ann Kollé by Joranger, Seattle, January 8, 1996; impressions from visit to Skandia Folkdance Society, January 5, 1996; brochures and announcements of activities of Skandia Folkdance Society for 1996; typescript histories of dance groups provided by Elizabeth Kollé; brochure containing history and activities of Leikarringen of Leif Erikson Lodge.

29. Jean Reek, "History of the Stoughton High School Norwegian Dancers Organized 1953" (typescript, n.d.); interview with Jean Reek by Joranger and Lovoll, Stoughton, Wisconsin, September 25, 1995.

30. Meetings and interviews with members of the Skål Klubb, Brainerd, Minnesota, March 15–16, 1996.

31. T. J. Jackson Lears, *No Place to Hide: Antimodernism and the Transformation of American Culture 1880–1920* (New York: Pantheon, 1981); and John Higham, "The Reorientation of American Culture in the 1890s," in John Higham, ed., *Writing American History: Essays on Modern Scholarship* (Bloomington: University of Illinois Press, 1972), 73–102, are excellent discussions of the reorientation of American culture in this period. E. John B. Allen, *From Skisport to Skiing: One Hundred Years of an American Sport, 1840–1940* (Amherst: University of Massachusetts Press, 1993), 5.

32. Odd S. Lovoll, "'Better Than a Visit to the Old Country': The *Stevne* of the Sognalag in America," in Øyvind T. Gulliksen, David C. Mauk, and Dina Tolfsby, eds., *Norwegian-American Essays* (Oslo: NAHA-Norway, 1996), 16, 22–25.

33. Allen, *From Skisport to Skiing,* 47–48; Odd S. Lovoll, *The Promise of America: A History of the Norwegian-American People* (Minneapolis: University of Minnesota Press, 1984), 190; Kenneth O. Bjork, "'Snowshoe' Thompson: Fact and Legend," *Norwegian-American Studies and Records* (Northfield, Minn.) 19 (1956): 62–88.

34. Interview with Bonnie Pine Haven and Jack Haven by Joranger and Lovoll, Portland, Oregon, January 17, 1996.

35. Harold A. Grinden, comp. *History of the National Ski Association and the Ski Sport in the United States 1840 to 1931* (Duluth, Minn.: NSA [1931]), 8–9, 14; Russell M. Magnaghi, ed., *Seventy-Five Years of Skiing, 1904–1979* (Ishpeming, Mich.: National Ski Hall of Fame Press, 1979); Allen, *From Skisport to Skiing,* 47–48.

36. Tom Harrington with Wally Wakefield, *On Wings of Wood: A Summary of the First 100 Years of the St. Paul Ski Club* (St. Paul: St. Paul Ski Club, 1985), 2–7. See Arnold R. Beisser, "The American Seasonal Masculinity Rites," in Marie Hart, ed., *Sport in the Sociocultural Process,* 2d. ed. (Dubuque, Iowa: Wm. C. Brown Company Publishers, 1976), 403–12, on how sport becomes a rite that encourages male camaraderie and affirms masculinity and sexual distinctness.

37. Lovoll, *A Century of Urban Life,* 249–52; Grinden, *History of the National Ski Association,* 19; Allen Guttmann, *From Ritual to Record: The Nature of Modern Sport* (New York: Columbia University Press, 1978), 26–36; *91st Annual Norge Ski Club Winter Ski Jumping Tournament, Fox River Grove, IL, Sunday, January 21, 1996;* LeRoy O. Ruud, "The Norge Ski Club 1905–1994," typescript; *Norden,* December 1930, November 1932; Olav Bø, *Skiing throughout History,* trans. W. Edson Richmond (Oslo: Det Norske Samlaget, 1993), 11–23, 53–55, 67–73, quote page 71.

38. Allen, *From Skisport to Skiing*, 104–16, 145–70; *U.S. Skiing Annual Guide 1996* (Park City, Utah: U.S. Skiing, 1996); interviews with LeRoy Ruud and Edward Waters by Joranger and Lovoll, Fox River Grove, Illinois, April 2, 1996.

39. Interviews with Jeff Hammel and Mark Hammel, father and son, by Joranger, Minneapolis, April 17, 1996; interview with Phillip T. Bland by Joranger, Westby, Wisconsin, July 16, 1996; interview with James F. Vatn by Joranger, Seattle, January 10, 1996; *Nordic Notes*, February-March, 1996; *1995–1996 U.S. Skiing Jumping/Nordic Combined Competition Guide* (Park City, Utah: U.S. Skiing, 1996); *Snowflake Ski and Golf Club: 1993 Subaru Large Hill National Championships, February 13 and 14, 1993, Westby, Wisconsin; International Ski Jumping Tournament, Silvermine Hill, Eau Claire, Wis., March 1, 1987.*

40. The American Birkebeiner is part of the so-called Worldloppet, or "world race," a premier international series of thirteen marathon races held in Japan, Switzerland, Sweden, Norway, France, Estonia, Germany, Austria, Finland, Italy, Canada, Australia, and the United States.

41. *American Birkebeiner Birch Scroll*, fall 1995: 6–9; *The American Birkebeiner—An Overview*, typescript 1996; *Sons of Norway Viking*, May 1996; Christine Maestri, *The Barnebirkie Book* (Hayward, Wis.: Country Print Shop, 1995).

42. Barbara Kvigne Rostad, ed., *If I Can Do This . . . The Saga of Ski for Light* (Minneapolis: Sons of Norway Foundation, 1985), 32, 34, 35, 78–79.

43. Interview with Olav Pedersen by Lovoll, Breckenridge, Colorado, February 15, 1996; résumé of Olav Pedersen; *Western Viking*, June 10, 1983; Sureva Towler, *The History of Skiing at Steamboat Springs* (Steamboat Springs, Colo.: Routt County Research, 1987), 51–52, 61–64; Leif Hovelsen, *The Flying Norseman* (Ishpeming, Mich.: National Ski Hall of Fame Press, 1983), 27–34, 128–29. Olav Pedersen at age 79 was still an active ski instructor at the time he was interviewed in February 1996.

44. Interviews with Bigton and Odden, July 16, 1996.

45. Interview with Ted R. Ahre by Lovoll, Woodburn, Oregon, January 18, 1996.

46. Interview with Shauna Sandner Chance by Lovoll, Sacramento, California, January 24, 1996.

47. Liv Aannestad, questionnaire response, dated March 9, 1996; interview with Lois Mickelson by Lovoll, Stevens Point, Wisconsin, September 20, 1995, and by telephone, June 25, 1997.

48. Interview with Mickelson.

49. Sister Cities International, 120 South Payne Street, Alexandria, VA 22314, facsimile message, June 20, 1996.

50. Attendance at planning committee for the Flekkefest in Elbow Lake, March 13, 1996, and several interviews and recording of impressions by Lovoll and Joranger; interview with E. T. Lowell Smith, president of the sister city committee, by Joranger and Lovoll, Elbow Lake, Minnesota, March 13, 1996.

51. Herbert J. Gans, "Symbolic Ethnicity: The Future of Ethnic Groups and Cultures in America," in Herbert J. Gans, Nathan Glazer, Joseph R. Gusfield, and Christopher Jencks, eds., *On the Making of Americans: Essays in Honor of David Riesman* (Philadelphia: University of Pennsylvania Press, 1979), 206–7; interview with Walter F. Mondale by Lovoll, Minneapolis, Minnesota, January 29, 1997.

52. Gans, "Symbolic Ethnicity," 206–7; Andrew T. Kopan, "Greek Survival in Chicago: The Role of Ethnic Education, 1890–1980," in Peter d'A. Jones and Melvin G. Holli, eds., *Ethnic Chicago* (Grand Rapids, Mich.: William B. Eerdman's Publishing Company, 1981), 115. For a discussion of the invention of historical tradition, see "The Invention of Tradition: The Highland Tradition of Scotland," in Eric Hobsbawm and Terence Ranger, eds., *The Invention of Tradition* (Cambridge: Cambridge University Press, 1984), 15–41.

53. Howard R. Bergen, *History of 99th Infantry Battalion U.S. Army* (Oslo: Norway: Emil Mostue, 1945); reunion of 99th Infantry Battalion, Minneapolis 1994.

54. See Lloyd Hustvedt, *Rasmus B. Anderson: Pioneer Scholar* (Northfield, Minn.: Norwegian-American Historical Association, 1966).

55. *Fargo Forum*, May 19, 1996; *North Dakota Quarterly*, autumn 1981: 80–88; Peter Thoresen Reite, ed., *Fra det amerikanske Normandi* (Moorhead, Minn.: privately published, 1912), 21; *Norway Times*, May 2, 1996; interview with Myron Peterson by Joranger and Lovoll, Minot, North Dakota, October 12, 1995; Odd S. Lovoll, "Swedes, Norwegians,

and the Columbian Exposition of 1893," in Ulf Beijbom, ed., *Swedes in America: Intercultural and Interethnic Perspectives on Contemporary Research* (Växjö, Sweden: Swedish Emigrant Institute, 1993), 192–93; Theodore C. Blegen, *Norwegian Migration to America, 1825–1860* (Northfield, Minn.: Norwegian-American Historical Association, 1931), 61; Lovoll, *A Century of Urban Life,* 241

56. John Bodnar, *Remaking America: Public Memory, Commemoration, and Patriotism in the Twentieth Century* (Princeton, N.J.: Princeton University Press, 1992), 13–20, 55–61.

57. Lester Seversike, ed., *The Fox Valley Norwegian-American Sesquicentennial 1825–1975* (Souvenir Booklet, 1975), unpaged; notes from visit to the Fox River valley by Joranger and Lovoll, October 30, 1995.

58. Interviews with Sally Christensen and Ivar Christensen, president of the Leif Ericson Society, by Joranger and Lovoll, Philadelphia, December 2, 1995; copy of the "Leif Erikson Day, 1984" presidential proclamation.

59. *Valhalla's Svar. The Official Sagaletter of the Viking Age Club,* November 1995, February 1996, April 1996 (The magazine is dated in a Runic calendar, 1991, for instance, being "2241 Runic Era."); "About the Viking Age Club," typescript; interviews with Dennis Rusinko, Gary Anderson, and Eric Anderson, members of the Viking Age Club, by Joranger and Lovoll, Minneapolis, June 18, 1996.

60. "The Ásatrú Alliance," World Wide Web site information; *Vor Tru,* fall 1991, spring 1995, fall/winter 1996; *The Runestone: Celebrating the Indigenous Religion of European Americans,* fall 1995; Stephen A. McNallen, *What Is Asatru?* (Nevada City, Calif.: Asatru Folk Assembly, n.d.); *Why Asatru?* membership brochure.

61. "The Loki Cult" World Wide Web page; William Fox, alias Thor Sannhet, copy of letter to Tom Roren, editor, *Norway Times,* December 11, 1994; *The Oregonian,* July 31, 1993; *The Oregonian,* July 11, 1993; *The Columbian,* July 8, 12, 1993.

62. "What Is the National Alliance? Ideology and program of the National Alliance," printed membership invitation.

63. Odd S. Lovoll and Kenneth O. Bjork, *The Norwegian-American Historical Association 1925–1975* (Northfield, Minn.: Norwegian-American Historical Association, 1975), 14–17, 46–48, 49–53; Odd S. Lovoll, "Norwegian-American Historical Scholarship: A Survey of Its History and a Look to the Future," in Dorothy Burton Skårdal and Ingeborg R. Kongslien, eds., *Essays on Norwegian-American Literature and History* (Oslo: Norwegian-American Historical Association-Norway, 1986), 223–39; John R. Jenswold, "Becoming American, Becoming Suburban," *Norwegian-American Studies* (Northfield, Minn.) 33 (1992): 21–23.

64. Marion J. Nelson, "Material Culture and Ethnicity: Collecting and Preserving Norwegian Americana before World War II," in Marion J. Nelson, ed., *Material Culture and People's Art among the Norwegians in America* (Northfield, Minn.: Norwegian-American Historical Association, 1994), 13–21, 26–34; interview with Darrell D. Henning by Joranger and Lovoll, Decorah, Iowa, May 15, 1996.

65. Nelson, "Material Culture and Ethnicity," 43–46, quotes on pages 44 and 45; Little Norway publicity brochure; *Sons of Norway Viking,* April 1983: 128–29; interview with Borghild L. Olson, publicity director, by Joranger, Norskedalen, La Crosse, Wisconsin, July 18, 1996.

66. *Crossings,* winter 1996; *Nordic News,* spring 1995; Bob Asp, *A Dream Is a Dream* (rev. ed., Moorhead, Minn.: privately printed, 1980).

67. J. Hart Rosdail, *The Sloopers: Their Ancestry and Posterity* (Broadview, Ill.: Norwegian Slooper Society of America, 1961), xii; Seversike, ed., *The Fox Valley Norwegian-American Sesquicentennial 1825–1975,* unpaged.

68. Rosdail, *The Sloopers,* 613–16. Richard D. Alba, *Ethnic Identity: The Transformation of White America* (New Haven, Conn.: Yale University Press, 1990), on page 69 supports the findings on gender influence on ethnic identity. Interview with Patricia Ainsley Hayes by Lovoll, Dayton, Illinois, November 1, 1995.

69. Interview with Patricia Peterson and Silas Peterson by Lovoll, Norway, Illinois, October 31, 1995.

70. Stanley Lieberson and Mary C. Waters, *From Many Strands: Ethnic and Racial Groups in Contemporary America* (New York: Russell Sage Foundation, 1988), 5; John Higham, *Send These to Me: Jews and Other Immigrants in Urban America* (New York: Atheneum, 1975), 229; U.S. Bureau of the Census, *Supplementary Report: Ancestry of the Population by State: 1980 Census of the Population.*

Index

171, 172; in community foundation, 63–64; increased diversity in, 95–102; unions and divisions in, 85–88, 94–95

Lutheran Medical Center (Brooklyn), 192

Lutheraneren, 209

Lyngli, Elisabeth, 83

Lysne, Per, 229, 231, 237

male dominance, 101, 187

male luncheon clubs, 204–7

marriage, 32, 97, 188–90, 216–17

Maryland, 64, 83

Massachusetts, 63, 141

May 17 (Syttende mai): and Sons of Norway, 201; as ethnic identifying symbol, 39–40, 66, 71; as most prominent ethnic celebration, 53, 70, 148; first celebrations, 29; incorporated into American holiday array, 54, 117, 262; inspiration for other festivals, 74

McKinney, William, 79

Methodists, 22–23, 79, 80

Michigan, 12, 47, 125, 240

Michigan Militia, 125

Mickelson, Lois, 248

Midelfart, Hans Christian, 193

Midelfort, C. F., 186, 187, 214

Midelfort Clinic (Eau Claire, Wisconsin), 193

Midelfort, H. C., 186, 214

migration, 1, 7–11

militant Norwegian Americans, 125–29

Mills, C. Wright, 208

Milwaukee, Wisconsin, 50

mining, 12, 76

Minneapolis, Minnesota: "downtown" Norwegians in, 178–79; headquarters of Sons of Norway, 198; "Norwegian-American capital," 16–17, 50–51; Norwegian hospital in, 192–93; site of centennial and other celebrations, 32, 70; Torske Klubben in, 205–7

Minneapolis *Star Tribune,* 93

Minneapolis Tidende, 24

Minnesota: and ethnic celebrations, 53–54, 70–71; and Sister Cities International, 242; and skiing, 242; and Sons of Norway, 198, 201; anti-Catholicism in, 79; census figures (1990) for, 47, 51; crime in, 174–78; early move into, 13; farmers in, 14, 145–46; fish clubs in, 205–7; increase in minority population in, 114; inter-

views with political figures in, 116–20; lutefisk dinners in, 90, 91–93; Lutheran church in, 85, 88, 96–97; Norwegian language in, 26–27, 108–9, 112–13; religious affiliation in, 81, 84; successful Norwegians in, 161. *See also* Minneapolis; St. Paul

Minnesota Daily, 172

Minnesota Genealogical Society, 46

Minnesota Scandinavian Genealogical Society, 46

Minot, North Dakota, 72, 250

Missouri, 229

Missouri Synod, 21, 87, 102

moderates, 110, 120

Moe, Clair B., 113

Moe, Roger D., 116–17

Mohr, Howard, 224

Molstad, Maynard O., 126

Mondale, Theodore, 119

Mondale, Walter F., 108, 116, 119–20, 126, 249

Monkman, Betty Claire, 170–71

Montana, 17, 48–50, 76, 125, 128

monuments, 53–54, 115, 251–52

"mooring holes," 5

Morkemo, Trygve G., 205

Mormons. *See* Church of Jesus Christ of the Latter-day Saints

Mortensen, Hjørdis, 64

Mount Horeb, Wisconsin, 65–66, 93

multiculturalism, 33, 96–98, 101, 215

Munch, P. A. (historian), 3

Munch, Peter A. (sociologist), 85, 93, 179

Murat, William, 121–22

Muskego, Wisconsin, 11, 21, 24, 98

mutual aid societies, 183–86

Muus, Bernt J., 103

Naeseth, Gerhard B., 45

Nansen, Fridtjof, 240

National Organization for Women (NOW), 115

National Ski Association (NSA) (Ishpeming, Michigan), 31, 240

Native Americans, 116, 173

Nelson, David T., 103

Nelson, Knute, 26, 108–9

Nelson, Lowry, 189–90

Nelson, Marion J., 258

Odd S. Lovoll immigrated to the United States from Norway with his family in 1946. He has been a member of the faculty of St. Olaf College since 1971 and was appointed to the King Olav V Chair in Scandinavian-American Studies there in 1992. He also teaches at the University of Oslo. He is the publications editor for the Norwegian-American Historical Association and has written many books and articles on immigration studies, including *The Promise of America: A History of the Norwegian-American People* (Minnesota, 1984).